TALES FROM OLD JAPAN:
FOLKTALES AND LEGENDS FROM
THE LAND OF THE RISING SUN

TALES FROM OLD JAPAN:
FOLKTALES AND LEGENDS FROM THE LAND OF THE RISING SUN

CHRISTOPHER KINCAID

KITSUNE PUBLISHING

Other Books by Christopher Kincaid

Teahouse Mysteries
Kanzashi

Japanese Folklore
Come and Sleep: The Folklore of the Japanese Fox
Under the Cherry Blossoms:
Tanuki: The Folklore of Japan's Trickster

The Hunted Series
Vixen Hunted
Shepherd Hunted
Memory Hunted

Contents

Introduction

With this collection, I wanted to make folklore more accessible. Often, folklore is couched in dated language and Victorian observations. You can even see the gods speaking to each other in Latin. I rewrote these Japanese folk tales for the reader who wants to simply read them for enjoyment. While I tried to stay true to the spirit of the stories, I had to make small changes such as substituting obscure references with more recognizable ones. Whenever I deemed it appropriate, I modernized spellings of places and substituted transliterations with the English synonym. When I encountered multiple versions of a single story, I opted to combine them into a single telling whenever possible. This collection also includes various Ainu stories.

I am indebted to all those who made Japanese folklore available to English speakers: William Elliot Griffis, Basil Hall Chamberlain, A.B. Freeman-Mitford, Lafcadio Hearn, Yei Theodora Ozaki, and many others.

Animal Stories

A Carp Teaches Perseverance

A great painter named Okyo lived in Kyoto. His work sold at high prices and earned him many admirers and students who wanted to learn his style. One student by the name of Rosetsu set himself apart—sadly, not in the best of ways. Rosetsu struggled to learn even the most basic painting skills. The young man worked hard, harder than any other student, but it seemed as if the gods themselves acted against him.

As Rosetsu saw his fellow students graduate to become great painters in their own rights, he grew discouraged. He had worked for three years and made little progress. One evening, he had finally had enough and left the school, giving up on his dream. He set off for home, not caring if he died on the way. In fact, he found that preferable.

All that winter night he walked until his lack of sleep caught up to him. He collapsed into a snowy grove of pine trees. A strange noise awoke him just before dawn. He sat up, listening and trying to figure out the direction of the odd splashing sound. But his exhaustion soon overcame his curiosity.

He awoke again three hours after dawn. As he shook the snow from his cloak, he noticed a partially iced-over pond nearby. A large carp leaped out of a break in the ice, then slipped back in. Again the carp leaped, and then Rosetsu noticed a rice cracker laying on the ice. Scales and blood flecked the jagged break, yet still the carp jumped after the rice cracker.

Rosetsu watched the carp's persistence with growing admiration. The fish tried everything it could to get at the cracker. It attacked the ice underneath. It leaped into the air and landed on the ice, trying to break it from above. Gradually, the ice gave away until the carp finally snatched the cracker.

Rosetsu cheered the carp as it swam away with its prize.

"I need to be like this carp," he said to himself. "I can't go home without my rice cracker." He stood with fresh resolve. "I won't give up until I have it, or I'll die trying."

He walked back toward Kyoto, stopping at a small temple along the way. He prayed for success and thanked the local god for showing him the carp's perseverance.

When Rosetsu arrived at the school, he told Okyo about the fish's determination. Okyo could see the new resolve in his student's eyes and welcomed him back. He redoubled his efforts to teach Rosetsu, and the young man progressed. Rosetsu eventually became one of Japan's greatest painters and took the image of a leaping carp as his family crest.

The Badger-Haunted Temple

Long ago in the southern town of Kumamoto, there lived a samurai who enjoyed fishing. He spent most of his days, from dawn to dusk, by the water. One fine day, fortune filled his large basket by late afternoon. As he returned home, he sang. Around dusk, he came across a deserted Buddhist temple with its half-opened gate hanging from rusted hinges. The temple had seen better days, with moss growing everywhere and a slumping roof. Curious, he peered inside.

Just inside the gate stood a pretty young woman. Her neatness and cleanliness clashed against the sad state of the temple. She smiled at him and beckoned. Something seemed off about her, but despite this misgiving, he felt compelled to approach her. She bowed and led the way up the stone path and into the temple. The temple's interior sagged as much as the exterior. Leaves covered the floor, and cobwebs hung from corners. She continued to walk, occasionally smiling over her shoulder to make sure he still followed. After they passed through the temple to the garden beyond, the samurai saw what used to be a priest's home. Surprisingly, the home stood in good repair. He followed the strange young woman inside where the tatami were presentable, and a well-kept screen divided the room.

The girl motioned for him to sit.

"Does the priest of the temple live here?" he asked as he sat.

"No. My mother and I came here yesterday. She's gone to the next village to buy some things and may not be back tonight. Why don't you rest? I will get you something to drink."

She went into the kitchen. The samurai listened to the stillness, and the moments lengthened without the girl's return. The moon rose and lit the room. His misgivings began to overwhelm his curiosity about the young woman. He crossed his arms and wished he had remembered his sword.

Suddenly a sneeze behind the screen startled him. He expected the girl, but instead a red-faced, bald priest stalked out. He stood close to seven-feet tall—his head almost brushed the ceiling—and carried an iron wand.

He lifted it. "How dare you enter my house without my permission!" he shouted. "Leave, or I will beat you."

The young man jumped to his feet and backed away. Once he reached the door, he ran. As he fled across the courtyard, laughter rang out behind him. He stopped once he left the gate, hearing the laughter continue. He then realized that he had forgotten his basket of fish inside the temple. He chided himself for his forgetfulness and cowardice. But despite that, he couldn't make himself go back for it. Berating himself, he returned home.

The next day he told his friends of his experience. "Are you sure you didn't just imagine them?" one friend asked. "It was a hot day."

"Bah, he is just making up an excuse to cover how he lost his basket to the river," another friend said. They shared a laugh.

The samurai's best friend crossed his arms. "It was likely a badger."

They looked at him.

"The badger likely wanted your fish. I know first-hand that no one lives in that temple. I will go there tonight and end the badger's mischief. We can't have it scaring the common people."

The man went to a fishmonger and bought a large basket of fish and borrowed his friend's fishing pole. When dusk arrived, he fetched his sword and went to the temple. When he arrived, he saw not one, but three girls!

"So that is how it is," he said to himself. "But I won't be so easily fooled."

The trio gestured for him to come inside. He followed them in and into the priest's home in the courtyard. The girls brought tea, cakes, and rice wine. The swordsman ignored the refreshments and studied the girls.

"Why don't you have some saké?" the prettiest of the girls asked.

"I dislike tea and saké but if you can dance or sing, I would be delighted."

"Such an old-fashioned man for being so young!" she said. "If you don't drink, you can't know anything about love. You must live a dull life! But we can dance a little for you."

So the three girls opened their fans and danced. The swordsman hadn't expected the skill and grace they showed him. Country girls didn't dance like samurai women. Despite himself, he became entranced.

Suddenly, the three girls' heads disappeared. He sat back and blinked. Each of the girls held her own head in her hands. They threw them into the air and caught them and then tossed their heads to each other. One of them tossed her head at the swordsman. It landed on his knees, looked up, and laughed at him. He shoved the head away and drew his sword. He attacked, but the girls glided around his slashes, continuing to toss their heads around him while they laughed.

"Why don't you catch me?" the prettiest girl's head said. She dodged his attack as if he was a child first learning how to use a wooden sword.

The girls replaced their heads and laughed at him. Then they vanished.

The swordsman's heart thumped from his efforts and anger. The moonlit night stood still, broken only by the chirping of insects. He gazed around for any signs of the badger and noticed his basket of fish was gone. Realizing that the badger had outfoxed him, he could only accept his defeat and return home.

The next day, the swordsman told his friends of his misadventure. The young fisherman sympathized with him, but their other friend, a doctor, spoke up. "Give me three days, and I will catch that old badger."

The doctor went home and cooked a meat dish with poison. He then cooked a second portion without poison for himself. He took both dishes along with a bottle of saké to the temple. When he arrived, the temple was deserted. He followed the example of his friends and went to the priest's house in the courtyard, but it too stood empty. The doctor knew badgers were crafty, and he knew they were dreaming up some trick for him. So he decided to wait. As time passed without any girls appearing, the doctor spread out his evening meal, hoping to lure the badger out.

"There's nothing like solitude," he said. "Especially on a perfect night. I'm lucky to have found this deserted temple to enjoy the autumn moon."

He ate from his portion and drank, making a show of how much he enjoyed the meal. He was about to give up on the badger when he heard footsteps. He watched the entrance, expecting to see the badger disguised as a girl. Instead, an old priest entered and sat with a weary sigh. He wore old, travel-stained clothes and looked to be between seventy and eighty years old. He held a rosary in his withered hands.

"May I ask who you are?" the doctor said.

"I am the priest who used to live here back when the temple prospered. During Saigo's rebellion, I was sent to another parish until that temple was burned to the ground during the siege of Kumamoto castle. Since then, I wandered until I decided to return here in my old age. You can imagine how I felt when I saw it in such a sad state. I want to collect money to restore it, but at my age...." The old man began to cry.

After wiping his eyes on the sleeve of his threadbare robe, he looked at the doctor's food. "Can I ask you to spare a little of your meal? I haven't eaten in several days."

At first the doctor thought the priest was a priest in truth. The man's story was plausible, and the doctor felt compassion for the old man. But the man's accent sounded strange. *I won't let myself be tricked by this badger. I will see how clever he is,* the doctor thought.

"I'm sorry to hear about your misfortunes. You are welcome to share the rest of my meal. In fact, I will bring you more tomorrow. I will also tell my friends about your plan to restore the temple, and I will help you as I can." The doctor pushed the plate of poisoned food to the priest. He stood. "Please enjoy yourself. I will return tomorrow evening."

The next morning, the doctor told his friends of his encounter with the badger. They doubted his story, thinking he had drunk too much, because it was too different from the previous two encounters.

"Come with me tonight, then," the doctor said.

That evening, they all went to the temple. Inside the priest's house, all they found was the basket the doctor carried the food in the night before. They searched the house for signs of the badger, but found nothing. Finally, in a dark corner of the temple, they came upon the body of an old badger. It was the size of a large dog. Its fur had turned gray from age. They agreed that the badger had to be several hundred years old.

The doctor carried the body home and put it on display. For several days, neighbors came to see the body. Several reluctantly admitted to being tricked by the old badger and shared their stories with the doctor. They also decided to rebuild the temple so no other badger would turn it into a home.

The Badger's Money

Once an old priest lived in a hut in Hitachi at a place called Namekata. Only the nearby village knew of him, and his neighbors made sure he was well. They brought him food and clothing and kept his hut in repair. He wasn't known for his wisdom, and neither did the concerns of the world trouble him.

One frigid night, a voice called from outside his hut. When he opened the door to see who braved such a cold night, he saw an old badger. The old priest didn't feel afraid as most commoners would have. Instead, he asked the creature what it was doing.

The badger bowed. "My home is in the mountains. The snow and frost never used to trouble me, but I am growing old. The cold of tonight is too much for me. Please let me come inside and warm myself at your fire so I won't freeze to death."

The priest felt sorry for the shivering badger. Frost even clung to the poor creature's fur. "Hurry inside and warm yourself."

The desperate badger hadn't expected such a welcome. He hurried inside and warmed himself as the priest returned to his prayers. After two hours, the badger left, thanking the old priest. The next night the badger returned to warm itself. And for each night after that. The badger started collecting dried branches and dead leaves for firewood as payment for the priest's kindness. Over time, the priest developed a friendship with the badger and welcomed its company. On the few nights the badger failed to appear, the priest found himself missing it. When winter ended, the badger stopped visiting. When winter began again, so too did the badger's visits. This went on for ten years.

One day, the badger said to the priest. "Thanks to your kindness, I've been able to pass the winter nights in comfort. I am grateful, and I will always remember your kindness. Is there anything I can do to repay you? If you have any wish, please tell me."

The priest smiled. "I don't have any desires or wishes. There is nothing that I can ask you to do for me. Don't worry about it. As long as I live, you are welcome here during the winter."

The badger admired the depth of the old man's kindness. Few would grant a creature such as the badger such kindness, but the badger also wanted to repay the priest. Time to time, he returned to the subject.

The badger's good intentions touched the priest's heart. "Since I've shaven my head and turned away from the pleasures of the world, I don't have any desires. But I have to admit that I would like three *ryo*. I don't need food or clothes. The villages provide them. They even promised to take care of my body when I die. I don't need money, but if I had three *ryo* I would offer them to a shrine so they might pray for my salvation. The money can't be obtained by violence or unlawful means, of course."

The badger gave him a puzzled and anxious look. The priest regretted saying anything because it seemed to trouble the badger so much. "Don't give my words any thought," the priest waved his hand. "I shouldn't entertain such thoughts anyway."

The badger returned to the mountain and didn't return to the hut, even on the coldest winter nights. The priest supposed the badger didn't want to come without the money and concluded it died trying to steal it. He blamed himself and regretted telling the badger his sinful thoughts. He focused much of his time praying for the badger.

Three years passed. One night, the old priest heard a familiar voice outside. He jumped up and ran to the door. There waited the badger. "You're safe! Why didn't you come back sooner? I missed you and worried about you," the priest said.

"If the money you wanted was for anything else, I would have gotten it sooner. But I knew stolen money wouldn't have worked for how you want to spend it. So I went to the island of Sado and gathered the earth that miners thought worthless. I extracted the bits of gold left within it." The badger produced three new gold *ryo*.

"And you worked that hard because of my foolish words?" The priest's eyes watered. "Thank you."

"I wished to show my gratitude. Just don't tell anyone."

The priest wiped tears from his cheeks. The badger's gratitude moved the old man as few things in his long life had. "I wish I could promise that. If I keep the money here, someone will steal it. I have to give it to someone to keep it for me or offer it at the temple. When I do either, people will see a poor old hermit with more money than he should have. They would suspect me. But I will tell them that you no longer come to my hut so you don't have to worry either. But I would like you to keep coming here in secret."

The badger understood the priest's dilemma and agreed that the priest may share their story. And as long as the old priest lived, the badger visited each winter night.

The Crackling Mountain

Once there lived an old man and an old woman and their pet hare. They lived in the mountains, far from any town. Their only neighbor was a malicious badger. Every night, the badger tore up the old farmer's fields. He did so much damage that the good-natured farmer decided to kill the badger. He tried waiting with a club for the badger to come out, but he could never catch the beast. He laid traps across the farm and tried to remain patient. He knew one day the badger would make a mistake.

And that day came. The old farmer found the badger trapped in a hole and bound the badger with a rope. When he returned home, he hung the badger upside down from the rafters of his storehouse.

"I've finally caught the bad badger." The farmer told his wife. "Watch him for me while I go to work. Don't let him escape. He is my stew for tonight." The farmer left to repair his fields.

The badger didn't like the idea of becoming a stew and struggled to think of a means to escape with all the blood flowing into his brain. The farmer's wife pounded barley just beyond the storehouse's door. She looked tired and old. Wrinkles seamed her face, and her skin was as brown as soft leather.

"Dear lady," the badger said. "You shouldn't work so hard at your age. Let me help you. My arms are strong."

"Thank you, but I can't untie you. My husband would be angry if you escaped."

"That's not very nice. What if I promise not to escape? I will even let you retie me after I finish pounding the barley. I'm sore from being tied like this. Just a few minutes, and I will be thankful. Please, untie me." He made of show of being in pain for good measure.

The old woman didn't suspect anything. A promise made was a promise kept, and she thought it was cruel to see the badger tied and in such pain. The ropes and knots cut into the creature's legs. Out of sympathy, she untied him and let him down. She handed him the wooden pestle and told him to work while she rested for a moment. He took the pestle and sprang on her, swinging the heavy piece of wood with enough force that it broke when it struck her head. She crumpled, dead on the spot. Then the badger assumed the woman's form and cooked her body into a stew.

The badger in the guise of the old woman welcomed the hungry old man home and served the stew. "Come, I've made a good stew from the badger your tied up. Sit down and eat."

The old man took off his straw sandals and sat at his small dinner tray. He relished the scent of the badger stew before him.

As soon as he finished eating, the badger flashed into its true form. "Foolish old man! You've eaten your own wife." The badger gestured to the kitchen. "Look at her bones!" He laughed at the horror on the old man's face. In a blink, the badger disappeared.

The horrified old man collapsed and wailed and cried at what had happened. The hare heard the man's cries and came to see what troubled his old master. His master told him. When the hare saw the horror in the kitchen, he vowed to avenge his family and immediately set off into the mountain. He found the badger not too far off, waddling under a bundle of sticks strapped to his back. The hare sneaked up behind the badger, who was too busy singing and laughing to himself to notice, and set fire to the sticks.

When the badger finally heard the crackling noise, he turned to see the hare behind him. "What is that noise?"

The hare shrugged. "This is called the Crackling Mountain. There's always noise here."

The badger thanked the hare and continued on its way, but as the fire spread, popping and snapping, the badger turned again. The hare put him at ease with the same explanation.

A sudden wind stoked the fire, causing it to engulf the badger's back. Yelping, he fled and jumped into the nearby river. Although the river put the fire out, his back was burned black. The hare met the badger at the river's edge and pretended to console him. He offered a poultice for the burn. The badger wanted nothing more than to be free of the pain and offered his tattered back. But the hare had mixed spices and other painful herbs. The badger fled in blind agony, bewailing his misfortune.

When the badger finally got well, he went to the hare's house. He had to confront the wicked hare for causing him such pain. But his goal fled him when he saw the hare had built a boat.

"Why did you build a boat?" asked the badger.

"I'm going to the moon," said the hare. "Won't you come with me?"

The badger shook his head. "I've had enough of you on the Crackling Mountain. Don't think I've forgotten your tricks. I would rather make a boat myself. I will make it to the moon first." The badger began to build a boat from the clay beside the river.

The hare laughed at this, ignoring the badger's boasts. When the badger finished, they launched their boats. The waves splashed, but the hare had learned some things from the old man. He had built his boat out of wood. As they river carried them away, the badger's boat began to crumble away. The hare waited until the right moment and grabbed the stick the badger used as an oar. With a few savage strikes, the badger's clay boat broke apart. The badger flailed and struggled, but the current of the river pulled him under, never to be seen again.

When the old man heard that the hare avenged his wife, his depression left him. He petted and loved the white hare. Together they welcomed the returning spring.

A Noble Sacrifice

Once there was a man who enjoyed shooting birds. He became quite skilled at it, and people often requested certain birds for their dinners. The man happened to have two daughters who devoted themselves to the teachings of Buddha. They tried again and again to convince him to give up hunting. After all, destroying any sort of life went against the Buddha's teachings. But the man enjoyed the hunt too much to give it up.

One day, a neighbor asked him to shoot two storks, and the man promised to do so. When the daughters heard of this they said:

"Let us dress in white and go down to the shore tonight. Father will certainly go there, considering how many storks we've seen there lately. If Father should kill either of us by mistake, it will teach him a lesson. He will surely repent of his ways then."

That night the man went to the shore, but the cloudy sky made it difficult to see. Finally, he saw two white shapes in the distance. He steadied himself and took the shot. The white shapes dropped immediately, and he ran to see his catch. To his horror, he saw his daughters lying dead. Only then did the lessons of his daughters hit him. In sorrow and regret, he burned his children on a funeral pyre. He shaved his head, went into the woods, and became a hermit for the rest of his days.

Gojiro's Dream

Gojiro was a studious twelve-year-old boy who lived in Fukui. His father had promised to give him a book of wonderful Chinese stories if he read through the five volumes of *The Ancient History of Japan*. Gojiro did just that! When his father returned from Kyoto, he presented his son with sixteen volumes. The books were bound with silk and illustrated with woodblock prints.

The stories delighted Gojiro. He read deep into the night until he fell asleep on his books.

He dreamed he was in faraway China, walking the banks of the Yellow River. He didn't understand the people's language, and they wore unfamiliar clothes. He watched a fisherman work with a set of odd birds. Each bird would dive into the water and return with a fish in its mouth. Gojiro wondered why the bird didn't just swallow the fish. Then he saw the bird had a ring around its neck. The fisherman would help the bird back onto the boat and take the fish from it. In return, he would feed it a sliver of fish he kept in a basket.

All along the river, trees blossomed and flowers bloomed. Fish swam in large schools beneath those trees. They swam and leaped against the current and up the waterfalls. Gojiro clapped and urged them on, greatly enjoying the fight between fish and current.

The boy came across an old, white-bearded sage standing on the bank. Gojiro took a stick and wrote with Chinese characters: "What is the name of this part of the river?"

"We call it Lung Men," the sage said.

"Can you please write it?" Gojiro wrote in the dirt. He pulled out his ink case and a roll of soft mulberry paper.

The sage wrote the two Chinese characters that meant "Dragon's Gate" and turned away to watch a carp swimming nearby.

"I see," Gojiro said to himself. "That's pronounced Riu Mon in Japanese. I'll keep going up stream. There must be some reason why the fish are climbing up the river."

The banks angled upward and changed into high bluffs. Fir trees topped them, and white clouds weaved through the trees. The river circled around the bluffs. Gojiro glanced back and saw the fish trying to reach where he stood.

A single carp leaped high into the air at the final leg of the cascade and slipped into the calm, mirrored water in front of Gojiro. It had made it inside the Dragon's Gate!

One of the fleecy white clouds dipped down and swirled into a waterspout above the river. The carp darted toward it. As it leaped into it, it transformed into a white dragon and rose along the waterspout. Its scales flashed white, and it looked at Gojiro with two red eyes.

The boy woke up.

"Odd that a carp would become a white dragon," he murmured.

The next day, he told his mother about his dream and his observation.

"It is a good lesson for you," she said. "The carp persevered, leaping up the waterfalls until he became a dragon. I hope you will do the same and enter a high government position."

Gojiro stroked his chin. "So that is what my teacher means when he says 'I'm a fish today, but I hope to be a dragon tomorrow.' And that's what Father means when he says 'That fish's son, Kofuku, has become a white dragon while I am still a carp.'"

Kadzutoyo and the Badger

Kadzutoyo and his retainer enjoyed fishing. On one fishing trip, they got caught in a storm, and they had to shelter under a willow tree. After some time passed, the storm showed no signs of abating, so they decided to continue home despite the downpour. They hadn't gotten far when they encountered a young girl crying. Kadzutoyo regarded her with suspicion—after all, what girl would sit in such a rain?— but his retainer could only see her beauty. The retainer asked why she was out in the storm.

"My stepmother hates me. Tonight she beat me, and I had enough. I decided to run away to stay with my aunt who lives in the next village. But a strange pain struck me just as the storm hit."

The kindhearted retainer reached out to her, his love for her evident on his face.

Without warning, Kadzutoyo drew his sword and cut off her head.

The retainer froze with shock as the head rolled to his feet. He turned toward Kadzutoyo in rage. "How can you kill a harmless girl like that? Didn't you hear all she had been through? You will pay for what you've done."

Kadzutoyo continued to watch the girl's body as if he expected it to spring up. "Be quiet. You don't understand the situation." Finally satisfied, he sheathed his sword and walked away. "Let's go."

The retainer glanced at the body. He couldn't just leave her unburied! But Kadzutoyo showed no signs of stopping. The retainer growled his frustration and followed. He fumed on the rest of their way home. When Kadzutoyo went to sleep, the retainer continued to think about the murder of the girl. Finally, he got up and went to Kadzutoyo's parents and told them what had happened.

After hearing the tale, Kadzutoyo's father stormed into his son's bedroom. He woke Kadzutoyo. "How could you kill an innocent girl without a reason? You've shamed yourself. You've shamed me and the family." He drew his sword. "There is only one way to reclaim our family's honor."

Kadzutoyo didn't flinch at the sword. Instead, he remained calm. "Like my retainer, you don't understand. I am not guilty of any crime as you think. In fact, I've followed the samurai code. The girl I killed wasn't a girl as everyone thinks. Go tomorrow and see for yourself. If you find a girl's body, I will kill myself to make amends."

At dawn, Kadzutoyo's father gathered his retainers and set out. On the side of the road, they didn't see the body of a girl as the father feared they would. Instead, they found the body of a large headless badger.

After the father returned, he asked his son, "How did you know the girl was a badger?"

"It appeared to be a girl, but her beauty was strange. She didn't have the beauty of an earthly woman. I saw her clothes remained dry despite how hard it was raining. I knew at once the woman was some sort of goblin or creature. It had taken the form of a maiden to bewitch us and steal our fish."

Kadzutoyo's father admired his son's cleverness and foresight. He decided to retire and proclaimed Kadzutoyo the prince of Tosa.

Koma and Gon

Long ago, a music teacher lived close to Kyoto with only a serving woman and a beautiful cat to keep him company. Gon was a wonderful cat with a sleek coat, bushy tail, and green eyes. His master loved him and often said as the cat purred by his side in the evenings, "Nothing will separate us, old friend."

Ume was a happy young woman who lived in the midst of the plum groves. She loved her little cat, Koma. "You are such a good cat, Koma," Ume said. "I'm sure your ancestors shed tears when our Buddha died. You will always be with me."

Unknown to their humans, Gon and Koma loved each other dearly. Gon's handsomeness made the other cats in the district jealous. And all the female cats wanted to be his mate. But his heart only saw Koma. The cat lovers had a problem. Gon's master would have gladly taken Koma in to live with him, but Ume wouldn't hear of this. Likewise, Gon couldn't leave his master.

So their hearts wrestled with the love they had for each other and the loyalty they had for their masters.

On the seventh night of the seventh moon, Gon and Koma left their homes and fled together into the moon-bright night. They scampered through the rice fields and across the plains. When day broke, they stood near a palace with a large park full of old trees and ponds covered with lotus flowers.

"Oh that we could live in that palace," Koma said. As she spoke, a fierce dog saw the cats and bounded toward them. Koma cried out and sprang up a nearby cherry tree.

Gon didn't move. "You will see that I am a hero, Koma! I will die rather than run."

The powerful dog was almost upon the brave cat when a servant arrived and drove the dog off. The man scooped up Gon and carried him into the palace, leaving Koma alone in the tree.

The princess who lived in the palace was overjoyed when the servant brought Gon to her. And days passed before he could finally slip out of her sight. He immediately went looking for Koma, but he didn't find her anywhere.

As Gon overheard from the servants while he searched for Koma, the princess lived in splendor and happiness, but a great snake loved her. At all hours the snake would try to come near her. A constant guard kept the snake back, but sometimes it succeeded in reaching the door to her room.

One afternoon, as she played her koto while Gon slept nearby, the snake slipped past the guards and into her room. Gon sprang on it and killed it. When the princess heard the noise and discovered that Gon had risked his life for her, she was moved. The entire household praised him and fed him some of the best treats. But Gon couldn't be happy. Not without Koma.

On a summer day, he sunned himself before the open door of the palace. Half asleep, he looked out and dreamed of the moonlit night he and Koma fled their former homes. He noticed a large cat mistreating a little one in the garden. He jumped up and flew to her aid. He drove the larger cat away and turned to the little cat to see if she was hurt. He froze when he saw her.

Koma!

She wasn't the sleek, beautiful Koma he remembered. She was thin and sad, but her eyes sparkled as she gazed at Gon. Immediately, Gon took her to the princess and shared their love story.

She smiled. "I'm so happy for both of you."

On the seventh night of the seventh moon—the same night when Kingen crossed the Silver River of Heaven to visit his Shakujo—Gon and Koma married. The princess watched over them and took good care of them. Years passed. Then, on a sunny day, the princess found them curled up together.

The two faithful hearts had stopped beating.

Mandarin Ducks

Sonjo lived as a falconer and hunter in the district called Tamura-no-Go in Mutsu Province. On his way from an unsuccessful hunting trip, Sonjo saw a pair of mandarin ducks swimming together in a river. Sonjo knew that killing such ducks was bad luck, but he was famished. His arrow killed the male. The female duck escaped into the far rushes. Pleased that he had managed to find dinner, he returned home.

That night, he dreamed. A beautiful woman came into his room and stood beside his pillow, crying. Sonjo felt his heart ache with her sobs. "Why?" she asked. "Why did you kill him? What did he do wrong? We were so happy together. You have also killed me. I can't live without my husband."

She wept for a time. Then she took a shuddering breath and said,

At the coming of twilight,
I invited him to return with me.

Now to sleep alone in the shadow of the rushes of Akanuma
  Unspeakable misery.

She shook her head. "You don't know what you've done. Tomorrow when you go to Akanuma you will see and understand." She turned away and disappeared.

When Sonjo awoke in the morning, the dream remained vivid in his memory. He left at once for the river. When he arrived at Akanuma, he saw the female duck swimming alone. The duck saw him and swam straight toward him instead of trying to escape. She stopped a short distance from the river bank. Suddenly, she tore open her body with her own beak and died as he watched.

Sonjo shaved his head and became a priest that day.

Nedzumi

Two rats made their home in a lonely farmstead surrounded by rice fields. They lived happily in their home for so long that other rats, who had to regularly find new homes, believed the couple was protected by Fukoruku Jin, the god of long life.

The couple had a large family of children, and every summer they led the little ones into the rice fields. Under the waving stalks, the children learned of the history and cunning of their people. After their lessons, the parents let their little ones run and play with their friends until dusk.

Nedzumi was the gem of these children and the pride of her parents. Her sleek silver skin, bright intelligent eyes, tiny upstanding ears, and pearly white teeth truly did make her the most beautiful of rats. Her parents worried that they wouldn't be able to find anyone good enough to marry their daughter. After much discussion they decided only the most powerful being in the universe would be worthy of her.

They discussed the problem with a trusted neighbor who said, "You must seek the sun to marry her because his empire extends across the entire world."

So the parents took to the skies. How, no rat can tell. The sun met with them and listened to their request. "Your daughter is indeed beautiful," the sun said. "And I'm honored you offer her hand to me, but why did you choose me?"

"Because we want our Nedzumi to marry the mightiest being, and you alone span the world."

"My kingdom is vast, but often when I want to illuminate the world, a cloud floats by and covers me. I cannot pierce the cloud, so you need to speak with him if you want your wish."

The rats thanked the sun and came upon a cloud as he rested from his flight. The cloud sighed at the intrusion, but mischief shined in his dusky eyes. "You are mistaken if you think I am the most powerful being. Sometimes I can hide the sun, but I cannot withstand the wind. He tears me to pieces and blows me wherever he wants. My strength isn't equal to his."

The rat parents felt sad as they heard this, but they refused to give up on their daughter's future. They waylaid the wind as he swept through a pine forest and told him of their mission.

"It is true that I have the strength to drive away clouds," the wind whispered. "but I am powerless against the wall men build to keep me back. The wall is mightier than me."

Anxiety riddled the well-meaning parents as they set out to speak with the wall. The wall listened to their story and answered, "I can withstand the wind, but a rat undermines me and makes holes through my very heart. I cannot overcome him. So you must wed your daughter to him if you want her to be the wife of the most powerful being in the world."

After hearing this, the parent rats returned to their home. Nedzumi rejoiced at their news that she was to marry one of her own people. She had already given her heart to a playmate of the rice fields. They married and lived many years as the king and queen of the rat world.

Shippeitaro

Long ago, a warrior sought adventure. For some time, he traveled without finding anything curious. One evening, he trekked through a thick forest on a lonely mountain. Not a single village, cottage, or hermit hut could be found. He hiked a faint, overgrown trail that became increasingly hard to see as night fell and the briars grew thicker with each step.

He stumbled into a clearing and upon a small temple. Broken walls and grass encroached paths lined the temple grounds. But the shrine appeared intact. With the night's cold falling, he took shelter in the ruin. He didn't have food, so he wrapped himself in his cloak and kept his good sword close. He fell asleep just a few moments later.

Around midnight, a dreadful noise woke him. At first, he thought he was dreaming, but the shrine resounded with terrible shrieks and wails. The young warrior snatched his sword and gazed through a hole in the ruined wall. Just beyond, a troop of hideous cats danced. Among their screeches the young warrior heard them say:

"Don't tell it to Shippeitaro. Keep it close and dark. Don't tell Shippeitaro."

The beautiful full moon cast its light on the grotesque dance. The warrior watched with amazement and horror, his grip tightening on his sword. When the midnight hour finally passed, the phantom cats suddenly disappeared. Silence returned. The rest of the night passed undisturbed, and the warrior fell back to sleep.

When he awoke, the sun shined overhead. The warrior wasted no time leaving the scene of last night's dance. Luckily, the sun revealed the traces of the path he was following. The path angled away from the mountain and toward an open plain. There he saw scattered cottages and a village further ahead. His hunger spurred him toward the village.

The sound of a woman crying reached him. He hurried toward the sound, forgetting his hunger, to see what was the matter and if he could offer help. Search as he would, he couldn't find the source of the crying. He asked the villagers he encountered about the sound, but they could only shake their heads.

"Every year," one old man said, "the mountain spirit claims a victim. Tonight he will devour our loveliest maiden. The crying you hear is hers."

The warrior seemed to have found the adventure he had searched for. He pressed for more information. The villagers told him they would put the victim into a cage at sunset and carry her to the same ruined temple he slept within. There, they would leave her. The next morning she would vanish. Each year they saw to the terrible ritual. As the warrior listened, he became determined to save the maiden. He also remembered the phantom cats from the night before and asked the old man if he had heard of Shippeitaro.

"Shippeitaro is a strong and beautiful dog. He belongs to the head man of our village who lives a little way from here. We often see him with his master. He is a brave, good dog."

The warrior decided to search out the connection and hurried to Shippeitaro's master. He begged the man to lend the dog for one night. At first the man was unwilling, but he relented on the condition that it was only overnight.

Next, the warrior went to see the parents of the maiden and told them to keep her in the house. He also told them to watch for his return. He placed Shippeitaro into the cage meant for the maiden. With the help of some of the village's young men, he carried it to the ruined temple. The young men refused to stay a moment longer than they had to and fled as if they were chased by demons. The warrior settled in to wait with only Shippeitaro for company.

When the full moon was high in the heavens, the phantom cats appeared. This time a huge black tom cat joined them. The tom stood fiercer and more terrible than any of the others, and the young warrior knew the cat was the mountain fiend himself. As soon as the fiend spotted the cage, it pounced on top with screeches of triumph. The cats paced and rattled the cage, seeking to torment the victim inside.

But this time, the fiend had met his match. When the fiend finally threw open the door, brave Shippeitaro attacked. The dog seized the cat and held him fast as the young warrior leaped from his hiding place. His sword whistled as he sliced the air, and the fiend died with the single stroke.

The other cats froze with astonishment, gazing on their dead leader. Shippeitaro and the warrior tore into them. In just a few moments all of the phantom cats lay dead.

The young warrior returned the brave Shippeitaro to his master and thanked him. Then, he went to the maiden's house and told her parents that she was safe and that the fiend had claimed its last victim from the village.

"You owe all of this to the brave Shippeitaro," the warrior said.

He left the village to search for new adventures and people to help.

The Faithful Cat

One summer, a man visited his friend in Osaka. "I've eaten an extraordinary cake today," the man told his friend.

"What was so special about it?"

"I received the cake from a family who were celebrating the one-hundred year anniversary of a cat's death. When I asked about the history of this cat, they told me about a young girl. When she was sixteen years old, a tom-cat followed her everywhere she went. This cat had grown up in the house, and the two were never separate. When the father finally noticed the cat's focus, he grew angry. You see, he thought the cat had fallen in love with his daughter and had forgotten all the kindness the family had given it. He worried that the cat intended to cast a spell on the girl, so he decided the cat had to die. As he worked out the plan, the cat discovered the father's intent and spoke with him one night."

"'You suspect me of being in love with your daughter. You're wrong. There is a large old rat who lives in your granary. This old rat is in love with my young mistress, and this is why I dare not leave her for even a moment. The old rat will carry her off. I am not a match for this rat, but there is a cat who is. The cat's name is Buchi and he lives in Ajikawa. Borrow him and we will soon end this old rat.'"

"When the father awoke from his dream, he went off to Ajikawa to find the house in which the cat lived. He had no difficulty finding the cat and called on his master. He told the cat's master of his dream and his wish to borrow Buchi."

"'Take him with you and put an end to that rat,' Buchi's master said. And so the father took Buchi home. That night he put both cats into the granary. In a short time, a terrible clatter erupted. After it ended, the father opened the door, and his family crowded inside. There they saw the two cats and the rat locked together, panting and wounded. The father cut the throat of the rat, which was as big as either of the cats, and tended to the two feline heroes. But despite the family's efforts, the cats grew weak from their wounds and died. The family threw the rat into the river and buried the cats with honor at the nearby temple.'"

The Hare of Inaba

Long, long ago, when all the animals could talk, there lived in the province of Inaba, a little white hare. His home was on the island of Oki, and just across the sea was the mainland of Inaba.

Now, the hare wanted to cross over to Inaba. Day after day he would go out and sit on the shore and look longingly over the water, and day after day he hoped to find some way of getting across.

One day as usual, the hare was standing on the beach when he saw a great crocodile swimming near the island.

"This is very lucky!" thought the hare. "Now I shall be able to get my wish. I will ask the crocodile to carry me across the sea!"

But he was doubtful whether the crocodile would consent. Instead of asking for a favor he would try to get what he wanted by a trick.

So with a loud voice he called to the crocodile and said: "Oh, Mr. Crocodile, isn't it a lovely day?"

The crocodile, who had come out all by itself that day to enjoy the bright sunshine, was just beginning to feel a bit lonely when the hare's cheerful greeting broke the silence. The crocodile swam to the shore, pleased to hear someone speak.

"I wonder who it was that spoke to me just now! Was it you, Mr. Hare? You must be very lonely all by yourself!"

"Oh, no, I am not at all lonely," said the hare, "but as it was such a fine day, I came out here to enjoy myself. Won't you stop and play with me a little while?"

The crocodile came out of the sea and sat on the shore, and the two played together for some time. Then the hare said, "Mr. Crocodile, you live in the sea and I live on this island, and we do not often meet, so I know very little about you. Tell me, are there more crocodiles than hares?"

"Of course there are more crocodiles than hares," answered the crocodile. "Can you not see that for yourself? You live on this small island, while I live in the sea, which spreads through all parts of the world, so if I call together all the crocodiles who dwell in the sea, you hares will be as nothing compared to us!"

"Do you think it possible for you to call up enough crocodiles to form a line from this island across the sea to Inaba?"

The crocodile thought for a moment. "Of course, it is possible."

"Then try it," the hare said, "and I will count the number from here!"

The crocodile, who was very simple-minded, agreed to do what the hare asked. "Wait a little while I go back into the sea and call my company together!"

The crocodile plunged into the sea and was gone for some time. The hare, meanwhile, waited patiently on the shore. At last the crocodile appeared, bringing with him a large number of other crocodiles.

"Look, Mr. Hare!" he said, "it is nothing for my friends to form a line between here and Inaba. There are enough crocodiles to stretch from here even as far as China or India. Have you ever seen so many?"

Then the crocodiles arranged themselves in the water, forming a bridge between the Island of Oki and the mainland of Inaba.

When the hare saw the bridge, he said, "How splendid! I did not believe this was possible. Now let me count you all! To do this, however, with your permission, I must walk over on your backs to the other side, so please stay still, or else I shall fall into the sea and drown!"

So the hare hopped off the island onto the strange bridge, counting as he jumped from one crocodile's back to the next: "Please keep quite still, or I shall not be able to count. One, two, three, four, five, six, seven, eight, nine—"

Thus, the cunning hare walked right across to the mainland of Inaba. Not content with getting his wish, he began to jeer at the crocodiles instead of thanking them, and said, as he leaped off the last one's back: "Oh! you stupid crocodiles, you are so easily tricked!" He laughed at them, making them lash their tails with anger.

And he was just about to run away when the crocodiles attacked. They surrounded the hare and pulled out all his fur. He cried out and begged for them to stop, but with each tuft of fur they pulled out they said "Serves you right!"

When the crocodiles had pulled out the last bit of fur, they threw the poor hare on the beach and swam away, laughing and satisfied with their revenge.

The hare was now in a pitiful plight. His bare little body quivered with pain, and his blood soaked the sand. He tried to move and failed. All he could do was to lie helpless on the beach and cry over the misfortune that had befallen him.

Just at this time a number of princes passed and, seeing the hare lying on the beach crying, stopped and asked what was the matter.

The hare lifted up his head from between his paws. "I had a fight with some crocodiles, but I was beaten, and they pulled out all my fur and left me to suffer."

Now, one of these princes had a bad and spiteful disposition. But he feigned kindness, and said to the hare: "I feel very sorry for you. If you will only try it, I know of a remedy which will cure your sore body. Go and bathe yourself in the sea, and then come and sit in the wind. This will make your fur grow again, and you will be just as you were before."

The princes then continued their journey. The hare was pleased, thinking that he had found a cure. He went and bathed in the sea and then came out and sat where the wind could blow upon him. But as the wind blew and dried him, his skin became drawn and hardened, and the salt increased the pain so much that he rolled on the sand in desperation.

Just then another prince arrived, carrying a great bag on his back. He saw the hare, and stopped and asked what had happened. But the poor hare, remembering that he had been deceived by a man who looked similar to this prince, didn't answer. He could only cry.

However, this man had a kind heart. "You poor thing! I see that your fur is all pulled out and that your skin is quite bare. Who treated you so cruelly?"

The man's kind voice coaxed the hare to share his story. When the hare finished, the man's face filled with empathy. "I am sorry for all you have suffered, but remember, it was only the consequence of the deceit you practiced on the crocodiles."

"I know," answered the hare, "but I've learned my lesson, so please tell me how I can cure myself and make my fur grow again."

"First go and bathe in that pond over there and try to wash all the salt from your body. Then pick some of those bulrushes that are growing near the edge of the water, spread them on the ground and roll yourself on them. If you do this, the pollen will cause your fur to grow again, and you will be quite well in a little while."

The desperate hare crawled to the pond pointed out to him and bathed in it. Then he picked the bulrushes growing near the water and rolled on them. To his amazement, he saw his nice white fur grow, and the pain stopped. When he finished rolling, he felt just as he had before all his misfortunes.

He was overjoyed at his quick recovery and hopped joyfully towards the young man who had helped him. He kneeled before the man. "I cannot express my thanks for all you have done for me! It is my earnest wish to do something for you in return. Please tell me what lord you are."

"I am not a lord." answered the man, "And those men who passed here before me are my brothers. They have heard of a beautiful princess called Yakami who lives in this province of Inaba, and they are on their way to find her and to ask her to marry one of them. I am only their attendant. That's why I carry this large bag on my back."

"I can't believe the man who told me to bathe in the sea is one of your brothers. I am quite sure that the princess will refuse all of them. She would prefer you because of your good heart. I am certain that she will ask to be your bride."

The prince shook his head and gazed at the sky. "I have to hurry to catch up to my brothers. Goodbye."

He found his brothers as they entered the princess's gate. Just as the hare had said, the princess didn't want anything to do with them, but when she looked at the kind brother's face she went to him and said: "To you I give myself," and so they were married.

The Kind Giver and the Grudging Giver

A man cast his net into a river and pulled out a large number of fish. A raven watched from a nearby branch. The bird seemed to be hungry, so the fisherman threw his best fish at it. The raven ate it with obvious joy. After it finished, it flew to the fisherman as he worked with his catch on the shore.

"Thank you for feeding me," the raven said. "If you come with me, my father will thank you too."

The fisherman blinked. "A talking raven!" Curiosity made him follow the raven home. They traveled a long way until they came to a large house. The raven flew into the house. After hesitating a moment, the fisherman followed. A girl stood before him, dressed in black with black, feathery hair. An old man and woman stood beside her. The fisherman supposed the girl was the raven because her hair looked like feathers.

"Thank you for feeding my daughter," the old man said. "I want to reward you for your kindness."

Two puppies appeared from behind the man, one was gold and the other was silver. He picked up the puppies and handed them to the fisherman. "I could give you treasure, but these puppies will benefit you more. The gold puppy will produce gold bars. The silver puppy will produce silver bars."

Uncertain what to think, the fisherman thanked them and returned home. He fed the puppies a little food at a time and sure enough they pooped gold and silver!

The fisherman's story soon circulated and inspired another man to try to find the raven family. He went into the river and cast his net until the raven arrived. The man smeared a fish with mud and threw it at the raven. The raven flew away, and the man chased her to the large house. He burst inside to find the old man.

"You selfish man," the old man said. "You gave my daughter a fish smeared with mud. Although I am angry with you, I will give you some puppies for at least attempting to feed my daughter. If you take care of the puppies properly, you will benefit." The old man gave the fisherman a gold puppy and a silver puppy.

On the way home, the man said to himself. "If I feed a lot to these puppies, they will give me all kinds of gold and silver. It would be foolish to feed them only a little."

So he fed the puppies everything he could, including garbage. The puppies pooped normally instead of pooping gold and silver. The man's house quickly filled with the puppies' poop. His house became so filthy that no one would go near it or the man.

The Snow Tomb

Rokugo Yakeji was a skilled swordsman for his young age. He had such skill that he was asked to teach swordsmanship at one of the best schools in Tokyo. One January, the students celebrated the New Year by telling ghost stories. Each lit a candle and placed it in the darkest, furthest end of the garden. After each person told their story, they had to cross into the darkness and return with their candle.

Soon Rokugo's turn came to tell his story. He gazed about the huddled assistants and students and said, "My friends, this story isn't dreadful, but it is true. Three years ago, when I was seventeen, my father sent me to Gifu in Mino Province. I reached a place called Nakimura at about ten in the evening. Outside the village, in a wild and unfarmed field I saw a strange fireball. It moved here and there without making a noise. It came close to me and sped away again, as if it was looking for something. It kept going around the same bit of land, but generally it stayed five feet from the ground. Sometimes it dipped lower. I wasn't frightened, but I was glad when I made it to the Miyoshiya Inn. The next morning my curiosity got the better of me. I told the innkeeper what I had seen, and he told me a story of his own."

"'About two hundred years ago, a great battle was fought here, and the defeated general was killed. When his soldiers recovered his body, it lacked a head. The soldiers thought the enemy had stolen it. And one soldier continued to search for his general's head even as the battle raged. He was killed while he searched. Since that evening, the fireball has burned after ten o'clock. We've called it *Kubi sagashi no hi.*' As the innkeeper told me this story, I felt uncomfortable. It was the first ghost I had seen."

The students agreed that the story was strange. Rokugo stood and went to fetch his candle from the far end of the garden. He hadn't gotten far when he heard the voice of a woman. The snow reflected the moon's wane light, but Rokugo didn't see a woman anywhere. He reached the candles when the voice called again. He turned and saw a beautiful woman. She wore a kimono patterned with pine and bamboo. Her sudden appearance and beauty struck Rokugo for a moment before he realized the woman couldn't be real.

He concluded the woman was a ghost, and he had a chance to distinguish himself in front of all his friends. So he drew his sword and with a single stroke cut the spirit in half. He seized his candle and ran back to where his students waited. He told them about his encounter and asked one of them to see the ghost.

After a few moments, Yamamoto Jonosuke volunteered and set off for the garden. The other students, feeling ashamed of their lack of pluck, followed him.

When they came upon the spot where the ghost was supposed to be, they found the remains of the snowman they had made earlier that day. It was cut in half just as Rokugo described, and they all laughed. At first, a few of the students thought Rokugo had played a prank on them, but when they returned, they found him to be all business.

"We indeed found the evidence of your swordsmanship," one student told Rokugo. "Even a small boy could do what you did."

Rokugo's temper flared, and his hand flew to his sword. "I will kill you for your insolence."

The student held up his hands in apology. "Your ghost was only the snowman we made this morning."

Rokugo frowned and apologized. He couldn't understand how he could mistake a snowman for a ghost. He asked the students not to say anything about it and left the house.

He passed near the gates of Korinji Temple and saw a woman running across the temple grounds. He leaned against the fence and watched her. Her hair and clothes were disheveled. A man appeared behind her with a butcher's knife in his hand.

"You wicked woman. You cheated on my friend, and I will kill you for it."

He caught up to the woman and stabbed her six times. Rokugo pushed away from the fence and walked toward home, thinking how good a friend the man was. A woman who dishonored her marriage vows should be rewarded with death.

He walked a short distance and suddenly came upon the woman he had just seen.

"How can a brave samurai watch a murder without doing anything? Did you enjoy yourself?" she asked.

Rokugo took a step back. "Don't talk to me as if I was your husband. I was pleased to see you killed for being unfaithful. If you are the ghost of the woman, I will kill you myself." But before he could draw his sword the ghost vanished.

Rokugo took a deep breath to gather himself and continued home. When he neared his house, another woman rushed up to him with her face contorted as if in agony.

He had had enough with women that evening. He assumed they were badgers or foxes that were playing a prank on him at that point. He remembered how foxes and badgers emitted a light about their bodies, and he studied the woman. Sure enough, he saw a faint light surrounding her.

Rokugo drew his sword and struck the air beside the woman. He had once heard foxes stood on the left side of their illusions. He felt his sword hit flesh, and the woman vanished. He ran into his house, calling on his family members to come out with lanterns. They followed him outside. They found the body under their two-hundred year old myrtle tree. But instead of finding a fox or badger as Rokugo expected, they found an otter. They carried the otter inside, and Rokugo invited all the students to see it, proving that he wasn't fooled by a snowman.

The Two Frogs

Osaka and Kyoto stand twenty-seven miles apart as the crane flies. One is a city of canals and bridges with streets bustling with trade. The other is the sacred city of the Emperor, ringed with green hills and clean, quiet streets. Long ago, a frog lived in a pond in Osaka and another frog lived in the wells of Kyoto.

The Kyoto frog often heard the maids who drew water from the well say "the frog in the well doesn't know the ocean." He grew tired of hearing it and decided to travel and see the ocean they kept speaking about.

"I will see it for myself," he told himself as he packed his clothes. "I bet it isn't half as deep or wide as they say."

In truth, the water in the well had dropped because of an earthquake, giving him a good reason to search for a better home. His wife cried a great deal and declared she would count the hours on her fingers until he returned. She also said she would set out his meal every morning and evening just as if he was home. She wrapped a small lacquered box full of boiled rice and snails for his journey. She bundled extra clothes and settled them onto his back for him. He seized his staff and set off with a final goodbye to his family. He would most certainly miss his two polliwogs. They watched him from their older brothers' backs with large, sad eyes.

The Kyoto frog set off, noticing that other animals didn't jump as he. Instead, they walked on their legs. He didn't want to attract undue attention, so he mimicked them, walking upright on his hind legs until they grew tired and then waddling on all four.

At Osaka, another father frog grew restless with his life on the edges of his lotus pond. His pond sat next to a monastery of Buddhist monks, so he heard everything they studied every day: Confucius and prayers and the classics.

The philosophical frog sat nearby one day when two monks came up to his pond.

"The babies of frogs will become but frogs. What do you think?" asked the first.

"The white lotus flower springs out of the black mud," the other said. They walked away, still in discussion.

"Humph!" croaked the frog. "The babies of frogs will only become frogs? If mud becomes a lotus, why can't a frog become a man? If my son travels to see the world, places such as Kyoto, why can't he become as wise as those shiny-headed men? I will 'cast the lion cub into the valley.'"

So the philosophical father frog told his eldest son to go on a journey to Kyoto.

The Kyoto frog and the Osaka frog happened to leave at the same time. Both had uneventful journeys. As luck would have it, both frogs met on a hill near Hashimoto, halfway between both cities. Both frogs were footsore and tired by then, with their hips hurting from walking instead of hopping.

The frogs exchanged niceties, both being properly polite frogs, and introduced themselves.

"I am Gamataro from Osaka, the oldest son of Lord Bullfrog, the Prince of the Lotus Ditch."

"You must be tired from your journey. I am the Frog of the Well in Kyoto. I started out to see the ocean, but my hips hurt so much that I may give up on my plan and just be content with the view of this hill. Maybe we can save ourselves the trouble of both our journeys. This hill is halfway. While I see Osaka and the ocean, you can get a look at Kyoto."

"That is a good idea," said the young Osaka frog.

Both frogs reared on their hind legs, stretching on their toes and propping each other up. They looked toward what they supposed were their goals. Of course, they had forgotten that their eyes were on the backs of their heads. So when they stood up, each gazed behind instead of toward their destinations.

They gazed long at their supposed destinations until they grew too tired to stand and fell down on all fours.

"Osaka looks just like Kyoto," said the Kyoto frog. "And as for the ocean those stupid maids talked about, I don't see that at all. Unless they meant that strip of river. I don't believe there is any ocean."

"I am satisfied that it is foolish to go any further," said the young Osaka frog. "Kyoto is as similar to Osaka as one grain of rice is like another. My father is a fool with all his philosophy."

They congratulated themselves for saving such time and effort with their clever plan and turned toward home. They dropped into a frog's hop and returned home in half the time—the Kyoto frog to his well and the Osaka frog to his pond. They each told the story of how both cities were exactly alike, and how the cities were an example of the foolishness of men. The philosophical frog was so happy to have his son return safely that he gave up trying to reason out the problems of philosophy he overheard.

And so the frog in the well continued to not believe in the ocean, and the babies of frogs still became frogs. But the glorious white lotus still grew out of black mud.

The Vampire Cat of Nabeshima

The prince of Hizen favored Toyo over all the other ladies of the court. One day, they went into the garden to enjoy the flowers. When they returned to the palace at sunset, a large cat followed them. The pair said their goodnights and departed.

The next day, the prince's strength began to fail. He became pale and listless, preferring to spend what strength he had with Toyo. At night, he suffered from nightmares that woke his wife and his councilors. In response, they appointed one hundred retainers to watch over him at night.

On the first night of the watch, an irresistible drowsiness put all the retainers to sleep. Nightmares harassed the prince until morning. Night after night this repeated until three of the prince's councilors decided to guard him themselves. But by ten o'clock, they too fell asleep.

The next morning, the councilors met to discuss what happened.

"This has to be a work of witchcraft," Ishahaya Buzen, the chief councilor, said. "There's no other way one hundred men would all fall asleep at once. We need to have Ruiten, the chief priest of Miyo In Temple, pray for us and for the recovery of our lord."

Ruiten proved happy to help and prayed for the prince each night. One night, around midnight, he prepared to sleep and heard a noise outside in the garden. It sounded as if someone was washing in the well. Curious, he looked down from the window. In the moonlight, he saw a handsome young soldier washing himself. After he finished, the young man prayed before the statue of the Buddha and prayed for the recovery of the prince.

After the young man finished, Ruiten called out. "Wait a minute. I have something to tell you. Why don't you come up here?"

The young man did as he was asked.

"I admire a loyal young man like you," Ruiten said. "What is your name?"

"I am Ito Soda. I serve as a soldier in Nabeshima. Since my lord has been sick, I think only of finding a way to help him. But I am too low of rank to be near him. So all I can do is pray."

"He suffers from a strange sickness. All the retainers who stay up to watch over him fall into a mysterious sleep," Ruiten said.

"If I could just sit up one night with my lord, I would see if I could resist the witchcraft and catch the creature doing it," Soda said.

Ruiten rubbed his chin. "I should be able to arrange that if you wish."

Soda bowed. "I would be honored."

"I will take you there tomorrow night."

Soda returned to the temple the next evening. Ruiten took him to Buzen and introduced the young man.

"It is impossible to allow a man of such low rank to watch over our lord," Buzen said.

"Why not raise his rank based on his fidelity?" Ruiten asked. Soda remained silent next to him.

Buzen studied the young man for several moments. "I must speak with the other councilors, and we will see what can be done for you."

Elated, Soda thanked Ruiten and left. The next day, the councilors sent for Soda and told him he could keep watch with the other retainers that night.

The prince slept in the center of the room with the hundred guards around him, trying to keep themselves awake with conversations and games. But when ten o'clock arrived, they dozed off where they sat.

Soda felt the irresistible desire for sleep creeping over him, and nothing he tried helped. Finally, he pulled out his knife and thrust it into his thigh. The pain jolted him awake, but moments later the spell washed over him again.

He twisted the knife to push back the drowsiness.

Suddenly, the doors opened, and a beautiful woman stalked inside. She peered around the room at the sleeping guards and smirked. She padded to the prince.

Soda twisted the knife. The motion made her look up at him. Her eyes widened.

"Who are you?"

"I am Ito Soda, and this is my first night as a guard."

"How is it that you are the only one awake?"

"There's nothing to boast. I'm asleep too."

She stared at him. Then turned to the sleeping prince. "How is my lord tonight?"

Soda tensed and watched for her to make a move. She seemed to sense this because she looked up at him, backed away from the prince, and left.

When dawn came and the guards awoke, they felt shame at how Soda had stabbed himself to remain awake—something they hadn't considered. Soda went to Buzen and accounted what he saw, taking care to describe the woman.

"That woman is Toyo, our lord's favorite court lady." Ruiten said.

The councilors praised Soda for his dedication and ordered him to watch again that night.

At the same hour, Toyo reappeared. All the guards slept except Soda. This time, she left without going near the prince. So the nights passed, and the prince began to regain his health. Toyo kept her distance from the room, and the mysterious sleep that afflicted the guards stopped.

Soda brought the correlation to Buzen. "She has to be the spellcaster," Buzen said. "Although it will anger our lord, go to the creature's room and try to kill her. Have eight men lie in wait for her in case she escapes."

Soda went to Toyo's apartment that night, pretending to have a message from the prince.

"What message does my lord send?" she asked.

"He gave me a letter," Soda said. He reached inside his clothes and pulled his knife, slashing at her in a single swift motion.

She jumped back and snatched a naginata with a hiss. She brought the polearm down. Soda managed to deflect it with his knife, realizing that she wasn't a samurai woman, or he would've been dead with only his knife as a defense. He thrust at her and drove her back.

She threw down the naginata and shimmered, making Soda blink. Before him stood a huge cat. It sprang up the walls and jumped through the window and onto the roof. Soda's men shot at it but missed. After Soda made his report, the Prince of Hizen organized a hunt for it. They eventually found the cat in the mountains and killed it.

The prince recovered from his illness, and Ito Soda was well rewarded for his loyalty.

The Wonderful Tea Kettle

Long ago, an old priest lived in the temple of Morinji in Hitachi Province. He cooked his own rice, boiled his own tea, and lived as an honest priest should.

One day he sat near his hearth. A rope and chain extended from the smoke hole in his ceiling and held his kettle above the fire. A pair of brass tongs stuck from the ashes, and the fire blazed merrily. Near the hearth, a tray filled with teacups, and all the necessary utensils waited. He finished sweeping the ashes from the hearth with his hawk-feather whisk. He was just about to put on the tea when the tea kettle's spout sang. Its lid flapped up and down. Suddenly the entire kettle began to swing.

The priest sat back. "What is going on?"

The spout of the kettle turned into a badger's nose, whiskers and all. The handle burst into a long, bushy tail.

The priest jumped back, spilling green tea leaves all over.

Four hairy legs appeared under the kettle. The strange half-badger, half-kettle jumped off the fire and ran around the room. It leaped onto a shelf and stopped. It puffed out a belly and slapped its stomach as if it was a drum.

The racket pulled in one of the priest's students. He chased the badger, scattering piles of books and breaking some of the tea cups in the process. At last, he seized the creature and shoved him into a pot used to store *daikon*. He plunked a heavy stone on the lid. They supposed the smell of the fermenting radishes would kill the creature.

The next morning, they called in the village's tinker and told him of the strange villager. The priest lifted the lid cautiously, but instead of a dead badger sat the old iron tea kettle. The old priest, worried that the kettle would play the same prank again, sold the kettle for a low price.

The tinker took it to his shop, feeling surprised at how heavy it was.

That night he heard a noise like an iron pot lid lifting and falling. He sat up in his bed and rubbed his eyes. In front of him sat the iron kettle, only it had fur and legs. After it finished its transformation, the badger grabbed a nearby paper fan and danced. When the man stood, it instantly turned back into a tea kettle.

The next morning, the tinker told his wife about the strange event. "I can earn a fortune with this tea kettle. I'll call it Bunbuku Chagama, the Tea Kettle Accomplished in Literature and Military Art. People will pay to see it!"

He hired a professional performer and built a small theatre. He called on his artist friend to paint a backdrop with Mount Fuji and a crimson sun shining through the bamboo. The mural featured stories from folklore, such as the Procession of Lord Longlegs. He stretched a tight rope of rice-straw across the stage.

On opening day, people packed the theatre. They brought their teapots and bento boxes full of rice, eggs, dumplings, and other goodies. Mothers brought children, and everyone settled in to spend the day.

The tinker, dressed in his best ceremonial clothes, took the stage with a big fan in his hand. He bowed and sat the wonderful tea kettle on the stage. He waved his fan, and four legs popped out of the kettle. It ran around the stage, clanking its lid and wagging its tail. He waved his fan again. The badger finished his transformation. It swelled its belly and drummed it. It danced with a fan on the rice-straw rope and tumbled across the stage. The tinker made a final flourish and the badger became the tea kettle once again.

The audience went wild.

As the fame of the tea kettle spread, people came from all over to see it. The tinker grew rich. After several years, he retired. To express his gratitude, he returned the tea kettle to the temple where it became a precious relic.

How a Man Got the Better of Two Foxes

A rope maker went into the mountains to find materials and came upon a fox standing near a hole. The fox called down into the hole until another emerged.

"I know of a profitable venture," the first fox said.

"What venture?" the second fox stretched as he left the hole.

"I will come tomorrow at lunch time. You have to be waiting for me then. If you take the shape of a horse, and if I take the shape of a man, we can go to the village by the shore. I will then sell you. Then I will steal and buy what I can from the village. When they lead you out to eat grass, I will return and help you run away. We will then split everything."

The second fox bounced with excitement. "What a splendid idea!"

The man waited in his hiding place until the foxes left. Then he returned home, thinking about how he might profit from the fox's plan. The next day he set out to the fox hole. Once there, he imitated the voice of the first fox. "Here I am. Come out now and turn into a horse so we can get to the village." The large fox stepped out of the hole and regarded the man.

"I've already turned into a man as you can see," the man said. "Hurry and turn into a horse before someone sees us."

The big fox shook himself and turned into a fine chestnut horse, and the two went off to the village. The man sold the fox and left with more coins than he had expected to get from the trick.

The fox's disguise proved too fine. The new owner decided the horse was too valuable to keep outside, so he locked it into a barn. After four days of being offered grass, the fox worried that he was about to die. He gave up his horse form and fled through the window.

He came upon the home of the other fox and wanted revenge for what he had endured. However when the second fox emerged from its den, the desire for revenge faded. The foxes were, after all, long-time neighbors. Together, they concluded the man the second fox had seen was behind the trick. They decided to kill him.

When they finally found the man, he feared for his life. "I did overhear your plot and wanted to stop you. I ask your forgiveness. Tell you what, I will brew you saké and build a shrine for you. There I will feed you fish whenever I have a good catch. This sounds better than just killing me, doesn't it? From here on, men will worship you forever."

The foxes liked the idea and immediately agreed. Thus, it came to be that men venerated the fox.

How a Man was Duped by Foxes and had His Head Shaved

A wealthy family lived in the village of Iwahara. The family made their wealth from trading wine and enjoyed throwing parties. On one occasion, a number of guests gathered together enjoying fish and wine. As they dined, conversation turned to foxes. Among the guests sat a carpenter named Tokutaro, an obstinate thirty-year-old man.

"You've been talking quite a bit about foxes tricking people. They must be tricking you now. How on earth can foxes do such things to men? Unless those men are fools. Let's talk about something else."

The man sitting beside him took offense to Tokutaro's tone. "You don't know anything about the world. We've already mentioned how twenty or thirty people were tricked by the foxes of Maki Moor. Many of us have seen it ourselves."

"Idiots," Tokutaro said. "I will go out to this Maki Moor tonight and prove you are fools. There isn't a fox in Japan who can trick me."

The guest grew angry with him. The man beside Tokutaro spoke again. "If you can return without anything happening, we will give you five bottles of wine and a thousand coppers worth of fish. But if you end up duped, you will give each of us that much."

Tokutaro puffed out his chest and took the bet. In his mind, it was an easy win. He immediately set out for Maki Moor by himself. By the time he reached the marsh, night had fallen, and he saw a red fox dash ahead of him. He scoffed, but his caution roused.

Just as he peered after the fox, a beautiful girl approached him. "Where are you going?" she asked.

Tokutaro knew the woman. She was the daughter of the Upper Horikane headman. Horikane sat just beyond the swamp. "I am going to the village," Tokutaro said.

"I'm going there too. Will you accompany me?"

Tokutaro thought it odd to see the woman so far from home during the night. He suspected she was a fox. "It has been a long time since I've had the pleasure of seeing you. I would be glad to escort you home." He gestured for her to take the lead.

As they walked, he watched the hem of her clothes, looking for the tip of a fox's tail to peep out. But the tail failed to show. They walked into the village of Upper Horikane and reached the girl's cottage. Her entire family rushed out, surprised to see her.

"We weren't expecting you this late. I hope there is nothing the matter," the girl's elderly mother said.

As they spoke and walked toward the kitchen, Tokutaro pulled her father aside. "The girl isn't your daughter," Tokutaro said. "I was going to Maki Moor and saw a fox. When it dashed into the bamboo grove, it took the shape of your daughter and offered to accompany me to your village. I went along with it, but now we—"

The old man cut him off and called for his wife. When she arrived, he repeated the story.

The wife turned on Tokutaro. "It is just a pretty way to insult my daughter. And she is our daughter. I would know. How dare you lie like that."

Tokutaro remained calm. "I am certain she is a fox."

"What do you plan to do to prove it?" the old man asked.

"I will take care of it. I will soon strip the false skin off and show you the beast's true form." Without waiting for a response, Tokutaro went into the kitchen, shutting and barring the door behind him. The girl turned to him with fear on her face. He grabbed her by the back of the neck. He slammed her to the floor close to the hearth and pinned her.

She gasped. "Mother. Father. Help!"

Tokutaro twisted her hands behind her back. "So you thought to trick me, did you? I saw you jump into the wood and knew you would try to dupe me. Now you will show me what you really are." He wrenched her arms until they popped, and the girl cried out.

"If this isn't enough," He snatched a burning piece of wood from the hearth and shoved up her clothes.

The two old people finally forced the door open, but it was too late. The old man shoved Tokutaro off his daughter and scooped her into his arms, ignoring the flames that still worked at her clothes and skin.

Tokutaro stared. He saw not a single sign of a fox's tail.

The old man seized Tokutaro by his collar. "Murderer! Servants," old man bellowed, "bring me ropes now."

After the stunned Tokutaro was tied to a pillar, the father confronted him. "Although I could kill you now, I need to report this to the lord of this area. He will see you dead."

A priest from Anrakuji temple and his acolyte happened to be passing through when the commotion of the servants drew his attention. He went to the old man's house, thinking his services may be needed and said, "Is everything well with the honorable master of the house? I've come to offer prayers should you need them. "

The old man heard and let the priest in. "We are in trouble." He shared the story.

The priest was stunned by the tale and saw the unfortunate Tokutaro tied to the pillar. "So that's him?"

"Oh, your reverence," Tokutaro said. "I thought the young lady was a fox, so I killed her to protect the village. Please help me. Convince them I had their best interests in mind. Please save me."

"If I save your life, will you become my disciple and enter the priest-hood?"

"If it will save my life, I will with all my heart."

The priest called the parents over. "It seems my arrival was well timed. I have a request for you. Putting Tokutaro to death won't bring your daughter back. I've heard his story, and I don't see malice in him. He was trying to protect you and the village. But he also wants to make amends by becoming my disciple."

The old man considered the priest's words and discussed it with his wife. After some time, he turned to the priest. "It is as you say. Revenge won't bring her back. But we want to see you shave his head and make him a priest right now."

The priest nodded and gestured for Tokutaro to be loosed. He ordered Tokutaro to kneel and join his hands together prayerfully. The priest took a razor and sang a hymn as he took three strokes of Tokutaro's hair. He handed the razor to his acolyte to finish the job.

When the acolyte finished the clean shave, laughter burst all around Tokutaro. At the same moment dawn broke, and Tokutaro found himself alone in the middle of the moor. At first, he thought it was just a dream and that he had been tricked in his sleep by foxes. Then he ran his hand over his head and found he was shaved bald. There was nothing to do for it, so he wrapped a handkerchief around his head and went back to his friends.

"Hello, Tokutaro. How about those foxes?" one of his friends said as Tokutaro entered.

He bowed to them. "I'm sorry for how I was. I'm ashamed of old them the story and, when he finished, pulled off his reveal his bald head.

His friends laughed and claimed their bets of fish and wine from Tokutaro. To make up for his prideful ways, Tokutaro never allowed his hair to grow again and became a priest under the name of Sainen.

Panaumbe, Penaumbe, and the Weeping Foxes

One day, Panaumbe went down to the bank of a river to hunt. He saw something moving on the opposite shore and, on a whim, called out. "Ferry me across!"

"We need to make a boat. Wait for us!" several voices said.

Panaumbe called out again.

"We don't have poles," the voices yelled back. "We are going to make some. Wait for us!"

Panaumbe waited for a time and called out again.

"We are coming for you!" came the reply. As the boat neared, Panaumbe saw it was full of foxes. He grabbed his club and feigned death.

The foxes arrived and gathered around him. "It looks like we took too long. Did he freeze to death or starve?" The foxes started crying.

Panaumbe waited just a moment, then he attacked. He left only a single fox alive, breaking one of the fox's legs so it couldn't follow him. He gathered his kills and returned home. The price of the meat and the pelts made Panaumbe a rich man.

After hearing about Panaumbe's good fortune, Penaumbe came to visit. "How did you kill such a number of foxes?" He wanted to know the secret so he too could become rich.

"I'll tell you how over dinner," Panaumbe said.

The next day, Penaumbe went to the river and cried out as Panaumbe had done.

"We need to make a boat. Wait for us!" called the voices on the opposite side of the river.

He called out again after a little time passed.

"We don't have poles," the voices yelled back. "We are going to make some. Wait for us!"

After a while longer, a boat filled with foxes approached. Penaumbe feigned death. When the foxes arrived, they gathered around him. "It looks like we took too long. Did he freeze to death or starve?"

One of the foxes limped over. "I remember something much like this happened before. Weep at a greater distance!"

So all the foxes sat far away and cried. When Penaumbe jumped u with his club, all the foxes safely ran away. He wasn't able to catch a s: gle one of them. Penaumbe remained poor and eventually died of ⸱ vation because of this failure.

Tamamo, the Fox Maiden

A peddler journeyed upon the great high road toward Kyoto. Along the way, he found a little girl sitting alone.

"Why are you sitting alone here?" he asked.

"Where are you going?"

"I'm heading for Kyoto and the Emperor's palace to sell my goods to the ladies of the court."

"Take me with you," the girl said.

The peddler frowned at the strange little girl. "What is your name, little one?" For some reason she reminded him of his own daughter who remained safe at home.

"I don't have a name."

"Where do you come from?"

"I come from nowhere."

The peddler's frown deepened. "You seem to be about seven years old."

"I have no age."

What a strange girl, the peddler thought. "Why are you sitting alone here?"

"I've been waiting for you."

The peddler knew how children imagined things. Something had obviously happened to her for the girl to be alone as she was. "How long have you waited?"

"For more than a hundred years."

The peddler laughed.

"Take me to Kyoto with you."

The peddler couldn't leave her by the roadside. Not in the age in which they lived. "You can come with me if you want." So they traveled together until they came to Kyoto and the Emperor's palace. There the child danced in front of the Emperor. Her grace rivaled a sea bird alighting on a wave's crest.

When she finished dancing, the Emperor called her to him. "Ask me anything and I will give it to you, child."

"I cannot ask anything of you. I'm too afraid."

The Emperor smiled at the girl. "You don't have to be afraid. Just ̣"

̣ me stay here with you."

̣. From now on you will be called Tamamo." The Emperor re- ̣eddler for bringing him such an interesting girl and sent ̣is way.

She quickly mastered every courtly art. She could sing and play any musical instrument. She painted better than even the most experienced painter in Japan. She was a wonder with both the needle and loom. The poetry she wrote made even hardened warriors cry and laugh. Chinese writing proved no challenge for her, and she could recite Confucius, the Scriptures of the Buddha, and the lore of China, too. People called her the Exquisite Perfection, the Jewel without Flaw.

And the Emperor loved her.

Soon he forgot about his responsibilities, preferring to keep her at his side day and night. He became jealous and short tempered to the point where everyone feared to approach him. But he also grew sicker and more listless. Even the best physicians could do nothing for him.

Yet, he remained madly in love with Tamamo.

She went with him to his summer palace, and he prepared a feast in her honor. All of the highest lords of the land were required to attend. Tamamo sat as the Emperor's equal, resplendent in her scarlet and gold clothing. She, and she alone, poured and served the Emperor.

"Other women are just toys beside you," he said for everyone to hear. "There's not a woman here that is fit to touch the end of your sleeve. I love you so."

As they feasted, a terrible storm raged. A fearsome wind burst into the summer palace and blew out every candle and torch in the feast hall. The rain fell in torrents. The combination of darkness, howling wind, and terrible rain struck fear in everyone attending the feast. Suddenly, a light flooded the room.

The radiance came from Tamamo, and it streamed in long streaks of fire from her body.

The Emperor cried out her name three times and collapsed from the shock.

He lay that way for days, and he didn't respond to anyone. He would've been mistaken for dead if he didn't breathe so deeply.

The wise and holy men heard of the event and met together to determine what they could do. They called Abe Yasu, the Diviner.

"Abe, you know much about dark things. Find the cause of the Emperor's illness and the cure," the oldest wise men said.

Abe performed a divination and returned to the assembly. "*The wine is sweet, but the aftertaste is bitter. Set not your teeth in the golden persimmon; it is rotten at the core. Fair is the scarlet flower of the Death Lily. Pluck it not. What is beauty? What is wisdom? What is love? Be not deceived. They are threads in the fabric of illusion!*"

The wise men pondered Abe's saying before finally they turned him. "What you say is dark, and we can't understand it."

"I will do more than just speak." Abe left them and spent the next three days fasting and praying. Then he took a sacred *gohei* and returned to the wise men. He touched the wand on each of them and explained what they had to do. Together, they made their way to Tamamo's room.

Tamamo sat in her room with her maids, dressing.

"My lords, why do you disturb me as I dress?" she asked.

"My lady Tamamo," Abe said. "I've composed a song in the Chinese style. Because you are so learned in poetry, I wanted your judgment."

"I'm not in the mood for songs. My husband is dying,"

"This is a song you must hear."

She sighed. "If you must."

"*The wine is sweet, the aftertaste is bitter. Set not your teeth in the golden persimmon; it is rotten at the core. Fair is the scarlet flower of the Death Lily. Pluck it not. What is beauty? What is wisdom? What is love? Be not deceived. They are threads in the fabric of illusion!*"

When he finished speaking, he crossed the room and touched Tamamo with the sacred wand.

She cried out in pain. In a flash of light her form changed into a great fox with nine tails and fur like gold. The fox leaped out of the window and fled into the plain of Nasu.

The Emperor recovered from his illness at the moment the fox fled. The wise men thought the problem was solved with the Emperor's recovery. They could not have known where the fox hid. But stories began to circulate about terrible things happening at the stone of Nasu. A stream of poisonous water flowed from under it and withered the plain. Anyone that drank from the streams died, and anything living that approached the stone died too. Birds that perched upon it fell over dead. Even a traveler who rested in the stone's shadow died. People named it the Death Stone and avoided it for more than a hundred years.

One day, Genyo, a holy man, took up his staff and begging bowl and went on a pilgrimage. He came to a village on the Nasu plain and learned about the Death Stone.

"Don't go near the Stone. Don't even rest in its shade," the villagers warned him.

"My children, know what is written in the Book of the Good Law: ⁔ trees, and rocks shall all enter into Nirvana.'"

⁔ at, he visited the Death Stone. He walked right up to it, the
⁔ not even a bird could perch, and struck the stone with his
⁔ Spirit of the Death Stone."

⁔ the Stone, and it split open with a great rending
⁔ erged from the cleft and the fire.

"I am Tamamo, once called the Jewel without a Flaw. I am the golden-haired fox. I was worshiped by the princes of India; I was China's undoing. I was wise and beautiful and evil. But the power of the Buddha has changed me. I have lived in grief for a hundred years. Tears have washed away my beauty and my sin. Genyo, free me. Let me have peace."

"Poor Spirit," Genyo said. "Take my staff and my robe and my begging bowl and start your journey of repentance."

Tamamo put on the offered robe. She took the staff and the bowl. After she did this, she smiled and vanished.

"Tathagata. Kannon. Please make it possible that one day even she may attain Nirvana," Genyo prayed.

The Fox and the Badger

In Shikoku, a hunter had trapped and shot so many foxes and badgers that only an old gray badger and a female fox with one kit remained. Although they starved, they didn't dare to touch a piece of food. A trap might be hidden under it. They could only safely leave their dens at night. One night, the fox and the badger met to decide what they should do. Should they leave or try to outwit their enemy? They debated deep into the night when the badger finally came up with a plan.

"I have it. Transform yourself into a man, and I'll pretend to be dead. Tie me up and sell me in town. Then you can take the money to buy us food. I'll get loose and return, and then I will sell you, and you can escape."

The fox thought it was a good plan and quickly agreed. She couldn't watch her kit go hungry any longer. She transformed into a man and tied the badger up with straw ropes. She slung him over her shoulder and made for town. There she sold the badger. With the money, she bought tofu and two chickens, enough for a feast. Once in the mountains, she waited for the badger to return. As for the badger, he had little trouble escaping the loose ropes the fox had tied, so the three feasted well that night.

The next week, the badger turned into a human and sold the fox, according to the plan. However, the badger had a greedy streak and didn't want to share the food with the fox and her kit. So he whispered in the buyer's ear that the fox only played at being dead. The buyer took a club and beat in the fox's head, killing her.

The badger bought a good dinner and enjoyed it alone without a thought for the fox's kit.

The kit waited a long time for her mother, and when she failed to return, the kit suspected something terrible happened. She came across the badger in his feast and knew immediately what had happened. The young fox vowed revenge and challenged the badger to a trial of transformation skill. The badger accepted immediately. After all, he knew he was better at transforming than even the kit's mother. He also despised the kit and wanted to be rid of her.

"You can go first," the badger said. "Do whatever you want."

"Stand on the big bridge leading into the city," the kit said. "And wait for me to appear. I will show you my skill with all my splendid clothes and followers. If you recognize me, you will win. And I will leave. If you fail, I will win."

The badger went and waited behind a tree. He couldn't wait to crush the kit's foolish hopes. Soon a lord and his followers came up the road. The lord reclined in a palanquin. Everyone in the train wore bright clothing. The badger caught himself marveling at the skill of the young fox.

He shook himself and went up to the palanquin. "I see through your disguise, fox. You lose."

The lord's guards surrounded the badger and beat him to death.

The kit watched all of this from a hill nearby and laughed. Pleased that she had avenged her mother, she scampered away.

The Fox and the Tiger

Version 1

One day the tiger challenged the fox. "Let us run a race from the top of the world to the bottom. Whoever wins it will be the lord of the world."

The fox agreed, and the tiger tore away at his fastest. But he failed to notice that the fox had caught hold of his tail and was pulled along behind.

Just as the tiger reached the end of the world, he whirled to jeer at the fox. He knew the fox couldn't have kept up with his speed. But the whirl threw the fox safely over the finish line.

The fox called out to the tiger. "Here I am. What took you so long?"

The astonished tiger left northern Japan in shame. And that is why you won't find any tigers in the lands of the Ainu.

Version 2

The fox and the tiger had long vied for who was the best. They raced, and they tricked each other to find who would be the craftiest of all creatures. Finally, one day the tiger decided he had enough of the rivalry. He would prove himself the best for all time.

The tiger approached the fox. "Let us see who can roar the loudest. Whoever can will be the lord of the world."

The fox consented as she always did, and the two stood beside each other. The tiger was to roar first. As he focused, he didn't notice the fox had dug a hole to hide her head in so she wouldn't be stunned by the tiger's roar.

The tiger roared so loud that he thought all of the world must have heard him. The roar most certainly had to have stunned the fox. As for the fox, she jumped out of the hole as soon as the roar ended.

"Why, I hardly heard you," the fox said. "I'm sure you can do better than that. You had best try again."

The tiger glared at the fox. He had expected the fox to be stunned to death from the roar. But he had to show the fox once and for all. So the tiger gathered himself. Again, he failed to notice the fox hiding in the hole.

The tiger's great roar burst something deep inside, and he fell over dead. This is why you won't find any tigers in northern Japan. Foxes remain crafty even today.

The Fox, the Otter, and the Monkey

In the first days, a fox, an otter, and a monkey lived together. One day the fox asked the other two, "What do you think about going somewhere? We can steal food and treasures from the Japanese."

His two companions agreed to the venture. Together, they traveled to the distant land. They stole a bag of beans, a bag of salt, and a mat from the house of a rich man.

"Otter, you had better take the salt," the fox said. "You can salt the fish you catch. Monkey, take the mat. Your children can dance on it. And I will take the bag of red beans."

The three returned to their homes. The otter went into the river to fish soon after, but he took his bag of salt with him. When he plunged into the water, the salt melted. The monkey was equally unlucky. He took his mat and spread it on the top of a tree. He made his children dance on it, and his children fell from the height, crushing their heads on the ground.

The monkey and the otter, enraged by what the fox had brought upon them, joined together to fight the fox. The fox took beans from his bag, chewed them into a pulp, and smeared the paste all over his body. Then he lay down and pretended to be sick. When the otter and the monkey came to kill him, they thought a dire sickness had struck him.

"See what happened to me? It's a punishment for deceiving you. My entire body is covered with boils. I'm dying, so you don't have to kill me. Just leave me, or you will catch it too. I will be dead soon enough."

The monkey and the otter believed the fox and left him. The monkey felt too sad to go home. He couldn't look upon his tree without remembering his children plunging to their deaths, so he left.

That is why you can't find monkeys in the land of the Ainu.

The Foxes' Wedding

Once upon a time, a young white fox named Fukuyemon decided it was time he found a wife. His father decided to retire into private life and offered the family's wealth to Fukuyemon. In gratitude to his father, the young fox worked even harder to increase his family's wealth. He soon set his sights on a beautiful lady-fox from a famous old family. Tales of her lovely fur and her charming character spread far and wide. Fukuyemon decided he had to be hers. His father arranged a meeting between the families, and no fault was found on either side. The families exchanged the customary gifts and speeches.

When the ceremonies concluded, the families agreed on an auspicious day for the bride to go to her husband's house. Her servants carried her off in a solemn procession during a shower of rain, yet the sun also shown all the while. After the happy couple finished the wine drinking ceremony, the bride changed her dress, and the couple left for home amid singing and dancing and merry making.

The fox couple loved each other dearly and soon had a litter of kits, much to the joy of Fukuyemon's father. He loved the little kits and treated them tenderly.

"They're the very image of their old grandfather," he repeated to anyone who would listen and to those who didn't.

As soon as the kits were old enough, he took them to the temple of Inari, the patron saint of foxes, and prayed over them. He prayed that the kits would be protected from dogs and the other problems foxes faced.

The grandfather and the fox family prospered. Fukuyemon and his wife had more children each spring, bringing the old grandfather new joy each year.

The Grateful Foxes

One spring day, two friends, tradesmen both, went to the mountains to gather ferns. A boy accompanied them to carry a bottle of wine and their lunch. At the foot of a hill, they saw a pair of foxes bringing their kits out to play. While they looked on, three children from the neighboring village rushed at the foxes with bamboo sticks. Caught by surprise, the foxes scattered, but the children managed to trap and beat them a few times with their sticks before the foxes could flee. Two of the boys managed to catch one of the kits by the scruff of her neck. They held the frightened creature up and shouted with glee.

One of the tradesmen stepped forward. "What are you doing with that fox?"

The eldest of the boys stepped up. "We're going to take it back to our village and sell it to a young man. He hired us to find one for a special meal."

"Well if it is all the same, I'd like to buy it," the tradesman said.

The eldest boy shook his head. "The young man promised us a lot of money."

"How much?"

The boy held up three fingers. "Three hundred."

"I will give you five hundred."

The boys chattered among themselves at this offer. The eldest looked at them, and they nodded in unison. He turned back to the tradesman. "We can sell her for that. What do you want us to do with her?"

The tradesman gestured at his servant boy. "Take the string from our lunchbox and tie it against that tree." After they did so, he gave them the coins and the boys ran away, shouting their excitement.

The tradesman's friend looked puzzled. "I didn't know you had a taste in fox."

The tradesman glared at his friend. "Don't insult me. If I hadn't intervened the kit would be dead. I can't stand by and watch a life taken for no good reason."

"That was a fair bit of money for a fox."

"I would've spent more if I had to." The tradesman frowned. "I thought you knew me better than that."

His friend stepped back and bowed in apology. "I thought you might have wanted the foxes to pray for your prosperity. The young one would've made a good hostage to make her parents do whatever you wanted. I'm sorry. I am ashamed I had the thought."

The tradesman accepted the apology from his old friend. He understood the temptation. A family of foxes would be a benefit to any family. He turned toward the fox and examined it as it cowered. It held its front paw aloft, and the tradesman saw a wound on it. He looked around the area and saw an herb that cleaned wounds and eased pain. He rolled a bit of it in his fingers and applied the paste. They offered boiled rice to the fox, but it refused. The friends took turns stroking its back while the herb worked at the little fox's pain.

The tradesman looked up to see the old foxes sitting not too far away. "Look there. The foxes have come back for their kit." He untied the twine around the kit's neck. When it saw its parents, it bounded off. When it reached its parents, the kit licked them all over for joy. The old foxes seemed to bow their thanks and left.

The friends shared a smile and enjoyed the rest of the day, becoming stronger friends than before.

The tradesman had a full household, with many servants and a good wife and son. When his son turned ten years old, a strange disease attacked. The tradesman brought in the best doctors and bought the best medicine, but nothing helped. Finally, one of the best doctors in the region prescribed a liver from a live fox. Nothing else would help. When the parents heard this, they summoned a hunter who lived in the mountains and charged him to go fox hunting.

The following night, a messenger from the hunter arrived. "Last night the hunter procured the fox liver you needed. He sent me to bring it to you." The messenger offered the tradesman a small jar. "In a few days you will know the price."

The tradesman took the jar and bowed. "You've saved my son. Thank you!"

His wife emerged. "Stay. We have to give you something as thanks."

The messenger held up his hand. "I've already been paid for my trouble."

"At least stay the night," she said.

"I have a relative in the village that I haven't seen in some time. He is expecting me." The messenger bowed and left.

The parents sent for the doctor, telling him of the liver. The next day, the doctor arrived and made the liver into a medicine. Shortly after taking the medicine the boy was sitting up and showing signs of his old self. The entire family celebrated.

Three days later, the hunter arrived, and the wife ran out to welcome him. "Thank you for sending the liver at once. The doctor used it to make the medicine my son needed. Thanks to you our boy is up and walking again."

The hunter blinked and frowned at her. "I didn't send a fox liver. I came to tell you that I failed to find a single fox."

Just then, the tradesman came from the house. He bowed to the ground in front of the hunter, thanking him.

The hunter shifted his feet. "There has to be a mistake. I didn't send a liver, and I don't know who did."

The tradesman stood, looking confused. He told the trader about the messenger and the liver, even taking the time to describe the messenger.

"I don't know of a man who looks like that." The hunter cocked his head and thought, but he couldn't come to any conclusion. Feeling uncomfortable about the situation, he bade the couple a good night and his gladness that their son was well again.

That night the tradesman lay awake, wondering about the odd event, when he felt someone watching him. He sat up to see a woman standing in his bedroom. Despite the sudden appearance, he didn't feel threatened by her.

"I am the fox that lives on the mountain. Last spring I had taken my kits out to play when village boys attacked us. We only lived because of your kindness." The woman looked at him with beautiful, otherworldly eyes. "I wanted to repay you. So when I heard about your son's illness and what he needed to live, I saw my chance. I killed my own son and took out his liver. My husband disguised himself as a messenger and brought it to your house."

She cried as she spoke, and the old tradesman cried with her. The sobs startled his wife awake. When she sat up, the room was empty of the mother fox.

"Why are you crying?" she asked.

He told her the foxes' story and the depths of their gratitude.

The Love of the Snow-White Fox

Many foxes lived in Idzumo. The wicked Ninko foxes carried away the souls of children, robbed poor men of their food, and bewitched anyone they came across. The Inari foxes, natural enemies of the Ninko foxes, were kindhearted. They loved children and protected the poor and came to those who were troubled by the Ninko foxes.

Centuries ago, there lived a young Inari fox. She was snow-white and her gaze was full of intelligence. The good people in the area loved her and looked forward to the knock of her tail against their windows. They opened their doors to her so she could play with their children and share their food. Inari protected those who were kind to her.

The Ninko foxes hated her, but they were not her only trouble. Several hunters wanted to kill her for her beautiful white fur. Several times they nearly succeeded, too.

One summer afternoon, she frisked about the woods with her fox friends when two hunters found her. They set their dogs loose on her and gave her a close chase. She dashed for the nearby Inari temple, thinking the temple would protect her.

Inside the temple meditated Yashima, the prince of the house of Abe. The exhausted white fox ran up to him and hid under the thick folds of his robe. The sight of the quivering and terrified fox moved Yashima, and he tried to soothe the poor creature.

"I will protect you, little one. Don't be afraid," he said. The fox looked up at him and seemed to understand. Her trembling stopped.

The prince went to the door of the temple just as the two hunters neared. They asked if he had seen a pure white fox. "It must have run into the temple," said the tall hunter. "We need its blood to cure the sickness of one of our family members."

"I've been praying in the temple, but I can't tell you anything about a fox," Yashima said.

The men turned to leave when they spotted a white, bushy tail behind the prince.

"Stand aside," the tall hunter said.

The prince refused, and the men tried to get past him. Yashima reached for the sword he had left against the temple's entrance. At the same moment, Yashima's father walked from around the temple and saw his son threatened. He rushed upon the hunters, but the two men killed him. In a rage, Yashima tore into the hunters, killing them in two strikes. He threw aside his sword and bent to his father. Grief froze his throat.

Behind him in the temple, a woman began singing. The beauty of the melody cut through his grief, and he went inside the temple to see its source. A beautiful young woman approached him, and the sympathy in her gaze tugged at him. He told her of the snow-white fox and all that happened moments before. She spoke her sympathy, and some-how her kind words soothed his grief. He could see that her heart was true and pure, and he fell in love with her. Right there, still covered with the blood of his father and the hunters, he asked her to marry him.

"I already love you. I know that you are brave and good. Let me be your comfort," she said.

So they married. Yashima didn't forget about the death of his father, but he also remembered how the event brought him his love. They lived happily together. And the days passed too quickly, as they tend to do. Yashima ruled his people well with the princess by his side. Each morning, they went to the temple and thanked Inari for their joy.

They had a son named Seimei, but the boy didn't bring the Princess happiness. Soon after his birth, she sat alone and cried for hours. Yashima asked her what made her so sad, but she didn't answer.

One such day, when Yashima patiently sat with her, she took his hand. "Our life has been beautiful, and I've given you a son. But now Inari tells me I have to leave you. She will protect you as you protected me from the hunters those years ago. Yes, my love. I am the snow-white fox you saved." She gazed deep into his eyes as tears ran down her cheeks.

And then she was simply gone, disappearing like a mirage in the heat of the summer.

Yashima and Seimei lived long and prosperous lives. Their people loved them, but no one saw the snow-white fox again.

The Man Who Changed into a Fox

A certain man had no idea how to work honestly. He made it is business to tell lies and blackmail people. He stayed in each region as long as he could before people became wise to him. Then he went to another place to start again.

One day he traveled to another region, his ill-gotten gains on his back, thinking of new schemes. He heard a voice, but he couldn't understand its words. He kept walking when he heard the voice again. He then realized the voice was his own. He glanced down at his body only to see a fox's body instead of a man's. In a panic, he thought to return to his own village for help, but he realized the dogs and hunters would kill him. Crying at his unexplained misfortune, he fled, leaving his possessions behind. He rushed toward the mountains. There he found a large oak and lay down to cry beneath it.

Once he was cried out, he fell asleep. In his dream, he came upon a large house. A divine woman came out of it and said, "What a bad man. You have become a demon as punishment for your misdeeds. Why do you come and stand by my house? You see, I am the oak tree. I can't have you dying and defiling me. I will give you a second chance as a man. Do not return to your old habits."

While the fox-man dreamed, the branches on the top of the tree broke and crashed down. He jerked awake and saw he had hands again. He bowed to the tree for the second chance and left for home. From then on, the man worked honestly and never swindled anyone else again.

The Stolen Charm

A wealthy man once prized a treasure above all others: a silver charm shaped like a ship. He also kept a fox kit and a puppy. One day while the man was out, his charm was stolen. He went throughout the house and village looking for it, but he couldn't find it anywhere. He fell into depression so deep that he refused to eat.

The kit saw how thin their master had become and said to the puppy, "If our master dies, we will starve to death too. We need to find that charm."

They discussed what could've happened to the charm for some time when the kit hit upon an idea. "You know that ogre on top of the mountain who is always watching us play? He might have stolen it and put it into his box. But we will need help if we are to rescue it. We need to see if Rat can help us."

So, the two went to Rat and told him of their problem. The rat agreed to help them, and they went up the mountain.

As they ventured toward the ogre's house, the ogre didn't notice them. He stared at the rich man's house and straight into the window, hoping the rich man would die. When the kit, rat, and puppy reached the ogre's house, the kit and the rat dug a passage into the house. The left it to the rat to get the charm by chewing through the ogre's box. To distract the ogre, the kit took on the shape of a little boy, and the puppy took on the shape of a little girl. They danced and played, and the ogre found them amusing. But he wondered how they got into his house because all the doors were closed. He decided to let them amuse him and kill them afterward.

Meanwhile the rat chewed a hole into the box and retrieved the charm. When he reached the hole they had dug, he chattered their signal and fled. Immediately, the boy and the girl disappeared from the ogre's sight.

He gazed about his house for where they went and thrust open his door. He saw the three fleeing down the mountain but hesitated. He had already been tricked once and surmised they wanted him to leave his house. He wouldn't be fooled twice, so he shut up his home and waited inside.

The three returned to the village. The puppy and kit thanked the rat for his help and went home with the charm. They placed it beside their master's pillow and tugged at his clothes until he awoke. He found the charm and cried out with gratitude and joy. That night, the kit and the puppy revealed to him in a dream what they and the rat had done. And the rich man venerated all three.

This is why the Ainu do not think poorly of the rat. And this is why sometimes the fox will make friends with the dogs that hunt her.

The Two Foxes, The Mole, and the Crows

Two fox brothers grew bored one day and said among themselves, "It would be fun to take human shape and visit a village."

So they made clothing out of leaves from various trees and made food for their journey. But the mole saw them doing all of this and decided to play a prank of his own. He made a place similar to a human village and disguised himself as an old man. He filled his home with beautiful treasures and made clothing out of various herbs and leaves. He also made good food out of mulberries and grapes. The mole invited all the nearby crows and other birds and gave them human shapes. He made them owners of the houses in the fake village.

The fox brothers came upon the village and didn't suspect anything. They visited the mole's house, and he bought everything the brothers carried with them. Then he showed the brothers his own treasures, dazzling the young foxes.

"There is a dance tonight," the mole said. "You have to stay for it."

All of the people in the village gathered and danced all sorts of dances. They even began to fly into the air. The sight amused the foxes as they ate of the mulberries and grapes. The foxes had a great time and didn't suspect anything odd, despite the flying dances of the villagers. After the dance, the foxes went home.

On their way home, they discussed the village. "The food humans have is even nicer than their treasures," said the youngest. "We need to go back and see what other food we can buy from them."

So they again made treasure out of herbs and returned to the village. The mole had sent away all the crows and birds, but he remained in the largest house. When the foxes entered the house, they saw a venerable mole god sitting inside instead of the human elder they had seen before.

"You foxes," said the mole. "You had made fake treasures out of grasses, leaves, and weeds. Then you assumed human form to complete your trick. I saw all of it. You think this is a human village, but it is mine. You always behave badly. Do not assume human shape anymore. If you keep to your true shape, you can eat your fill of mulberries and grapes. The crows will drop the fruits from the tops of the trees, and it will be more profitable for you than trying to trick humans."

The foxes stopped trying to trick humans by assuming their shapes, and from that day on they ate as many mulberries and grapes as they pleased.

The Monkey, the Crab, and the Persimmon Seed

One bright autumn day long ago, a monkey and a crab played together on the bank of a river. As they scampered, the crab found a rice-dumpling, and the monkey found a persimmon seed. However, because of his greed, the monkey couldn't celebrate his friend's find. After all, a persimmon seed might as well be a stone for the hungry monkey. He offered an exchange.

He proffered the seed to the simple crab and said, "I will make you a deal, my friend. Your rice-dumpling for my seed. You can eat the dumpling now, but just think of all the persimmons you will enjoy once this seed grows into a mighty tree. Think about your future. You wouldn't want to be sorry you passed up such an exchange."

The simple-minded crab quickly gave in to the monkey's argument. In a flash, the monkey gobbled the dumpling and had second thoughts about giving up the seed. But he knew how sharp the crab's claws were, so he decided not to anger the crab. Soon after the crab returned home to his stones along the river, he planted the seed.

Spring came, and the crab was delighted to see the seed sprout. Each year the tree grew taller and stronger until one spring it blossomed. That autumn large persimmons awarded the crab's patience. And the crab enjoyed spending each day watching the fruit ripen in the sun.

"They will be delicious!" he said to himself.

Finally they were ripe enough, but he quickly learned that a crab's legs weren't meant for climbing trees. After several failures, he sat at his home and thought of his old playmate the monkey. Monkeys could climb trees better than anyone else he knew. Once decided, he set off to find the old monkey.

He ran up the river and into the dark forest where he found the monkey taking a nap in a pine tree. The monkey awoke and listened to the crab's story. At once, the monkey devised a plan to take all the persimmons for himself. He promised the crab he would pick the fruit.

When they reached the tree, the monkey gazed up, astonished at how fine a tree the seed had become. Ripe persimmons festooned its branches. The monkey climbed and feasted on the persimmons as fast as he could pluck them. He savored the best and ripest the tree offered until he thought he would burst. He made sure not a single one reached the hungry crab waiting below. By the time the monkey finished, only hard, unripe fruit hung from the tree.

During the monkey's feasting, the disappointed crab scuttled around the tree, calling on the monkey to remember his promise. The monkey grew irritated at the little crab's noise and threw the hardest fruit he could find at the crab's head. The hard-as-a-stone persimmon struck the crab with a ping. Amused by the sound and wanting to get at the annoying crab, the monk threw the fruit as fast as he could pluck them. The fruit cracked the crab's shell and bruised him. Still, the monkey didn't stop until the crab lay dead at the base of the tree.

When the monkey noticed he had killed the crab, he panicked and fled as fast as he could.

The crab had a son who was off playing with a friend. The son came upon his father on his way home that evening. All around his father's shattered body lay the unripe persimmons. The young crab collapsed and cried at the terrible sight.

After some time, the young crab told himself that crying would do little good. He had to avenge his father. He knew unripe persimmons wouldn't have fallen as they had on their own. Gazing up into the tree, he noticed the branches missed all the best fruit. Bits of peel and seeds littered the ground too. He knew only monkeys could climb so tall a tree. He also knew how much monkeys coveted persimmons.

And there was only one monkey in the area.

His anger drove him to attack the monkey at once, but second thoughts stopped him. The monkey was an old, cunning animal. The monkey had conned his father, after all, and his father was the head of their crab village. The young crab knew he needed help if he was to kill the foul monkey.

He left at once to find his father's old friend, the mortar. When he told the mortar of what had happened, the mortar promised to help. He also warned the young crab that they had to be careful. The monkey wouldn't be easily fooled. So the mortar called upon the bee and the chestnut. The chestnut and bee agreed to help after they heard what had befallen their old friend.

It took them some time to devise a plan. After they had, each went to do their part. The mortar went home with the young crab to help him bury his father.

While this was happening, the old monkey worried and celebrated in turn. He felt happy that he now had such a grand persimmon tree to himself, but he worried that someone might discover his role in the murder. The old crab's family and village would be sure to seek revenge should they discover the truth. So he kept to his forest home, but as the days passed he grew bored.

Finally, he left home saying, "No one saw me. He was certainly dead when I left him, and a dead crab can't speak. There's no use brooding over it. Done is done, so I might as well go have fun."

Despite his words, he sneaked into the crab's village and tried to listen to the gossip. He had to be sure. But the crabs didn't know who had murdered their chief. Most had already moved on to their normal daily routines and gossip.

"They are all such fools," the monkey said to himself. "They don't know and don't even care about who murdered their chief."

The monkey failed to realize that the lack of concern was a part of the young crab's plan. He wanted to lull the monkey into complacency.

One day, while the monkey sat at home, a messenger from the crabs arrived. The monkey hadn't expected to hear anything from the crab village.

"I've been sent by my master to tell you that his father died. He died by falling from a persimmon tree while trying to get its fruit. Because this is the seventh day since his death, my master has prepared a festival in his father's honor. He invites you to come since you were one of his father's best friends. My master hopes you will honor his house with your kind visit," the messenger said.

When the monkey heard these words, relief cooled his stomach. The crabs didn't suspect a thing. He kept his feelings from his face and made a show of crying instead.

"I'm so sorry to hear about your chief's death. We were close friends. We once exchanged a rice-dumpling for a persimmon seed. "The monkey squeezed out a few more tears for effect. "It hurts me to know that the seed was the cause of his death. It will be my pleasure to honor my old friend."

The messenger hid his reaction. The monkey's false words and falser tears hurt him as the unripe persimmon must have hurt his chief. *In a short time he shall shed real tears,* the messenger thought. He thanked the monkey and went home.

The monkey laughed his relief. He changed into his formal clothes and left for the feast, wondering what sort of food the crabs would offer.

He found all the members of the crab's family waiting. They led him into the hall where the young crab waited to receive him. After expressing their condolences, they sat to a great feast and entertained the monkey as the guest of honor.

When the feast finished, the young crab invited the monkey into the tea room. The young crab excused himself and left the monkey alone.

Soon, the monkey grew impatient. "This tea ceremony is a slow affair. I'm tired of waiting. I'm thirsty after drinking so much saké at dinner."

He stood and approached the fireplace. He reached toward the kettle boiling there when something burst out of the ashes and smashed him in the neck. The chestnut had hidden himself in the fireplace, waiting for the right moment. In pain and startled, the monkey fled the room.

The monkey's flight signaled the bee to strike. The bee flew from its hiding place outside the screens and stung the monkey on the cheek. Burned by the chestnut and now swelling from the drilling bee-sting, the monkey ran screaming from the crab's home.

The mortar waited with several stones on the top of the crab's gate. As the monkey ran underneath, the mortar and the stones fell onto the monkey, pinning the murderer to the ground. The monkey struggled to get up, but the rocks and mortar had his arms and even his tail pinned.

As he struggled helplessly, the young crab strolled up. The monkey recoiled when the crab lifted his great claw scissors.

"I'm sure you remember what happened to my father now. The persimmons and these rocks are quite similar."

"It was your father's fault. Not mine!" the monkey said.

The young crab sighed. "Even now you lie. Farewell, wicked monkey." The young crab's great claw swept down and cut off the monkey's head.

The Monkeys' Request

A young priest lived in Kinoto Temple during the reign of the Emperor Ichijo. He would read the sermons of the Buddha aloud twice each day. His voice carried into the quiet hills and forests despite his soft speaking.

One day, the young priest saw two monkeys listening to his reading with serious expressions on their faces. He smiled and kept reading. As soon as he finished, the monkeys went off into the hills without causing mischief.

On the next day, the monkeys returned and again on the third day. He couldn't help asking why they were coming regularly.

"We've come because we like to hear you read the Buddha's words. We want to learn the virtues you recite. Can you make a copy of the book you read from?"

The priest blinked with astonishment. "It would take a lot of work. But it's unusual for animals like you to show interest in the Buddha's words. I will do my best to honor your interest."

The monkeys bowed and left the monk, pleased with the young man's promise. The priest began copying the thick book. Seven days later, five-hundred monkeys came to the temple, each carrying a sheet of parchment. They lined up and laid their sheets in front of the monk. Then, each monkey left until only the original two monkeys remained. These monkeys brought food. Each day, they went into the mountains and returned with wild fruits and potatoes, honey and mushrooms, and other food. The priest copied steadily until he copied five volumes of the sacred book.

When he reached the end of the fifth volume, the two monkeys failed to appear at the usual time. The priest worried about them. They had come each day without fail. On the second day of their absence, he went looking for them. He found the traces of their forages. Branches were broken from wild fruit trees. Holes littered the forest floor from their searches for potatoes. The two monkeys had worked hard for the monk, and he grew increasingly worried.

Near the top of the mountain he found them in a deep hole. Both monkeys were dead. Tears sprang to the priest's eyes. No doubt the monkeys had worried he would think they had deserted him. Their efforts to climb stood out all along the hole's walls.

He buried the monkeys and prayed for them. A few days later, the priest learned he was called to serve in another temple. He put the five volumes he had copied into a compartment built into one of the temple's pillars and left.

Forty years later, the governor of the province came to the temple. He had heard of the unfinished copy of sermons. The priests sent for a servant who still worked in the temple. The eighty-five year old man had worked at the temple when the monkeys visited. The governor asked his question.

"It is still in the compartment in one of the main pillars. I will get it for you," the old man said.

When the old servant returned with the document, the governor held it with appreciation. "I came for these documents because of who I was in my previous life. I was the eldest of the two monkeys who requested this. Now that I've been reborn as a man, I want to complete them."

The priests allowed the governor to take the five volumes with him, and he worked to complete them. He made three thousand copies, and it is said the originals are now kept at the Kinoto Temple as its most sacred treasure.

The Sagacious Monkey and the Boar

Long ago, a traveling entertainer lived in the province of Shinano. He earned his living by putting on shows with his trained monkey.

One evening, the man came home angry and told his wife to send for the butcher in the morning.

"Why do you want the butcher?" she asked.

"There's no point in keeping that monkey anymore. He's too old and forgets his tricks. I beat him with my stick, but he won't dance properly. At least if I sell him to the butcher I can get something out of him. I can't do anything else at this point."

The woman felt sorry for the monkey and tried to change her husband's mind. But he wouldn't relent.

The monkey sat in the next room and overheard the conversation. "I've served my master faithfully for years and this is the thanks I get?" the monkey said to himself. "Instead of letting me end my days in peace and comfort, he is going to let the butcher turn me into a stew! I have to do something."

The monkey thought hard and remembered hearing about a wise boar that lived in the nearby forest. He decided to seek the boar's help. He slipped out of the house and dashed into the forest. Following his luck and the little he had heard, the monkey managed to find the boar and told his story between gasps.

"I'm in trouble, Mr. Boar. I've heard of your wisdom and came for your help. My master wants to sell me to a butcher because I can no longer dance in my age. Please tell me what to do."

The boar thought a moment. "Doesn't your master have a baby?"

"He does. An infant son."

"Doesn't his wife lay the baby by the door each morning while she works?"

The monkey nodded.

"I will come by and seize the child and run off with it. The mother will be terrified. And before she and your master know what to do, you will run after me and rescue the child. After you save their son, they won't have the heart to sell you to the butcher."

The monkey thanked the boar many times and returned home. Anxiety kept the monkey awake all night. It seemed to take his master's wife forever to start her daily routine. Finally, she opened the house's shutters and doors and placed her child near the door as she cleaned and prepared the day's food.

The child crooned happily in the dappled sunlight. Suddenly a noise and the child's cry snatched the mother's attention. She ran out of the kitchen just in time to see the boar race off with the child balanced on its snout. She cried out and rushed to wake her husband.

He sat up and rubbed his eyes. "What is it, woman?"

She was incoherent with terror. He finally figured out what she attempted to tell him and rushed outside in time to see the old monkey running after the boar as fast as he could. The apparent bravery of the monkey struck the man. The monkey and boar disappeared into the forest's undergrowth. A few moments passed and the monkey returned, carrying the child.

The wife collapsed with relief as she saw the monkey coming toward them with their child. "And you wanted to kill him. If he hadn't been here, we would've lost our baby forever."

"For once, you are right," the man said as he retrieved his son from the monkey. "Send the butcher away when he comes, and be sure to make breakfast for the monkey too."

When the butcher arrived, the wife asked him to bring boar's meat for their dinner. The couple took good care of the monkey from then on. His master never struck him with a stick, and the monkey spent the rest of his days in peace.

Birds and Insects

Akinosuke's Dream

Miyata Akinosuke was a samurai who lived in Yamato Province. In his garden grew a large, ancient cedar tree. He and his friends often spent hot summer days resting in its shade. One afternoon, he sat under this tree talking and drinking wine with his buddies. Suddenly, he felt so tired that he couldn't keep his eyes open. He begged his friends to excuse him for taking a nap and fell asleep as soon as he settled into the grass. He dreamed.

He lay in his garden when a procession topped the nearby hill. He got up to watch it, for it was a grand procession. The young men wore rich clothes and carried a great lacquered palanquin with bright blue silk. The procession halted a short distance from Akinosuke's home. A richly dressed man dismounted from his resplendent stallion and walked from the train. He bowed to Akinosuke.

"I am a vassal of the Shogun. He commands me to be at your disposal and to bring you to see him. Will you please follow me?"

Akinosuke grasped for the right response and could only splutter from his shock. He, a country samurai, summoned by the Shogun? He entered the palanquin without saying anything. What else could he do?

Somehow, the journey took less time than he expected. The procession stopped in front of a huge two-storied Chinese gate.

The vassal dismounted. "I will announce your honorable arrival."

Akinosuke had waited in the palanquin for some time when two men dressed in purple silk robes and the high caps of rank appeared. They bowed to him, helped him from the palanquin, and led him through the gate and across a vast garden. The palace stretched for miles ahead of him. The men showed Akinosuke into a reception room where serving maids brought him refreshments.

After he drank, the purple-dressed men bowed. "It is our honorable duty to tell you, that the Shogun wants you to marry his daughter today. We will soon take you to him, but you will first need to dress appropriate to the ceremony."

The men walked to the alcove and opened a chest decorated with gold leaf. They pulled out various robes and girdles of silk and a royal headdress. When they finished dressing him, Akinosuke looked like a prince. The men led Akinosuke to the Shogun. The man sat upon the dais, flanked by dignitaries arranged by rank. Akinosuke, feeling out of his element, shuffled forward and bowed low three times.

"You've been told why I called for you," the Shogun said. "We've decided that you will wed our only daughter. And the ceremony will now be performed."

As the Shogun finished speaking, music began to play, and a line of beautiful court ladies appeared from behind a curtain. They led him to where his bride waited. The room he entered was immense, but the number of guests made it feel close. The guests bowed before Akinosuke as he took his place facing the Shogun's daughter on the kneeling cushion. The girl's robes were as beautiful as the summer sky, and the room rejoiced as the marriage rites ended. The couple received wedding gifts beyond counting.

Some days later, the Shogun summoned Akinosuke. "In the southwestern part of our dominion lies an island called Raishu. We have appointed you to be its governor. You will find the people loyal and docile, but their laws are not aligned with ours. We entrust you with the duty of improving their social condition and ruling over them with kindness and wisdom. The preparations for your journey are already made."

So Akinosuke and his bride left for Raishu. When they arrived, the people of the island welcomed them. Akinosuke jumped into his new duties, which proved easier than he had expected. He spent the first three years framing and enacting laws with the help of the counselors assigned to him. The country was healthy and the land fertile. Sickness and hunger were unknown. The people lived so well that the laws were never broken. So Akinosuke ruled in Raishu for twenty more years. During this time, he and his wife had seven children, five boys and two girls.

On his twenty-fourth year, his wife suddenly became sick and died. He buried her on the summit of a beautiful mountain in the district of Hanryoko and set up a monument. Akinosuke felt such grief that he lost his will to live.

Just after the mourning period ended, a messenger arrived. "The Shogun commands you to return to your own people and country. As for the seven children, they are the grandsons and granddaughters of the Shogun. They will be cared for, so don't worry about them."

Akinosuke settled his affairs and held the necessary ceremony to bid farewell to his counselors and officials. He boarded the awaiting ship with honor. As the ship sailed, the shape of the island itself turned blue. Then it turned gray and vanished.

Akinosuke awoke under the cedar tree in his garden. He gazed about in a daze. His friends still sat close to him, drinking and talking.

"How strange," he said to them.

"You must have been dreaming," one of them laughed. "What did you dream about that was so strange?"

Akinosuke told them of his dream, and they were astonished at it. He had only slept for a few minutes.

"That was a strange dream," the other friend said. "We also saw something odd while you napped. A little yellow butterfly fluttered over your face for a moment. It landed on the ground beside you, close to the tree, and a big ant came out of the hole and seized it. It dragged the butterfly into the hole. Just before you woke up, that same butterfly came out of the hole and fluttered over your face as before. Then it disappeared."

"Maybe it was Akinosuke's soul," the first friend said. "I think I saw it fly into his mouth, but even if the butterfly was his soul, it wouldn't explain his dream."

"The ants might explain it. They are odd things, and there is a big nest under this tree."

"Let us look," Akinosuke said. He left to retrieve his spade.

Under the cedar tree, the friends found a strange ant colony. The assemblies of straw, clay, and stems looked similar to miniature towns. In the middle of the colony stood a large structure with a swarm of small ants around the body of a big ant with yellow wings and a long black head.

"Why, that is the Shogun of my dream," Akinosuke said. "And that looks like the palace. Raishu ought to be southwest of it, to the left of that big root. Yes! Here it is. Now I'm sure that I can find the mountain of Hanryoko and my wife's—the princess's—grave."

He searched the wreck of the colony and discovered a mound. A water-worn pebble, resembling a Buddhist monument stood at the top. Underneath it he found, embedded in clay, a dead female ant.

How Yogodayu Won the Battle

During the reign of Emperor Shirakawa, a general by the name of Yogodayu built a fort in the wilds of Yamato, not far from Kasagi Mountain. A few months after he finished the fort, his wife's brother attacked. The army overwhelmed his fort, but he managed to escape into the mountain with twenty other warriors. And they hid in a cave for two days.

On the third day, Yogodayu and his men emerged. There were no signs of pursuit. As they scouted, Yogodayu saw a bee struggling in a large spider's web. As the bee struggled, more webbing tangled over it. He felt sympathy for the bee and freed it.

"Fly back to your hive, little bee," he said. "I wish I could do the same."

That night, Yogodayu dreamed of a man dressed in black and yellow. The man saluted him. "Sir, I want to help you and fulfill my decision this morning."

"Who are you?" Yogodayu asked.

"I am the bee you freed from the spider's web. I am deeply grateful, and I want to help you out of your web. I have a plan that will let you defeat your enemy and regain your lost fortune."

"How can I defeat an enemy with only twenty warriors?"

"It's simple." The man smiled and held up a finger. "Follow my instructions and you will see."

"I can't attack the enemy with the numbers we have. We don't have walls to work against their numbers either."

The bee's smile widened. "You don't want walls. You will be attacked, but you will outnumber them by ten million. The bees of Yamato will join you. When you decide on the day and place to fight your brother-in-law, build a wooden house and place within it as many empty jars as your men can find. We bees will hide in them. You and your men need to live in the house and let the enemy know where you are. We will attack them. Your victory will be certain, so don't worry."

Yogodayu was about to ask another question when the bee disappeared. He awoke from the dream. He relayed it to his men, who listened with wonder. After he finished the story, he split the men into pairs and sent them to their home regions to bring back other supporters. They set the cave as their meeting place and vowed to see each other after thirty days. Yogodayu went off alone.

A month later, eighty men gathered at the cave. Yogodayu selected a site at the entrance of the valley, and the men built a house as the bee had instructed. The men also collected two thousand jars. Once the house was finished and the jars placed, bees arrived in swarms that defied counting. Yogodayu sent one of his men to spread the location of the house and gathering.

Two days later, his brother-in-law arrived with his army.

Yogodayu led his men into the enemy's lines to draw them out. The plan worked, and the army broke their ranks to come after them. The bees swarmed out of their hiding places and flew into the extended army. They blackened the sky and fell on the soldiers, stinging their eyes and down their throats. The army held for a moment longer before they broke and ran.

Yogodayu and his warriors descended on the fleeing men, cutting them down without resistance. Yogodayu found his brother-in-law amid a swarm of bees and killed him with a single slash. They pursued the army all the way back to the fortress and took it back.

The next day, Yogodayu sent his men to collect all the dead bees that helped him. He built a small temple at the back of Mount Kasagi and buried the bees on the temple grounds. For the rest of his life, Yogodayu visited the shrine once a year and offered his thanks to the bees.

Fireflies

An old farmer named Kanshiro used to live in the village of Funakami in the province of Omi. He was well known for his honesty, charity, and piety, such that no one could find a man like him even among priests. Each year, Kanshiro journeyed to various parts of the country to pray to various gods. He wasn't strong and suffered from dysentery during hot weather, but he never thought of these problems or his age.

One year, Kanshiro felt he couldn't live much longer. He decided to make one last pilgrimage to the shrines at Ise and to risk the heat of August to do so. The people of his village gathered one-hundred yen so he might have the honor of presenting a decent offering to the shrines. So, he set out with the money stuffed in a bag around his neck. He walked from sunrise to sunset for two days, but on the third day the heat had gotten the better of him. He arrived at the village of Myojo, weak from dysentery.

Kanshiro considered himself too impure to carry the money that had been entrusted to him by the village. He staggered to the cheapest inn he could find and told the innkeeper his story. "I'm an old man sick with dysentery. If you will take care of me for a day or two, I will get better. Please keep the money I intend to offer. I don't want to defile it with how I am now."

"Don't worry. I will place your money in a safe place and watch it myself until you are well. Good men like you are rare," said Jimpachi, the innkeeper.

For five days Kanshiro lay sick in his small room, but the old man's pluck finally returned. On the sixth day, he decided to set out. The day was fine too. He paid his bill, thanked the innkeeper for his kindness, and received his moneybag as he left. He didn't look inside the bag. The common room teemed with laborers and pilgrims, and Kanshiro didn't want them to see how much he carried. He stuffed his clothes into a bag and set off.

About midday, he stopped to rest and to eat his cold rice under a pine tree. He pulled out the moneybag and opened it. Inside, he found stones instead of the money. The old man quivered with a mix of anger and anxiety. He jumped to his feet without finishing his rice and headed back to the inn.

He reached the inn at dusk. He tried to keep his anger in check as he spoke with Jimpachi. The innkeeper listened with a show of sympathy until Kanshiro asked for him to return the money.

"You old thief," Jimpachi said. "You are trying to blackmail me with that story. I will show you how well it will work." He punched the old man in the chest and seized a nearby staff. He struck Kanshiro and called to the laborers in the room. "Come help me. This man is trying to blackmail money from me." The laborers joined Jimpachi and thrashed the old man.

Kanshiro managed to crawl away. And three days later he somehow managed to reach the Ise shrines. He said his prayers and started back to Funakami. When he arrived home, the beating and illness and heat made him collapse. His friends tended to him, and he told them what had happened. But not everyone believed him. To make amends, he sold his small property and repaid everyone who had given money for the pilgrimage. With the meager leftover funds, he continued his pilgrimages to various temples and shrines. When he had exhausted the money, he resorted to begging on his journeys.

Three years later, he returned to Myojo village on his way to Ise, and he learned that Jimpachi had made a lot of money and lived in a large home.

Kanshiro traveled to the house and confronted the man. "Three years ago, you stole the money entrusted to me. I sold my property to refund the people who trusted me. Since then, I've become a beggar and wanderer. Don't think you've gotten away with it. I am old, and you are young. I will be avenged, and soon."

"You dishonest old man. If you wanted a meal, just tell me, but don't you dare threaten me." As Jimpachi spoke, a village watchman on his rounds saw them. The watchman rushed forward and seized Kanshiro and dragged him out of the village.

"If I see you in the village again, especially bothering Mr. Jimpachi, I will arrest you," the watchman said.

By that time, hunger and illness had finally gotten the best of Kanshiro, and he died just outside the village. The priest of the neighboring temple was called, and he knew Kanshiro from the old man's visits. He buried Kanshiro with respect and offered prayers for the faithful old man.

The encounter with Kanshiro tugged at Jimpachi's conscience to the point where he became sick with what he had done. One night as he lay in bed, thousands of fireflies rushed out of Kanshiro's tomb and flew into Jimpachi's bedroom. They surrounded his mosquito net and tried to force their way in. The top of the net pressed down with them. The air teemed with their lights, hurting the sick man's eyes. Several villagers heard his cries for help and rushed in to kill the fireflies. But no matter how many they killed with torches or boards, still more rushed from Kanshiro's tomb.

One of the villagers noticed how the fireflies only streamed into Jimpachi's room. "It must be true that he stole the old man's money. This is his spirit's revenge."

The villagers backed away, afraid to kill the fireflies. The swarm grew thicker around Jimpachi's bed until the mosquito net finally tore. The fireflies flooded in, choking off his cries as they filled his mouth, nose, ears, and eyes. Then, just as suddenly, the swarm left Jimpachi's room and returned to the tomb. For twenty nights this repeated until, finally, Jimpachi died. After his death, the fireflies disappeared.

Panaumbe, Penaumbe, the Fish, and the Insects

One fine day, Panaumbe went down to the shore, squatted on the sand, and opened his anus as wide as possible. He called out to all the whales, salmon, and other fish, saying he had found a beautiful cavern. They all swam toward it and crowded inside. When Panaumbe's anus was full, he closed it and ran home. When he got home, he closed the doors and windows, and let out all the whales, salmon, and fish that had crowded into him. The house filled up, and they couldn't escape. So Panaumbe caught them all. He ate some. The rest he sold and became a rich man.

Penaumbe came to visit. "You were poor just a few days ago. How did you manage to get so rich so quickly?"

"I'll tell you over dinner," Panaumbe said.

The next day, Penaumbe did what Panaumbe did. He opened his anus wide toward the sea and called to the various sea creatures. Then he felt all the whales, salmon, and other fish crowding in. When he was filled, he closed his anus, and ran home. He closed all the windows, doors, and filled even the smallest holes. Then he opened his anus again so all the creatures of the sea came out. Only instead of whales, salmon, and fish, his house crowded with wasps, horseflies, spiders, centipedes, and other poisonous insects. Unable to get out, they stung him to death.

Princess Firefly

On the southern, sunny side of the moats of Fukui castle, the water had long ago become shallow enough for lotus lilies to grow. Deep in the heart of the largest pink lotus lived the King of the Fireflies and his daughter, the Princess Hotaru. The king kept the princess at home, and she dreamed of seeing the world abroad. As she matured, the fire in her body grew until it illuminated her lotus home like a lamp.

Finally, her father deemed her old enough to join him in his flights around the kingdom. He hoped her light would attract a proper suitor. So she flew with her father among the lilies of the moat and out into the rice fields and even further into the meadows edging against the forest.

Wherever she went, a crowd of suitors followed. Her light dazzled them, but she didn't like their attention. Oh, she remained polite as a good princess should, but she did not encourage them.

One night, she sat with her mother. "I've met many admirers, but I don't want any of them to be my husband. Tonight I plan on staying home and giving a task to anyone who visits me. If they are wise, they won't do it. If they love their lives more than they love me, I don't want any of them. But whoever succeeds will be my husband."

"If that is what you want," her mother said. She helped the princess dress in her most resplendent robes.

She settled onto her throne in the center of the lotus and ordered the guards to keep the suitors a safe distance from her. She worried that some of them might hurt her in their frenzy to get close to her light.

First, a golden beetle approached. "I am Lord Green-Gold. I offer my house, my fortune, and my love to you."

"Go and bring me fire. Only then will I marry you," said Princess Hotaru.

The beetle bowed and flew off.

Soon after the beetle left, a shiny, black bug appeared, and the princess gave him the same task.

So the insects came. Next a fuzzy moth. Then, a scarlet dragonfly who tried to dazzle her with his iridescent wings. All night the suitors arrived and tried to woo her. She told each to go and bring her fire. Each thought he had the secret necessary to achieve her impossible quest.

The beetle whirred into a house through a hole in the paper window. But he misjudged the hole and dashed his head against a nail sticking from the wood as he flew at his fastest speed. The nail cracked his head, and he fell dead.

The black bug flew into a room where a student studied. The student's lamp was an earthenware dish filled with rapeseed oil and a wick. Not understanding the nature of oil, the black bug crawled into the dish to snatch the flame and drowned.

The dragonfly managed to get inside the house's common room and flew straight into the hearth. The heat of it burned off his iridescent wings, and he roasted before he could touch a flame. At the same time, a moth hovered around a candle's flame, coming nearer with each pass. With a burst of courage, he dived into the flame and tried to snatch the fire with his furry legs. His wings and body singed, and he fell to the table to die.

So the princess's suitors died. Some to candle. Some to incense. Yet others to lanterns. A few even tried to catch the fire from a cat's eyes. Morning brought a series of funerals across the land of the fireflies. The funerals grabbed the attention of Himaro, the Prince of the Fireflies on the north side of the castle. He soon learned about the glittering princess, and he decided to see what beauty could cause so many deaths in a single night. He gathered his retainers and set off for the Princess's lotus.

Although he and his men were wrapped with their own glorious light, their light still couldn't match that of the princess. Yet, as soon as Himaro and Hotaru saw each other, they fell in love. After a short period of courting, they married and lived the rest of their lives, uniting the north and the south sides of the moat into a single kingdom.

Many generations have passed since the marriage of Himaro and Hotaru. But since then, all of the firefly princesses send their suitors on the same quest as Hotaru. Night after night, suitors succumb to their passion and their hope to win the heart of the shining firefly.

The Fire Quest

The Wise Poet sat reading by candlelight. The night of the seventh month filled with the sound of cicadas and the songs of frogs. The moon shone with the stars in the cloudless sky, and the air smelled sweet. But the Poet wasn't happy. He watched dragonflies and moths and other insects fly into his candle. Their suicides grieved the Poet.

"Little harmless children of the night," he said. "why do you still go on the fire quest? You won't succeed, yet you keep trying and dying in the process. Haven't you heard of the story of the Firefly Queen?"

The moths and dragonflies and other insects ignored him and continued to flutter around the candle.

"You haven't heard of it, obviously. Please listen. The Firefly Queen was the brightest and most beautiful of all the small creatures that fly. She lived in the center of a lotus that grew on a still lake. Her home swayed upon the lake and glowed like a star from her brilliance."

"You need to know, children of the night, that the Firefly Queen had many suitors. Creatures like you: moths, dragonflies, and all of the night's small creatures. She filled their hearts with love, yet she ignored their desires. At last she told them. 'Prove your love if you truly love me as you say. I will wed the first who brings me fire.'"

"And so the children of the night whirred on their wings, as you do tonight, on the Fire Quest. But the Firefly Queen laughed at them, as she laughs at you. The lovers flew all over in their search. In one room a girl cried and read a letter by the light of a candle. In another room, a woman sat in front of a mirror, putting on her makeup, by candlelight. In yet another place, a dying man asked his servants to light a lamp.

Firefly Queen's suitors died to all of these flames. All the while, the Firefly Queen sat safe in her lotus with her beloved, who shone as bright as she. This great Lord of the Fireflies carried his own flame beneath his wings and had no need for the Fire Quest."

"So the Firefly Queen deceived her lovers and laughed at their folly, as she laughs at you tonight. Don't be deceived, little children of the night. The Firefly Queen is always the same. Give up the Fire Quest."

But the moths, dragonflies, and other children of the night didn't listen to the Wise Poet. They continued to flutter into his candle's flame, burning their bright wings and dying.

Saddened, the Poet blew out the candle. "I can only save them by sitting in the dark."

The Procession of Lord Long Legs

On a bright day in May, the time of rice planting, Lord Long Legs learned that it was time for his journey to Edo. Lord Long legs ruled over four acres of rice fields in Echizen. His retainers, who were all grasshoppers, numbered over six thousand. His court included only noble insects like the Mantis and the Beetle. His queen, Katydid, was served by the most beautiful ladybugs and butterflies. Lord Long Legs employed dragonflies and fireflies as his messengers. Every once in a while, he sent beetles on an errand, but the clumsy fellows often plowed into things, hitting their heads hard enough to forget their tasks. He ruled over a kingdom of several million, including the spiders, fleas, ants, and ticks.

Across his kingdom, the insects worked. Silkworms kept spinning wheels in their heads. They could turn mulberry leaves into silk. Wasps made paper, and bees made honey. The resources of his kingdom were so great that even men took notice.

Once a year, Lord Long Legs took a trip to Edo to pay his respects to the Shogun. There, he and his court would spend several weeks before returning home. The trip required work from across his domain and a long procession to carry what his honored court needed for their stay. Each member of his court tried to outshine each other in their dress and behavior.

The leader of the procession, Locust, gathered everyone together. Locust prided himself on living to be seventeen years old and didn't hesitate to remind the others they were children compared to him. He read from a piece of wasp nest paper all the rules of the journey.

"Don't leave the line to suckle flowers. We will stop for that," he read.

The bumblebee brushed the pollen off his legs, and the blue-tailed fly washed his face and hands for the journey. Behind the procession, ladybugs cried because they couldn't join their Queen. Crickets chirped sadly because the journey was too far for their short legs. Locust wrangled them to readiness and then sent them home. The journey would start at six in the morning, as announced by the flea.

Flea sat on the back of the cat that lived within the fields and watched the cat's green eyes. When they closed to a certain width, the flea knew it was time to ready the procession and sent the mosquito to wake the Locust.

Exactly at six, the procession passed beyond the gates of their home and toward Edo. All the servants of the kingdom gathered to bow and see them off. They bowed low as Lord Long Legs passed in his palanquin.

The tall mantis led the procession, waving a baton of grass, and crying out: "Down on your knees! The Lord comes." And all the ants, bugs, and lizards would bend their forelegs. Even the toads bobbed their noses in the dust. Grubs, worms, and other creatures that lived in the trees and high grasses gathered on the ground. The Lord had forbidden any insect to remain on a high stalk of grass, lest they looked down upon their ruler. The law required parents to cover their high nests with leaves so their children wouldn't look down upon their lord.

After the mantis came two lantern-bearers, holding glow worms for lanterns. Behind them buzzed six fireflies, adding further light. Weevils followed in rows of four, and each carried morning glories for umbrellas.

Four grasshoppers strutted with their spears, and just ahead of the palanquin walked two noble spiders. They carried the insignia of their lord. Behind the palanquin walked the praying beetle, the priest in his robes. Finally, guarding the back of Lord Long Legs walked four great black spiders. The rest of the servants and baggage followed behind them.

And so, the creatures of the domain came out to see their lord off. Worms stopped crawling, and every creature came to bow as the train passed. Bug mothers carried their babies on their backs and taught them how to bow respectfully. No one dared speak aloud as the lord passed in his palanquin.

The palanquin rivaled the splendor of the court. It was made of delicately woven grass, bound by bamboo threads. It was lacquered and finished with gauze curtains made from dragonfly wings. Four strong grasshoppers bore it on their shoulders, flanked by the personal guard of Lord Long Legs.

And so the common insects had to bow and wait for the long train to pass. Most of the train consisted of the food, luggage, furniture, and other courtly needs. Only after these too passed could the insects return to their climbing, crawling, and other work.

The Tongue Cut Sparrow

Long ago there lived an old man and his wife. The old man was a good, kindhearted, and hard-working fellow, but his wife was a cross, unhappy woman. She spent her days grumbling about everything. They didn't have any children, which was just as well. She would've grumbled about them too! The old man had long ago grown used to her grumbling and didn't notice it. He spent most of the day working in his fields. When he came home, he wanted nothing more than to play with his tame sparrow. He loved the little bird as if she were his child.

When he came back at night, he would open her cage and let her fly about the room. They would play together, and he would teach her little tricks, which she learned quickly. He always saved a little from his dinner for her.

One day the old man went into the forest to chop wood. The old woman went about the house, readying to wash clothes. The day before she had made starch, but the bowl she had filled yesterday stood empty.

While she wondered who could've stolen the starch, the sparrow flew down and bowed her little feathered head as the old man had taught her. "I took your starch. I thought it was food put out for me, and I ate it all. I didn't know it was for your washing. Please forgive me." The sparrow spread her wings and bowed her apology.

The old woman didn't like the sparrow and often fought with her husband for keeping the dirty bird and making more work for her. She cursed the little sparrow and seized it. She fetched a pair of scissors and cut off the little bird's tongue.

"You used that tongue to steal my starch. See what it is like to go without it." She drove the bird out of the house. Then she made more rice starch and continued her laundry.

That evening when the old man came home, he expected his feathered friend to meet him at the gate as she did whenever she flew free. But she didn't appear. He dashed into the house and kicked off his straw sandals. Still no sparrow. He supposed his wife had shut the sparrow into its cage again.

"Where is the sparrow?" he called.

"Your bird? I don't know. I haven't seen her all afternoon. The ungrateful thing has flown away no doubt."

The old man knew better than that, so he kept asking her. Finally, she confessed what she did and even showed the old man the sparrow's tongue. "Here is the tongue. Horrid bird didn't have to eat all my starch."

"How could you be so cruel?" the old man asked. He was too kind to punish his wife. "She won't be able to chirp or maybe even eat. Not to mention the pain! What can I do?"

After his wife went to sleep, the old man cried. While he cried, he decided to go look for the sparrow as soon as the sun rose. With that thought, he managed to finally sleep.

The next morning, he rose before the sun and set off after eating a fast breakfast. He stopped at every hill and clump of bamboos to call for the bird. "Where does my tongue-cut sparrow stay?"

He didn't stop for lunch, and the afternoon grew late when he found himself near a bamboo forest. He knew such forests were favorite shelters for sparrows. As he approached, he saw his dear sparrow waiting for him. He ran toward her, and she bowed her head and showed off a number of her tricks. He apologized for what had happened to her, as joyful tears flowed down his cheeks.

"Please don't think about it," she said.

"How can you speak without your tongue?" the old man asked.

She opened her beak and showed him that her tongue had grown back. "Don't worry about the past. I am quite fine now."

The old man then knew that his sparrow wasn't a common bird. His relief overwhelmed his hunger and his exhaustion.

The sparrow asked him to follow her, and she led him to a beautiful house in the heart of the bamboo forest. The beauty of the place astonished the old man. The house was built from the whitest of wood. Inside, he found beautiful vases and boxes and fine furniture. The sparrow sat him in the place of honor and thanked him for his kindness over the long years. She introduced her family to him. Her daughters brought all kinds of delicious foods and entertained him with dancing.

The old man had never enjoyed himself so much. The hours flew by until the darkness reminded him he was far from home. He thanked the sparrow and her family and begged she forget all that she had suffered because of his wife. He told the sparrow that he was happy that she had such a beautiful home and family and said he could return with a light heart. If she ever needed him for anything, she had only to send for him.

The sparrow begged him to stay and rest, but the old man said he had to return to his wife and work. As much as he wanted to accept her invitation, he had to go, but he promised to visit. The sparrow ordered her servants to bring two boxes and asked the old man to pick whichever he wanted.

He chose the smallest box. "I am too old and feeble to carry the heavy box. This one is easier for me to carry."

The sparrow family saw him off and asked him to come back whenever he had the time. The sparrow felt bad for all the old man had to deal with throughout his life.

When he returned home, his wife launched into him. "Where have you been? Why did you come back so late?"

He showed her the box he brought back and told her everything that had happened and how wonderful the sparrow's house was. He had his wife help him open the box.

Gold and silver coins filled the box to its brim. The old man hadn't expected such a gift. He would be able to give up work and live the rest of his life at ease with such wealth.

"Thanks to my good little sparrow," the old man said many times.

After the old woman's surprise faded, she reproached the old man for not bringing home the large gift box he told her about. "You stupid old man. Just think what we lost. We might have had twice as much as this. You are a fool."

The old man wished he hadn't mentioned the big box.

The next morning the old woman got up early, determined to bring home the box her fool of a husband had left. She made the old man describe the way to the sparrow's house and left for a visit. She never once considered that the sparrow family might want to punish her for what she had done. As for the sparrow family, they had talked of little else. They loved the old man, but they hated the old woman and determined they would punish her whenever they had the chance.

After walking several hours, the old woman found the bamboo grove. "Where is the tongue-cut sparrow's house?" she called.

She saw the eaves of the house peeping from the bamboo foliage and hastened to knock on the door.

When the servants told the sparrow that the old woman was at the door, she was surprised. She hadn't expected the old woman to be so bold. The sparrow was a polite bird, however, so she went to greet her.

The old woman didn't waste any time. "You don't need to entertain me as you did my old man. I've come to get the box he stupidly left behind. I will leave as soon as I get it. It is all I want."

The sparrow immediately consented and ordered her servants to bring out the big box. The old woman grabbed it and hoisted it onto her back. Without even a thank-you, she hurried home. The box was so heavy that she couldn't walk quickly, and she often had to rest. Her desire to look inside the box grew with every step until she couldn't wait any longer. A box that heavy had to be full of gold and precious jewels.

She sat it down and carefully opened it. As soon as she lifted the lid, a number of demons leaped out of the box and surrounded her as if to kill her. Even in her nightmares she had never seen such horrible creatures. A demon with a single eye glared at her. Another with gaping mouths looked ready to eat her. A huge snake threatened to squeeze her.

She ran.

When she burst through the door of her home, she fell to the floor and told the old man what had happened to her. Then she began to blame the sparrow, but the old man stopped her at once.

"Don't blame the sparrow. Your wickedness has at least seen its reward. I just hope you learned your lesson."

The old woman repented of her ways and worked toward becoming a good old woman. She made such progress that the old man wondered if she was the same person. They spent their last days together happily, living off the treasure the old man received from the tongue-cut sparrow.

The Sparrow's Wedding

Chiyotaro, a prosperous sparrow, lived in the heart of a pine tree forest nestled in a remote part of the Land of the Dragonfly. Chiyotaro had many beautiful children, but Tsuchiotaro stood out among them. He was the life of the household, merry and talkative as only a sparrow could be. He would often fly far through the woods and across the surrounding plains. He would even come within sight of the peaks of the Matchless Mountain. But as soon as sundown approached, he would wing homeward to tell the story of the day's adventure. Laughter echoed throughout the forest as the sparrow family listened to Tsuchiotaro's chatter.

One sunny morning, Tsuchiotaro chirped his goodbye and flew off without a destination in mind. He flew at random until he came upon the shadowy bamboo grove where Kosuzumi, the tongue-cut sparrow, lived. There he saw Kosuzumi's daughter. While Kosuzumi was beautiful, her daughter Osuzu was even more lovely. Tsuchiotaro loved her at fight sight and could see she was warmhearted and winsome.

He approached her, hopping around her quietly. When he saw Osuzu smile and peep coyly at him, he risked talking to her. Gradually, their reserve fell away as they spoke with each other. All too soon, dusk came, and Tsuchiotaro promised Osuzu that he would return. As he flew through the summer air, full of the fragrance of wildflowers, deep joy filled his heart. Back in her grove, Osuzu played over the day's memory and her feelings of love as the soft breeze rocked her to sleep.

Tsuchiotaro rushed to tell his father about his love. In his joy, he neglected to tell his father that Osuzu belonged to the family of the honored Kosuzumi. His father listened with surprise. As rich and respected as he was, he couldn't let his son marry just any little sparrow. But as Chiyotaro sat in a quiet nook of his rustling home, he considered his son's happiness.

"If Osuzu is good and true," he concluded. "I will give my consent."

After a day or two, the eldest of sparrows confirmed Tsuchiotaro's story. When Chiyotaro heard that Osuzu's mother was the famous tongue-cut sparrow, he determined to make his son happy. According to tradition, he sent a messenger to Kosuzumi with a formal request of marriage. After some consideration, they consented to meet Chiyotaro. Luckily for the young couple, the parents found each other agreeable, and they set the date of the wedding.

The families built the couple's new home high in a beautiful cherry tree. Its pure white flowers would give the couple peace and fill their springtime with perfume. Gifts came from all over to furnish the new home.

Just before the wedding day, the couple visited their future home and rejoiced at the rich furnishings. Tsuchiotaro presented his love with a headdress made from the slender petals of a rare mountain flower and a pair of tiny moss sandals, so soft that she put them on immediately. Osuzu's parents sent a robe woven from peach blossoms along with rice wine and fine fruit for Tsuchiotaro.

Finally, the day of the wedding arrived. The wedding procession came from all over, such that no one had ever seen such a collection of sparrows. Tsuchiotaro was widely loved, and the beauty of Osuzu was of such renown.

When the couple arrived at their new home, the couple sipped three times from the three cups of rice wine, consecrating their union. All of the sparrows celebrated until late evening, long after the sun faded behind the hills.

Tsuchiotaro and Osuzu lived happily and had children as graceful as themselves.

Gods and Goddesses

Autumn and Spring

A young woman once slept in a rice field while the sun was at its height. A god watched her, captivated by her inner beauty, a beauty that rivaled the dreams of heaven. The god waited for her to wake and descended. He asked her to be his wife, and she accepted. They married immediately, and a wonderful red jewel came out of their happiness.

Long after the wedding, a farmer found the jewel. He prized it and always carried it with him because he knew how rare it was. Sometimes when he looked at it by the light of the moon, he thought he saw a pair of eyes looking back from the jewel's depths. Sometimes he would wake in the depth of night, thinking that a voice called him by his name.

One day, the farmer prepared the midday meal for his workers. The sun burned down on him as he loaded a cow with bowls of rice, dumplings, and beans. As he worked, Prince Ama Boko approached. The prince grew angry at the farmer, thinking the farmer meant to kill the cow. Despite the farmer's truthful protest, the prince grew even more angry. The farmer feared what the prince would do and pulled the red stone from his pocket and offered it to the powerful prince. The gem captivated Ama Boko, and he allowed the farmer to continue to the fields.

The prince returned to his home. When he pulled out his new treasure, the stone transformed into a goddess of indescribable beauty. He fell for her, and they married before the moon waned that night. The goddess provided for his every need. She cooked meals that only gods ate. She made wine that mortals never got to taste. Their children flourished.

But after a while, the prince became proud and began to treat his faithful wife with contempt.

This saddened the goddess. "You are not worthy of my love," she said. "I will now return to my father."

Ama Boko ignored her. He didn't believe she would leave him. On the next day, she escaped the palace and fled to Naniwa, where she was worshiped as the Goddess of Light, Akaru-hime.

When the prince learned of her escape, he raged and set out after her. When he neared Naniwa, the gods refused to let him in. Then he understood that he had lost his priceless red jewel. He returned to his ship and went to the north coast of Japan, landing at Tajima. He was well received because of all the treasures he brought with him. Of course, none of the pearls, gems, or even a mirror that controlled the wind and ocean waves were as great as the treasure he lost. Prince Ama Boko lived in Tajima and became the father of a mighty race.

His granddaughter became a princess so renowned for her beauty that eighty suitors vied for her hand. But she rejected all of them. Finally, two young brothers came before her, the God of Autumn, and the God of Spring.

The eldest brother, the God of Autumn, approached her first, but she refused him. He returned to his brother. "The princess doesn't love me. You won't win her heart either."

"I bet you a cask of rice wine that I will," the God of Spring said.

His older brother accepted the bet, expecting it was a sure win.

The God of Spring went to his mother and told her about his desire for the princess and of his wager. To help him, she wove a robe and sandals from the unopened buds of the lilac and white wisteria for him to wear. She also made him a bow and arrows.

As the God of Spring approached the princess, every bud opened, filling the air with their fragrance. The sight filled the princess with joy, and she accepted the God of Spring as her husband.

When the God of Autumn heard how their mother helped his brother, he grew angry and refused to fulfill his side of the bet. When his mother heard of how he had broken his word, she placed stones and salt in the hollow of a bamboo cane, wrapped it in bamboo leaves, and hung it in the smoke of a fire. She then cursed her first-born son. "As the leaves wither and fade, so must you. As the salt sea ebbs, so must you. As the stone sinks, so must you."

And so the God of Autumn was cursed to grow old, withered, and sad while the God of Spring remained ever young, fragrant, and merry.

Broken Statues

There once lived two princes. The elder brother lived as a hunter. He loved forests and hunts, spending each day from dawn to dark with his bow and arrows. He could run like a deer and was strong and intelligent. His younger brother was a gentle intellectual. From dawn to dark he would read or sit with his thoughts. He would sing of love and any subject that caught his interest. He told stories of fairies and of the time of the gods.

Upon a fair summer day, the hunter went off to the woods as was his habit. The intellectual took his book and walked along the stream, smiling at the flowers that grew there. He continued for some time and came upon a holy shrine. One hundred moss-covered steps led to the shrine. Beside the great stairway sat stone lion guardians, and Mount Fuji rose behind the shrine, white and beautiful.

The intellectual looked up the mountain. "Mount Fuji, such a wonder. To see you is to hear sweet music without sound, the harmony of silence."

He climbed the steps, and the stone lions rose from their pedestals to follow behind him. Lost in his thoughts, the intellectual didn't notice them. They followed him to the inner gates of the shrine and stopped.

The interior of the shrine was quiet, and a soft light bounced from gold and bronze mirrors. Smoke from incense curled in the still air. The intellectual felt tired from his walk and settled into a corner to take a short nap.

Singing awoke him, and he saw a man towering beside him. The ageless man bounced a sleeping one-year old child in his arms while he sang a strange melody. When the child relaxed into sleep, the man smiled.

"Is that your child?" the intellectual asked.

"This isn't a child. It is a spirit."

"Then, my lord, what are you?"

"I am Jizo, and I guard the souls of children. Do you know how pitiful it is to hear their cries when they come to the riverbed *Sainokawara?* They come alone, wailing and wandering. They have to pile stones for a prayer. But a demon comes at night and scatters the stones, terrifying the children."

"What happens to the children then?" the intellectual asked.

"I come to them and call the children to me. They fly to me and hide in my long sleeves." He lifted his arm to show off his sleeve. "I carry them like this one. They are as light and cold as a mountain's mist."

As he spoke, the child stirred and murmured. He rocked her and paced across the temple.

The intellectual saw a lady approach the temple. She wore a gray robe and silver sandals. She answered the intellectual's unspoken question as he noticed her. "I am called the Merciful. For all of humankind, I have refused eternal peace, and I was given one thousand loving arms. Dreamer, when you dream you will see me in my lotus boat when I sail upon the mystic sea."

The intellectual recognized the goddess. "Lady Kannon."

Yet another goddess appeared, dressed in blue. "Hello, Dreamer. I am Benten, the Goddess of Sea and Song. My dragons live with me and beneath my feet." She gestured at the dragons that swirled about her. "Look at their green scales and their opal eyes."

After her came a band of boys, laughing and clasping their arms together. "We are the sons of the Sea Goddess. Come with us to our cool caves."

The God of Roads and his three ape messengers topped the stairs. The first ape covered his eyes with his hands so he could see no evil thing. The second covered his ears so he could hear no evil thing. The third ape covered his mouth so he could speak no evil thing.

Behind the apes and the God of Roads walked the goddess who takes the clothes from the dead who cannot pay their toll. She forced those unfortunate souls to stand shivering at the entrance of the Three Ways.

The intellectual saw many more gods and goddesses approach the shrine until darkness arrived with a storm that battered the roof.

"Brother, wake up!"

The intellectual awoke to see his brother standing over him.

"Thank the gods you are safe," said the hunter. "I've looked for you half the night. I shouldn't have left you by the stream." He took his brother's face between his warm hands.

"I've been with the gods here in this shrine." The intellectual gazed about the empty shrine. He could almost see the outlines of the gods and goddesses in the darkness. "This place is holy."

The hunter lifted his lantern so the shrine's mirrors caught the light. "I don't see anything. All I see are rows of broken, gray statues with moss growing on their feet."

"They are gray because they are sad. They've been forgotten."

The hunter took his brother by the hand and helped him stand. He led his brother into the night.

"The forest always smells so nice after the rain," the intellectual said.

"Tighten your sandals," the hunter said, "and I will race you home."

Prince Ninigi

Amaterasu spoke with her grandson Ninigi who was also known as Prince Rice Ear Ruddy Plenty. "Descend from your heavenly seat and go rule the Land of Fresh Rice Ears." She gave him many gifts to help him with her request, including precious stones from the mountain steps of heaven, the purest white crystal balls, and the cloud sword of her brother Susanoo. She also entrusted him with the mirror that enticed her from the cave.

"Guard the mirror well," she told him. "When you look into it, you will see my face." She also commanded several gods to join him, including the beautiful dancer Uzume.

So Ninigi and his company descended through the clouds to the eight forks of heaven. There stood a giant god statue with fierce, fiery eyes. The sight of the god froze the entire company with fear, including Ninigi. Only Uzume remained brave. She left the company and approached the statue alone.

"Who are you? Why do you stop our journey?" she asked.

The statue-god felt pleased that she would address him so bravely. "I am a friendly earth spirit, the God of the Field Paths. I've come to guide Ninigi. Please return and tell him that I, the Prince of Saruta, greet him."

Uzume smiled at the god. "We will continue to earth and there I will tell Ninigi of you."

"I will wait for you on the mountain of Takichihi, in the country of Tsukushi."

Uzume returned to the company and related the message. When Ninigi heard her, he immediately left for the Bridge of Heaven on the summit of Takachihi. After joining with the Prince of Saruta, Ninigi traveled across his new kingdom, visiting the mountains, the lakes, the plains, and the vast pine forests.

"This is a land where the morning sun always shines," he said. "It is a good land."

He built a palace with pillars that extended into the bedrock and with cross beams that rose to the Plain of High Heaven.

"The God of the Field Paths will return to his home. Because of his help as a guide, he will wed the beautiful goddess Uzume. She will be the priestess of his mountain," Ninigi said.

Uzume and the Prince of Saruta obeyed Ninigi's commands, and Uzume continued to be admired for her courage, mirth, and beauty.

As Ninigi traveled along the coast, he saw a lovely young woman. "What is your name?" he asked her.

"I am the daughter of the God Ohoyama. My name is Konohane, Princess Tree Blossom."

Ninigi was struck by her beauty and her inner character. He traveled to her father and asked for Konohane's hand. But Ohoyama had an elder daughter Ihanaga, known as Princess Long As the Rocks. Unfortunately, Ihanaga lacked the beauty of her younger sister. Ohoyama wanted Ihanaga and Ninigi to wed and have children that could live as long as rocks and mountains could live. So he sent both Ihanaga and Konohane to Ninigi. But Ninigi loved Konohane and didn't even look at Ihanaga.

Ihanaga said, "If you had chosen me, you and your children would have lived long lives, but because you love my sister, all your descendants will die like the blossoms of the trees."

For some time, Ninigi and Konohane lived happily. She had the delicate grace and freshness of a cherry blossom. She loved the sunshine and the soft west wind and the cool rain on a quiet summer night. But Ninigi grew jealous of other men despite his wife's faithfulness. Unable to take his jealousy any longer, Konohane locked herself in her palace and set it on fire. The flames rose high as Ninigi watched. Three little boys sprang out of the flames and called for their father, followed by an untouched Konohane.

He asked her forgiveness and named their sons Hoderi (Fire Flash) Hosueri (Fire Climax) and Howori (Fire Fade). After his sons had grown, Ninigi divided his kingdom among his sons and returned to the Plain of High Heaven.

The Creation of Heaven and Earth

Before time began, the Heavens and the Earth were one swirling ocean of chaos. Land and water, solids and gases, light and darkness mixed together. Eventually gases rose from the ocean, forming the sky and heavens. The heavier parts sank and cohered, forming the earth. Water settled into the four seas. Between these seas and the newly settled earth and heaven, a presence floated, resembling a white cloud. Out of this came forth three beings: The Being of the Middle of Heaven, the High August Being, and the Majestic Being.

Out of the warm earth a rush sprouted. Its bud shone clear and bright like a crystal, and a god bloomed from it. The rush sprouted five more buds and five more heavenly gods. Pairs of gods came from the muddy earth and the settling air until the first man and woman appeared. The first man was called Izanagi. The first woman was called Izanami.

Izanagi and Izanami lived in the Heavens. The world below floated on the surface of the water. The sun, earth, and moon were still attached to each other like a head to the neck or arms to the body. Slowly the parts that joined them grew thinner, forming a thin strip called Heaven's Floating Bridge. Izanagi and Izanami stood on this bridge when they saw a pair of wagtails singing together. The birds entranced the couple, and they imitated the birds. And so man and woman began the art of love.

While talking together on the Bridge of Heaven, they wondered if a world existed beneath them. They gazed down into the green seas but saw nothing. Then Izanagi took his long, jeweled spear and plunged it into the torrent below. He stirred the waters for a time. As he lifted the spear, drops trickled from it and hardened into dry earth. Izanagi lifted his spear and cleaned it the rest of the way. The lumps of muck and mud that flew from it careened off into space, turning into stars and comets.

The couple named the earth The Island of the Congealed Drop. They descended from Heaven and landed on the island. Izanagi struck his spear into the ground and made it the axis of the world. He then built a pillar around the spear. When he was finished, the couple walked separately around the island to examine it.

When they met on the other side, Izanami cried out, "What a lovely man!"

But Izanagi berated her for speaking first, and said they had to try again. So the couple walked around the island once more. When they met, Izanami remained quiet.

"What a lovely woman!" Izanagi said.

They laughed and began the work of creating Japan. The first island brought out of the water was called Awaji. After that, the couple brought up eight large islands and six smaller ones. The several thousand islets that make up the archipelago of Japan were formed when the foam of the sea coalesced.

After they were finished with the land, the divine couple created eight million gods and ten thousand living things on the earth. Plants sprang up all over the misty land. Izanagi breathed and created two gods, the male and female of the wind.

The island children of Izanagi and Izanami grew larger as time passed, just as people grow from tiny infants. As the land and sea gradually separated and the islands grew, foreign countries coalesced from the foam of the sea.

The divine couple also had a child, the god of fire who proved to have a temper. Izanami created the gods of metal, clay, and fresh water to keep the god of fire quiet. She told them to put him out whenever he got out of hand.

Although the divine couple were together just a short time, they began to fight. Izanami had once told her husband not to look at her when she hid herself. But Izanagi spied upon her when she was unwell and wanted to be alone. Izanami grew angry at this intrusion and went down into the lower world of darkness. She stayed in this dark world for a long time until Izanagi finally went after her. But the underworld horrified him, and he tried to escape back to the light of the surface.

As he struggled during his escape, several gods were created. One came out of his staff. When he finally reached daylight, he found a large rock to close the hole he used. He turned the rock into a god and commanded it to watch the hole. Then he rushed into the sea to wash himself. He blew out the polluted air of the underworld, and two evil gods sprang from his nostrils. Izanagi knew these two would cause trouble and so created two other gods to balance them.

When he washed his eyes, two more gods appeared. Out of his left eye came the glistening maiden, Amaterasu. From his right eye appeared Susanoo, the Ruler of the Moon. Izanagi felt joy when he saw these two children.

"I have begotten so many children. No more. These two are the jewels of all my children," he said.

Amaterasu's beauty shone throughout Heaven and Earth. Izanagi admired her and said to himself, "None of my children are like this one. She can't stay here." He took off his jeweled necklace and gave it to her. "I want you to rule over the High Plain of Heaven."

At that time, the distance between Heaven and Earth wasn't great. He sent her up to the sky via the pillar he had built. Amaterasu climbed it easily and made her home in the sun.

Izanagi turned to his other child, Susanoo, and said. "I want you to rule over the newborn Earth and the sea."

Susanoo took the moon as his home.

And so everything that exists was created, leaving Japan directly opposite the sun when it separated from the Earth.

The Divine Messengers

The gods looked down from the High Plain of Heaven and saw the earth was filled with wicked spirits. The earth didn't see peace even through the night. So the gods commanded Oshihomi to go down and govern the earth. As he walked on the Floating Bridge, he heard the sounds of the earth below. The chaos and confusion he heard made him turn on his heel.

"I can't do this work," he told the gods. "Send someone else."

Amaterasu called a meeting of the eight hundred gods in the Tranquil River of Heaven. "Trouble and disorder plague the central Land of the Reed Plains," she said. "One of you needs to descend and prepare the earth for our grandson Ninigi. He is to rule over it. Who will go and do this?"

The gods replied. "Let Amenoho do it."

So Amenoho descended to the earth. But soon after he arrived, he felt happy with his life on the lower plane. He forgot his mission and took to living with the spirits of the earth. Confusion still reigned.

For three years Amaterasu and the gods waited for him. News never arrived. Finally, Amaterasu said, "We will send Amewaka. He won't forget his mission."

She gave Amewaka a heavenly deer bow and feathered arrows that always fly straight to their target. "Take these and bring order to the land below, even if you have to declare war."

When Amewaka landed on the seashore, the beautiful earth spirit, Princess Under Shining, stood before him. Her beauty entranced him, and they married. Eight years passed. Amewaka spent them with his wife, enjoying the food and joys of the earth instead of seeing to his charge. He didn't attempt to raise an army, nor did he have any desire to rule over the Land of the Reed Plains.

Again, the eight hundred gods assembled at Amaterasu's call. "We haven't heard anything from Amewaka. Who will go to discover why?"

The gods brought forward a faithful pheasant hen. "Go to Amewaka," they told the hen, "and remind him of his mission to pacify the earth. Ask him why we haven't heard from him these past eight years."

The pheasant flew to earth and perched on the cassia tree that over-looked the gates of Amewaka's palace. She spoke the message, but no one in the palace stirred. The pheasant tried again, and Amanosagu heard.

She went to Amewaka. "There's a pheasant outside the gate, and its cry brings trouble. Take your bow and arrows and kill it."

Amewaka, angered that a bird would trouble him, shot the pheasant through the heart. The divine arrow continued past its target and up into the heavens. It pierced the clouds and fell still at the feet of Amaterasu. The goddess saw the blood that stained the arrow's feathers and picked it up. "If this arrow was shot by our messenger at evil spirits, don't hit him. But if it was shot out of the foulness of his heart, kill him." So she threw the arrow back to the earth.

At this moment, Amewaka slept under a tree after enjoying the harvest feast. The arrow screamed through the air and pierced him through the heart. Princess Under Shining cried out when she found the body of her husband a few moments later. Her cries rose to the heavens and to the ears of Amewaka's father. The god stirred the wind and carried the body of his wayward son back to the heavens.

For eight days and eight nights, the god and his family mourned the death and folly of Amewaka. Ajishiki came to see his brother one last time. Ajishiki looked so much like Amewaka, that his grief-stricken parents thought Amewaka had returned to life. This angered Ajishiki. He drew his sword and tore apart the shrine that housed his brother's body.

By that time Amaterasu had had her fill of failures. "Takemika and Toribune will go and subdue the earth once and for all."

So the two gods went down to the earth, landing on the shore of Inasa. As soon as their toes touched the sand, they drew their swords and declared war against the earth spirits. The pair succeeded where so many other gods had failed. After they finished their mission, they returned to the High Plain of Heaven.

The Legend of Kannon

In the age of the gods, they traveled between heaven and earth using the Floating Bridge of Heaven, *Ama no hashidate*. They carried their jeweled spears, magnificent bows, and divine arrows. But as all things must end, so too the direct way between earth and heaven closed. But people continued to call the area *Ama no hashidate*.

Saion Zenji was a holy man from Kyoto who followed the Way of the Gods since he was young. He also followed the doctrines of the Buddha. He spent long hours in meditation and memorized many scriptures.

One day, he took a pilgrimage to *Ama no hashidate* and found the area beautiful. "The foolish believe trees and rocks and the sea aren't sentient. But the wise know that they sing praises to Tathagata. I will stay here and sing with them," he said.

So he climbed Nariai Mountain and settled on location to build a shrine to Kannon the Merciful and a hut for himself. After he finished building both, he began a routine of singing Holy Sutras from dawn to twilight. Lost in the music, he floated on the ecstasy. His voice resonated until the blue bell flowers of the mountain bowed to him. The white lilies offered their incense for his shrine, and even the cicada joined their voices to his. Dragonflies and butterflies of all sorts fluttered around his hut in time with his chanting. Even the farmers deep in the valley heard his voice. Time to time, they climbed the mountain to kneel at the shrine he built and to bring him rice. Sometimes he would follow them back home to tend to their sick and teach their children. The villagers said even his clothes shined like his voice.

One winter, a storm that defied the memory of the oldest man blew from the north. Snow fell for nine days. While the villagers fared fine, Saion struggled in his hut. The snow piled so high that the shrine of Kannon disappeared. Saion made due with his scant food stores and meditated as he could. But even he couldn't ignore the needs of his body. He collapsed from starvation.

"Forgive me, merciful Kannon. I will die without food."

He rose and pushed opened the door of his hut. The snow had stopped. It lay thick and glaring in the sunlight.

"Forgive me, Kannon," he prayed. "I don't know why, but I am reluctant to leave this world yet. Please save my life."

He trudged into the snow in the direction of the village. He walked only a short distance when he saw the dappled hide of a deer in the snow. The deer appeared to have died from the cold.

"Poor creature. You won't run again or nibble on the grass and flowers." He stroked the deer's soft flank. "It's forbidden for me to eat you by both the Buddha and Kannon." Yet he knew the deer would make a delicious stew that would save his life.

As he stroked the cold fur and wrestled with his morals and his stomach, a voice spoke to him from the snow. "If you die of hunger, Saion Zenji, what shall happen to my people living in the valley below? They won't have you to help them or teach them the Sutras of the Tathagata. Break the law to keep the law, my love."

Saion knew deep inside that the voice belonged to Kannon. He took his knife in his trembling hand and cut a piece of meat from the deer's flank. He gathered fir cones and made a small fire in his hearth and cooked the meat in an iron pot. When it finished cooking, he ate half of it and felt his strength return. He sang out his thankfulness, and even the embers of the dying fire leaped up to hear him.

Saion looked outside his door toward the deer that saved his life. "I need to bury the poor deer." He went outside, but the deer was gone. Not even a mark remained in the snow to betray where it had been.

He pondered for a moment before returning to his hut. He had taken up a chant when a small group of villagers appeared at his door.

"Thank Kannon you are well," they said. "We worried that you might have died from the cold and hunger."

"I would've if it wasn't for a deer." Saion told them his story. "I cut only a hand's width of meat and half of it remains in that iron pot."

When the villagers bent to look in the pot, they found a piece of cedar gilded with gold on one side. Even Saion was surprised. Saion took the cedar to the shrine. The villagers cleared the shrine of snow. Inside sat a smiling golden image of the lady Kannon. A gash stood out on her right side where the gilded wood had been cut away. Saion placed the wedge of cedar into the gash, and the statue's wound sealed so not a single seam could be seen. The villagers fell to the floor and bowed. Saion stood and sang praises to the goddess.

The villagers remained until the sun began to set. A cold moon appeared to shine down upon the area. Through a hole in the ceiling, the moonlight shined on the face of Kannon. Saion Zenji continued to sing his gratitude with tears sliding down his cheeks.

Life-Giving Wine

Between Totomi Province and Suruga Province stood the mountain Daimugenzan. Few people ever visited its rugged, wild peaks. The forest grew thick and dark. About halfway up the forest sat a lonely, forgotten shrine dedicated to Kannon. Moss and weather ate its wooden frame. Only one girl and her parents ever visited.

The girl was named Okureha and lived at the foot of the mountain. As the daughter of a samurai, she didn't fear the darkness of the forest and the shrine. She made it a point to keep the forlorn place company. One day, she returned from praying for her mother to recover from her illness when a rough-looking man appeared and grabbed her by the arm.

She cried for help. Her voice echoed through the forest, and she knew the man could do anything he wanted to her. She struggled, but the man had the strength of a warrior.

Suddenly, a piercing cold wind blew through the trees. The autumn leaves rose in columns around them. The wind seemed to drain her assailant's strength. Okureha felt weakness steal upon her too, but she fought against it and against the man.

The man fell down as if he had fallen asleep, releasing her as he fell. She felt drowsy too until the wind became hot. She looked up and saw a beautiful girl walking toward her. The girl didn't look any older than she and glided over the needles and leaves. The girl's face was as white as the snow that capped the mountain. Her eyebrows bent in perfect crescents, and her lips formed a small flower.

"Don't be surprised or afraid, my child." The girl's silvery voice calmed Okureha. "I saw you were in danger and came to you. The man isn't dead. I can revive him or keep him as he is if I wish. What is your name?"

Okureha fell to her knees and bowed. "Thank you for saving me. My name is Okureha. My father is a samurai who owns the village of Tashiro. My mother is sick, so I came here to pray. My father and mother prayed here when they couldn't have a child. Then they had me. I don't doubt that my prayers will be answered."

The Mountain Goddess smiled. "Come here whenever you want, and I will protect you. Children as dedicated as your parents deserve all that is good. Come back tomorrow and we can talk. Bring me flowers from the fields if you come. I enjoy them but rarely get to smell them. You had better go home now. When you've had enough time, I will let this vile man go. He won't bother you again."

"I will return tomorrow," Okureha said.

That night, Okureha remained awake. As soon as dawn broke, she gathered wild flowers and went up to the shrine. The goddess waited for her. They discussed a variety of topics, enjoying each other's company.

Whenever Okureha had free time, she visited. This continued for nearly a year.

One day, Okureha went up to visit with flowers, but she couldn't feel happy no matter how much she tried.

"Why are you so sad?" the goddess asked.

"This is the last day I can visit you. I'm now seventeen and have to marry. My father arranged for me to marry the son of his friend Tokue of Iwasakimura. The wedding is in three days. After that, I will have to stay home and won't be able to visit you again." Okureha began to cry.

The goddess smiled and touched the girl's shoulder. "Don't be sad, dear child. You are about to start the happiest stage of your life. If people didn't marry, they wouldn't produce children to inherit the new spirits of life. You will be happy and doing your duty for the world." She produced a small gourd. "Take this rice wine with you. When you are married, give some to your husband. You will remain as you are now and live for centuries. Farewell, my child."

Okureha wiped her tears and accepted the rice wine. She mustered all her pluck and left the goddess, her friend. Three days later, she married.

It was the year Emperor Toba came to the throne, 1108 AD.

As they celebrated their marriage, Okureha gave her husband some of the rice wine and poured the rest for herself. They sat alone in a meadow. The fragrance of wild violets danced on the air, and a mountain stream gurgled not far off. As they drank, cherry blossoms suddenly fell around them.

They looked around, puzzled. No cherry trees stood nearby. Then they happened to look up. A single white cloud sailed over them, and seated on it was the goddess.

"It's the goddess that gave us the rice wine," Okureha said.

The goddess flew to the top of the mountain and hovered there until night fell and the newlyweds had to go home.

Okureha and her husband never grew any older. They enjoyed centuries of life around Mount Daimugenzan.

The Man Who Married the Bear Goddess

Some time ago a village prospered. Its villagers enjoyed plenty of venison, fish, and every type of food. However, one year a terrible famine set in. The villagers were unable to find even the smallest fish to eat, and all the wildlife fled. One by one, all of the villagers died until only the village chief and his son and daughter remained. Soon, the father too died, leaving the eldest daughter and her younger brother alone.

The daughter gathered their family's treasures, stuffed them into a bag, and gave them to her brother. "Take these and buy food with them. Don't think about bringing the food back to me. Eat it and live. It doesn't matter if I die. I'm a girl and can't inherit father's property. But you can. Don't let our family die."

The boy didn't want to leave his sister, but he knew if he stayed they both would starve to death. So he set out along the coast. He walked through the sand for some time when he came across a beautiful house. Near it was the fresh carcass of a large whale. The boy went to the house, knocked, and waited for a response. After a little time, he left his bag of treasures outside and entered. Inside sat a man who looked like a god. His speckled clothing sparkled, and his face shined. Beside him sat the man's wife. She wore the finest black clothing.

The boy stopped in the doorway, uncertain what to say for intruding on them.

"Welcome," said the god. "Care to join us for a meal?"

The couple prepared a meal of whale meat, and the boy feasted on it. Throughout the meal, the woman never looked at him.

When they finished, the boy asked them to wait for a moment. He retrieved his bag of treasures from outside and offered them to the couple. "I will give you these in payment for the food."

The god took the bag and peered inside it. His face twitched with his excitement. "These are beautiful treasures, but you don't have to pay me for the food. Tell you what. I will take these treasures to my other house and bring you treasures of my own to exchange for them. Please eat as much as you want." The god left with the bag of treasure.

The boy remained with the woman. He kept quiet, feeling awkward being alone with a beautiful woman like her. After a few moments, the woman leaned toward the boy. "Listen close. I am the bear goddess. This supposed husband of mine is the dragon god. There's no one more jealous than him. That's why I didn't look at you. Those treasures you offered are so special that not even the gods have them. He took them to make counterfeits. When he returns he will offer you similar counterfeits. You need to tell him: 'We don't need to make an exchange. I want to buy the woman.' Even though he is jealous he is also as greedy as the sky is large. Do you understand?"

The shaken boy nodded.

"I will marry you if you do this. We will have a happy life together. I promise," she said.

A sound outside separated them. The woman returned to looking outside the window. The god entered with the boy's bag of treasures and a finer, larger bag. "Lad, I've returned with your treasures and my best ones so we can exchange equally."

"I wouldn't mind your treasures, but I want your wife even more. Please sell me your wife."

As soon as he spoke the words, a clap of thunder sounded. The boy felt as if a giant had boxed his ears. He gazed around him. The house had disappeared. The god was also gone, but the boy's bag of treasure and the goddess remained.

"The dragon god left in a rage because he sensed how we want to be together," the goddess said. "That was the noise you heard. Now we can live together."

This is why the bear is a creature half like a human being.

The Palace of the Ocean Bed

Howori, the son of Ninigi, was a great hunter. His elder brother, Hoderi lived as a great fisherman, but even with his skill he was at the mercy of the sea. He would often spend hours in the rough ocean and catch nothing. When the Storm God roamed, Hoderi had to stay home while his brother would return with success from his mountain hunt.

After many days of this, Hoderi felt frustrated. "Let me borrow your bow," he said to Howori. "And I will become a hunter. Here, take my fish hook and give fishing a try."

At first Howori refused, but he eventually relented to stop Hoderi's pestering.

Hoderi didn't know how to track game, nor could he run or shoot with any accuracy. Howori proved as poor a fisherman. Day after day he went out to sea and returned without a single fish. One day he even lost his brother's fish hook.

That evening, Hoderi returned from a day of fruitless hunting. "Mountains have their luck and then there is the luck of the sea. You can have your bow and arrows back, and I will take back my hook. I had better luck at sea."

Howori looked away. "I lost your hook today."

The elder Hoderi paused. "You lost my hook."

Howori nodded.

At that Hoderi grew angry and demanded his brother go and get it. Howori knew it would be impossible to find the hook out in the great ocean, so he took his best sword and made five hundred fish hooks. Hoderi refused the offer. He wanted his lucky hook.

Howori couldn't take the anger and disappointment his brother felt toward him. He went out to the shore and sighed. As he sat there pondering what to do, the Old Man of the Sea appeared and asked what was the problem. Howori explained the fish hook situation, and the old man promised to help. He gathered bamboo from the forest nearby and weaved a boat out of it. The stripes of bamboo were so tight that water couldn't pass through them.

"Take this boat to sea," said the old man. "As you sail, it will sink and carry you into the Kingdom of the Sea."

Howori didn't hesitate at a chance to make amends with his brother, so he set sail and, as the old man said, the boat slowly sank into the sea. Howori descended into the waters, magically able to breathe thanks to the boat, until he came upon a palace made of glittering fish scales. In front of the palace grew a great cassia tree, and his boat entangled in its branches. Beneath it sat the lovely Toyotama, the Peerless Jewel, the daughter of the Sea King Watatsumi. Her strange beauty with her long hair and soft blue eyes entranced Howori as he gazed at her from the tree's branches. When she saw Howori's reflection in the jeweled bowl she held, she dropped it, and it shattered.

She fled to her father. "A man sits in the branches of the cassia tree. He looks like a god. I have seen his image in the waters of my bowl."

The Sea King knew she had seen the great hunter Howori. After all, he knew all that happened in the sea. He left the palace and stopped under the cassia tree. He looked up at Howori. "Come down, son of the gods, and enter my Palace of the Ocean Bed."

Howori descended the tree and was led into the palace. A banquet was prepared to celebrate his arrival. The wealth of the feast astonished Howori. The plates were made of the best mother-of-pearl. He sipped wine from cup-shaped ocean blooms. Howori had never seen such an exotic feast.

When it ended, he went with Toyotama and her father to the roof of the palace. The sun filtered through the waters above them. He saw the ocean's mountains and valleys and the great waving forests of seaweed. As he enjoyed the sights, Howori told Watatsumi of the lost fish hook. The Sea King summoned his retainers, but not a single fish had seen the hook.

However, the lobster spoke up. "As I sat one day in my crevice, the red sea bream swam near me. His mouth had swelled and he didn't greet me as he always does."

Watatsumi noticed the sea bream was absent from his retainers. He sent his fastest messenger to find him. When the sea bream appeared, the lost fish hook dangled from his lip. Howori removed the hook from the unfortunate fish.

Watatsumi was pleased by the Howori's dedication. He also noticed how his daughter looked at the young man. So he decided to offer Toyotama's hand. Howori happily agreed.

The new couple lived in a small fish-scale palace of their own, and Howori learned of the ocean's secrets. He learned how the chopping waves of the upper sea didn't touch the ocean bed. Each night, the gentle motion of the lowest waters rocked Howori to sleep.

Time passed, and Howori grew depressed. He told Toyotama that he missed his home on the earth and how he wanted to see it again. Toyotama turned to her father for help. So the Sea King gave Howori the two great jewels of the sea: the jewel that controlled the flow of the tide and the jewel that controlled the ebb of the tide.

"Return to the earth on the head of my trusted sea dragon," Watatsumi told his son-in-law. "Give your brother his fish hook. If he's angry with you, use the flow jewel to summon the water over him. If he forgives you, use the ebbing jewel."

Howori left the Palace of the Ocean Bed, and the sea dragon carried him to his shore. As he walked onto the sand, he removed his sword and tied it around the neck of the sea dragon. "Take this to the Sea King as a token of my love and gratitude."

When he returned to his brother, he presented the hook. Pleased to have his brother and hook back, Hoderi repented of his anger.

The Serpent with the Eight Heads

After Amaterasu emerged from her cave, she and the other gods banished Susanoo to earth for flaying the celestial horse.

He walked along the bank of a river, remembering what it was like in Heaven. He came upon an old man and an old woman with their arms around their daughter. The old couple cried.

"What is the matter?" Susanoo asked.

The old woman looked up. Tears streaked her cheeks. "We once had eight daughters, but in a marsh near our home lives a huge eight-headed serpent. It comes out once a year and eats one of our daughters." She hugged the young woman. "She's our last."

"And today is the day he will come for her," the old man said. "Can you not help us?"

"I can," Susanoo said. "Don't worry any longer. I will save your daughter. I need you to brew some beer and build a fence with eight gates in it." He instructed the family with what he had in mind.

They finished just as the serpent appeared. Its body trailed over eight hills and eight valleys as it slithered along. With eight heads, the serpent could smell better than any other creature, and the scent of the brewing beer caught its attention. It glided toward the eight large vats. Each head went through its own gate and dunked into a vat. It drank until the alcohol put it to sleep.

When the last head fell asleep, Susanoo leaped from the hole within which he was hidden and drew his sword. With a single swing, he severed the first head. In a blink, he severed the other heads and chopped the body to pieces. But when he struck the tail, his sword snapped.

"What could be so hard?" Susanoo asked. He drew his knife and carefully cut open the tail. Inside the snake's viscera was a sword. Gems glittered on the hilt of the sword, and the blade gleamed sharply. Susanoo took the sword.

"Thank you for saving us," the old woman said.

"If you want to have her, I'd like you to marry our daughter," the old man said.

Susanoo married the young woman and was kind to her. The sword he found within the snake passed through his family and became part of the treasures of the Imperial family.

The Son of Thunder

People who fear storms say Raiden, the God of Thunder, is a cruel god. They also say that his son Raitaro is just as cruel. But they are wrong.

Raiden lived with Raitaro in the Castle of the Clouds high in the blue heaven. And Raiden loved his son dearly. Each evening, the pair would walk the ramparts of the castle and look down upon the Land of Reed Plains. They found the actions of humans amusing and troubling. Raitaro often leaned far over the castle walls so he could watch the earth's children.

One night Raiden turned to his son. "Pay careful attention to what humans are doing tonight."

They gazed over the northern rampart and saw great lords and their soldiers fighting. From the southern rampart, they saw priests and acolytes serving in a holy temple dimmed by incense. Statues of bronze and gold gleamed deep inside. From the eastern rampart, Raitaro saw a lady listening to a group of female musicians. Children played with a small cart of flowers as the lady relaxed.

"Look at those children," Raitaro said.

From the western rampart they saw a peasant toiling in a rice field. He straightened to knuckle his back before bending back to his planting. His wife worked beside him. She looked more tired than he did.

Raitaro turned to his father. "Don't they have children?"

Raiden shook his head. "Have you paid careful attention to the doings of men tonight?"

"I have, Father."

"Then choose, my son, which you will live with. Tonight I am sending you to live among them."

Raitaro stepped back. "Do I have to go?"

"You must."

Raitaro gazed over the walls. "I won't go to the soldiers. I am not a fighter."

Raiden smiled. "So you will go then to the lady?"

Raitaro shook his head. "I'm a man. And I won't shave my head to live with the priests."

"So you choose the peasant. You will have a hard life and little food, Raitaro."

"They don't have children. I can be their child for them so they will have someone to love."

Raiden touched his son's shoulder. "You've chosen wisely. You will descend as a Prince of Heaven should."

The peasant worked his field which sat at the foot of Hakusan Mountain. He sat on a stone at the edge of the field, despairing of his work. It felt useless. He didn't remember the last time rain had fallen. The rice seedlings withered and burned under the relentless sun. As he despaired, he drifted to sleep.

When he awoke, clouds blackened the sky. Although it was the early afternoon, it looked like night had fallen. The leaves in the nearby trees shuddered, and the birds fell silent.

The tired man smiled. "Raiden rides his black horse and beats the drum of thunder. We will finally have the rain we need."

Lightning flashed and thunder clashed. Rain fell in torrents across the man's fields until the man began to fear everything would be washed away.

"Great Raiden, you've sent enough rain," he said.

Lightning lit the raging sky, and a ball of living fire fell to the earth, making the man fall to the ground and cry out to Kannon for protection.

Silence followed.

The man rubbed his eyes and gazed about him. In front of him lay a baby. Rain ran in rivulets from his cheeks and hair. The man couldn't believe what he saw. He crept to the baby and scooped it into his arms. As he did, the sun chased the clouds from the sky, but a gentle rain continued to fall from the refreshed blue. The man knew without a doubt that the child was the son of Raiden. He returned to his cottage with the baby cooing at him.

"Wife, I've brought you something," he said.

"And what could that be?" she called from inside.

He entered his home and proffered the child. "Raitaro, the eldest son of Raiden."

Raitaro grew to be a strong and happy boy. His foster parents and his neighbors loved him. When he was ten years old, he worked the rice fields and was a wonderful weather forecaster. He brought good fortune to his family, and the family prospered.

When Raitaro turned eighteen, his family invited all the neighbors to the celebration. The feast had plenty of rice wine and food for everyone, and they enjoyed themselves. However, Raitaro remained sad and quiet.

"What's bothering you, Raitaro?" his foster mother asked. "You seem so sad."

"It's because I have to leave you."

"Why would you have to leave us?"

Tears slid down Raitaro's cheeks. "I have to."

His foster mother then understood he had to return to his heavenly home. She began to cry. "You've been the best thing in our lives. You've given us so many things. What have I given you, my son?"

"I've learned how to work, how to suffer, and how to love." Raitaro smiled through his tears. "I understand more than any of the gods."

A white cloud suddenly formed under his feet. With a final goodbye to his foster parents, he rose into the sky, where Raiden waited for him. Together, they took to the ramparts to look down on the earth.

The foster-mother looked into the sky as she continued to cry. Her husband walked up to her and took her hand. He had understood it wasn't their place to keep the Son of Thunder.

"My dear, we will see him again soon enough."

The Souls of the Children

Far below the roots of the mountains, further than the bottom of the sea, lay the river Sainokawara. Ages ago, its current took the souls of the blessed dead to the Land of the Eternal Peace. Wicked demons watched in anger as the good spirits flowed out of their reach. Every so often, the snow-pure soul of a child would wash ashore. The demons would come for the soul, but a lotus bloom also waited to carry the little one to safety. This spirit of a kindly old man, whose heart remained forever young, would thread its way through the demon horde with the child's soul cupped to his breast.

The demons decided to dam the River of Souls, forcing every soul to find their way across their land. The souls of children particularly struggled without guides. The souls wailed for their mothers and fathers. Their cries never ended, rising and falling in an unceasing rhythm.

The lost souls gathered stones from the bed of the river and made towers to pray for help:

Help from their mothers.

Help from their fathers.

Help from their brothers and sisters.

All the while, even the eldest children cried out for their family.

Each night, the demons taunted them and kicked down the prayer towers. "You parents can't hear you. No one hears your prayers." The demons wanted the little children to become like them.

So Jizo, the Never-Sleeping, took to guarding the souls of these children as he had when the river still flowed. His voice eased the fears of the lost children, and his love made the sea look like a shallow puddle. He gathered the babies too young to walk into his sleeves. He gathered the rest around him with this comforting words. He hugged them as a mother and a father would because he was mother and father to all the children lost in the Dry Bed of the River of Souls.

With the Never Sleeping Jizo to watch over them, the children no longer had to build prayer towers. During the night, they slept peacefully and safe from the taunts of the demons.

The Star Lovers

The beautiful Shokujo lived on the banks of the Silver River of Heaven. Despite being the daughter of the sun, she didn't care for games or worry about her appearance. She preferred diligence and work over play and socialness. She made so many garments for others that she was called the Weaving Princess.

The King of Light noticed her serious personality and how she avoided others. He tried various ways to get her to have more fun before finally settling on marrying her off. Without consulting her, he arranged her to marry Kingin. Kingin kept a herd of cows on the banks of the celestial stream and had always been a good neighbor. The King of Light surmised Kingin would make a good son-in-law, and the young man would also help his melancholy daughter.

As soon as Shokujo and Kingin met, they loved each other dearly. Shokujo's worry for her wedding day turned to joy. Kingin wanted nothing more than to see the lovely Shokujo smile. But soon after Shokujo married, her personality changed for the worse. She gave up her duties entirely. She spent her nights and days playing and laying around idle. The King of Light didn't like the change and surmised he had misjudged Kingin. He regretted trying to change his daughter and determined to separate the newlyweds. He ordered Kingin to move to the other side of the Milky Way. The King of Light called a large flock of magpies to make a bridge for the young man.

Kingin had little choice but to sadly say goodbye to his new wife and cross the bridge of magpies. As soon as he stepped off, the magpies flew away, filling all the heavens with their chatter. Shokujo remained on her side of the shore, crying and gazing at her husband. Finally, the pair had to leave each other. Kingin returned to his cattle. Shokujo returned to her weaving. The King of Light once again felt pleased with his daughter's industry.

But the king's pleasure soon turned to worry as he saw how despondent she had become. The clothes she made for the gods lacked the bright colors they had before. The gods were reluctant to wear such drab, gray, and sad clothes as she made. So her father approached her one day.

"I am pleased with how much you work, dear daughter. But the spring clothes should show more happiness."

"How can I be happy, Father?" She looked up with tears in her eyes. "You took away my husband."

The King of Light met her gaze and was struck by the depths of her sorrow. "I can't break my decree."

She hung her head. "I know."

The King of Light couldn't bear to see his daughter worse than she had been before her marriage. He turned his back to her. "On the seventh day of the seventh month, I will summon the magpies. They will make a bridge over the River of Heaven. I can only grant you both one night a year." The King of Light knew he bent the decree too far and hoped the other gods wouldn't find out.

When Shokujo heard this, her heart filled with hope and joy. So her weaving took on her feelings. She worked diligently until the seventh night of the seventh month.

When night finally came, and only the lamps of heaven shown, the lovers sneaked away and stood by the banks of the starry river. There, they gazed at each other and waited for the seventh night of the seventh month.

At last the night came, but Shokujo feared only one thing. Whenever she thought of it, her heart lurched.

Rain.

The River of Heaven always flowed near its brim. Just a single extra drop of rain would cause a flood that would spoil their meeting.

But the rain didn't come. The magpies returned and formed a bridge on that seventh night. Shokujo trembled with joy. Her heart fluttered more than the bridge of wings as she crossed. Kingin waited for her.

So the star lovers spent the night together until dawn forced them apart once more. Once a year, on the seventh month and on the seventh night, the lovers had a chance to meet. But on some years, rain flooded the River of Heaven and the magpies stayed away. So every year the people of the earth prayed and hoped for clear weather so the lovers could meet for their single night.

The Sun Goddess

Amaterasu, the sun goddess, sat in the Blue Plain of Heaven. Her light brought joy to the other celestial deities, and it allowed plants of all sorts to flourish, such as the cherry and the plum, rice and hemp. However, her brother Susanoo, the Moon God, grew jealous of his sister's glory. He resented how even her whisper was heard throughout the world. His voice wasn't so clear. His smile wasn't so radiant. Despite how much he lashed out at his sister, Amaterasu continually forgave him, but this only made him more angry.

One day, Amaterasu sat in her court, weaving. She and her celestial weavers gathered around their lotus fountain singing of the clouds and of the wind and of the sky. Suddenly a horse fell from the dome of the sky and landed at their feet. The horse, known as the Beloved of the Gods, had been flayed. Amaterasu knew at once who did the terrible act. She trembled with horror and anger, pricking her finger on her shuttle. Despondent at how she could have such a cruel brother, she shut herself into a cave.

Heaven and earth plunged into darkness, and with it came evil spirits. Their grim laughter replaced the joy and love that Amaterasu shined everywhere.

The other gods feared for their safety and the safety of creation, so they gathered at the dry river of the Milky Way. They discussed what they could do to ease Amaterasu's anger. They discussed for quite some time before they settled on a plan. But they wasted no time once they had made it.

Amenoko uprooted holy *sakaki* trees that grew on the Mountain of Heaven and planted them at the entrance of the cave. The gods hung the string of jewels Izanagi had given the sun goddess from the top of the trees. From the middle branches, they hung a dazzling mirror forged from the rarest of heaven's metals. Amaterasu's weavers made a robe of white and blue and hung it on the lowest branches of the *sakaki*. Finally, the gods built a palace that was surrounded with delicate plants and flowers planted by the God of Blossoms.

With everything ready, Amenoko called for Amaterasu to come out and see what they had made for her. He called loud and often, but the goddess refused to show herself. The gods prepared a festival and selected Uzume to take the lead. She put on a crown of the pine tree and adorned herself with a sash made of moss from Mount Kagu. She bound her long sleeves with a creeper vine and made a baton and flute out of bamboo. The other gods lit great bonfires and set up a large drum for her to dance upon. Crows began to crow and so Uzume began her dance. All the other gods joined in, dancing or playing as their skills allowed.

Uzume danced, stripping off her clothes until she danced naked. The gods laughed at her foolishness, shaking the entirety of creation.

Deep in her cave, Amaterasu felt the laughter and became curious of its cause. She peered from the mouth of the cave. "What is this? I thought heaven and earth went dark. The light is blinding, and Uzume and the other gods are partying."

"We are dancing because we have a goddess whose glory equals your own," Uzume said. "Take a look." She gestured.

Amaterasu gazed into the mirror and wondered at the beautiful goddess that stared back. She stepped from the cave to get a closer look. As soon as she cleared the cave, the strongest god sealed it behind her. Her presence revived the trees and the grass. It drove the evil spirits back to their dark corners. The gods celebrated Amaterasu's warmth, and the goddess of colors returned to tinting the flowers.

And so the gods averted the calamity and also invented the arts of metal-working, weaving, carpentry, jewel making, and the other useful skills of humans. They also were the first to put music to use, to dance, and to create comedy. They started the foolish games that children continue to play.

The White Serpent God

Harada Kurando taught the art of the sword and served the Lord of Tsugaru as his top samurai. Next to Harada in rank stood Hira Gundayu, who also taught the sword. But Gundayu felt jealous of Harada's skill.

One day, the Lord of Tsugaru summoned all his retainers and ordered them to show their skills. He wanted to encourage them to improve themselves. After the younger vassals dueled, the Lord ordered Harada and Gundayu to have a match. He offered a gold statue of the goddess Kannon to the winner.

Both men fought their best. Gundayu had never fought so well, but Harada remained his better. He won the match and received the reward. Gundayu boiled with jealousy and vowed revenge. Four of his friends left with him, and they planned to ambush Harada that evening as Harada returned home.

For three hours they waited on the road Harada often walked. At last, the moonlight revealed Harada staggering from too much drink. The men pounced at him.

"Fight me to the death," Gundayu said.

Harada tried to draw his sword, but he was slow from drinking. Gundayu didn't hesitate to strike. With a great slash he struck Harada to the ground and killed him. Gundayu and his friends hunted through Harada's clothes and retrieved the golden Kannon. With their treasure in hand, the five men left Tsugaru.

The next morning, Harada's body was found on the side of the road. When word reached Harada's son, Yonosuke, he vowed revenge. It was no secret that Gundayu was behind the murder. His disappearance offered enough evidence. So Yonosuke got permission from the Lord of Tsugaru to kill the man and set out that day to find him.

Five years passed as Yonosuke wandered. Five years without a clue to where Gundayu disappeared. Eventually, the Buddha allowed him to catch word that his enemy lived in Gifu and taught swordsmanship for the area's lord.

Yonosuke knew it would be hard to get at Gundayu. The man rarely left the safety of the castle. So Yonosuke decided to change his name to Ippai and apply for a position in Gundayu's house as a private attendant. As divine providence had it, Gundayu was looking for an attended as Ippai arrived in Gifu.

On the 24th of June, Gundayu's house celebrated the fifth anniversary of his service for the lord. He put his stolen golden statue of Kannon out and set out offerings. He then held a dinner where he and his friends drank until they fell asleep.

The next morning, they awoke to find the statue of Kannon missing.

A few days later Ippai became sick. Unable to afford the medicine he needed, he grew increasingly weaker. His fellow servants cared for him the best they could, but he didn't improve. He only asked that they keep a branch of the Nippon lily in a vase next to him so he could see it continually.

That autumn, Ippai passed away. After the funeral, the servants were cleaning out his room when they found a small white snake had curled around the lily and its vase. They tried to remove it, but the snake coiled tighter. They threw the vase into the nearby pond to remove the snake. To their astonishment, the snake continued to cling to the vase. The servants grew anxious. They used a net to retrieve the vase and snake and threw them into a stream. The snake only shifted enough to keep the lily from falling out of the vase.

By then, news of the strange snake had spread. A few samurai came to the stream and found the snake sitting exactly as described. One of them drew his sword and slashed at the snake. The snake released the vase and lily and escaped. The vase shattered and the statue of Kannon fell into the stream along with Ippai's stamped permit from the Lord of Tsugaru to kill a certain man. The name on the permit remained blank.

The samurai who broke the vase left to tell Gundayu of his find. Gundayu grew pale with fear as the samurai accounted the story. He then knew that Ippai was Yonosuke. However, he was a proper samurai and kept himself together. He rewarded the samurai for returning the statue of Kannon and threw a feast to celebrate. Curiously, the samurai fell sick and was unable to come.

That night, Gundayu jerked awake, gurgling and twisting enough to wake his wife. She lit the lantern and saw a white snake coiled around her husband's throat. His face turned purple and his eyes bulged. She cried out for help, but she was too late. By the time the samurai arrived, Gundayu's face had turned purple-black.

The next day messengers were sent to the Lord of Tsugaru to learn about the history of Ippai. When the Lord of Gifu heard of the Harada's murder from the messengers, he admired the samurai spirit Yonosuke had shown and sent the statue of Kannon to the Harada family. The Lord of Gifu also built a shrine to the white snake at the foot of Kodayama. The spirit is still known as Hakuja no Myojin, The White Serpent God.

Heroes and Warriors

How a Spider and Two Doves Saved Yoritomo

Following his defeat by Lord Oba, Yoritomo and six of his retainers fled into a large forest. Hampered by their heavy armor and the thick undergrowth, they made slow progress. Just as their exhaustion threatened to overwhelm them, they came upon an enormous cypress tree. The tree's interior had rotted, providing enough space to hide them all.

On the outskirts of the forest, Lord Oba stopped his men and summoned his cousin Kagetoki.

"Go into the forest and find Yoritomo while our men surround the forest. He won't escape us," Lord Oba said.

Kagetoki bowed, to his displeasure. Before the war, Yoritomo and Kagetoki had been friends. But he also couldn't disobey Lord Oba, so he went into the forest alone. After just a half hour of searching, he came upon the cypress and the exhausted Yoritomo. When Kagetoki saw the state of his friend, he couldn't carry out his duty. Instead, he returned to Lord Oba and suggested Yoritomo had managed to escape the forest.

Lord Oba exploded. "You're lying. No one could've escaped from the woods that quickly. I will give you another chance, cousin. Show us where you went." The threat on Kagetoki's life hung unspoken in the air. After all, Lord Oba also knew of Kagetoki's friendship with Yoritomo.

Lord Oba gathered twenty soldiers, and Kagetoki took the lead. Kagetoki led them away from the cypress, but the path he chose proved too treacherous and muddy for men in full armor.

Lord Oba lost his remaining patience. "Enough. We will stick to the road. They would not have taken this path. In full armor and exhausted as they are, they wouldn't have gotten even this far."

Unfortunately, Lord Oba chose the road that led straight to the cypress. Without hesitation, the lord moved toward the tree. Kagetoki thought about how he could save his friend, but no ideas came. When Lord Oba was about the enter the hollow of the great tree, Kagetoki noticed the spider's web.

"Wait." He gestured at the web. "There's no use wasting time by going in there. Can't you see the spider's web? No one could've gotten inside without breaking it."

Lord Oba stopped, knowing his cousin was right. But he still didn't trust Kagetoki's truthfulness. He thrust his bow inside the tree. Just as his bow was about to hit Yoritomo's armor, two beautiful doves few out of the hollow.

Lord Oba stepped back and laughed to hide his surprise. "You're right, cousin. We're wasting time. No one can be in there with a nest of wild doves in it and a web closing the entrance."

So it was that a spider and two doves saved Yoritomo's life. When he became Shogun a few years later, he built two shrines to show his gratitude to the God of War for watching over him that day.

How Tajima Shume was Tormented by A Devil He Created

Long ago, the ronin Tajima Shume decided to see the world he had read so much about. He traveled to Kyoto on the Tokaido road and came upon a priest heading the same way. They agreed to travel together and spent their days speaking about every topic imaginable. As the days wore on, they became friends and shared their private affairs.

"For some time," the priest said. "I've wanted to set up a bronze statue in honor of the Buddha. I know. It's not something a priest like me should worry about, but I managed to gather two hundred ounces of silver. Enough to fund a handsome statue."

Shume heard this and felt envy. Here he was, a forty-year-old wanderer without any chance to marry and have a family. *With that amount of money, I could live well for the rest of my life. I could find a wife and have children,* he thought. He began to wonder if he could arrange some way to steal his new friend's money.

"From the womb to the grave, man's life is made up of good and bad luck," he said.

The priest regarded him. "Luck is merely how we view things. Events are neutral."

They continued their traveling and discussions. All the while Shume plotted.

They came to the town of Kuana and had to board a ferry to continue their journey. They joined twenty other passengers. Halfway through the crossing, the priest felt sick from the motion of the boat and rushed toward the railing. Seeing his chance, Shume thrust out his leg, tripping the priest and plunging him into the sea.

"Help," Shume called. "My cousin!"

The ferriers and the passengers heard the splash and threw ropes to try to save the priest. But the wind gathered in the boat's sails and carried them past the drowning man. Before the handlers could turn the boat, the priest sank into the sea.

"He was my cousin," Shume said to the nearby passengers. He screwed up his face to look dismayed and grieved. "We were both going to Kyoto on business. Now he is dead, and I'm alone."

The passengers tried to comfort him, and Shume turned to the boatmen. "We need to report this to the authorities, but please let me take care of it when I reach Kyoto. I will tell my cousin's patron and send a letter back to our family. We don't have to stop or go back."

The passengers were pleased with this. Many had worried about being late if they had to turn back. So they agreed to continue.

When they reached the shore, Shume gathered the priest's luggage—including the hidden money—and continued to Kyoto. When he reached the capital, he changed his name to Tokubei and used the priest's money to become a merchant. Tokubei proved more skilled with money than with his sword. Soon he built a fortune and found a good wife with whom to start a family.

Three years passed.

On a fine summer's night, Tokubei walked the gardens of his house, trying to enjoy the cool air and moonlight. Despite his success and realizing his dreams, the events on the ferry troubled him. He had stolen from his friend and killed him.

"Here I am, fat and rich on his money." He shook his head.

Remorse ate at his heart, and his guilt gripped his mind. As he stood in his garden wondering if life could've played out differently, the faint outline of a man appeared next to the fir tree. The man appeared thin and worn. His eyes sunk into his skull, but Tokubei knew the man—no, the ghost of the man—before him.

Tokubei shivered as the ghost smiled, a scornful press of bloodless lips. He took a step back, but the ghost's withered arm thrust out and grabbed Tokubei by the back of his neck. The ghost priest glared at him, but Tokubei was still a warrior deep down. Those instincts rushed back from where they slept, and he cast the ghost's arm aside and struck at the ghost with the dirk he carried. As soon as the metal struck the ghost priest's stomach, the ghost disappeared. It reappeared further in the garden only to vanish again and reappear in yet another place. Tokubei backed into his home and shut the door.

The ghost appeared in the window. It stared at him with that mocking smile.

After that night, the ghost continued to appear. It followed him in the garden or stared at him from the windows or from the corner of the bedroom. Tokubei resisted the best he could, but he fell sick. He moaned and twisted.

His wife fretted for him and called a doctor, but nothing the doctor could do helped. The entire neighborhood gossiped about how Tokubei had gone mad. This gossip reached a certain wandering priest who rested a street over. He sent a friend to Tokubei's house to offer the priest's prayers. Tokubei's wife, driven half-wild herself from worry, readily agreed.

When the priest entered Tokubei's room, the stricken man cried out. "Forgive me. Forgive me. Forgive me. Don't torment me anymore. Forgive me." He shuddered under his blanket.

The priest made everyone leave the room and leaned to whisper in Tokubei's ear. "Three years ago, at the Kuana ferry you flung me into the water. Do you remember?"

Tokubei's lips quivered, but he could only tremble. He couldn't even nod.

"Luckily," the priest said. "I learned to swim and dive as a boy. I reached the shore and continued to wander through many provinces. I even managed to set up that Buddha statue I told you about. On my way back home, I stopped a street over from you and heard of your sickness. You have done a hateful deed, but I'm a priest. I've given up the things of this world. I can't very well hold a grudge and still be a priest."

Tokubei's friend chuckled. "I forgave you as soon as I got back on that shore. But you need to repent and change your evil ways. Nothing would make me happier, my friend. Now look at me and see that I'm not some ghost or goblin come to torment you."

As the priest spoke, Tokubei cried. His gaze focused on the priest's warm face. "I don't know what to say. In a fit of madness, I tried to kill you. I robbed you. Fortune befriended me, but I always remembered that day. I saw you as a ghost. I don't understand how you could've escaped the sea."

The priest's smile widened. "A guilty man shudders at the rustling of the wind. A murderer's conscience preys on his mind until he sees what isn't there. Poverty, too, drives a man to commit crimes he repents of after he is rich." He patted Tokubei's hand. "The heart of man is pure by nature, but circumstances corrupt it."

"Please forgive me," Tokubei said.

The priest waved him off and stood up. "I forgave you three years ago. Just change your ways and live a life of virtue." The priest left the room to tell the news of Tokubei's recovery to rest of the family.

As the priest made his leave, Tokubei came out with a heavy bag. "Half of this is the amount I stole from you three years ago. The other half is interest or a gift. Please take it."

"I can't."

Tokubei pressed it into the priest's hands. "I won't let you leave without it."

The priest shook his head and chuckled. "All right." He accepted the money and gave it to the poor and needy in the area.

After Tokubei's health recovered, he used his wealth to help those around him. He lived peacefully with his family and his neighbors and became known as a good, generous man.

The Quest of the Lost Sword

The rain buffeted Jurobei as he walked toward the house of Shusen Sakurai. He thought on the past seven years and the day he had let his anger get the better of him. Because of that anger, Sakurai had to dismiss him from his service, and by extension the service of Lord Tokushima. Jurobei hoped to earn his former master's forgiveness. His wife Yumi prayed each day for his honor. Yumi prayed she would have a chance to return to the daughter she was forced to leave in her mother's care.

Tonight, he would see their prayers answered. Jurobei gripped his umbrella and rushed onward.

Meanwhile, the enemy of Sakurai, Gunbei Onota, ordered two of his men to wait for Sakurai's return from the Shogun's palace and kill him on his way home. Gunbei had long vied against Sakurai for the attention of Lord Tokushima.

Jurobei arrived at Sakurai's house and right into the ambush. In the deluge, the men jumped out and drew their swords.

"Stop!" one of the men said.

"I recognize that voice," Jurobei said. "You serve Gunbei! Have you come to kill my lord?"

"We have."

Jurobei stood straighter. "Kill me instead."

"Your life isn't enough." The assassin stepped forward. Jurobei recognized the man. He was the same man he had tried to kill seven years ago. He was the same man who contributed to Jurobei's dismissal. "It's time I collect my revenge for what you did."

Jurobei fell to his knees in the mud and bowed. "I don't care if you kill me. Just accept my life instead of my lord's."

The man kicked Jurobei. Jurobei caught the leg and held it tight. "So you won't grant my request?"

"Of course not!"

Jurobei stood and confronted them. The two men attacked. He pulled his sword out and met both attacks head on. The storm's violence matched the men. Rain fell, and thunder shook the muddy ground. The two attackers soon realized that Jurobei was too skilled for both of them together. As they turned to run, Jurobei struck.

Lightning flashed.

The two would-be assassins lay still in the mud. Their blood blossomed around them.

Jurobei thanked the gods for his victory, pleased that he had rescued his master from death. As he did, the storm lessened, and he heard approaching footsteps. The moon cut through the storm clouds, revealing Sakurai.

"My lord!" Jurobei said. "Are you safe?"

"Who's there?" Sakurai asked. "Jurobei? Why are you here?" Then Sakurai saw the two dead men. "What happened here?"

"Gunbei sent these men to kill you. They attacked me when I found them."

Sakurai gazed at the men and frowned. "I knew these men. I wanted to convince them to join me and confess the crimes of their master."

Jurobei realized his mistake and sank to the ground. "I didn't think about that. I only thought of saving your life no matter what. I've made a terrible mistake by killing them. Please forgive my stupidity." He drew his short sword and moved to plunge it into his stomach.

Sakurai seized his wrist. "If you kill yourself here, you will be no better than a dog. You need to do something worthy of a samurai. Then I will call you my retainer again." He shook his head. "You are too rash, Jurobei. You need to think before you act."

"Will you really forgive me?"

"I will if you prove yourself," Sakurai said. "The Lord of Tokushima has entrusted my house with his most valuable talisman, the Kunitsugu sword. Last year, someone stole it from me. I suspect Gunbei plans to attack Lord Tokushima. I can't spare any time to find the sword. I need you to find it before March. Otherwise, my house will be disgraced."

"I will not fail you." Jurobei turned to examine the two bodies for money for his journey.

"Don't take anything from them. You don't want to be accused of being a thief before you even begin your search," Sakurai said.

Jurobei bowed. "I am a stupid man for not thinking of that either. I will do better. I will find the sword."

***

Weeks passed, and Jurobei failed to discover any leads. Because he lacked funds, he was forced to become a thief as he searched. His journey eventually took him to Osaka where he rented a small house on the outskirts of town. Yumi and Jurobei stayed there together, creating a small resemblance to normal life. There he met a man named Izaemon, a fellow retainer of Lord Tokushima. Izaemon had followed the half-sister, Takao, of Lord Tokushima to the town. She had sold herself into a brothel to help her mother's family. Izaemon intended to pay off her family's debt, but the money lender refused to budge, knowing the girl would earn more than her debt.

This troubled Jurobei, and he tried to figure out some way to help Izaemon. While he went out to town to figure out what to do, Yumi received a letter from one of Jurobei's followers. The police were on to him! The letter urged them to run.

"Don't they understand that my husband does all he does in the service of his lord?" she asked the letter. "At this rate, he will only be remembered as a thief."

Feeling helpless, she knelt before their little shrine that was dedicated to Kannon, the Goddess of Mercy. She prayed that her husband would be able to live long enough to return the sword. As she prayed, a child's voice sang a pilgrim's song dedicated to Kannon. Yumi stood and looked outside. A little girl of about nine years of age stood on the porch. She wore a pilgrim's pack. She looked at Yumi and sang another traveler's song. When the girl finished, Yumi gave her a few coins.

"Thank you!" the girl said. Yumi could tell that the girl wasn't a common pilgrim despite the stains on her clothing. Her eyes held Yumi's gaze, and the woman could see the girl's intelligence. The girl swayed from exhaustion, and she was too thin.

The girl reminded Yumi of her daughter she had had to leave behind seven years ago.

"Tell me." Yumi said. "Where do you come from?"

"Tokushima of Awa."

"I was born there too! Are you taking a pilgrimage with your parents?"

The little girl shook her head. Her voice held a tinge of sadness. "I haven't seen my parents for seven years. I left my home in Awa to try to find them."

Yumi froze. "What are their names?"

"My grandmother said my father's name is Jurobei and my mother is called Yumi."

Yumi stared. Her daughter had been two years old when she had been exiled. But the girl she studied resembled her. Then she saw the mole on the girl's forehead. There was no doubt that the girl was her Tsuru. She wanted to hug the girl and say her journey was over. But she didn't want her daughter to also be caught by the police when they arrived.

She swallowed her heart. "You certainly have come a long way. Your parents would weep for joy for your faithfulness. I'm sure they had a good reason for leaving you. Please don't resent them for that."

"I can't resent them. Grandmother told me they didn't have a choice. They did what they could to protect me. But It makes me feel sad that I may never see my mother again." Tsuru wiped her eyes on her dirty sleeve as she began to cry.

Yumi reached for the girl. She barely managed to stop herself from pulling the crying girl into a hug. "It's not likely that you will find them." Yumi felt her heart tear. "You don't even know their faces. You should give up and return to your grandmother."

The girl shook her head. "I will spend all of my life looking for them if I have to. If only someone could tell me where they are!"

Yumi couldn't take it anymore. She hugged her daughter.

"I can't tell you how much I feel for you," Yumi whispered. "Someday you will be reunited with your parents. But if you keep going as you are, you will ruin your health. Return to your grandmother. I'm sure your parents will find you if you return home and wait."

"You're right," Tsuru said. "I feel as if you were my mother. Please let me stay with you. Grandmother...she died. No one has been as kind as you've been since I left home. I will do whatever you say if you let me stay."

Yumi's voice broke. "Your grandmother is...."She gathered herself. "I feel as if you were my daughter, but I can't keep you with me. For your sake, you can't stay with me right now." Yumi went into another room and returned with all the money she had. "Take this, and use it to return home."

Tsuru refused the money. "I can't take that much money." Her shoulders slumped. "I will leave, then."

Yumi brushed away the dust from the girl's legs. "I don't want to let you go. You remind me so much...." She hugged the girl again.

When Tsuru finally left for home, Yumi watched the road long after the girl disappeared. Her memories of leaving Tsuru burst from where she had stuffed them. As the memories and emotions engulfed her, she couldn't help but despair until she couldn't endure any more.

"If we part now, we will never see each other again!" She ran down the road to find Tsuru.

Jurobei returned home some time after Yumi went to find their daughter. He failed to find the money Izaemon needed. As he walked, he came upon a group of beggars surrounding a little girl dressed as a pilgrim. The beggars tugged at her pack, but she defended herself with spirit that caught Jurobei's attention. Jurobei rushed over and drove the beggars away.

"Are you all right?" he asked.

The little girl--Tsuru--nodded.

"Why don't you come home with me tonight? The beggars will return if you don't." Without waiting for her to respond, he snatched her hand and led her home.

When he reached home, he called out. "I've returned, Yumi!"

Entering the empty house, he looked around. "Where has she gone this late in the day?" He lit the lanterns, thinking about how far he and his wife had fallen. He felt hopeless. He couldn't even help Izaemon.

He regarded the little girl. "Those beggars were really after your money. How much do you have with you?"

"Several kind people have given me a fair bit."

"Can I see?"

She held out a few coins.

"Is this all you have?" Jurobei asked.

She shook her head. "I have several gold coins too."

"Oh, so you have several gold coins." Jurobei suddenly saw a means to help Izaemon. "Let me take care of them so the beggars won't attack you."

"I can't!" Tsuru said. "My grandmother told me to never show them. She made me promise to her as she lay dying." Tsuru backed toward the door, clutching her bag.

Jurobei snatched her by the collar, and Tsuru yelled for help. Jurobei laid his hand over her mouth to muffle her screams. The girl struggled against him like a bird caught in a net. She soon stopped struggling.

"You don't have to be afraid," Jurobei said. He tried explaining his situation. "I will even take you to Kannon's temple and go every day to see the city if you lend me everything you have."

Thinking she had calmed because of his explanation, he lowered her to the floor. She collapsed.

"What is—" Jurobei bent over her. She didn't move.

He fetched water and sprinkled it over her face, but she didn't respond. Just then, he heard his wife outside. He dragged the little girl's body to one side of the room and threw a quilt over her.

"Help me look for her!" Yumi said as she burst through the door. "Our daughter Tsuru found us! I wanted to tell her I was her mother, but I just couldn't. I sent her on her way, but now....help me find her."

"How was she dressed?" Jurobei asked.

As his wife described her down to her pilgrim's pack, Jurobei went cold. "She is already here." His voice rasped.

"Where is she?" Yumi gazed about the room.

Jurobei turned away. "U-under the quilt."

His wife lifted the quilt and wailed. "Tsuru, wake up. Tsuru! S-she's dead. Breath for me, Tsuru. What happened, Jurobei?"

Jurobei turned and met his wife's tearful gaze. "I put my hand over her mouth to keep her from screaming." The event rushed out of him. "I didn't mean to kill her." His voice gave out.

Yumi rocked Tsuru.

"Words are useless," Jurobei clenched his fists. "If only I hadn't known about her money. Money is a curse!" He bent over the girl and pulled out her wallet. A few low-value coins rested inside. "I killed her for this?" A letter rested under the coins. Jurobei pulled it out and read it. "This is my mother's handwriting." He began to read:

"I've learned that Onota Gunbei had the lost Kunitsugu sword. I tried to get evidence but failed. Tsuru and I were going to come to you, but I became sick. As I write this, I'm dying. As soon as you read this, come home and restore the sword to its rightful owner. I will await the return of your honor beneath the flowers and grass."

Jurobei, unable to read any further, offered the letter to his wife.

"My greatest worry is for little Tsuru. She will be alone on a journey to find you. If by the mercy of the gods she reaches you safely, bring her up tenderly and carefully. She is clever. She writes and plays the koto. She can sew silken clothes. I have instructed her in everything I know, and I'm proud of her." Yumi took a shuddering breath. "Let her show you what she can do. Praise her. She also brings a special medicine. If she ever gets sick, give it to her. I beg you to take care of my precious grandchild."

Yumi crumpled the letter and bent over Tsuru and cried.

A clamor arose outside. Jurobei peeked out the window to see armed police marching toward them.

"It has to be Butaroku!" Jurobei said. "We have to take Tsuru and hide. Hurry!"

Jurobei lifted Tsuru's body and they fled to the back room. Moments later, their front door crashed inward. A stream of police stormed inside. Finding no one, they smashed open the cupboards and walls and the ceiling. Jurobei snatched his sword from the backroom and attacked them. The officers weren't expecting such skilled and fierce resistance. They fought back for just a moment--Jurobei easily cut down all who tried—and then they fled.

"Now's our chance!" Jurobei shouted at Yumi.

"Have you forgotten our child?" Yumi came out of the back room, cradling Tsuru.

"She is safe from the suffering of this world." Jurobei saw that his wife wouldn't accept that as an answer. "We can't take her with us." He sighed. "Fine. We will bury her here before we leave."

They gathered the pieces of the shattered cabinets and heaped them upon the little girl. Jurobei lit a torch and started the pyre. As the flames rose, Jurobei and Yumi stood side by side, praying and watching their child's soul rise with the embers into the night.

***

Before Jurobei returned home, he and Izaemon decided to free Takao by force. They waited until the police had given up their search for Jurobei and struck one night. Butaroku's guards fled as soon as they saw the two samurai. The samurai stormed into the brothel, amid the screams of the women and the shouts of the customers. Jurobei and Izaemon split up in the chaos. Izaemon was to find his sister while Jurobei killed anyone who came after them.

Izaemon kicked down the door to Takao's cell. "Takao! We're leaving."

She shook her head. "I can't. I'm honor-bound to repay my debt."

Jurobei stepped into the room. Red painted his sword. "You don't have to worry about that. Butaroku is dead."

Takao's eyes widened. "Then I no longer have a debt to him." She smiled.

"I will take you to Sakurai," Izaemon said. "My lord will give you refuge in case any of Butaroku's associates come for you."

The sounds of the police drifted through the window.

"We had best get away while we can," Jurobei said.

***

In the town of Tokushima, the cherry blossoms bloomed. March had arrived, and Onoto Gunbei relished the upcoming demise of his rival Sakurai. Tomorrow, Sakurai had to take the Kunitsugu to the palace and lay it before his lord. Gunbei couldn't wait to see his rival's disgrace.

Gunbei reached the temple when one of his retainers stopped and knelt before him. "My lord, Jurobei is in a nearby teahouse. What do you want us to do?"

Gunbei smiled. It was a fortuitous day. "We will hide, and when he leaves, we will ambush him."

When Jurobei left the teahouse, he was occupied with the problem of retrieving the sword and trying to figure out what plan Sakurai had working. Although he was distracted, when Gunbei's men pounced, his muscle memory kicked in and saved him. As he fought, he saw Gunbei just behind the men. Jurobei snatched one of the retainers as a shield and charged toward the man. The battle moved through the streets until the news of it reached Sakurai.

Sakurai and his men ran to join the fight and saw Jurobei.

"How dare you attack your superior!" Sakurai shouted at Jurobei. He met Jurobei's gaze with a slight nod. "Surrender."

Sakurai turned to Gunbei. "I will take him. Put your sword away."

Jurobei understood what his lord planned and gave himself up. Sakurai handed him to Gunbei, who took Jurobei to his mansion.

Gunbei had Jurobei tied to a tree in the mansion's courtyard. "You know, Jurobei, I still have a grudge to pay. Why did you kill two of my men three months ago?"

"They tried to murder my master."

Gunbei smirked. "Aren't you the man who stole the Kunitsugu? You must have connived with your master to do that. Confess your sin!"

"You can say whatever you want about me, but you lie about my master."

Gunbei quivered and gestured at his men. His men used their sheathed swords to tighten the ropes around Jurobei until they cut into his flesh. Just as they did this, Takao passed by the garden. Gunbei had sent his retainer Dotetsuke to steal her from Sakurai in order to make her his mistress. Unknown to Gunbei, Sakurai wanted this to happen, and Dotetsuke had served as Sakurai's spy for several years. He had told her about the sword and wanted her to look for it while she repelled Gunbei's advances.

"Brother!" Takao rushed to Jurobei. She confronted Gunbei. "Why have you done this to my brother? Let him go."

"Are you really brother and sister?" Gunbei hesitated. "If you do what I say, I will let him go. If you disobey, I will have him tortured with fire and water."

Takao wept into her sleeve. "How can you call yourself a samurai? Doesn't your heart know mercy?"

"All you have to do is accept my love, and he will go free."

"I can't decide that for myself. My elder brother has to make that decision," Takao said.

"Fine." He gestured for Jurobei to be released. "Talk with him and make your decision. I will leave you both for a little while. But if you reject my proposals, I will kill you both."

Unfortunately for Gunbei, he didn't realize Takao was higher in birth. His threats were little more than air. Jurobei and Takao made a show of sitting down to discuss the proposal. Jurobei kept a respectful distance from Takao.

"We have to take the sword tonight," she whispered. "We don't have time to think of our rank differences. But Gunbei always carries it with him. I'm sure you also saw it."

"You should listen to Gunbei's wooing to make him drop is guard," Jurobei whispered. "Once he does, you should be able to make certain the sword he carries is the Kunitsugu. Then give me a sign and I will attack."

Takao frowned. "I despise the man, but I will do what I have to. As for the signal, I will go to the stream and throw cherry blossoms into it. I will then say 'The cherry is the first among flowers: the warrior first among men.'"

Jurobei nodded, and they separated just as Gunbei returned. Takao's dejection at what she had to do attracted Gunbei even more.

"What did you decide?" Gunbei took her hand. He didn't notice her shudder. "It can only be yes."

She nodded.

"You are as beautiful as the moon. I will make you my wife." He pulled her toward the room off of the courtyard. He paused and looked at Jurobei. "You may go. I am a man of my word, after all."

Jurobei bowed his head and left to await Takao's signal.

As Gunbei and Takao left, the man spoke of his dreams for them. She listened with half a mind until finally the chance arrived for her to reach for the short sword.

"What are you doing?" Gunbei jerked her around.

"I will use this sword to cut off my hair and become a nun. No other man will touch me for the rest of my life." She attempted to pull his sword out.

He shoved her away. "So you scorn me? You will soon understand what my hatred means." He clapped to call a servant. "Dotetsuke!"

The man appeared and bowed.

"Tie that woman to the cherry tree."

Dotetsuke dragged Takao back into the garden and tied her to the same tree Jurobei had been bound to. Gunbei retired to his room to let his hate and love war within him. But a priest approached him as he walked the veranda.

"According to your wishes, I've prayed for seven days for the Lord of Tokushima to die of an illness. Where is my reward?" the priest, Kazoin, asked.

"Don't speak so loudly. I will pay you later. This is not the time."

"Don't forget to give me the money soon." The priest fingered his rosary a moment and left.

Meanwhile, Takao was left alone to struggle against her ropes. "Jurobei must be waiting for my answer. I need to get free to find the sword for Sakurai." She twisted against the tree. "I can't let Sakurai be ruined tomorrow." As she struggled, the branches above her shook, knocking several blossoms into the stream.

"Buddha has surely come to help me," she murmured. "Jurobei will see the flowers in the water."

In his hiding place, Jurobei watched the stream impatiently for their signal. Just when he was about to see what the problem was, a cluster of white blossoms floated past. Elated to finally act, he crept along the shadows of the garden toward the room where he expected to find Takao.

When he saw her tied to the cherry tree, he gasped.

"Finally, you've come," she said.

"What happened?" He moved to free her. She explained everything as he worked.

"Follow my lead." Jurobei abandoned the shadows and strode across the garden, followed by Takao. He shoved the screens aside to come face to face with Gunbei.

"How dare you release that woman," Gunbei said.

"I brought her to comply with your wishes," Jurobei said.

"So you brought her to her senses, did you?"

"I don't know which I am, an elder brother or a go-between, but I am at your service if you have more work that needs to be done."

Gunbei laughed. "Well, we are members of the same family now. Take this as my congratulation." He drew his sword and slashed at Jurobei.

Jurobei had seen Gunbei's fingers twitch on his sword. He managed to snatch a nearby bucket and parried the man's attacks.

"This is too much attention from a relative," Jurobei said. "This ceremony isn't really necessary."

Gunbei swung wide, and Jurobei dodged. While Gunbei focused on Jurobei, Takao slipped behind him and stole Gunbei's second sword—the Kunitsugu.

"I've got it!" she said.

Gunbei whirled. "I will kill you both." He raised his sword to kill Takao, and Jurobei grabbed him from behind.

Just then, Dotetsuke and Sakurai entered the room.

"There's no way for you to get out of this," Sakurai said. "Confess and pray for mercy."

Gunbei flung off Jurobei and charged at Sakurai. Sakurai parried Gunbei's blade and hurled him into the garden. Jurobei lunged onto Gunbei and pinned down his sword arm.

"Dotetsuke, help Jurobei," Sakurai said.

"Even you are on Sakurai's side?" Gunbei shouted. He went limp. "I give up. I stole the sword in an attempt to ruin you. Take the sword and go."

"The sword is just the smallest crime you've committed," Sakurai loomed over Gunbei. "You've betrayed our Lord Tokushima. You conspired to have him killed."

"That's a lie," Gunbei said. "I've always hated you, but I never wanted anything to happen to our lord. What proof do you have?"

Sakurai clapped his hands. Izaemon entered with Kazoin, the wicked priest.

"My witnesses." Sakurai smiled.

Gunbei roared and tried to get up, but Dotetsuke and Jurobei held him to the dirt.

"Lord Tokushima will judge you, Gunbei. Bind him."

After Jurobei and Dotetsuke did as ordered, Sakurai regarded them. "Jurobei, I promote you to my service. You are a true and faithful samurai. With your help, we have defeated our enemy."

Takao brought the sword to Jurobei. "We found it just in time. Dawn breaks on the third of March."

Jurobei knelt in front of Sakurai and presented the sword. "At last, the stolen treasure of Lord Tokushima has been restored to your care, my Lord Sakurai."

Makino Heinei and the Giant

The Lord of Kishu ordered a hunting party on Toma Island. Sixty ships landed with some eight hundred men. Soon after landing, they scattered to hunt boar and deer. That afternoon, a storm came upon them, forcing the men to return to the ships.

They set sail for the mainland just as the storm tore trees from the ground. The sea threw the ships like they were floating leaves.

Makino Heinei, whose nickname was Wild Boar, noticed the lack of progress, so he pushed a small boat off the ship and jumped into it. He took the oars.

"You all seem too afraid to make any headway," he laughed. "Follow me. I'm not afraid of the waves, and neither should any of you be." He shot out into the wild sea and managed to get three hundred yards ahead of the fleet before the gale became too violent for even him. The waves threatened to engulf him. All he could do was hold on with closed eyes, awaiting his fate.

A powerful squall struck his boat, lifting it as if it were truly a leaf, and blew him far from the fleet. Heinei clung tight to the disintegrating boat. For eight hours, the storm tried to break his grip until, at last, the sky gave up. Stars shown from the breaks in the clouds. Heinei, though tired, felt encouraged by the sight.

Crack!

The boat slammed into rocks, throwing Heinei to a damp, sandy shore.

Heinei recovered himself and thanked the gods for saving him. He prayed for the welfare of his lord and friends before he snatched a little sleep.

He awoke stiff and hungry. He didn't know where he was, but he found plenty of shellfish for his hunger. While he ate, he studied the island, deciding to climb a hill that rose in the middle. From there, he might get a better idea of where he was. He didn't recognize the trees, and the undergrowth appeared thick. However, he soon saw a path leading from the shore and toward the hill. He wondered who or what had made the path, but he also wasn't one to disregard good fortune.

Along the path, he came across footprints that could only belong to a giant.

"A warrior of Kishu must fear nothing," Heinei told himself. He found a strong stick.

He walked for a time before coming upon a cave near the top of the hill. An enormous man, eight feet in height, emerged from the cave. The man's skin was nearly black, and he had a wild, angry expression. His long, matted hair floated around him. And his mouth stretched from ear to ear. Two rows of teeth gleamed. The man wore the skin of a wild cat tied around his waist and nothing else.

"Who are you? Why have you come here?" the man-creature asked.

"I'm Makino Heinei." He explained what had befallen him.

"And where are those places? I am the only one who lives here. My name is Tomaru, and my father was Shoun Yamaguchi. I've heard of your lord, but I want nothing to do with him. I just want to be alone. You can take my old boat. Sail northwest, and you will reach Kishu. But it is a long, very long, way."

Tomaru walked toward the beach, taking a basket with him. Heinei followed.

"The boat is nearly rotten, but with some luck it will last until you get home. I can give you dried fish and fruit. And I must also give you a gift for your lord. It is a special type of seaweed I've discovered. No matter how badly you are cut with a sword, it will stop the bleeding and heal it at once." Tomaru handed him the basket. "You can speak of your adventure, but don't mention my name. I like to be alone. Goodbye."

Heinei could only do as Tomaru bid. He rowed off. The currents favored him, and he found himself off the coast of Kishu in only three days. Everyone was astonished that he was still alive. The Lord of Kishu relished Heinei's story and had the seaweed planted in the sea. He renamed the coast District of the Famous Seaweed.

Some months later, the lord asked Heinei to return to the island for more seaweed, but the giant was nowhere to be found.

The Dragon King and the Lord Bag of Rice

Hidesato Fujiwara couldn't stand being idle. So he took his two swords along with his great bow and arrows and set off to find adventure. He hadn't traveled far when he came to the bridge of *Seta no Karashi*, which spanned Lake Biwa. He started across the bridge when the lake's mist cleared to reveal a serpent dragon. Its body was as wide as a large pine tree. Its claws rested on one side of the bridge, and its tail lay against the other. The monster appeared to be asleep. Each time it exhaled, fire and smoke escaped its nostrils.

At first, Hidesato felt alarmed at the sight. He considered going back, but it would take far too long to walk around the lake. Hidesato was a brave man, so he gripped his sword and walked forward. He stepped over the dragon's body.

He stepped into its coils.

He only relaxed when both of his feet were clear of the creature. Without looking back, he continued on his way.

"Sir," a voice came from behind.

Hidesato turned and was surprised to see the dragon had disappeared. In its place stood a strange man. The man knelt and bowed his head to the wood of the bridge. His red hair fell over his shoulders, and he wore a crown in the shape of a dragon's head. He wore sea-green clothing patterned with shells. Hidesato knew that this wasn't a normal man. Had the dragon transformed into this man?

"Did you just call me?" Hidesato asked.

"I did. I have a request. Do you think you can grant it?" The man stood.

"If it is in my power." Hidesato removed his hand from his sword. "But first, tell me who you are."

"I am the Dragon King of the Lake. I live in the waters just under this bridge."

"And what do you want of me?"

"I need you to kill the centipede that lives on the mountain." The Dragon King pointed to the high peak on the opposite shore of the lake. "I have many children, and each night the monster steals one of them. I've tried to save them, but I can do nothing. If this continues, I will lose all of my children and become a victim myself. So I decided to turn to a human for help, but everyone ran away from me. You are the first man to see me and not be afraid. Will you please help me?"

Hidesato felt sorry for the Dragon King. He also felt excited. This was just the sort of adventure he was seeking. "I will kill it for you. Tell me exactly where it lives."

"It's on Mikami mountain. I don't know exactly where, but it comes down to my palace each night. It would be best to wait for it."

The Dragon King showed Hidesato to his palace under the bridge. The water parted in a bubble around him. He had no trouble breathing, nor did his clothes get wet as he descended. He had never seen anything as beautiful as the King's palace under the lake. The palace's white marble shimmered in the water-filtered sunlight. The palace thrust up from the lake and formed a tower in the center of the lake. Goldfish, red carp, and silvery trout acted as servants and prepared a feast for Hidesato while he waited.

The dishes were made of crystallized lotus leaves and flowers, and the chopsticks were made of ebony. After the King and Hidesato sat, sliding doors opened, and ten lovely goldfish dancers entered. Behind them came ten red carp musicians, playing koto and shamisen and drums. So they passed the time until midnight.

The Dragon King was offering Hidesato a fresh cup of wine when the palace shook. Hidesato didn't need to look at the King to know the centipede had come. He rushed to the balcony and saw two great balls of fire falling from Mikami mountain.

Beside him, the Dragon King trembled. "The centipede is coming. Those two balls of fire are his eyes. Now is the time to kill it."

Hidesato looked closer and saw a long body behind the two fireballs. The centipede wound around the mountain, and its one hundred legs glowed like distant lanterns.

"Don't be afraid," he told the Dragon King. "I will kill the monster. Just bring me my bow and arrows."

When the Dragon King returned, Hidesato saw he had only three arrows. He notched the first, aimed, and fired.

The arrow hit the centipede in the middle of its head, but it glanced off and fell to the ground.

Undaunted, Hidesato notched the second arrow and fired. It hit the middle of the centipede and glanced off again. When the Dragon King saw this, he trembled with fear. "Your weapons won't work against it."

Hidesato took out his last arrow. It was his last chance to kill the creature.

The monster wound seven times around the mountain and prepared to enter the lake. The fireball eyes threw reflections into the lake's still waters.

Hidesato suddenly remembered that human saliva was supposed deadly to centipedes. But this wasn't an ordinary centipede. Hidesato had no other idea, so he put the end of the arrow into his mouth, notched it, aimed, and fired.

He again hit the centipede in the middle of its head, but instead of glancing off as before, it pierced all the way to the creature's brain. Its great body shuddered and collapsed. The fiery light of its eyes went out as if a giant had blown out a candle. The one-hundred lantern feet went black.

In the sudden darkness, thunder and lightning flashed, and the wind kicked up. The palace shook. The Dragon King, his children, and his retainers crouched in fear. Hidesato stood unmoved on the balcony, enduring the rumbling of the palace and the buffeting of the wind. The chaos lasted only moments. They stopped as soon as the sun's rays shot over the horizon. When the sunlight pushed back the darkness, the centipede was gone from the mountain.

"Dragon King, come and see for yourself. The centipede is gone."

All the inhabitants of the palace rushed to the balcony. Hidesato pointed to the body of the great centipede floating in the water. The lake shimmered red with its blood.

The family cheered and bowed to Hidesato, calling him the bravest warrior in all Japan.

The Dragon King ordered another feast, grander than the previous night's feast. They brought the warrior the best wine he had ever tasted. They brought all sorts of fish and other food for him to enjoy.

While he enjoyed the feast, Hidesato began to feel the itch to move on. The Dragon King tried to convince him to stay a few more days, but Hidesato insisted on leaving.

The Dragon King made Hidesato take a few small tokens of his gratitude. As the warrior waited to leave, a train of fish came and transformed into men. Each wore the dragon crown and the Dragon King's colors. Each carried a gift.

The first carried a large bronze bell.

The second carried a bag of rice.

The third carried a roll of silk.

The fourth carried a cooking pot.

The last carried a small bell.

"I can't accept all of these gifts," Hidesato said.

The Dragon King walked with Hidesato to the bridge. "My servants will carry them for you. It's the least I can do to thank you."

Hidesato couldn't refuse without insulting the grateful Dragon King, so he led the procession to his home.

When Hidesato's servants, who were worried about his unannounced disappearance, saw him, they called all his house outside. Everyone wondered about where he had gathered the procession and gifts and banners.

As soon as the Dragon King's servants put down the gifts, they vanished.

Hidesato accounted all that happened to his amazed family. When he was finished, he took a closer look at the gifts.

The bronze bell proved ordinary, and Hidesato had no use for it. So he gave it to the nearby temple where it was hung to chime the hours of the day for the neighborhood.

The bag of rice proved magical. No matter how much rice was taken from it, the amount inside never lessened. The supply proved inexhaustible, and Hidesato had tried to exhaust it too!

The roll of silk never grew shorter no matter how much was cut from it.

The cooking pot proved wonderful too. No matter what Hidesato put into it, it cooked the food perfectly without needing fire or heat of any sort.

Hidesato and his family grew wealthy because he didn't have to spend money on rice, silk, or cooking fires. He soon became known to everyone as My Lord Bag of Rice.

Raiko and the Demons of Mount Oye

During the reign of Emperor Ichijo, stories of a demon circulated around Kyoto. The stories spoke of a demon who lived on Mount Oye. The demon could transform into many different forms, everything from a human to a spider. People whispered that the demon kidnapped people and ate them. The Imperial Court considered these whispers to be just the foolishness of the commoners.

Until the daughter of the court official Kimitaka disappeared.

A guard happened to see a demon that looked like the Demon King Shutendoji leaving the official's home.

The Emperor called his court to decide what to do about this. His ministers suggested sending the samurai Raiko to handle it.

Raiko accepted the mission and chose five companions to help him kill the Demon King. They disguised themselves as mountain priests, concealing their weapons and armor in knapsacks such priests carried. Before going on the journey, they divided into pairs and prayed at the temple of Hachiman, the God of War, the shrine of Kannon, the Goddess of Mercy, and at the temple of Gongen.

They reached the province of Tamba without any problems and came to the daunting Mount Oye. Sheer cliffs and dark forests obstructed their path no matter which way they went. They also encountered ravines so deep that they appeared bottomless.

Just as the group began to feel disheartened, three old people suddenly appeared on the trail ahead of them. The group were wary of the elders at first. After all, they were in demon country.

"Be at ease," one of the old men said. "We are the gods you prayed to before you left."

The old woman presented Raiko with a jar of rice wine. "This is *Shimben Kidoku Shu*. It is a magical rice wine that is poison to demons. You need to get Shutendoji to drink it. It will paralyze him, leaving him vulnerable to you."

Raiko took the rice wine. As soon as he did, a light shone around the three elders and they vanished.

Raiko and his companions smiled at each other. How could they fail when the gods themselves helped them? They continued on their way with a faster pace. They came upon a stream and saw a beautiful woman washing bloody clothes. She cried and wiped at her eyes with the long sleeve of her kimono.

Raiko approached her cautiously. "Who are you?"

"I am the daughter of a lord, and I was kidnapped by the Demon King. He makes us work for him until he decides to eat us."

"You don't have to worry any more. I am Raiko, sent by the Emperor to end the Demon King."

The woman's face brightened at the news. "I will help you get in." She led the men toward a gate of black iron, guarded by a pair of hideous demons.

"They are poor mountain priests who need shelter for the night," she said.

The demons shared a knowing smile and let them inside.

After passing through several long corridors, Raiko and his companions entered a huge hall. At one end sat the Demon King. He dominated the space. His bright red skin shined in the lantern light, and his long white hair billowed about him.

Raiko bowed. "Sorry to intrude, grand king. We are poor mountain priests looking for food and a place to stay for the night."

The Demon King gestured. "You have good timing. We are just going to enjoy a feast." He clapped his great red hands together. Immediately, a group of young women came running with trays covered with food and drink. Raiko recognized several of the women from Kyoto.

Raiko and his men sat to eat. Raiko waited until the Demon King settled in before taking out the jar of magic rice wine. "Please, great king, try this rice wine as my thanks for this feast."

The monster let Raiko pour the wine and downed it in a single gulp. "Mmm. That is good." He held out his cup for a second pour.

All the other demons wanted a taste of what pleased the Demon King. Raiko left the jar with them and motioned to his companions to dance with him.

The power of the rice wine quickly worked. In a few moments, the Demon King and his fellow demons fell asleep.

"Now's our chance," Raiko said. He and his companions quickly donned their armor.

While they did this, the three gods appeared. "We have tied the hands and feet of the demons so you will have nothing to fear if they would wake up. While your men cut off the Demon King's limbs, cut off his head. Then kill the rest of them." The gods disappeared again.

Raiko and his men drew their swords and approached the Demon King. With a mighty slice, Raiko's blade cut off the demon's head. Instead of rolling to the ground, the head shot into the air. Smoke and fire exploded from its nostrils, scorching Raiko. He ignored the pain and slashed out, cutting the head in half. Both halves hit the floor and didn't move again. His men descended on the sleeping demons. The great hall soon ran red.

Raiko's men took the remains of the Demon King's head and skewered it on their spears. They led the freed women back home to Kyoto.

The Adventures of Hachiro Tametomo

Hachiro Tametomo was the son of General Tameyoshi Minamoto and the younger brother of Yoshitomo. As a child, Tametomo showed a natural skill in archery; his left arm was four inches longer than his right. As he grew into adulthood, he could fire an arrow further than anyone. But he also had a wild, disrespectful personality. He obeyed no one and fought with everyone.

One day, when Tametomo was thirteen, Shinsei Fujiwara gave a lecture about the history of Japan.

"No one was better at archery than Kiyomori Taira and Yorimasa Minamoto," he said.

Tametomo laughed. "You're right about Yorimasa, but you are a fool if you think Kiyomori is that good. He's a coward."

Fujiwara glared at the boy but continued his lecture. Afterward, he sent for Tametomo and demanded an apology for his insolence.

"You're wasting your time, old man." Tametomo said. "You should apologize to me for trying to teach me something false."

At this, Fujiwara told the boy's father. The father had had enough of his son's antics and how they dishonored the family. He exiled Tametomo to Kyushu.

Despite being only thirteen, this suited Tametomo rather well. He felt like a hound freed from his leash. As soon as he landed in Kyushu, he stirred up trouble. He gathered several fighters like himself, and they proceeded to fight anyone willing or unwilling to fight them. The young Tametomo won twenty battles in a row, capturing villages and land in the process. By the time he was eighteen, he and his growing band of outlaws had taken over all of Kyushu. His exploits earned him the name Chinsei. *Chin* means "to put down," and *sei* means "the West."

Some time later, the Emperor heard about Tametomo's conquest and sent a regiment to take him prisoner. Tametomo and his band chipped at the more numerous army until the general returned to Kyoto to confess his failure. Determined to rein in the upstart, the Emperor ordered Tameyoshi imprisoned.

When Tametomo heard of what had happened to his father, he felt responsible. Despite everything, he still felt a sense of duty toward his father. The injustice of the imprisonment drove Tametomo to give up Kyushu and go to Kyoto.

As soon as he arrived, he sent a document signed and sealed with his blood to the Imperial Court. The document asked the court to pardon him and to release his father. Tametomo fully expected to be punished for leading what amounted to an uprising. So he waited calmly for the sword to slice.

The Emperor and the court were surprised and moved by Tametomo's conduct. After all, not just anyone would give up all of his land to receive punishment and free his father.

"Even a man who behaved like a demon can feel for his father," Emperor Go-Shirakawa said.

So the court merely rebuked him for his lawlessness and freed his father. Tametomo was fortunate with the timing. Within that same week, a civil war erupted between the Emperor and his elder brother Sutoku. Their father had surmised this would happen and left a letter just before his death. The letter contained an order for all the principle generals to support Go-Shirakawa.

The country split. The Taira clan and Tametomo's eldest brother Yoshitomo sided with Go-Shirakawa as the letter ordered. Others like Yorinaga and Shinsei Fujiwara sided with Sutoku. Tametomo's father— and by extension Tametomo himself—also sided with Sutoku. Despite the pardon, they couldn't forget the injustice Emperor Go-Shirakawa had done them.

By this time, Tametomo was twenty years old and stood nearly seven feet tall. Tametomo told Sutoku about his banishment to Kyushu and the lessons he had learned fighting on the island. The young man's bearing and confidence convinced Sutoku that Tametomo would offer sound advice as a general.

Sutoku called Yorinaga, Tametomo, and the other generals together for a war conference. "How should we defeat my brother?" Sutoku asked.

"We always fought at night," Tametomo said. "That's why we never lost. If you would attack the Palace of Go-Shirakawa by night and set fires at three sides of it, you could funnel the men right into yours. You would be certain to win."

Yorinaga heard Tametomo's plan and shook his head. "Only cowards attack at night. We don't need dishonorable tactics like that to win."

The other older generals nodded their agreement.

Tametomo gazed at the men. He shook with anger and wanted to strike them down, but he settled with turning on his heel and leaving the council at that moment.

He returned to his men and told them what had happened. "Yorinaga knows nothing of fighting. His thoughts are worthless. What battles has he won? How many has he lost? I've never lost a battle." Tametomo's anger faded as he spoke. Finally, he sighed. "Sutoku will be defeated because of this."

On the same night, Kiyomori and the armies of Go-Shirakawa attacked. Tametomo and his men were guarding the southern gate when Kiyomori's army appeared in the fading sunlight. Tametomo took his great bow and killed a samurai named Roku Ito. The thick arrow— more like a spear, so great was Tametomo's strength in archery— pierced the man's chest and continued on to nick the forearm of his younger brother Go Ito.

Go Ito took the arrow to Kiyomori to caution him.

"This looks more like the arrow of a demon than of a man," Kiyomori said. He gazed up the castle walls. "We should find a weaker point. One without archers like these."

So Kiyomori and his men left off their attack of the southern gate.

Yoshitomo heard of what had happened to make Kiyomori withdraw and knew only his brother could fire such arrows. "Tametomo may be a wild fool and a great archer, but even he won't kill his elder brother," he said. So he led his men to the southern gate.

He rode close to the gate and called out. "Is that you, Tametomo? Do you guard this gate? It's Yoshitomo. Will you sin and fight against your elder brother? Just open the gate and let me in, and you will be forgiven."

Tametomo's laugh echoed into the night. "If it's wrong for me to fight you, brother, are you not also an undutiful son to fight against our father?"

Yoshitomo kept silent.

Tametomo saw as his brother made a perfect target and was tempted to shoot at him for fun. He wouldn't hurt him of course. His conscience wouldn't allow it. So he took aim at Yoshitomo's helmet and loosed. The arrow hit the star that stood on top of the helmet and pierced it through.

Yoshitomo sat on his horse, frozen with astonishment at his brother's skill. He soon regained himself and ordered the attack.

Although Tametomo and his men fought bravely, they were outnumbered. They gave up ground grudgingly until they fought inside the palace itself. The enemy armies set fires, and Sutoku's forces descended to confusion.

Sutoku and Yorinaga attempted to escape, but both were taken prisoner. When Tametomo heard the news, he and his father and his brothers fled to Omi province. The journey proved too difficult for Tameyoshi, who was an old man.

He sat on a rock, spent and unable to move. "I can't go any further. With Sutoku taken, you only have one hope of getting out of this. Go to Kyoto and surrender yourself to the Taira." The brothers and the men listened and agreed to do what the old man wanted.

All except Tametomo.

After his family left him behind, Tametomo decided to right his only defeat. He traveled east, but the wound he had sustained in the fighting slowed him down. He stopped at a hot spring to rest. There his enemies found him and took him prisoner.

By the time Tametomo reached Kyoto, his father and brothers had been put to death. His captors said he would have the same fate, but the leaders of the court considered execution a waste of Tametomo's rare archery talents and the symbol they could make of him. They decided to spare him.

Before they released him, they cut the tendons of both his arms and sent him to the island of Oshima. They bound him and sent fifty men to guard him on his journey. Twenty more carried his heavy palanquin.

Despite everything, Tametomo was undaunted. As the twenty men carried him, he would use his great strength to rock the palanquin, and all twenty of the men would fall. This alarmed his fifty guards. They began to treat him as if he were a caged tiger and tried not to anger him throughout the journey.

At last they arrived in Idzu province and the shore closest to Oshima island. They hired a boat and left Tametomo on the island. Tametomo found himself treated by the locals as a brave, though vanquished, foe instead of a prisoner. The islanders took good care of him, and he lived quietly and comfortably.

One day Tametomo stood on the beach, gazing at the sea and thinking of his past adventures. He wondered if he was destined to continue his quiet life on the island when a sea gull came flying toward him. "There has to be an island where that sea gull came from," he said. He found a boat and set sail.

As he had expected, he came to an island after sailing all day. But instead of finding people on the shore, he found a village of creatures. The creatures had dark red faces with bright red hair. The locks hung over their foreheads and eyes. They stood on the sand when Tametomo landed, gesturing wildly among themselves. After he set foot on the sand, they stopped gesturing and formed up what looked to be battle lines and started toward him.

Tametomo didn't have anything to defend himself with, but a pine tree grew not far away. He sprinted to it and uprooted it as if it were a weed. He held it over his head. "Come and fight me, demons, if you want. I am Chinsei Hachiro Tametomo, the Archer. If you will become my servants and look up to me as your master in everything, I will spare you. If not..." He hefted the tree.

When the demons saw Tametomo's strength and courage, they trembled and looked at each other. After a brief discussion, what could only be the demon chief stepped forward. He stopped in front of Tametomo and prostrated in the sand. All the demons behind him followed suit. Tametomo spent a few days on the island to make sure the demons knew who ruled them before returning to Oshima.

The islanders rejoiced at how Tametomo had subdued the demons their ancestors had feared.

Not too long after, Tametomo walked along the shores of Oshima when he saw a little old man riding on top of the waves. Tametomo had never seen anything like it. The old man stood perhaps a foot and a half high and sat on a round straw mat.

Tametomo walked to the edge of the shore just as the waves deposited the old man in their shallows. "Who are you?" Tametomo asked.

"I am Small Pox."

"Why do you come to this island?"

"Oh, I've been here before. I came to sight see and to seize the inhabitant to—"

Tametomo straightened and his eyes narrowed. "You are the Spirit of Pestilence the islanders spoke about. I am Chinsei Hachiro Tametomo. Get out of my sight and away from my island. Or I will make you rue the day you ever came here."

As Tametomo spoke, Small Pox shrank until he became the size of a pea. "I'm sorry I intruded on your island," Small Pox said as he shrank. "I didn't know you owned the island." The waves caught the round straw mat and pulled it back out to sea.

After these exploits, the islanders had come to regard Tametomo as a king. They bowed as he passed and gave him every honor. Eventually, word of this reached Kyoto. The Ministers of the State decided that this couldn't continue. Tametomo's reputation could threaten the Emperor. So they sent a decree to General Shigemitsu in Idzu to kill Tametomo.

Tametomo stood on the beach watching the sea, as was his habit, when he saw fifty war ships coming toward the island. He heard the war drums and the singing of the soldiers. His honed gaze could see their weapons and armor.

He smiled. "Now I have a chance to try my archery." While he had long ago healed, he hadn't tested his abilities other than at practice. He took his bow and aimed at the foremost ship. The arrow slammed into the prow, upsetting the ship and sending the soldiers into the sea.

Until that moment, Tametomo feared his arms had lost their archery strength. He also noticed that his arms had grown longer, and he could pull his bow wider than before. He gazed at his hands with wonder as joy filled him.

He shook himself and gazed at the oncoming ships. He knew the government had sent them to take him. But he also didn't want the kind islanders to be punished because of him. They didn't need to know war. Oh, he could sink all the ships. He knew that now. But fifty more would follow. And fifty more after that.

The islanders didn't need that.

Tametomo had lived the past ten years well. He had lived when he should've died many times in the past. He didn't feel shame or regret. He felt only concern for the kind folk who had named him king.

So Tametomo turned away from the beach and went home. There he killed himself to spare the islanders and his honor. He was thirty-two.

***

Some people say there is a different ending to Tametomo's story. After he sank the fifty ships, he fled Oshima and reached Sanuki. There he visited the tomb of the previous Emperor and prayed before deciding to kill himself. Just as he was about to stab his stomach, a vision fell upon him. In it, the Emperor, Yorinaga, his father, and all the loyalists who died during the civil war appeared to him in the clouds. They told him to remain alive. His work wasn't finished.

As Tametomo gazed at the vision, sunlight washed over him. His knife fell from his hands.

Tametomo gave up on suicide and left for Kyushu. On Mount Kihara, he collected his former followers and set off toward Kyoto. Using the tactics that had won him Kyushu when he was young, he struck a blow against the House of Taira.

As they escaped toward Kyushu, a storm blew their ship into the rocks. Everyone except Tametomo died. He washed up on Ryukyu. There he awoke to find himself in the middle of an uprising. The loyalists had found him and restored him to health, so he sided with them. He helped them free their lord from the rebels and restore peace to the province. The grateful lord adopted Tametomo into his house and offered his daughter to be Tametomo's wife.

So Tametomo lived happily. He and his wife had a son named Shuntenno, and they lived well into old age. Shuntenno would eventually become the Lord of Ryukyu.

One day, while the elderly Tametomo walked the palace, his attendants saw a cloud coming toward him. As soon as the cloud touched him, he rose into the air. Frozen with amazement, they could only watch as the cloud carried Tametomo higher until he disappeared into the high clouds of heaven.

The Adventures of Jiraiya and Tsunade

Ogata lived as the lord of Kyushu. He had only one son who went by his nickname Jiraiya. As so often happened in the past, a civil war erupted. During the war, the enemy took the castle and killed Ogata. Jiraiya, though only a boy, would've died as well if it wasn't for a faithful retainer who spirited the boy north to Echigo. Jiraiya grew up in that lawless province, under the protection of the retainer.

When Jiraiya had just become a man, thieves attacked them while they traveled. The retainer died defending his charge. And Jiraiya killed the rest of the thieves using the sword skills the retainer had drilled into him. Jiraiya found himself alone and homeless, but he was determined to restore his family's honor. He used his swordsmanship to gather together a band of outlaws to steal from the rich. Jiraiya often came up with disguises which allowed him to sneak into the houses of rich men, learning the positions of the gates and the guards and where they slept. Success came easily.

Jiraiya heard about an old man who lived in Shinano. He and his band had already robbed most of the men of wealth in the area, so the fables of the old man's wealth came as welcome news. So Jiraiya disguised himself as a pilgrim and went up into the mountains where the old man lived. A snow storm blew out of the heights without warning, catching Jiraiya out in the open.

He struggled onward. The wind tried to throw him off the mountain path. The snow threatened to bury him and freeze him to death. Just as he grew desperate, a cottage came into view. Without hesitating, he burst inside.

A beautiful woman calmly regarded him from her seat by the fire. "A traveler in this weather?" She seemed not the least surprised at his entrance. She stood and gestured at the hearth. "Come and warm yourself. The stew is almost ready, and I made enough for two."

Jiraiya's teeth chattered as he shuffled closer to the fire. The woman did all she could to warm and feed him before she excused herself to her bedroom. By midnight, Jiraiya felt like himself. Despite the kindness of the woman, he wondered what sort of riches he could steal from her.

He unsheathed his sword and padded into her room. The woman looked up from her book as he lunged inside. Jiraiya swung his sword as if he was going to strike her neck. He didn't intend to actually cut her, merely scare her with his skill. But she shimmered like light dancing on water as his steel closed the distance.

An ancient man caught the blade with two fingers and snapped the steel as if it were a stick. Jiraiya froze with shock.

"So much for my disguise," the old man said. "My name is Senso Dojin. I've made these mountains my home for about three hundred years. Although I look like an old man, I'm actually a huge frog. Much too large for this house, so please excuse me for not showing you my true form." The old man smiled and tossed the steel shards to the floor.

Jiraiya recovered from his shock and readied himself to fight if need be.

"Oh please. If I wanted to kill you, you'd be dead already. I have other plans for you. How about I teach you magic and how to do what I just showed you?"

Jiraiya knew if he could change his shape like the old man had, he would be untouchable. He put his pride aside and bowed his head to the floor. "Thank you for your mercy. Please teach me."

The old man wasted no time in the lessons. For the next several weeks, Jiraiya spend every moment learning the skills of frogs. He learned how to call a storm and control the wind. He learned how to summon frogs and how they could enlarge to the size of elephants.

At the end of the instruction, the old man regarded Jiraiya as he prepared to leave. "I've taught you everything you could learn. But I demand payment in return."

Jiraiya stopped packing his supplies. "Payment?"

"From now on you will not steal or hurt the poor. Instead, you will take from those who get their money dishonestly. You will use that money to help those in need."

Jiraiya nodded. "I will, Teacher."

"One more thing. You can control frogs, but frogs must beware the poison of snakes. There is an influential thief called Orochimaru that preys on the weak and the strong alike. Beware his poison. One day you will have to face him." The old man turned into a huge frog and hopped into the forest.

Jiraiya frowned at the news, but he wasn't the type to worry for long. He would deal with Orochimaru when fate determined it. He shouldered his supplies and descended the mountain to be about his work.

Jiraiya quickly gained a reputation among the poor that were swindled by money-lenders and greedy merchants. The money-lenders and merchants grew to fear him. Besides stealing from the wicked rich and giving to the poor, Jiraiya also helped the honest and generous rich with their problems.

One day a merchant named Fukutaro was wrongly sentenced to death. When Jiraiya heard of this—people in the area knew Fukutaro for being a generous and fair man—he went to the magistrate.

"What is your case?" the magistrate didn't look up from his paperwork as Jiraiya entered.

"You sentenced Fukutaro wrongly. I was the one who stole," Jiraiya said.

The magistrate looked up then. He shrugged. "Then you will take his place, and he will go free." He motioned for the guards to take Jiraiya. They freed Fukutaro and hanged Jiraiya from a large oak tree.

But that night, Jiraiya's "dead" body turned into a bullfrog which hopped toward the mountains of Shinano.

While Jiraiya did all of this, the beautiful Tsunade lived in Shinano. She was obedient to her parents and kind to her friends. Each day, she went into the mountains to cut brushwood for her family. One day while she went about her task, she came upon an ancient man with a long, sweeping beard.

"Don't be afraid," he said. "I've lived in this mountain for hundreds of years. But I'm not an old man in truth. I'm a snail. We were fated to meet so I could teach you magic. You will be able to walk on the sea or cross any river, no matter how swift it is."

"I don't believe you," she said.

"Watch then." He transformed into a tiny snail and then back into the old man.

Tsunade believed him then and began her lessons the same day. Each day when she went to the mountain to cut brushwood, she met with the old man and learned all she could.

"You've learned all I can teach," the old man said after several weeks. "I want you to use your powers to destroy wicked thieves. Help those who defend the poor. But you are also sentenced to two tasks by fate."

"Two tasks?"

"You have the magic of the snail, but it isn't enough to defeat a villain that preys on the weak and strong alike. You've heard of Orochimaru, yes? No one can destroy him except you and Jiraiya. Jiraiya has frog magic, but alone neither of you are strong enough. You need to find Jiraiya and marry him. Only together can you defeat Orochimaru before he takes over the country."

Tsunade bowed. "If I can stop the death Orochimaru is causing, I will be glad."

The old man smiled and shriveled into a snail and crawled away.

Instead of returning home, Tsunade set off to find Jiraiya. She had heard of his adventures and the good he was doing. She felt pleased to be able to do the same.

She found him shortly after he crossed into Shinano. Jiraiya paused at the sight of such a beautiful woman coming toward him. As she neared, he sensed her power.

"My name is Tsunade. I was sent to marry you so together we can defeat Orochimaru."

Her bluntness surprised and charmed him. Jiraiya couldn't well say no to someone who shared his fate. He asked her many questions. They both found each other agreeable, so Jiraiya sent one of his frog messengers—transformed into a human—to her parents to ask for her hand. The messenger returned a few days later with the parents' blessing. The couple found a shrine and a priest to seal the marriage, and they set off to find Orochimaru.

Jiraiya discovered that he didn't need to summon a frog to cross rivers as he had in the past. As long as they held hands, the couple could walk across any water as if it were made of unmoving rock.

They quickly learned war had again broken out between the Tsukikage and the Inukage. Tsunade and Jiraiya both knew Orochimaru served the Inukage. So when the Tsukikage asked for their help, they didn't hesitate to join.

Now Orochimaru had thousands of followers. They ravaged the country side, stealing and murdering everyone. Orochimaru, whose father was a man and whose mother was a snake, used his serpent magic to kill all warriors who dared to challenge him. The dead outnumbered the living. Burned villages and fields covered the country.

Jiraiya and Tsunade led their own army against Orochimaru's. They fought each other to stalemates again and again. After one such fight, Jiraiya and Tsunade took refuge in a monastery with a few trusted vassals to rest. They discovered a princess named Tagoto hiding in the monastery. She had fled from Orochimaru, who wanted to marry her. Somehow Orochimaru heard that his enemies and the target of his love were together. He changed into a snake and went to finish off his enemies himself. He came upon the room where Jiraiya and Tsunade slept and crawled into the ceiling over them. He opened his mouth, bared his fangs, and poured his venom over them. The fumes knocked out Jiraiya's warriors and the monks that lived in the monastery. Orochimaru, supposing Jiraiya and Tsunade were dead, turned into a man and seized Tagoto and fled.

When the retainers awoke, they found Jiraiya and Tsunade near death. No one knew what to do. As they looked at their pale master and mistress, they grew desperate and called the abbot to see if he knew of a cure.

The abbot examined them and shook his head. "There's nothing in Japan that can sure them. But there is a cure in India. If we could get that, they would recover."

The retainers felt sad at the news. India was just too far away.

Just then, Rikimatsu, one of the youngest of those who served Jiraiya spoke up. "How long will they live?"

"They will be dead in thirty hours," the abbot said.

"I will go and get the medicine."

The other retainers scoffed at him. "There's no way you can go to India and return in thirty hours!"

"I can and will." Rikimatsu chanted in the language of the Tengu, and Tengu wings sprouted out of his back. With a few more words, a white cloud zipped out of the air and toward him. He climbed upon it and sped off.

He returned a day and a night later, just as Jiraiya and Tsunade took a turn for the worst. Rikimatsu gave them both the elixir. Within just a few moments both husband and wife sat up. Sweat streamed from them, and they swayed with weakness. But they lived.

After they recovered, they learned Orochimaru planned on ending the war with a single great battle. Jiraiya and Tsunade gathered their forces and met him in the field. The battle raged, hot and bloody. Orochimaru used all of his serpent magic against them, but this time the combined powers of Jiraiya and Tsunade proved the strongest. Jiraiya fought with his sword. Tsunade fought with her naginata. Together, they managed to finally kill the snake and rescue Tagoto.

For his service, Jiraiya was named the lord of Idzu. Jiraiya and Tsunade were glad to settle into a peaceful life. Jiraiya spent the rest of his days reading the books of the sages, writing poetry, and playing with his children and grandchildren.

The Adventures of Kintaro

Long ago, a brave soldier named Kintoki lived in Kyoto, where he fell in love with a beautiful woman and married her. Not long after the wedding, his jealous friends ruined his reputation with the Imperial Court. Kintoki was dismissed. The betrayal troubled him until he died of despair, leaving his pregnant young wife alone. She fled the capital and her husband's enemies until she reached the Ashigara Mountains. She entered a forest so lonely that only woodcutters visited. There she gave birth to a son. She named him Kintaro, the Golden Boy.

As Kintaro grew, his strength amazed even his mother. By the time he was eight, he could cut down trees as quickly as the woodcutters. His mother gave him a large axe and he would go out to help the woodcutters. They called him the Wonder Child and called his mother the Old Nurse of the Mountain. Besides cutting wood, Kintaro enjoyed smashing the boulders that scattered across the forest.

Other than the woodcutters, Kintaro grew up alone in the wilds of the mountains. He learned how to speak the languages of the animals that lived there and made friends of all of them. His best friends were the bear, the deer, the monkey, and the hare.

The bear often brought her cubs for Kintaro to play with, and when she came to take them home, Kintaro would ride on her back to her cave. He didn't fear the great antlers of the deer nor any other creature of the forest.

One day, Kintaro went up into the mountains with his friends. After walking for some time up hills and down vales, they came upon a wide grassy plain bursting with wild flowers. They agreed that this was the perfect place to play.

"What do you say to a wrestling match?" Kintaro asked.

"That's a great idea," the bear said. "I am the strongest so I will make a platform." She picked a spot in the meadow and dug up the earth to make a raised wrestling platform.

"I'll watch you wrestle," Kintaro said. "And I will give a prize to whoever wins each round."

At that, the deer, the monkey, and the hare helped the bear build the platform. They finished in short order.

"Monkey. Hare. You're up first," Kintaro said. "Deer, you can be the judge."

The monkey and the hare climbed onto the platform and took their places. The deer stood between them. He gestured at the monkey with a dip of his antlers. "Red Back, are you ready?" He turned to the hare. "Long Ears, are you ready?"

The little wrestlers faced each other while the deer raised a leaf in his mouth. When he dropped the leaf, the monkey and the hare rushed each other. While they grappled, the deer encouraged them and gave warning as they pushed each other near the edge of the platform. At last, the hare managed to shove the tired monkey close to the edge one more time. With a last push, the monkey flew from the platform and sprawled on his back. The deer signaled the match was over.

Kintaro opened his lunch box and took out a rice dumpling. He gave it to the hare. "And here is your prize. You've earned it."

The monkey stood up. "That wasn't a fair match. My foot slipped, and I fell. Let me try again."

Kintaro nodded and the monkey and hare set up to wrestle again. This time, the cunning monkey was determined to get the best of the hare no matter what. At the deer's signal, they crashed into each other. As they grappled, the monkey grabbed one of the hare's long ears and gave it a hard tug. The pain stopped the hare, and the monkey caught one of the hare's legs and tripped the hare in the middle of the platform. Kintaro gave the monkey his rice dumpling, and the monkey forgot about his sore back.

The deer asked the hare for a round. The hare nodded. As they took their sides, the bear took her place as the judge. The deer with his long antlers and the hare with his long ears made for a strange match. But the little hare quickly had the deer on one knee. The bear used her leaf to declare the match for the hare.

And so the animals spent their afternoon wrestling back and forth as Kintaro watched and handed out prizes.

Finally, Kintaro got up. "That's enough for today. Let's come back here tomorrow to wrestle. It's time to go home." So Kintaro led his animal friends as they walked toward home.

They came upon a river without any way to cross. The animals didn't like the speed of the water. They wondered just how they could cross and get home before evening fell.

"Just a moment." Kintaro said. "I will make a bridge for us."

He walked among the trees that grew along the river banks until he found a suitably large one. He wrapped his arms around the trunk and pulled at it. With each pull, the tree shuddered, and its grasp on the earth loosed. At the third tug, it came free and fell across the river with a great crash.

Kintaro grinned at his friends. "What do you think of my bridge?" He crossed the bridge first to prove how safe it was. The four animals followed, wondering at how strong the boy was.

A man watched all of this from a rock overlooking the river. He rubbed his eyes to make sure he wasn't dreaming, that he truly saw what he had just seen. "That is no ordinary child. I have to find out whose son he is." He followed behind Kintaro and the animals.

Once back home in their part of the forest, each of the animals went their ways. Kintaro continued to his cottage in the heart of the pines.

"Mother, I'm home."

"You're late, Kimbo. I worried something had happened to you. Where did you go?" His mother smiled her relief despite trying to sound stern.

"My friends and I found the perfect place to wrestle." Kintaro accounted the events of the day.

"Now tell me. Who is the strongest?" she asked.

"Oh, Mother. You know I am. Next is the bear."

"And after the bear?"

Kintaro thought a moment. "That's a hard one. The deer, the monkey, and the hare about equal in strength."

A voice outside startled them. "Next time you go wrestling take this old man. I want to wrestle too."

Kintaro's mother cracked open the door. "Who are you?"

The man who had followed Kintaro opened the door the rest of the way and crowded in. "It doesn't matter who I am. Let's see who has the strongest arm. Me or your boy."

Kintaro stepped forward. "We can try if you are sure, but don't be angry when you lose."

Kintaro and the man set themselves on the table and clasped their right hands together. His mother gave them the signal, and the two bent their arms against each other. The old man proved an even match for the boy. They struggled for some time before the old man declared the game a draw.

"You are indeed a strong boy," the man said. "Few men can match the strength of my right arm. I saw you on the banks of the river. When you are full grown you will be the strongest man in Japan. It is a pity you are hidden in these mountains."

He turned to Kintaro's mother. "Have you considered taking him to the capital? He would make a superb samurai."

"Thank you for your interest in my boy," she said. "But as you can see, he is wild and uneducated. I hid him here because of his strength. I often wish I could see him wearing the twin swords of a samurai, but we don't have any connections."

"I will sponsor him. You see, I am Sadamitsu, one of the great generals of Japan. I am the vassal of Lord Raiko Minamoto. He ordered me to travel and find boys who could become soldiers in his army. I disguised myself as a woodcutter, as you see, to make it easier to travel. If you want your boy to become a samurai, I will personally take him to Lord Raiko."

As the general spoke, Kintaro's mother was filled with joy. She dreamed her son could follow in his father's footsteps. She bowed her head. "I will trust my son to you if what you say is true."

Kintaro laughed and shouted. "I get to be a samurai. I get to be a samurai."

Kintaro and the general left the next morning. Although Kintaro's mother felt sad to see him leave, she hid her grief. She knew it was for the best. Kintaro promised that he would build her a home and take care of her as soon as he became a samurai.

As Kintaro and the general traveled through the forest, all his animal friends came to see him off as word got around. They wished him their best. General Sadamitsu felt pleased he had found such a strong boy that even the forest animals respected him.

When they arrived at the capital, the general took Kintaro straight to Lord Raiko and accounted of their meeting. The story delighted Lord Raiko, and he commanded Kintaro be made a vassal.

Lord Raiko had a famous unit called The Four Braves. He selected only the bravest and strongest warriors for this unit. When Kintaro came of age, Lord Raiko selected him as the commander. Soon after this promotion, news arrived of a man-eating monster terrorizing a village. Lord Raiko ordered Kintaro to put an end to the creature.

Kintaro traveled to the monster's den and made short work of the creature. He cut off its head and brought it back to Lord Raiko. Whenever a similar story reached the Lord's ears, he would send Kintaro off to deal with it. Over time, Kintaro rose to be the greatest hero of his country. He grew in honor and wealth, but he remembered the promise he made to his mother. He built her a comfortable house in Kyoto where she lived happily with him until the end of her days.

The Adventures of Momotaro

Long, long ago, an old woman and an old man lived together. Despite their many married years, they never had children of their own. Each day, the old man went out to cut grass for the farmers in the area while his wife took care of the house and tended their small rice field.

One day, the old man went into the hills as usual, and the old woman took some clothes to the river to wash. The country was bright with the green of late spring. The grass on the banks of the river waved. The willows dipped their soft tassels into the brisk water. A warm breeze touched each of the older folk as they went about their separate tasks.

The old woman found a nice spot on the river bank and sat her basket of laundry down. She set to work rubbing the clothes on stones and washing the previous day's dirt away. She watched the tiny fish in the clear water as she worked.

She heard a soft bumping noise and looked up to see a peach as large as both her hands meandering down the stream. In her long life, she had never seen a peach so large. A couple larger rocks snagged it just a little way from her.

"I bet that peach is delicious," she said. "It would make quite a treat for my old man."

The peach bobbed just out of her reach, so she looked for a stick long enough to knock it toward her. Nothing nearby was quite long enough when she remembered an old song her grandmother had once taught her.

Distant water is bitter,
The nearby water is sweet.
Pass by the distant water,
And come into the sweet!

As she sang, the peach rocked in its cradle of rocks. It rolled back into the stream and bobbed toward her. So she repeated the little song, and the peach gently rolled across the direction of the stream to stop in front of her. She laughed and clapped her hands and scooped the peach up. She couldn't wait to see the look on her old man's face, but she had to be sure to make it home first. She put all the clothes back into her bamboo basket, nestling the peach on top, and set off for home.

The old man returned at dusk with a huge bundle of grass on his back. He almost disappeared into it. He walked slowly, leaning on his scythe like it was a walking stick. He had barely dropped his load outside and walked in when she rushed toward him with the peach behind her back. The peach felt heavier than before.

"I've been waiting for you for so long today!"

"Did something happen? What is the matter?" the old man asked. He bent and washed his feet.

"No, no. Nothing has happened. I just found a nice present for you." She proffered the peach with both her hands. "Just look at it! Have you ever seen such a large peach?"

The old man's bushy eyebrows climbed. "Where did you buy it? I've never seen one that large."

"I didn't buy it. I found it in the river while I washed our clothes."

The old man smiled. "Let's eat it for dinner. I'm starved."

They went into the kitchen, and the old man brought out their knife. He placed the peach on their cutting board and was just about to slice it when the peach split in two. A clear voice came out of the peach.

"Wait a minute!"

A beautiful boy stepped out of the peach.

The suddenness stole the strength from the old couple's legs, and they fell to the floorboards.

"Don't be afraid," the little boy said. He smelled of peach. "I am not a demon or a fairy. Heaven has decided to have compassion on you. You've always wanted a child, and the gods have heard. They sent me to be your son!"

The old couple couldn't believe what they heard. They had often cried together and prayed together for children of their own. The old man gathered the boy, who had somehow grown to be the size of a normal child as he spoke, and hugged the boy close. The old wife joined him.

They named the boy Momotaro because he had come out of a peach.

The years passed happily, and Momotaro grew to be a good, kind boy. When he turned fifteen, he stood taller and had more strength than any other boy of his age. He was also wise and courageous.

The day after his fifteenth birthday, Momotaro approached his father. "Father, your goodness has been higher than the mountain grasses you cut every day. Mother's kindness is deeper than the river she washes our clothes in. I can't thank you enough."

The old man felt awkward. "There's no need to thank us. You are our son, after all. When you are older, you will repay our kindness by taking care of us when we are too feeble to do so."

"I have to ask you a favor, Father."

"You aren't like the other boys, so I will let you do whatever you wish. I trust you."

"Then you will let me leave?"

The old man blinked. "Leave? Why do you want to leave? Where do you want to go?"

"I heard in the northeast there is an island, and on that island is a band of demons. We've both heard the stories of how they kill and rob people."

"We have," the old man said.

"They also carry off people and eat them. I must go and kill them. I must go and bring back what they have robbed."

The old man felt surprised at hearing this from a boy of fifteen. He knew Momotaro wasn't a common child. The boy was sent from Heaven, so he doubted demons could hurt him.

"You may go if you wish," he said. "Go and destroy the demons and bring peace to the land."

Momotaro bowed. "Thank you for everything." He left to prepare for his journey.

The old man and his wife went to the kitchen to make rice cakes for Momotaro to take with him. They handed the bundle to him with tears in their eyes.

"Be careful," they said. "Come back victorious."

Momotaro wished them well and left quickly so his parents couldn't see the tears in his eyes. He traveled until midday when he stopped under a tree to eat lunch. He pulled out one of the rice cakes and sat down when a dog the size of a colt ran out of the high grass.

The dog bared his teeth. "How dare you pass through my field without asking. If you leave me all your food, you can go. Otherwise I will kill you."

Momotaro laughed. "Don't you know who I am? I'm Momotaro, and I'm on my way to end the demons on their island in the northeast. If you try to stop me, I will cut you in two."

Momotaro's tone of voice made the dog's tail drop between his legs. He bowed so low that his forehead touched the ground. "You are *the* Momotaro? Please forgive me my stupidity. If you don't mind someone as rude as me, can I come along and help you?"

"If you want to go with me, you can."

"Thank you," the dog said. "But I am very hungry. Can I have one of your rice cakes?"

"This is the best rice cake in Japan. I will give you half of this one."

After they ate, they continued their journey. They walked over hills and through valleys. The weather remained fine, allowing them to cover many miles. They were up on a forested hill when a monkey jumped down from a tree ahead of them.

"Good morning, Momotaro," the monkey said, "I've heard of your journey, and I want to go with you."

The dog growled. "He already has me to go with him. What use is a monkey? Get out of our way."

The monkey chattered and jumped at the dog, pulling at his fur. The dog tried to bite her.

"Stop fighting!" Momotaro stepped between them.

"It's not dignified for you to have such a creature following you," the dog said.

"What do you know about it?" Momotaro asked. He pushed the dog aside and turned to the monkey. "Just who are you anyway?"

"I am a monkey who lives in these hills. We've also had trouble with the demons. That's why I want to come with you." She bared her fangs.

"You have good courage," the boy said. He dug into his sack of rice cakes. "Here is a piece of my rice cake. You can come with us."

The monkey and the dog didn't get along. They kept snapping at each other and threatening to fight again. It slowed their pace until Momotaro had enough of them. He sent the dog ahead with a flag in his mouth and put the monkey behind with a sword. He walked between them.

They came to a large field. A bird landed on the trail ahead of them. Momotaro hadn't seen a bird so beautiful. Its feathers layered as if it wore five different robes. The dog dropped his flag and went after the bird, but the bird flew up and snatched the dog's tail with its talons.

As he watched the two scuffle, Momotaro admired the spirit of the bird. It would certainly make a good fighter for their mission. He stepped forward. "You are in our way. Surrender and I will take you with us. If you don't, I will let this dog bite your head off."

The pheasant settled back to the ground and bowed. "I know of you, Momotaro. Please forgive my rudeness. I would be happy to join you."

"So you are going to take this bird too?" the dog asked.

"Didn't you hear what I said?" Momotaro asked. "I will take the bird with me because I want to. Now all of you listen to me. An army needs harmony. From now on you three must be friends. I will make whoever fights leave."

The three promised to stop fighting, and they made every effort to become friends as Momotaro ordered. The days passed until they came upon the shore of the northeastern sea. Although the companions had traveled the high hills and dark forests bravely, the sight of the sea unnerved them. How were they going to cross the sea and get to the island in the distance?

"Why do you hesitate?" Momotaro asked. "Are you afraid of the sea? Cowards! If that scares you, how can you fight demons? You can all stay here, and I will fight them alone."

"Please, Momotaro. Let me stay with you," the dog said.

"We've come this far," the monkey said. "We are not afraid of the sea. It is just a puddle."

"Please let us go with you," the pheasant said.

Momotaro's rough words did their trick. He found a small ship, and the fair weather pushed their ship as fast as an arrow across the water. At first the companions were afraid of the waves and the rolling of the ship, but they quickly grew used to it. They all gazed with anticipation at the island as it enlarged on the horizon.

When they got tired of watching, they shared stories of their exploits before they had met. Momotaro enjoyed listening to their stories and watching their antics. He forgot his exhaustion from the journey, but he couldn't shake his homesickness. He itched to kill the demons so he could return home sooner.

The ship made good time. On the morning of the next day, the island loomed ahead of them. The demons' castle stood on a cliff overlooking the shore. Momotaro watched it from the railing and considered his plan of attack.

At last he motioned the pheasant over. "Your wings give us an advantage. Fly to the castle and fight with the demons. We will follow you."

The pheasant flew from the ship and landed on the roof in the middle of the castle. "The great general Momotaro has come to take your castle," the pheasant shouted. "If you want to live, surrender. Break off the horns that grow on your foreheads as a token of your submission. If you don't, we will kill you."

The horned demons looked up and laughed. "A wild pheasant! What do you think you can do to us other than become dinner?"

The demons equipped themselves for fight, donning their tiger-skin pants and arming themselves with iron bars. They tried to knock the pheasant down, but the nimble bird dodged and attack their faces. He tore the demons' red hair from their heads.

In the meantime, Momotaro landed his ship and approached the castle. Atop the cliff, the castle had high walls and large iron gates. The companions walked the path that led to the castle. About midway to the cliff, they came upon two women washing clothes in a stream. Blood stained the clothes, and as the young women washed them, they cried.

"Who are you? Why do you cry?" Momotaro asked.

"We are prisoners of the Demon King. He kidnapped us despite how we are daughters of powerful lords. We have to be his servants, and one day he will kill us and eat us." They cried more at the thought.

"I will rescue you," Momotaro said. "Don't cry anymore. Show me how to get into the castle, and I will end this."

The women led him to a small back door in the lowest part of the castle. The door was so small that Momotaro could barely crawl inside. When they emerged, the pheasant saw them and redoubled his efforts to distract the demons. Momotaro and his companions wasted no time. They attacked the demons, who fell back in surprise. Although they were only a boy and three animals, they attacked with the ferocity of a hundred warriors. Demons fell from the castle walls to their deaths on the rocks below. Others fell into the sea to drown. The rest died to the boy and his companions.

Finally, only the Demon King remained. He threw down his iron bar. The red-haired creature knelt before the boy and snapped off his horn. He presented it and bowed his forehead to the dirt. "I know I can't win against you. If you spare my life, I will give you all the treasure I've hidden in the castle."

"It's not like you to beg for mercy, is it?" Momotaro laughed. "No matter how much you beg, I can't spare your life. You've killed and tortured too many people."

He tied the king up and gave him to the monkey. He went into all the rooms of the castle, freeing the prisoners and gathering all the treasure he found. He handed a measure of the wealth to each of the prisoners and to his animal companions. Then they all set off for home.

Momotaro took each of the prisoners safely home. He paraded the captive Demon King to show everyone that the threat had ended. He gave the king to the lords whose daughters he had rescued and left them to decide justice.

With his quest completed, Momotaro returned home. The treasure he brought allowed his family to live in peace and plenty to the end of their days.

The Adventures of Tokoyo

When Takatoki Hojo ruled Japan, Oribe Shima lived. The samurai had offended Takatoki and ended up banished to the island of Kamishima. Oribe had a beautiful eighteen-year-old daughter named Tokoyo. She loved her father dearly.

When she heard of her father's banishment, she still lived in Ise. She spent that night crying. By morning, she had cried herself out and come to a decision.

She would find her father or die trying.

She sold the house's furnishings to get enough money for the search and set off. She traveled alone for many long weeks until she reached Akasaki, near the Islands of Oki where her father had been banished. There, she searched for a fisherman to ferry her across.

"I need to hire you and your boat," she told a fisherman. "I need to get to the Oki Islands."

The man looked her up and down. "You had better go home."

"I will offer you what I have left." Tokoyo didn't have much money left, but she intended to offer her last penny.

The fisherman laughed. "That isn't enough, even if I wanted to take you. And I don't. Those islands are forbidden. You'd best go home to your father or husband."

Tokoyo wasn't to be deterred. She spent what she had on provisions and waited until nightfall. She crept to the beach and selected the lightest boat she could find. She struggled to get it into the water.

Fortune watched over her that night. The breeze blew strong, and the current swept her skiff along. But she hadn't counted on how exhausting sailing could be nor the heat of the sun when it broke over the sea. By the evening, s exhaustion and the heat had overwhelmed her. But her boat touched the shore of a rocky bay.

She found a sheltered spot and slept until late morning. She awoke sore but refreshed and ate from her meager provisions before heading toward the nearby village.

"Do you know of my father Oribe Shima?" she asked the first fisherman she saw.

The weathered man shook his head.

"Please, he was banished here."

"I've never heard of your father. If you know what is best for you, you won't ask for him. "

She went about the village, but most everyone said something to the same effect. Luckily, some of the villagers felt sympathy for her and offered her a place to sleep and a meal. She continued to wander across the island, but it was as if her father had vanished.

One evening, she came to a rocky cape. A wind-beaten shrine stood there. Exhausted from another fruitless day, she prayed for help in her search. After she finished, she settled close to the shrine to sleep out of the wind.

She had slept for about an hour when the sound of clapping hands and a crying girl woke her. In the bright moonlight stood a fifteen-year-old girl. Beside her prayed a priest. Both wore white. When the priest finished, he pushed the girl toward the edge of the rocks.

Tokoyo leaped up and caught the girl's wrist just as the priest shoved her over the ledge. Tokoyo wrenched and threw the girl to safety.

The old priest looked surprised. "It seems you are a stranger. I don't want to kill this girl, but we are under the curse of an evil god called Yofune Nushi. He lives at the bottom of the sea and demands a girl just under fifteen years sent to him once a year. We have to do this on the Day of the Dog, June 13th, between eight and nine in the evening. If we don't, Yofune Nushi sends terrible storms that kill many more."

"Let this girl go, and let me take her place. I am the daughter of the samurai Oribe Shima. I came to find him, but he seems to have vanished." She felt tears well in her eyes. "My heart breaks, and I have nothing to live for. Please take this letter and give it to him."

Tokoyo took the white robe off the girl and put it on. She knelt before the Buddha statue in the shrine and prayed for strength and courage to kill the evil god. She took her dagger, which had belonged to one of her ancestors, and placed it between her teeth. Without waiting for the priest, she dived into the sea.

She swam down through the moonlit water until she reached the bottom. A cave lit with phosphorescent lights glittered before her. Inside the cave sat a man. She swam toward him with her dagger ready to strike. As she neared the god, she saw that she was mistaken. Inside the cave sat a wooden statue of Takatoki Hojo. Anger made her snort air bubbles. She was tempted to wreck the statue, but there wasn't any reason to. Instead, she decided to rescue the statue. She unwrapped her sash, tied it around the statue, and hauled it from the cave.

As she cleared the entrance, a serpentine creature with legs and glowing scales came from the depths. She gripped her dagger, feeling certain this was the evil Yofune Nushi.

When the creature came within six feet of her, she lunged sideways and buried her dagger into its right eye. The god shivered and made for its cave, blinded from its wound and the blood that clouded the water. Tokoyo swam to its left, twisting and stabbing it between its scales. Her dagger struck its heart. It froze from the pain, stiffened, and collapsed to the sea floor.

She gathered the statue and the carcass and made for the surface, certain she had killed the god that plagued the island.

The priest and the girl still stood on the rocks when Tokoyo broke the surface. The priest dashed down and pulled Tokoyo, the statue, and the slain monster to land. The girl went off to get help from the village.

After Tokoyo was settled and resting in the village, the priest left to report the event to Lord Tameyoshi. The lord sent word to Takatoki Hojo, who was suffering from a disease that resisted all treatment. Takatoki believed the statue was a figure used to curse him. Now that it was found, he should recover. When he heard that the daughter of his old enemy, Oribe Shima, was behind the breaking of the curse, he ordered Oribe released from prison.

Oribe and Tokoyo reunited and returned to Shima Province, where the story of Tokoyo's bravery had also spread.

As for the island of Kamijima, the death of Yofune Nushi brought peace. The villagers placed the body of the evil god in a shrine called the Tomb of the Sea Serpent. The statue of Takatoki came to rest at Honsoji.

The Adventures of Yamato Take

The Silver Robe Disguise

King Keiko ordered his youngest son Prince Yamato to kill the thieves Kumaso and Takeru. Before he left, the prince prayed at the shrines of Ise and asked Amaterasu to watch over him on his mission. He told his aunt, who was the high priestess at one of the Ise shrines, about his task. She was pleased that someone was finally going to do something about the thieves and gave her nephew a silk robe, saying it would bring him luck.

Prince Yamato set out with his wife, the Princess Ototachibana, and his most loyal followers. They traveled to the southern island of Kyushu, the base of the thieves. When they landed, Yamato immediately noticed how rough the island was. He would never be able to directly assault the thief brothers on their own land. So he had to come up with a plan.

He asked Ototachibana to bring him the robe his aunt had given him. She helped him put it on and let down his long hair. She tucked one of her combs into the locks and adorned him with some of her jewelry. When she finished, he gazed into a mirror and found he made a handsome woman. He told his followers to stay and protect his wife and set off alone toward the area where the thief brothers were said to stay.

He found them in a large tent discussing King Keiko's order to have them killed. When they looked up, they failed to see anyone except a fair woman.

"What is a woman like you doing out there?" Takeru asked.

Yamato covered his face with his sleeve and answered in his best falsetto. "I came searching for you. I had heard of your greatness and came to serve you."

"It's about time our fame attracted good attention." Kumaso smiled and gestured at their rice wine jars. "Go ahead."

Yamato walked with minute steps and tried to mimic the shyness Ototachibana had when they had first met. He did his best to serve the rice wine, but he didn't have to worry much about his thick wrists. The brothers quickly drank more than what was good for them and kept on drinking.

When Kumaso passed the point of awareness, Yamato slipped his dagger from its hiding place and stabbed him to death. Takeru still had enough of his wits to try to flee once he saw what happened, but he lacked the motor skills to pull it off. Yamato leaped at him and thrust the dagger deep.

Takeru fell to the floor of the tent. "Who are you?" He gasped. "Where did you come from? We thought we were the strongest and craftiest men."

"I am Yamato. The son of the king. I was ordered to kill men like you."

Takeru offered a pained smile. "From now on you should be called Yamato Take because you are the bravest man."

He fell back and died.

The Wooden Sword

On his way back to the capital, Yamato encountered another famous outlaw named Idzumo Takeru. He asked his princess and his men to stay back. He cut a sword out of wood and replaced his steel sword with it. Then, he went on ahead. He caught up to Idzumo while the outlaw swam in a river. Yamato sneaked up to Idzumo's clothes and exchanged swords. Yamato waited until the man emerged and dressed.

"Hello! What a fine day," Yamato called as he approached.

Idzumo watched him with narrowed eyes. "It is that."

"I couldn't help but notice you wear your sword well." Yamato gestured. "I'm a traveling swordsman too." He smiled with this best insolence. "I am your better, however."

Idzumo reached for his sword. "You are a pert one."

Yamato shrugged and partially turned his back on the man. "Then prove me wrong."

Idzumo's glare darkened, and he tried to free his sword. The wooden sword refused to come out of the sheath, and it wouldn't have helped him in any case. Yamato drew his sword, turned, and took off Idzumo's head in a single motion. He collected the head as proof of his bounty and returned to his men and princess. When they reached home, his father was pleased and rewarded him with priceless gifts.

The Grass Cutting Sword

Yamato wasn't home for long when the king ordered him to stop an Ainu uprising in the eastern provinces. The king gave him a spear made from a holly tree. The spear was named The Eight Arms' Length Spear. Before he left, the prince visited the shrines of Ise and his aunt. He told her of his adventures and of his new mission. She felt pleased that her gift of the robe had served him so well.

"Wait here just a moment," she said and went into the shrine. She returned with a sword and a bag of flint. "This is the Sword of Murakumo, the sword Susanoo himself wielded. May it protect you."

Yamato took the priceless sword and bowed to his beloved aunt.

Yamato, Ototachibana, and his men set out once again. They traveled to Suruga Province where the governor welcomed them. The governor organized a deer hunt as entertainment. The hunt took place in a wild plain covered with high grass. Yamato became separated as he tracked the largest deer he had ever seen.

He felt the heat before he noticed the smoke. Fire had overtaken the dry grass. In a blink, flames surrounded him without any means of escape. Such a fire was never natural.

He had fallen into a trap.

He opened the bag of flint his aunt had given him and set the grass near him on fire. He pulled out the Sword of Murakumo and slashed the blades down all around him. The wind kicked up behind his cuts and blew the flames away from him, creating a firewall against the enemy's fire. The fires clashed like swordsmen for several long moments before they both burned out.

Yamato trudged over the charred grass. His quick thinking and the forethought of his aunt had saved him from the trap without the slightest burn. So, too, the Sword of Murakumo came to be called the Grass Cutting Sword.

The Sacrifice of Ototachibana

Throughout all of Yamato's adventures, his loyal wife Ototachibana followed him and helped him. Despite this, Yamato looked down on her and treated her with indifference. The traveling had marked her. Her once-fair skin had become sunburned and leathery. Her once-fine clothes had become torn and stained. Yet she never complained. She tried to retain her sweet elegance, but Yamato's indifference depressed her.

Through their travels, Yamato had met the fascinating Princess Miyadzu. Her robes were as charming as Ototachibana's once were. Miyadzu's skin resembled the petals of cherry blossoms. Yamato came to love her and even swore he would make the princess his wife right in front of Ototachibana. The prince saw how this affected his wife, but he hardened his heart. He would keep his promise to Miyadzu next time he returned to her home.

They traveled along the coast of Idzu. His men wanted to rent several boats so they could cross the Straits of Kazusa.

"You worry too much," Yamato said. "This is just a brook. Why do you want so many boats? I can jump across it!"

So they used the single boat they had and started across the strait. A storm arose, turning the waves into water mountains. The wind screamed while lightning blazed across the black clouds. The wrath of Rin Jin, the King of the Sea, targeted them because of Yamato's pride. The storm grew worse when the crew took down the sails. Nothing they could do could ease the threat.

Ototachibana stood. Despite everything Yamato had done to her, she loved her husband. She wouldn't see him die. She walked to the edge of the pitching craft and shouted toward the sea. "Rin Jin, I know my husband has angered you with his boasting. I want you to spare him. I, Ototachibana, will give you my life in place of the life of Yamato Take. Please let my love make it safely to shore."

She leaped from the craft. The sea surged around her and carried her away. As soon as she disappeared, the lightning stopped. The waves settled, and the wind quieted. Sunlight sliced through the dark clouds and chased them away.

Yamato Take and his men made it safely ashore, and they succeeded in ending the Ainu uprising. He forgot about the Princess Miyadzu as he remembered the time he and Ototachibana had spent together. His wife's love throughout his journeys and her sacrifice remained with him for the rest of his life.

The Slaying of the Serpent

Yamato and his friends traveled to Omi Province, where they had heard rumors of trouble. They encountered many people mourning along the roads. They told him about a serpent that came down from the mountains every night and ate the people of the villages. Yamato left his friends to defend the villagers and went up into Mount Ibaki. He traveled only halfway up when he encountered the snake on its way down to eat. He wrapped his arms around the creature and twisted until he felt something snap deep within it and it stopped moving. Darkness suddenly descended, and rain fell. Yamato took shelter beneath a pine tree and waited until the weather improved before climbing down the mountain.

By the time he returned to his friends, his feet burned with a strange pain, and he felt sick. He collapsed at the edge of the village, too sick to move. Luckily, his friends awaited him and carried him to a mineral hot spring near the village. A long soak restored his health. This was the closest he had come to dying other than the time his wife sacrificed herself for him. He praised Amaterasu for watching out for him and returned home.

The Adventures of Yorimasa Gen

Long ago, a samurai by the name of Yorimasa Gen served as a warrior of the Third Rank in the Imperial Court. His skills in archery and combat rivaled his ancestor Raiko, who killed the demons of Oyeyama. Yorimasa served as the Chief Guard of the Imperial Palace.

His duties allowed him to glimpse the Lady Ayame, the loveliest lady-in-waiting in the court. Her mind was as sharp as her face was beautiful, and the Emperor and Empress were fond of her. The nobles in the court fell in love with her, but no matter how handsome or wealthy they were, Ayame only granted them a fleeting smile. She answered their poems with silence.

Yorimasa wasn't immune to her charms, although he had only caught fleeting looks at her. He never saw her face, but his heart didn't need to see her to love her. He attempted his poetry, but she gave him the same silent reply as the nobles. Over the three years he served the Imperial Court as the Chief Guard, he waited and despaired. He settled on just the glimpses he could steal of her as she went about her duties in the distance.

When Yorimasa's third year turned, the Emperor became sick and could not sleep at night. He complained about noises and a sense of being watched from sunset to sunrise. Noblemen took turns staying up to see if they could find the cause of the Emperor's problems. His bodyguards kept vigil around the Emperor's bedroom. All anyone saw was a black cloud that traveled across Kyoto and rested on the roof of the Purple Hall of the North Star, where the Emperor slept. The guards and nobles that ringed the bedroom heard scratches and noises on the roof as if a beast stood on it. Everyone concluded that the cloud hid some sort of monster. And that monster had to die before the Emperor grew any weaker.

The Ministers of the Right and of the Left, who were in charge of the Emperor's security, asked who could rise to the challenge. Yorimasa's name kept coming up, so they sent for him.

Yorimasa read the letter, and he felt the great responsibility settle on his shoulders. Although he protected the Emperor in his current post, this was different. He strung his bow carefully and placed two steel-tipped arrows in his quiver. He donned his armor and put on his hunting cloak. Instead of a helmet, he wore a ceremonial cap so he could at least look a little courtly. He selected the bravest and strongest of his garrison to come with him.

The Ministers told him about the cloud and the strange noises and the nightmares that plagued the Emperor and the court.

"We need you to kill the monster," said the Left. "All of our innermost guards are too frightened and weakened to do the job. None of them were able to fire their bows well enough to hit the mark."

Yorimasa listened with a grave look on his face. He had noticed how the palace was in chaos as he walked to the Minister's Hall. "I will do what I can." He bowed.

He found a spot on the roof and settled in to wait. Night brought a storm with lightning and thunder that shook the palace. The archer and his retainer waited in the rain as if the storm wasn't raging at all. Around midnight, he saw a thick black cloud sweep down and settle on the roof of the palace just as the ministers said. He had his retainer light a torch and ready his sword.

Yorimasa watched the cloud's movements. His retainer remained behind him. When lightning flashed, Yorimasa saw a large animal in the midst of the cloud. He locked his gaze on the spot that appeared to be the animal's head. In the darkness that followed the lightning flash, he saw the glare of first one eye and then the other as the creature moved across the roof.

"This must be the monster," Yorimasa said.

He fitted an arrow to his bow and aimed to the left of where he saw the left eye flash red. He pulled his bow string back as his concentration centered on the target. He let out a breath and let the arrow fly. The arrow flitted through the rain and disappeared into the cloud. A howl of pain erupted, followed by a heavy thud. The sounds of scratching and thrashing against the roof tiles shrilled.

Yorimasa gave his retainer the signal. The man rushed toward the monster who could now be seen as the cloud swirled away. The retainer fell upon the beast, stabbing it nine times in the throat and body.

"Come up and look upon the beast," Yorimasa shouted to the men below. The roof tiles clicked under his feet.

In all of Yorimasa's hunts, he had never seen such a strange creature. It was as large as a horse but looked like it was sewed together from all the animals in a zoo. It had the head of an ape, the body and claws of a tiger, the tail of a snake, the wings of a bird, and the scales of a dragon. Yorimasa had read about such a creature, but he had thought it was a story told by grandmothers to scare grandchildren into behaving. The Imperial guards and nobles gasped behind him as they saw it.

Yorimasa and his retainer skinned the creature, and the Imperial bodyguard presented the pelt to the Emperor. The Emperor ordered the pelt to be stored in the treasury as a curiosity and sent for Yorimasa and for a suitable reward that instant.

The samurai and his retainer felt some trepidation toward being in the Emperor's presence and bedroom, wet and bloody and filthy as they were. But the Emperor praised them from behind his screen and offered Yorimasa a sword called *Shishi-wo*, the King of Lions.

The Minster of the Left gave the sword to Yorimasa. "Bird of wonder, even your name climbs ever upward to Heaven."

Yorimasa sat on his knees with his head bowed, as was proper, and felt the sword settle into his hands. "Not through your own, but through the merit of a moon-shaped bow." He finished the Minister of the Left's poem. Yorimasa's modesty pleased the minister.

After Yorimasa left, the Emperor wanted to reward the man in a more fitting way than just a sword. When one of the nobles mentioned how Yorimasa had written love poems to the Lady Ayame, an idea struck the Emperor. He sent for her.

As soon as she arrived, he said, "Is it true you've received many letters and poems from the warrior Yorimasa?"

She blushed like a peach blossom in the glow of dawn. "May it please the Son of Heaven to send for Yorimasa and ask him?"

He sent her away and summoned Yorimasa. The warrior arrived in his best spring attire and prostrated himself in front of the Emperor's screened throne.

"Do you love Lady Ayame?" the Emperor asked.

Yorimasa was confused by the suddenness of the question and didn't know how to reply. He knew it was forbidden by court etiquette to write love-letters to any lady-in-waiting. The Emperor saw the warrior's confusion and felt sorry for him. He decided to have a little fun and whispered an order to his Master of Ceremony.

The Master of Ceremony left and returned after a few moments with three ladies in tow. The women dressed alike, and even their hair was in the same style. Unless someone knew them well, it would be impossible to tell one from the other. They looked as beautiful as plum blossoms.

"The Lady Ayame is here," the Emperor said. "If you can choose her from these ladies, you can marry her."

Yorimasa bowed, overcome with the kindness of the Emperor and the chance to wed his beloved. He had never seen his lady love up close. He had only glimpsed her from his station in the courtyard as she passed through the corridors of the palace.

The Emperor smiled inwardly, pleased at how Yorimasa was visibly perplexed.

I am a soldier, not a member of the court, Yorimasa thought. *I don't presume to gaze upon a lady above the clouds. Nor can I be sure which is Ayame. Were I to make a mistake and choose the wrong lady, I would be disgraced and disappointed.*

As he considered what to do, he whispered a short poem. "In the rainy season when the waters overflow the lake's banks, who can gather the iris?"

The Emperor understood that the poem referred to Yorimasa's life and his inability to select the Lady Ayame. The warriors modest reserved touched him as he thought about how great Yorimasa's love must be. The Emperor stood and descended the dais. He walked to Ayame and took her by the hand. He led her to the warrior.

"This is Lady Ayame. I give her to you."

They married that day and lived happily together.

Some years later, a band of discontented priests came to the gate Yorimasa guarded. They demanded to enter. Yorimasa saw how well armed the priests were and how quick they would be to use the weapons. A shrine rested among them. Fifty men carried the mobile shrine on their shoulders. When they noticed Yorimasa watching, the priests ordered the shrine lifted. The men groaned and hefted the shrine over their heads, staggering under the weight.

Yorimasa wasn't in the mood to fight. It seemed a waste to send his men against the priests. His men were the best archers and fighters. The priests of Mount Hiei were troublesome, and Yorimasa didn't want to encourage them. He smiled as an idea came to him. It was time to have a little fun at their expense.

When the procession stopped opposite the gate, Yorimasa and his men left their posts. They stopped in front of the mobile shrine and bowed. The priests had expected a difficult reception and gaped with surprise. After some confusion, their spokesman stepped forward. "We have a petition for the Emperor."

Yorimasa sent his captain forward.

"My lord welcomes you," he said. "He wishes for me to say he worships the same god as you. He is averse to shooting the shrine with his arrows. Besides this, we are few in number. If you chose to fight us, you would be dishonored and called cowards for fighting at the weakest gate. The next gate is guarded by Heike soldiers. They outnumber us. If you go and fight them, you could gain better honor."

The priests were pleased at the flattery. They didn't notice how Yorimasa was manipulating them to bother his rivals. The priests shouldered their shrine and left toward the other gate. As soon as they arrived. the priests fought with the Heike, but the guards beat the priests and sent them running for their lives.

Yorimasa lived many decades with his wife, and they had many children together. When Yorimasa turned seventy-five years old, political winds had changed. The Heike and Taira clans grew stronger until Kiyomori gained power. He filled the government posts with his sons and relatives. He treated any samurai who didn't belong to the Heike clan poorly. Yorimasa numbered among them. As he watched the conduct of Kiyomori and his family, he longed to punish them. He spent a lot of time considering how to do this.

Kiyomori's power grew to the point where he confined the Emperor in the Imperial Palace. Yorimasa had enough. He worked with Prince Takakura, the Emperor's son, to raise an army against the Heike. But by then the Genji clan lacked the numbers of the Heike, and the army was defeated. Yorimasa fled with the remnants of the army and sheltered in the Temple of Byodoin on the Uji River.

When the Heike army came for them, Yorimasa made a stand with his remaining soldiers. He could only buy time for Prince Takakura to escape. He divided his men into two divisions. He stationed the first as a reserve in the temple grounds and prepared the other for battle along the river's banks. They tore down all the bridges and waited.

The Heike came with 28,000 men. For some time, the two forces faced off on each side of the river, exchanging arrow volleys.

A huge priest named Tajima Bo rushed into the front ranks of the Genji. He brandished his halberd and stood on the remains of the bridge. The Heike shot arrows at him. When arrows came for his head, he dodged them. He jumped high into the air when arrows flew at his legs, and he swept all others away with his halberd. This inspired another priest, Jomyo, to come beside Tajima with his bow. Jomyo shot and killed about a dozen enemies.

After a time, Jomyo threw down his bow and took up his sword. He and his fellow priests swarmed the few boards that remained of the bridge. The Genji forces held out against the Heike until a young Heike warrior came forward.

"It comes to this!" He shouted and plunged his horse into the river.

The river had swelled from the rains the days before. His action caused a surge among the Heike. They charged into the river and made it to the bank where the Genji waited. Three hundred of them broke through the Genji lines and drove the defenders back into the temple.

The Genji fought desperately. Kanetsuna, Yorimasa's second son, died trying to defend his father. They fought valiantly, knowing they were going to die. Yorimasa took several wounds before he slipped away from the front lines to beg Prince Takakura to flee. The man had remained in the temple instead of following the original plan. Eventually, the prince conceded to Yorimasa's plea.

After making sure the prince escaped, Yorimasa went into the inner part of the temple's garden and knelt under a large tree. His retainer Watanabe followed him. Yorimasa removed his armor and drew his short sword. He decided he would die with honor. Watanabe took his place behind his master, sword drawn.

Yorimasa stabbed himself in his stomach and drew his blade across. At the right moment, Watanabe cut off his head. He tied a large stone to Yorimasa's head and dropped it into the river so it wouldn't become a war trophy.

Several years later, Yoritomo destroyed the Heike and fulfilled Yorimasa's goal.

The Adventures of Yoshitsune

Yoshitsune's father, Yoshitomo, died in a great battle against the powerful Taira clan. The clan's leader, Kiyomori, did what he could to end Yoshitomo's bloodline. But Tokiwa wasn't the wife of Yoshitomo for nothing. She fled with her children and arranged to marry Kiyomori in exchange for their safety. Kiyomori allowed her to keep the young Yoshitsune with her. She quietly urged her son not to forget his father and his heritage as a Minamoto. She planted the seed of revenge in the boy.

When Yoshitsune was seven years old, Kiyomori sent him to a monastery to become a monk. The boy took to his studies, but he never forgot the words of his self-sacrificing mother. He often sneaked out of the monastery and into a deep valley. There, he would practice with a wooden sword and sing fragments of war songs. He wanted nothing more than to right the wrongs the Taira clan had committed against his family.

One night as he practiced, a great thunderstorm blew down on him. At the head of the storm came a giant with a long red nose, enormous eyes, bird claws for hands, and great feathered wings. Yoshitsune gripped his wooden sword and stood his ground. When the giant stopped to glare down at him, Yoshitsune met his gaze.

"Who are you?" the boy asked.

"I am the King of the Tengu." The King smiled. "I know much about you, Yoshitsune, and about your family. I've watched you practice with that wooden sword, and I admire your persistence."

"I cannot let my mother down."

"That's why I've come to teach you how to use a sword properly."

Yoshitsune accepted the stated offer without hesitation. Each night, the King of the Tengu taught him the art of the sword and the ways of agility over brute strength. Soon Yoshitsune could defeat twenty small Tengu at once.

The lessons continued until Yoshitsune turned fifteen and heard that a warrior priest named Benkei lived on Mount Hiei. The warrior priest attacked samurai who attempted to cross the Gojo Bridge of Kyoto. He wanted to collect one thousand swords. By the time Yoshitsune heard of him, Benkei had collected nine hundred and ninety-nine swords. At this news, Yoshitsune decided to test what he had learned and kill the warrior priest.

That evening, Yoshitsune left for the bridge. He brought a flute with him, which he played as he traveled. When he came upon Gojo Bridge, a gigantic man wearing black armor barred his way. Benkei looked Yoshitsune up and down and stepped aside.

"You can go."

Yoshitsune frowned. "Aren't you the Benkei who collects swords from warriors?"

"I am, but you are not worth my time. You look more ready to write a poem about the moon or continue playing that flute than offer any challenge."

Yoshitsune narrowed his eyes and kicked at Benkei's halberd.

"You fool." Benkei swept his great halberd in a slicing arc, but Yoshitsune skipped back.

He jumped around the black armored man, moving from the man's front to rear and back again so fast that the man couldn't keep up. Yoshitsune mocked the man and laughed. All the while Benita sliced the air with his halberd.

At last even Benkei's great strength gave out. Yoshitsune knocked the halberd from the man's hand and tripped him. Benkei fell on his hands and knees, and with a cry of triumph Yoshitsune climbed on the man's back as if Benkei was a horse.

"You win," the man panted. "Just who are you?"

"I am Yoshitsune Minamoto, the son of Yoshitomo. And I will avenge him against the Taira."

Yoshitsune got off the big man's back and stood with relaxed tension, ready for the big man to try something.

Benkei bowed his forehead to the bridge. "I knew your father. Please do the honor of making me your retainer."

From that day forward, Yoshitsune and Benkei became the best of friends. They fought together against the Taira with great success.

Some time later, Yoshitsune and Benkei sailed to *Dan-n-ura* as a great storm hit. Above the sounds of the storm, the pair could also hear the marching of men, the clash of weapons, and the sound of arrows. The noise grew louder until an army of Taira appeared floating above the sea. The ghostly men wore tattered and blood-stained armor and reached out toward the boat as it to stop it. Yoshitsune recognized that these were the ghosts of the Taira who had lost the Battle of *Dan-n-a* to his family the Minamoto decades ago.

Yoshitsune unsheathed his sword and cried out his revenge against even the ghosts of the Taira.

"Please put aside your sword," Benkei said. "Prayer would serve us better." Benkei dug out a rosary and recited a number of Buddhist prayers.

The ghosts stopped wailing as Benkei prayed. One by one, the ghosts slid into the calming sea until the warriors were left alone on their boat.

The Chrysanthemum Hermit

Long ago, an old man named Kikuo lived at the foot of the Nambu Mountains in Saitama Prefecture. He was a faithful retainer of Tsugaru. Back then, Kikuo went by the name of Sawada Hayato. Kikuo was a strong and handsome man. He managed Tsugaru's bodyguards and all his estates.

Despite his best effort, one day the small force was overwhelmed. The lord and Kikuo with a few other survivors managed to escape to the mountains where they plotted their revenge. Kikuo knew his lord enjoyed flowers, especially chrysanthemum, so he devoted his spare time to cultivating them. He hoped it would reduce the pain of exile. He was right; they pleased his lord. But Tsugaru still worried. The chance for revenge didn't present itself before Tsugaru grew sick and died. Kikuo cried over his lord's humble and lonely grave. As he cried, he gave up on the possibility of revenge.

In order to please his master, Kikuo decided to plant chrysanthemums around the grave and tend them each day. The flower bed soon grew to be thirty yards wide and struck everyone with wonder. People began to call him Kikuo—the Chrysanthemum Old Man.

The Forty-Seven Ronin

Asano Takumi no Kami, the Lord of Ako Castle, lived at the beginning of the eighteenth century. The Shogun assigned Asano and Lord Kamei Korechika to receive an envoy from the Emperor. The Shogun appointed Kira Kotsuke-no-Suke to teach Asano and Kamei the proper ceremony. So the two samurai went to the castle each day to listen to

Kira. The two men brought Kira gifts in return for his instruction, but Kira felt dissatisfied with what they offered. Instead of teaching them, he made fools of them in front of their fellow samurai. Asano felt duty-bound to endure the insults, but Kamei had a hotter temper.

He decided to kill Kira.

One night after he finished his duties, Kamei returned to his manor and summoned his counselors. "Kira has insulted Asano and me during our lessons. He went against all decency. I wanted to kill him right there, but if I did so in the castle, I know not only would my life end, I would also ruin my family and all of you. I've decided to kill him tomorrow, and I wanted you to hear it from me."

Kamei's chief advisor knew he couldn't change Kamei's mind. "Your words are law. We will make the needed preparations. If Kira is insolent, let him die."

When the adviser returned home, he remained troubled by the news. Kira's greed wasn't a secret. He surmised the man would be open to a bribe. It was better to be out a large sum than to join his lord in ruin. So he gathered his servants and money and set off for Kira's manor.

When he arrived, Kira's retainers received him. The advisor bowed. "My master owes much to Lord Kotsuke-no-Suke for his great pains at teaching. I hope that this shabby gift will commend you to favor my lord." He offered one thousand ounces of silver and one hundred ounces for each of the retainers.

After the retainers told Kira of this, he summoned the advisor to him. "Thank you for your gift. Tomorrow I will teach your master carefully in all the different points of court etiquette."

The advisor felt pleased and relieved at Kira's words and returned home.

That morning, Asano and Kamei met Kira at the court. Kira treated them with every courtesy. "You have come early this morning, my Lord Kamei. I admire your dedication. Today, I will call to your attention several points of etiquette. I beg that you will excuse my past conduct, which must have seemed rude. I am naturally cross-grained, so please forgive me."

As Kamei listened, he changed his mind about killing Kira.

However, Kira didn't spare Asano. He ridiculed him more than he had yesterday. But Asano patiently endured all the insults and sneers.

This incensed Kira even more. "My Lord of Takumi, the ribbon of my sandal has come untied. Be so good as to tie it for me."

Asano seethed inside at being treated as a servant. But he felt bound by his duty, so he tied Kira's sandal.

"How clumsy you are. You can't even tie a sandal ribbon properly. Anyone could see you are a country bumpkin and don't understand anything about Edo." Kira laughed and strolled toward the inner room.

Asano couldn't take anymore. "My lord, stop."

"Well, what is it?" Kira asked.

As Kira turned, Asano drew his dagger and sliced at him. Kira's cap deflected the blow, but the dagger still ripped into his forehead. He fled, and Asano charged after him. Asano aimed another stab but missed. His dagger buried itself into a pillar. Just then an officer named Yosobei Kajikawa rushed forward and seized Asana, allowing Kira to escape.

More people arrived, and Asano was arrested. They confined him in one of the apartments while a council was held. The Lord Tamura Ukiyo-no-Daibu took Asano into his own house while the council debated. The council decided that Asano's behavior was outrageous. They ordered him to commit suicide by disemboweling himself. They also ordered his possessions forfeited and his family exiled.

So Asano killed himself. The Shogun confiscated Ako Castle, and Asano's retainers became *ronin* or entered the service of other lords. Other retainers gave up their status as samurai and became merchants.

Among Asano's retainers was a man called Oishi Kuranosuke. Oishi felt at fault for the incident. If he had been at the castle, he would've bribed Kira and have prevented the death of his master. He had to make amends, so he and forty-six of his fellow samurai formed a pact to avenge their master's death.

They vowed to kill Kira.

This wouldn't be easy. Lord Uyesugi had taken Kira under his protection because Kira had married the man's daughter. The forty-seven decided they had to wait until Kira wasn't on guard, so they agreed to separate and disguise themselves as carpenters and craftsman and merchants until Kira felt safe. Oishi went to Kyoto and built a house in Yamashina. He spent his time getting drunk and visiting with prostitutes to make people believe he had no interest in revenge. The forty-seven knew spies would be watching them.

One day, Oishi stumbled home drunk and collapsed on the street. Passersby laughed and derided him, and among these people was a man from Satsuma.

"Is this not, Oishi Kuranosuke?" the man asked. "He was the adviser to Asano Takumi no Kami, yet he doesn't have the heart to avenge his lord. Instead he lies drunk for everyone to see. The coward isn't worthy of being called a samurai." He walked on Oishi's face and spat on him.

When Kira heard of this incident from his spies, he finally felt at ease.

In another incident, Oishi's wife, who hated seeing what her husband had become, confronted him. "You told me, at first, that your debauchery was just a trick. But it has gone too far. Please restrain yourself!"

"Don't bother me. I won't listen to your whining. Since my way of life displeases you, we will divorce. I will buy some pretty young girl and marry her. I can't stand the sight of an old woman like you. The sooner you leave, the better."

"Please unsay those words," she said. "I've been faithful for twenty years and had three of your children. I've been with you through everything. Don't throw me out now."

"Shut up. I've made up my mind. You must go and take the children with you."

She went to their eldest son, Oishi Chikara, and begged him to intercede with his father. But Oishi wasn't to be persuaded. So he divorced his wife, and she took their two youngest children with her. Oishi Chikara remained with his father.

Kira's spies reported his incident, and Kira felt more confident that Oishi and the other *ronin* weren't planning to take revenge. He sent back half of the guards his father-in-law had lent him and began to relax.

By this time, a few of the forty-seven had managed to get into Kira's home as workman and peddlers. They memorized the layout and sent Oishi regular reports about Kira's security. Finally, Oishi decided Kira had relaxed his guard enough to strike. Oishi slipped out of Kyoto.

Oishi and the other *ronin* met on a cold midwinter night. The snow fell heavily—the perfect night to see their plan to the end. They divided into two groups and assigned a post to each man. Oishi would lead the attack on the front gate. His son, Oishi Chikara was to lead the attack on the rear. Oishi assigned Yoshida Chiuzaymon to watch over the sixteen-year-old.

They decided on using a drum to signal the attack. Anyone who cut off Kira's head was to blow a shrill whistle to signal everyone to the location. They planned to take the head to Sengakuji Temple and offer it before the tomb of their dead lord. Then they would report their deed to the government and wait for their death sentences. They all pledged themselves to the plan and sat down to a feast.

"Tonight, we will attack our enemy in his palace. His retainers will resist us, and we will have to kill them. But killing old men and women and children is terrible. Be careful not to kill a single helpless person," Oishi said.

When the hour finally came, the men set out. The wind howled, and the snow beat at them. At last, they reached the home of Kira and divided themselves according to the plan. Four of Oishi's men used a rope ladder to slip inside the inner garden and came upon a guard sleeping near the back gate. They tied up the guard, who begged for mercy. The men agreed to spare him if he would give up the keys to the gate.

"Our officer keeps them," the guard said.

The men didn't have the patience or time to find this officer. Instead, they smashed the wooden bolt and threw the doors open. At the same time, Chikara's men broke through the back gate.

Oishi sent a messenger to the nearby houses with the following message: "We, the *ronin* who were formally in the service of Asano Takumi no Kami, are about to break into the palace of Kotsuke-no-Suke to avenge our lord. Because we are not thieves, no harm will come to the neighboring houses. Please don't worry." Oishi knew the neighbors despised Kira, but he also stationed ten of his men with bows on the roof around the courtyard. He ordered them to shoot anyone who might attempt to leave the palace. He hoped it would prevent anyone from summoning help.

Oishi beat his drum, signaling the attack.

Ten of Kira's samurai woke to the drum and drew their swords. They rushed into the front room just as the *ronin* burst through the door of the front hall. As they fought, Chikara led his men through the garden and into the back of the house.

Kira and his wife and his female servants hid in a closest.

The commotion brought out the rest of Kira's men from their barrack outside the house. But by then, Oishi's assault had killed the first ten men and had joined up with Chikara's group. The barrack troops clashed with Oishi's men, but they found themselves outmatched. They attempted to send runners for help, but the archers Oishi had posted shot them down.

"Kira alone is our enemy," Oishi shouted. "Someone go inside and bring him to me. Dead or alive!"

Three brave retainers guarded Kira: Hehachi Kobayashi, Handaiyu Waku, and Ikkaku Shimidzu. They were excellent swordsman and held the *ronin* at bay.

When Oishi saw this, he ground his teeth with frustration. "Didn't every one of you swear to die? And now you are driven back by three men. Cowards! To die fighting in a master's cause is the noblest ambition of a samurai!" He turned to Chikara. "Go fight them, and if they are too strong for you, die."

Chikara seized a spear and attacked Handaiyu. He did his best, but the more experienced samurai drove him into the garden. Chikara slipped into a pond, but Handaiyu hesitated just a moment too long. The sixteen-year-old slashed Handaiyu's leg. The samurai fell heavily to the ground, giving Chikara enough time to climb out of the pond and finish him.

Meanwhile, Hehachi and Ikkaku died to the other *ronin*. Chikara saw how all of Kira's men were dead and went back inside to search for the man. He found Kira's son, Kira Sahioye. Sahioye attacked with a *naginata*, but Chikara wounded him with little trouble and allowed Sahioye to flee.

All around the home lay Kira's dead retainers, but the man remained elusive.

Oishi divided his men, and they searched the home. They found only crying women and children. The men worried that Kira had escaped them. Several, in their despair, agreed to kill themselves after they gave it one last search.

Oishi went into Kira's room and touched the blankets. "The blankets are still warm. He can't be far off. He has to be hidden somewhere in the house."

A picture hung on the wall in the room. Jiutaro Yazama removed it and found a large hole in the plaster. He thrust his spear inside and felt nothing beyond it. So Jiutaro climbed into the hole and found a court-yard. In the courtyard stood a shed for holding charcoal and firewood. He looked into the outhouse and saw something white. He was about the strike it with his spear when two samurai lunged at him. He managed to defend himself until two of his fellow *ronin* engaged them. Jiutaro entered the shed and used his spear to feel about the darkness. He saw something white and stabbed it.

A cry of pain rewarded him.

Jiutaro seized the man in white clothes, who was bleeding from his thigh. The man drew a dirk and tried to stab him, but Jiutaro disarmed him, grabbed him by the collar, and dragged him out of the shed.

The man was about sixty-years old and wore a satin sleeping robe. The men were convinced they had Kira and asked for his name. The man remained silent, but they whistled the signal anyway.

Oishi came with a lantern. The man had the scar on his forehead from when Asano had attacked him. Oishi had no doubts that they had at last found their man.

Oishi went to his knees. "My lord, we are the retainers of Asano Takumi no Kami. Last year you and our master fought in the palace. As you know, our master was ordered to kill himself, and his family was ruined. We've come to avenge him. I hope you realize the justice of our goal. I ask you perform *seppuku*. I will have the honor of being your second. After I cut off your head, I will lay it as an offering on the grave of Asano Takumi no Kami."

Each of the *ronin* asked him to kill himself honorably, but Kira crouched, silent and trembling. Oishi saw it was useless to urge Kira to die like a warrior. So he forced Kira down and cut off his head with the same short sword upon which Asano killed himself. The *ronin*, elated they had succeeded, placed Kira's head in a basket. They extinguished all the lights and fires in the house as they left. They didn't want a fire to accidentally break out and engulf the neighboring houses.

Day broke on their way to Sengakuji. People flocked to see the blood-stained men. The *ronin* remained alert, expecting Kira's father-in-law to attack and take back the head. However, Lord Matsudaira Aki-no-Kami, the Prince of Sendai, had heard of the night's work and made sure Kira's father-in-law wouldn't harass them. When the *ronin* came close to his palace, the lord sent one of his advisors to Oishi.

"I am an adviser for the Prince of Sendai. You must be tired from all you've been through. Come in and enjoy what poor refreshment we can offer you."

"Thank you," Oishi said. "We will accept his kindness gratefully."

The forty-seven went into the palace and ate. All the retainers of the Prince of Sendai praised them for their actions.

Oishi turned to the adviser. "We are indebted to you for your kind hospitality, but we still have to journey to Sengakuji. We must now take our leave." They thanked their hosts and left.

When they reached Sengakuji, the abbot of the monastery received them and led them to the tomb of Takumi no Kami.

They took the head of Kira, washed it clean in a nearby well, and laid it before the tomb. They asked the priests to read prayers while they burned incense. Oishi burned incense first, followed by his son Oishi Chikara. Then each of the forty-five remaining men performed the same ceremony.

Oishi gave all the money he had to the abbot. "When we've performed *seppuku*, I ask you bury us well. I can only offer this trifling amount. Please spend it on prayers for our souls."

The abbot, with tears in his eyes, promised to do as they wished. So the forty-seven, with their minds at peace, waited until they received orders from the government.

The Supreme Court eventually summoned them and passed the following sentence. "Neither respecting the dignity of the city or fearing the government, and forming a pact to kill your enemy, you violently broke into the house of Kira Kotsuke-no-Suke by night and murdered him. For this, the Court sentences you to perform *seppuku*."

After receiving their sentence, the forty-seven divided into four groups and went into the custody of four lords. The court sent representatives to make sure they carried out their sentences. But the forty-seven had decided from the start that they were to meet this end. They met their death as samurai. Their bodies were carried to Sengakuji and buried in front of the tomb of their master Asano Takumi no Kami.

The History of Sakata Kintoki

Long ago, Sakata Kurando served as an officer of the Emperor's body-guard. Despite his experience in the art of war, he had a gentle and loving personality. He loved the young Yaégiri, who lived in Gojozaka, Kyoto. However, Kurando attracted the jealousy of powerful officials in the Imperial Court who eventually forced him into disgrace. He became a *ronin and* disappeared from Kyoto. Yaégiri heard of this and left her family to search for him.

Kurando had given up his swords and worked as a tobacco merchant. He chanced upon Yaégiri while he traveled from village to village. They spent a long night together, but Kurando couldn't live with his disgrace.

That morning, he killed himself.

Yaégiri buried her lover and traveled to Ashigara Mountain. She stayed in a lovely, distant spot where she gave birth to a little boy. The boy had the strength of his father and played all over the mountain. A woodcutter saw the boy and eventually grew fond of him. He called the boy Little Wonder and called Yaégiri the Old Woman of the Mountain.

One day, as Little Wonder played, he saw a tengu nest at the top of a high cedar tree. He shook the tree with all his might until the nest fell. As luck would have it, the hero Yorimitsu Minamoto and his retainers Watanabe Isuna and Usui Sadamitsu were hunting in the mountain. They saw the boy shake the mighty cedar and concluded he was no ordinary child. Yorimitsu ordered Isuna to get the boy's name and find his parents.

Isuna learned about the boy from the woodcutter and paid them a visit.

"Who are you?" he asked Yaégiri as she opened the door of her cottage.

Yaégiri knew about Isuna. She mustered her old presence. "I am the wife of Sakata Kurando and the boy is our son." She told Isuna of what had befallen her lover.

Isuna had heard of Kurando. "The boy shows his father's strength. If you will trust me with him, I will make him the retainer of my Lord Yorimitsu."

Yaégiri knew this was her son's chance to follow in the footsteps of his father. She consented. Isuna brought the boy to Yorimitsu and accounted his findings. Yaégiri remained in her mountain home.

After he listened to the story, Yorimitsu gazed at the boy. "From today on your name will be Sakata Kintoki."

Sakata Kintoki grew up to become a famous warrior.

The Plot of the Blind Flute Player

During the first year of the Meiji period, 1868, Saigo Takamori defeated the Tokugawa army at Fushimi. Remnants of the army escaped. The Imperial army marched along the Tokaido, seeking the remnants. The advanced guard reached Hiratsuka, near Mount Fuji.

The troops arrived on the 5th of April with the cherry trees in full bloom. The country folk came out to watch the troops pass. Beggars and peddlers numbered among the people, begging money from the troops and selling food in turn. Toward evening, rain settled into the area, but by then the soldiers had settled into their lodgings.

Saigo and the staff officers set up at the main inn of Hiratsuka. They made the best of the poor weather, but they were feeling disheartened. Then they heard the soft notes of the *shakuhachi*, the bamboo flute, outside.

"That is a poor blind beggar we saw playing near the temple today," one officer said.

"The poor fellow must be wet and miserable. Let's call him in," said another officer.

"That's a good idea," Saigo Takamori said. "Let's have him play and raise our spirits." He called the landlord and ordered him to bring in the blind flute player.

The flute player bowed when he entered. "Thank you for doing me this honor and showing me kindness on this rainy night. I will play my best for you as repayment. It is my only means of earning a living since I became blind. Not many people stay at the inn while Imperial troops are in town. These are hard days."

"These may be hard days for you, but don't speak against the Imperial troops. We have to be cautious. Anyone can be a spy for the Tokugawa," an officer said.

"I don't mean to speak against the Imperial soldiers," the man said. "It is just hard for a blind man to earn enough rice. I'm only called once a week to play at private parties."

"Well, we will see what we can do for you," Saigo said. "Go around the room and take whatever is offered, and then you can start playing."

The man did this and collected five or six yen. When he approached Saigo, the general added to the money. "So what do you think now? Don't say the Imperial soldiers make you starve. Rather, say that if you lived near them you would get fat. Let's hear your music now."

"This is too much for my poor music," the blind man said. "Take some of it back."

"Just keep it. We don't know what will come tomorrow. Money may not do us any good then."

The blind man played long into the night. He played lively songs and songs as sorrowful as the wind that blew through the cherry trees. The officers were pleased by the man's skill and enjoyed spending the night listening. The blind man remained until the officers retired for the night. The inn's proprietor, Kato Shichibei, locked the inn behind him.

Hedges and clumps of bamboo surrounded the inn. At the far end sat an artificial mountain with a lake. Near the lake sat a summer house and a towering, ancient pine tree. One of its branches stretched back over the roof of the inn. At about one o'clock, a man climbed this tree and clambered along the branch that hung over the inn. He aimed to enter the upper floor.

Unfortunately for him, a small branch of dead wood cracked under his weight, causing the posted watchman to look up. The watchman shouted for help, waking Saigo and his officers inside. The man was trapped on the branch and in short order was taken prisoner.

The man turned out to be the not-so-blind beggar.

"He has to be a Tokugawa spy," said one of watchman. "Take him to headquarters for questioning."

The soldiers brought the man before Saigo Takamori and his Imperial officers, and they recognized him as the blind flute player. They forced the man to kneel.

"Look at me and tell me your name," Saigo said.

"I am Watanabe Tatsuzo. I have the honor of being a bodyguard for the Tokugawa Government."

"You have courage," Saigo said. "Why did you masquerade as a blind beggar and then try to break into this inn?"

"The Imperial Ambassador sleeps here. Killing ordinary officers isn't enough for us to win."

"You are a fool. How much better off would you be if you killed Yanagiwara, Hashimoto, or Katsura?"

Watanabe gazed with defiance. "Your question is stupid. Each of us can only do a little. My effort is just a fragment, but those fragments will add up."

"You have an accomplice here?"

Watanabe shook his head. "We act alone as we think best. I intended to kill anyone of importance. It didn't matter who. "

"I admire your loyalty," Saigo said. "But our victory at Fushimi ended the Tokugawa. The Imperial family is now back in power. Have you heard the proverb 'No single support can hold a falling tower?' Do you really think the Tokugawa have another chance?"

"If you were anyone else, I would refuse to answer you," Watanabe said. "But I admire you, Saigo Takamori. After our defeat, two hundred of us samurai swore to die for the cause in any way we could. I regret that nearly everyone ran away, and as far as I know, I am the only one left."

"Will you join us? The Tokugawa are dead, and too many faithful but ignorant samurai have died for them. The Imperial family has to take over, and they need men as loyal as you. Think carefully before you answer."

Watanabe answered immediately. "No. I will not be unfaithful to my cause. Kill me before the day dawns. I see the fact the Imperial family will rule, but I will not change my decision."

Saigo stood and addressed his officers. "Here is a man we need to respect. Too many Tokugawa have joined us because of their fear. They continue to hate us. Don't forget Watanabe. He is a noble man and true to the death."

Saigo bowed to Watanabe. He turned to the guard. "Behead him as soon as the day dawns."

The Story of Benkei

Benkei was the son of a Buddhist priest named Bensho who served the Temple of Gongen at Kumano. His mother was the daughter of a high court official. According to those who know, his mother was pregnant for one year and six months, and he had teeth and long hair when he was born. He quickly grew strong and tall.

Sadly, his mother died soon after he was born. Bensho had loved her dearly and thought Benkei had caused her early death. He wanted to abandon the boy altogether, but his aunt stepped in.

"If you are going to be so cruel," she told Bensho. "I will take him as my own child. He isn't responsible for his mother's death. It was just fate."

"Take him then," Bensho said. "I don't care what happens to him. I just can't bear to see him anymore."

So his aunt adopted Benkei and took him to Kyoto. Under her care, he grew into a fine boy—as strong as boys twice his age and far more clever. Unfortunately, he was also a serious boy. His grim face made the neighbor nickname him Oni Waka, Demon Youth.

His family decided to send him to study in the monastery of Eizan. There, Benkei studied under the famous priest Kwankei. Benkei made rapid progress at first, but he chafed at the rigid discipline of the monastery. Whenever he had the chance, he led the other boys into the mountain to wrestle and play fight. Of course, he was naturally stronger and bigger than any of them, so victory came easily. Soon, Benkei neglected his lessons in favor of his games and feats of strength.

Kwankei tried to reign in the boy, scolding him about how his antics brought dishonor to the temple. Benkei would listen respectfully, but the scolding didn't stop him. Eventually, Kwankei had enough and locked the Demon Youth inside.

One night, Benkei sneaked out and found a huge log. He took the log and smashed the temple's gate. He crushed the fences around the temple and smashed the shutters inside. He destroyed everything he could. The noise soon woke all the priests, but no one could stop Benkei. When he finished, he threw down the heavy log and left the temple.

He was seventeen and called himself Musashi Bo Benkei, after the famous swordsman who was also said to have been a wild young man.

But as he thought about the destruction, Benkei felt ashamed. Instead of returning to his aunt and uncle, he decided to travel. He traveled to Osaka and to Awa and back to the mainland, eventually finding himself at Shosa monastery. Benkei asked the abbot if he could stay as a student.

Among the temple's students, Benkei found others who shared his appetite for mischief. One day, a student named Kaien found Benkei asleep and wrote the Chinese character for clog on his cheek. When Benkei awoke, everyone laughed at him and no one would tell him why.

He glanced into a bowl of water and saw the character. He grew angry at the trick and grabbed a stick and rushed to his fellow students. "You must have thought yourselves clever when you scribbled on my face. Kneel and beg my forgiveness, each and every one of you. If you don't..." He hefted the stick.

Most of the students feared him, but a group of four came forward. "Why are you complaining? You were the lazy one sleeping in the middle of the day. If you keep grumbling, we will throw you out of the monastery."

They intended to scare Benkei, but instead he attacked them.

Kaien happened to come around as Benkei beat the other students. "Coward! Fight someone your own size." He grabbed a large log of wood from a fire and faced Benkei. "I wrote on your face. Come at me."

Benkei wasted no time attacking, but Kaien proved an even match. The sounds of their sticks reverberated through the courtyard. Benkei had grown used to his easy wins, so he grew impatient. He threw down his stick, seized Kaien by his belt and collar, and heaved the young man over his head.

"Apologize, Kaien!" the other boys called.

Kaien did just that, but Benkei didn't hear him. Anger had gotten hold of him. "You will die as the coward you are!" Benkei shouted. He shook Kaien as a dog shakes a rat.

He threw Kaien to the tiled roof of the nearby chapel, a height of fifteen feet. Somehow, Kaien held onto the flaming log. He rolled down the tiles, spreading the fire to the roof. Unable to catch himself, he fell and smashed his head on a rock.

He didn't move.

The breeze kicked up and fanned the flames on the roof, the fire engulfed the building and spread to the neighboring structures. Everyone scattered to battle the fire, leaving Benkei alone with Kaien's body.

Benkei laughed. "It will do the lazy priests good to hurry around for a change." He slipped away and made his way back to Kyoto.

Benkei decided that he had studied enough and needed a life of adventure. First, he had to find a man stronger than himself. Someone who would be worthy of serving. Of course, he had to prove how strong he was first. He decided he would collect one thousand swords as proof.

Each night, he went to Gojo Bridge and attacked strong-looking samurai. He never chased after those who ran. They were cowards, after all. In this way, he fought against nine hundred and ninety-nine men, collecting their swords and never finding his match. Most of the swords proved poor weapons, especially compared to his sharp naginata. The entire adventure left him disheartened. Such poor men were little proof of his ability, but he decided to get one last sword. It was stupid to give up on his goal after needing just one more.

It was the night of August 15th. The harvest moon sat above the velvet pines in the distance. Benkei leaned against the bridge, enjoying the moon's soft wash of light. The gurgle of the water below was the only sound.

The sound of a flute broke the quiet.

A slim figure approached, playing the flute. At first, Benkei thought that it was a woman. The moonlight revealed the figure's slender grace. As it approached, Benkei saw the figure was a young, aristocratic man. He didn't have the heart to attack such a gentle looking man. As Benkei wondered what brought such a different looking person out, the youth sauntered right up and kicked Benkei's naginata out of his hand.

"Just what are you doing?" Benkei shouted.

He recovered his naginata and noticed the gold-mounted sword at the young man's hip. He smiled at his good fortune and clutched the sword. The young man seized his hand with strength that far belied his feminine appearance.

The man swung a heavy iron fan at Benkei's face. "You think yourself brave, don't you?"

Benkei spluttered at the insult and the man's smirk. He sliced with his naginata but caught only air. The young man danced around his swings and thrusts. Benkei had never seen such agility. He too was by no means slow. The young man appeared in front of him and suddenly behind him with such speed that Benkei wondered if he fought twins. Benkei felt himself grow tired and realized he must be fighting a tengu or some other supernatural being. So far, the young man hadn't used his sword in the offensive. Benkei knew that if the man did, he was dead.

The young man then attacked. In a flash, he held Benkei's naginata as if Benkei himself had given it to him.

The Demon Youth knelt on the bridge. "Will you please tell me your name?"

The young man laughed. "My name is Ushiwaka Minamoto, the youngest son of Yoshitomo Minamoto. Please, stand up."

"I've heard of you. I am simply Musashi Bo Benkei. For a long time, I've been looking for a man stronger than myself. I've found him if you would have me as your faithful vassal."

For his part, Ushiwaka had heard of Benkei's great strength and had purposefully come to the bridge to find him. "I've heard of you too, Benkei," Ushiwaka said. "I would welcome you as a vassal."

From that day, Benkei changed. He gave up his wild ways and served Ushiwaka well. He fought beside Ushiwaka (whose adult name was Yoshitsune) against the Taira. Together, they won many victories and drove the Taira to the sea.

Yoshitsune's brother, Yoritomo, heard of these victories and Yoshitsune's popularity. One of his generals, Kajiwara, made sure Yoritomo felt threatened by his brother, even suggesting Yoshitsune planned to take power from Yoritomo.

So when Yoshitsune returned home with Munemori, the leader of the Taira clan, Yoritomo stopped him. Yoshitsune tried to dissuade his brother with the stories of his hardships in battle, but Yoritomo ordered his arrest. He sent a man named Tosabo to kill him.

Yoshitsune was in Kyoto when Tosabo caught up to him. Tosabo knew how good a warrior Yoshitsune was, and he doubted his ability to kill Yoshitsune directly. He decided to wait until Yoshitsune dropped his guard.

The people of the neighborhood warned Yoshitsune of Tosabo. In turn, Yoshitsune told Benkei about the man.

Benkei went off to question the man. Outside Tosabo's house, he shouted. "My Lord Yoshitsune wants to see you. Come back with me right now."

Benkei's voice alarmed Tosabo. "I'm sorry. I'm too sick to visit today," he said through the door.

"If you don't come out now, I will come in after you!" Benkei burst into the house. He scooped the stricken Tosabo under his arm as if the man were a child and carried him to Yoshitsune.

Tosabo claimed he was a poor priest in Yoritomo's service, claiming to be in Kyoto for a religious fast. No matter how much Yoshitsune and Benkei questioned him, Tosabo clung to his story. Because they lacked evidence, they had to let Tosabo go. Neither believed him, but they felt confident they could defense themselves against him.

As soon as Tosabo returned home, he gathered his men to attack.

Yoshitsune assumed he had some time before Tosabo attacked, so he drank with his men that night. He and his men all passed out, leaving just his wife, Shizuka, to stand watch. She heard Tosabo's raid and tried to rouse the men, but they were lost to their stupor.

An idea struck her. She retrieved Yoshitsune's armor and dragged it over his head. She banged on the armor, awakening his warrior instincts. He awoke, shaking off his drunkenness, and, with Shizuka's help, donned the armor. Benkei and the rest of the warriors joined him, and they met Tosabo's attack. Tosabo managed to escape, but Yoshitsune's men followed him into the mountains of Kurama and killed him.

When the news of Tosabo's failure reached Yoritomo, he disowned Yoshitsune.

Yoshitsune disliked how unjust his brother had treated him, but he also knew he couldn't win against Yoritomo. He decided to leave Kyoto and go somewhere out of Yoritomo's reach. He and Benkei took a ship to Saikoku.

About halfway through their journey, a terrible storm threatened. The waves rose high and the rain threatened to drown them. Above the darkening storm, they heard the sounds of battle—the shouts of men and the marching of their feet, the sounds of arrows whizzing in the air.

From amid the rolling waves, ghostly forms arose. They wore blood-stained, ruined armor. The forms extended their hands and wailed. A figure with a great naginata led them.

"Finally, I will have my revenge. I am the ghost of General Tomomori Taira," the figure said. "I've waited here to kill you all. Only then can the Taira rest."

Yoshitsune held his place near the railing. He faced the ghosts of the men he had slain in battle years ago and drew his blade. "Have you forgotten I drove you before me like dust? I thought you wouldn't want to see me again."

Benkei stepped forward. "Swords are useless against ghosts. It's not a good idea to anger them. Let me help them find peace."

Benkei pulled out his rosary and began to recite his prayers. The spirits' howling fell silent as his chanting wrapped them. One by one, they vanished into the sea. When the phantom general slid under the waters, sunlight drove the storm's dark clouds away.

They reached their destination safely and fled into the mountains. Yoshitsune intended to find help with General Hidehira in Oshu.

On their way, they came to a frontier station in Ataka. Benkei and Yoshitsune's followers disguised themselves as wandering priests, and Yoshitsune disguised himself as their servant. The younger men wanted to storm the frontier station.

"No, we can't afford to lose anyone. There are few of us as it is," Benkei said. He gave Yoshitsune a wide-brimmed bamboo hat and had him carry their supplies. Benkei took the lead and walked right up to the frontier station. "We are traveling priests seeking money to rebuild the shrine of the Great Buddha at Todaiji Temple. We ask permission to pass."

The captain of the frontier station approached. "I will need something to verify your story if you want to pass."

Benkei hesitated a moment. "I will read you my commission, written by the High Priest himself." He pulled out a random scroll and touched it to his forehead. He opened it and improvised an imaginary letter. When he mentioned the priest's name, the captain went to his knees out of respect and bowed.

When Benkei finished, the captain stood. "I'm satisfied. You can pass."

The party moved through the station when the captain walked toward Yoshitsune. "Wait a minute, servant."

Benkei thought they were discovered. His heart lurched, but he knew he couldn't hesitate. "What do you want of our servant?"

"My soldiers say your servant resembles Lord Yoshitsune. I wanted a closer look."

Benkei boomed a laugh. "Are you serious? But actually, he has been mistaken for Lord Yoshitsune several times on our journey. Trust me, his white skin is all he has going for him. He's nothing but trouble."

He turned to Yoshitsune. "It's your fault we are under suspicion all the time. You shuffle like such a coward and draw attention to yourself. Walk like a man." He struck Yoshitsune on the back with his staff. "Get on your knees when a guard addresses you!"

"That's enough. You can go. It was my mistake." The captain waved them off. The captain knew no vassal would dare strike his lord.

When they were safe in the forest, Yoshitsune and his men praised Benkei, but Benkei would have rather been beaten to death than to hear their praises.

Back in Kamakura, Yoritomo heard of Yoshitsune's whereabouts from his spies and sent a large army to put an end to him. The army found Yoshitsune and the men he had gathered with General Hidehira's help on the bank of Koromo River. Under the army's onslaught, Yoshitsune's small camp crumbled. Benkei, however, refused to budge. He stood on the bridge as arrows flew everywhere about him as Yoshitsune escaped. Several soldiers cautiously approached the unmoving giant. His open eyes glared at them without seeing. Arrows stuck out all over his body. He was long dead, yet remained standing guard for his lord.

The Story of Kato Sayemon

Kato Sayemon lived during the Ashikaga Shogunate. He had a charming wife and a healthy son along with a large household. The days passed full of peace and joy.

One evening, Sayemon strolled through his garden, watching the fireflies and listening to the sounds of the approaching night. He passed the window of his wife's room and gazed inside. She and his favorite concubine played *go* together. They appeared to be happy, but when he looked more closely, he saw the shadows of their hair fighting as if the locks were snakes.

He crept closer to get a better look, but other than the shadows, nothing seemed amiss. They had acted like sisters for as long as he could remember, but now he believed they hated each other. What else could explain the shadows?

He spent the night meditating, trying to decide how to best live a peaceful life. By morning, he decided the best course was to run away and become a priest. So he slipped away before anyone awoke.

His wife sent out their servants when she learned he had disappeared. By the sixth day of searching, she sent everyone in the household away to save money, leaving just herself and her son Ishidomaro. Even the Shogun worried what had befallen Sayemon. After a year of having others search, Sayemon's wife decided to search for him herself. So she took the five-year-old Ishidomaro with her and spent the next five years wandering.

One day, they entered a village in Kishu and encountered an old man. When she asked after her husband, the old man said, "I knew him. I often saw him as a palanquin bearer for the Shogun. He was the priest of Koya Temple a year ago."

Ishidomaro and his mother didn't sleep that night. At last they had a lead. She knew she couldn't go with her son. Women were forbidden to go to the temple or on the mountain. She worried about her son and felt excited at the prospect of seeing her husband. Waiting for them would be a challenge.

At daybreak, the eleven-year-old Ishidomaro prepared to set out. "I will bring back father this evening," he told his mother. "Don't worry about me."

"Remember, your father has a black mole over his left eye, just like yours," his mother said.

Ishidomaro nodded and gazed up the trail. "I know he is up there. I sense him."

Ishidomaro followed the trail into the forest. The path wound up the mountain, ending at the temple's gates. The boy ignored his exhaustion and went to the first house he saw. Inside, an old man prayed.

"Please, sir." The boy bowed. "Could you tell me if there is a priest named Kato Sayemon? My mother and I have searched for him. We both love him and want him to come back home with us."

The old man finished his prayer. "I'm sorry. I don't know of anyone by that name here." Sayemon turned toward the boy and froze. He knew the boy was his son and instantly doubted his decision to swear off his old life. He gathered himself. "I've heard of him as a friend of the Shogun Ashikaga, but I don't remember hearing of him living here."

The boy peered at him. "You have the same mole my father has." As he spoke, his eyes filled with tears. He stretched out his arms. "Father?"

Sayemon trembled. "There are many men with moles over their left eyes and even over their right. I am not your father. You need to go elsewhere to find him."

The chief priest entered. "It's time for the evening prayers."

Sayemon passed the boy who stood frozen with his arms still outstretched and followed the chief priest toward the prayer hall.

The Story of Sano Genzaemon

Long ago, during the reign of Emperor Go-Fukakusa, lived a regent named Saimyoji Tokiyori. When he turned thirty, he resigned his office to his son and retired to a monastery. Whenever a tale of injustice or cruelty reached him, he would travel and see if it was true. His life's goal was to learn how to govern well, and he had decided the best way to do this was to live as most people do. So he disguised himself and traveled among them. He even staged his own death so people wouldn't suspect him.

One day he arrived at Sano, in Kozuki Province, during a heavy snowstorm. He soon became lost. As night loomed and he resigned himself to weathering the storm under a tree, he came upon a cottage. He trudged up the hill and called out.

"I've lost my way in the storm. Please let me take shelter for the night."

A window opened, and a beautiful woman peered out. "I'm sorry. I would offer you shelter, but my husband is gone. The village of Yamamoto is not far that direction. They have an inn."

"I'm too tired to go further. Please let me stay in your storehouse at least. "

Genuine sympathy laced the woman's voice. "I'm sorry. If he was home, we would help you, but it isn't safe for a woman like me to be alone with a stranger these days. I will pray that you make it to the village." She shut the window.

Tokiyori admired the woman's modesty and caution. He bowed to the cottage and set off in the direction she pointed. As he plodded along, the storm's intensity increased until he couldn't see even a foot in front of him. He stopped and wondered what he could do. Exhaustion and the cold threatened to overwhelm him.

"Stop!" a voice came from behind.

Tokiyori turned to see a man approach through the white curtain.

"I'm the husband of the woman who turned you away. I'm sorry I didn't get home sooner. Please come with me and out of this terrible storm. I don't have much to offer, but it is yours. If you keep going you will freeze to death. "

Tokiyori sagged with relief. "Thank you."

The man led him back through the storm and into the cottage. As Tokiyori took off his sodden cloak, the woman came forward.

"I'm sorry I had to turn you away on such a terrible night."

Tokiyori shook his head. "Don't mention it. You were right to refuse me. In fact, I admire your prudence."

The man arranged cotton cushions around the fire and ushered Tokiyori to them. "I'm a poor man," the host said. "And I can't give you a meal worthy of your station, but you are welcome to what I have."

"I am grateful for anything you offer." Tokiyori bowed. "I haven't eaten since this morning."

Dinner was millet and vegetables. The ex-regent hadn't eaten such poor fare, but he enjoyed every bite.

After dinner, they sat around the hearth, sharing stories. Time passed quickly as they laughed and as the storm raged outside. It was midnight before they knew it, and the fire had burned low. The host noticed that his stock of wood and charcoal had run out.

"Please excuse me a moment," he said and left out the backdoor. He returned with three bonsai—a pine, a plum, and a cherry. "A good fire is necessary on a cold night like this and with such a good guest. I should've bought more charcoal or split more wood, but these will do."

Tokiyori recognized how old the bonsai trees were and how well tended. "Wait! These trees are too good to be used as fuel. They are too valuable to burn."

The host smiled. "Don't worry about it. When I was a rich man, I used to have many of these. Now that I'm poor, what use are they?" He snapped them apart and fed them to the fire. "If they could speak, I'm sure they would say they are pleased to warm you."

Tokiyori had guessed the man and his wife weren't common farmers. They spoke too well and showed too much etiquette. "Will you tell me your real name? You are obviously a former samurai."

The man shook his head. "I can't without feeling ashamed."

"Please tell me. I would like to know."

"My name is Sano Genzaemon Tsuneyo."

Tokiyori blinked. "I've heard of you. You are a high ranked samurai. How did you end up here?"

Sano sighed. "It's a long story. Let's just say a family member slowly stole my property without my awareness. Eventually, what you see is all I had left."

"Why didn't you sue him? I'm sure you could recover everything he stole."

"I considered it, but he died, and his son is young. I doubt my petition would be heard. But in my heart, I remain a samurai. If war breaks out, I will be the first to go to Kamakura with my armor and weapons, as sad as they are. The thought keeps me going." Sano smiled.

"Like a true samurai," Tokiyori said. "I know you will return to your old status. In fact, I will see and congratulate you in Kamakura on that day."

Morning light slipped through the window. Outside, the storm had stopped. Tokiyori stood and readied to leave.

"Thank you, but I need to hurry on. Remember what I've told you," Tokiyori said and trudged into the snow.

Only then did Sano and his wife realize they hadn't asked the traveler's name.

That spring, a call to arms rang out. When Sano heard of this, he gathered his rusted arms and armor and hurried to Kamakura. When he reached the city, warriors from all over crowded it. Each wore their most resplendent armor. Silver and gold shimmered in the sun. As he rode his old farm horse through their ranks, they scorned and insulted him. But he sat proud in his rust and shabbiness.

These men are not samurai in heart, no matter what armor and weapons they wear, he thought.

He found a spot in the ranks just as a herald rode along them.

"The Regent summons the samurai who wears the shabbiest armor and rides the most broken-down horse," the herald shouted.

The Regent must want to reprimand me for appearing in such a state, Sano thought. He urged his horse forward.

The herald led him to the Regent's house and ushered him through the corridors to a great hall. Sano found himself in front of General Tokimune. The young general sat armed with a helmet of golden horns and expensive scarlet armor.

Sano bowed.

"Are you Sano Genzaemon Tsuneyo?" Tokimune asked.

"I am." Sano kept his head down.

He heard the inner screens open and the sounds of an armored man stepping forward. He also heard the swish of silk rubbing against that armor.

"It's been awhile since that snowstorm, hasn't it, Sano Genzaemon?" a familiar voice said.

Sano looked up. "You are that traveler!"

"I am. I am also the Regent Saimyoji Tokiyori."

Sano bowed again. "Please forgive my rudeness that night. I didn't know whose presence with which I was honored." He felt a lump in his throat.

"There's no need to apologize. I remember what you told me that night. And here you are. I give you back the thirty villages of Sano that your family member stole from you. "

Sano looked up with astonishment.

"I also remember how you burned your prized bonsai to keep me warm," Tokiyori said. "The glow of that fire remains in my heart. I want to thank you. For the pine tree, I give you the village of Matsuida in Kadzuke Province. For the plum tree, Umeda in Kaga Province. And for the cherry tree, you will have Sakurai, a village in Etchiu Province."

Sano wiped the tears that flowed. He struggled to speak, but no words came. He sat overwhelmed for a time until he realized he was alone. He left the mansion in a daze. As he passed through the ranks of the men who had scorned him, they bowed. News of his promotion had spread.

So Sano Genzaemon returned home as a lord befitting his samurai heart.

The Sugawara Tragedy

Chiyo and her son Kotaro knelt in front of the Lady Sugawara. Chiyo bowed. "I don't like to think that a great lady such as you cannot step outside during the day without worrying about your enemies. You must feel like a prisoner. You endure so much since you can't see your son and daughter. Your husband didn't deserve to be removed as Prime Minister and exiled. I only wish my husband could've rescued them as well! But you will join your husband and children sooner than you may think."

"I won't forget your kindness, but I doubt I will see my family again. My husband's banishment likely destroyed him. Kotaro reminds me of my son." The lady began to cry, and Chiyo couldn't help but cry with her. Her husband had served Lady Sugawara's husband for years as a samurai. The plight of Chiyo's liege woman just tore at her. She couldn't imagine being separated from Matsuo and Kotaro.

One of their servants announced that an emissary had arrived.

The women jumped to their feet, and Chiyo rushed Lady Sugawara to an inner room just as Shundo Gemba, the imperial emissary, entered. Matsuo appeared, much to Chiyo's relief. After the exiled noblewoman settled, Chiyo joined her husband.

"Please overlook my lack of proper dress. I've been sick," Matsuo said. He faked a cough.

"However sick you may be, you must listen to the command of Lord Tokihira," Shundo said. "Sugawara's son has been found in the house of Takebe Genzo. He poses as a teacher of Chinese writing, but he is a secret supporter of Michizane. He passes the young lord off as his own son. Only you know Kanshusai, so our lord commands you to identify the head. You will be rewarded with sick leave and will be named the Lord of Harima. You need to leave at once."

"Our lord is kind," Matsuo said. "We couldn't have received a greater honor. I will leave at once, but because of my illness, I can't leave as fast as I wish. If Genzo would hear I was going to attack him, he might try to escape."

"Don't worry about that. He only lives in a hut."

"This teacher can't be a common man. We must be careful."

Shundo stroked his chin. "If they were to escape, we both would be blamed."

"Why not have your men watch the exits at night?"

"I will do just that," Shundo said.

"I will join you tomorrow." Matsuo bowed.

After exchanging the necessary pleasantries, Matsuo watched Shundo leave with a troubled heart. When he turned, Chiyo glared at him.

"How could you?" she said. "How can even consider betraying them to Tokihira? I heard everything."

Matsuo smiled as if he was pleased with himself. "At long last, I have my chance to gain the fortune and honor I've always wanted."

Chiyo gaped. Her husband hadn't given a hint of any sinister intent toward Lady Sugawara and her son. "Since when? I know it bothers that your father disinherited you. But I—"

Matsuo laughed. "What silly woman's talk. It would be foolish for me to forget our son's welfare for the sake of exiles. I do this for our son."

"What about Lady Sugawara's feelings toward her son?"

"Be quiet," Matsuo said. "If Lady Sugawara hears us and escapes, everything will be ruined. Whatever you do, don't try to stop me." He pushed past her and stalked toward Lady Sugawara's room.

Chiyo grabbed him, but he threw her to the floor. She sat there stunned for a few moments. "What happened to my husband? We had been so happy." She shook her head. "I can't let Kotaro grow up a degraded man. It will be better if I killed him and then myself so his pure soul can come with me. Maybe then Matsuo will come to his senses."

Just then Kotaro scampered into the room. "Mother, the lady is calling you. Hurry, she says!"

Tears sprang to Chiyo's eyes as she gazed at her son. She grasped his shoulders. "Listen close. The lady in the inner room is the wife of your father's lord—your lord. We owe them a debt for all the good things they've given us. But your father wants to kill the Lady Sugawara. I've decided that we need to go with her to the next world." She paused. "Do you want to stay here with your father?"

"If you die, I want to die with you."

Chiyo stroked his cheek. "You always understand without needing to be told." She pulled her dagger and raised it to stab her son.

"Wait!" Matsuo appeared with Lady Sugawara standing behind him.

Chiyo blinked and lowered her dagger.

"I guess I have played my role too well if even my wife doesn't understand my heart," Matsuo said. "Sit. Everything I've done was to help our lord. Father disowned me because he thought I had betrayed Lord Sugawara, but all this time I've worked to find his son. But with so many enemies, I couldn't well make it known. But Lady Sugawara gave me an idea."

Lady Sugawara couldn't hide the hope in her eyes.

"Kotaro looks like your son," Matsuo said.

Lady Sugawara stiffened. "I can't have you kill your son to save mine! You've already lost everything. You have to save both my son and Kotaro."

"There's no other way." Matsuo turned to his young son. "Kotaro, you are too young to understand these things, but for the sake of Lady Sugawara's son and your parents, you need to die without regret."

Kotaro looked up at his father without fear. Matsuo felt a surge of pride and protection that threatened to overwhelm his resolve. He closed his eyes and shuddered. When he opened them, Kotaro still gazed up at him with courage and absolute trust.

"Take Kotaro to Takebe's house," Matsuo said.

Chiyo grasped her son's hand.

"Do I have to go now?" Kotaro asked. "Father, will you not say goodbye and call me a good boy for the last time?"

***

The school Takebe Genzo and his wife Tonomi owned looked well kept. But Chiyo didn't like how some of the older boys lazed in the shade and hassled the younger boys who tried to study.

Not that it really mattered. She swallowed against the thought.

"His name is Kotaro," Chiyo said.

"What an intelligent-looking boy!" Tonomi said. She beckoned to the little Sugawara. "Doesn't he look clever?"

The boy studied Kotaro. "He looks like me."

"I'm going to the next village," Chiyo felt an odd pride about how steady her voice was. "Don't forget what I've told you."

"I want to come with you," Kotaro said.

"Don't be naughty. You know what we need to do."

"Why don't you come with me, and I will give you something nice," Tonomi said. "There are many boys who will be your friend here. Like this one." She gestured at Sugawara.

Chiyo gazed a long moment at her son before turning to leave. She didn't look back.

Takebe walked up. "Why don't you send those two boys to play in the inner room?" Tonomi noticed how the tension around her husband's eyes eased at the sight of Kotaro.

"Go run along as your teacher says," she said. After Kotaro and Sugawara left, she turned to her husband. "Something happened."

"Matsuo of the house of Sugawara has decided to take the head of our young lord."

"They know we have him," Tonomi said. "We have to—"

"Our new student looks identical to our lord."

"But Matsuo has known Kanshusai since he was three. How could even that boy fool him?"

"What choice do we really have?" Takebe asked. "Kotaro looks close enough that even Matsuo might be fooled. If he isn't, I will kill him and try to cut my way through the guards the best I can. But if that boy's mother returns before—"

"Just leave her to me."

Takebe shook his head. "She will have to die too. We can't risk our lord."

"This will make us demons, you know." Tonomi looked at the house. "These boys are like our own children, but heaven must have given us that boy just when we need him for a reason."

A few moments later, Shundo and Matsuo along with a number of villagers arrived at the gate. The villagers pleaded with them not to make a mistake and select one of their children. Matsuo almost laughed. As if a village boy could pass as Lord Sugawara's son!

"You don't have to worry about your children," Shundo said to the villagers that bowed to the dirt. "You are free to take your children home with you." Shundo turned to Matsuo. "We can't be too careful with these villagers. They know Sugawara is in the school. I wouldn't put it past one of them to try to pretend he is one of their sons."

He turned back to the villagers. "Call your children's names one by one. I will look at each face. Rest assured your sons will return home with you."

An elderly man stepped forward. "Chomatsu!"

A pock-marked boy ran out. Ink smudges covered his face, but Matsuo studied him. "This boy is charcoal to snow. He may go!" So they examined each of the villager boys as their parents called them. None resembled Kanshusai. When the villagers finally left, Matsuo and Shundo entered the school.

"Genzo," Shundo addressed Takebe. "You promised to behead young Sugawara. I've come for that head."

"We cannot just kill him like some animal. Please wait a little bit," Takebe said.

"We have the rear guarded by a hundred men," Matsuo said. "And don't think you can trick me with another boy's head."

Takebe studied Matsuo. "After your illness, your eyes may not see clearly, but I will give you the head you demand."

"Get to it, then!" Shundo said.

Takebe went inside and stalked past his wife. Tonomi was pale and anxious at what she had heard. Matsuo looked through the open door.

"It's rather strange," he said. "I saw eight students return home, yet you have nine desks."

"We have a new student," Tonomi said. "He—"

Matsuo glared at her.

She swallowed. "That is young Sugawara's desk."

In the next room, the sound of a sword being drawn hissed. Matsuo and Shundo shared a look and started toward it when Takebe appeared, carrying a white wooden tray. A wooden cover hid what was on it, but a thin trail of blood ran from the edge. He kneeled before the two men and offered the tray.

"May heaven forgive me," he said. "Please look at it carefully." Takebe gripped his sheathed sword, ready to cut down Matsuo the moment he realized the deception.

Matsuo gestured at the soldiers that accompanied him. "Surround them." Tonomi gazed with wide eyes as the men ringed her and her husband. Each man stood ready to strike.

Matsuo lifted the cover from the tray to see the lifeless eyes of his son.

He blinked to hide the tears that threatened him. His face hardened. Finally, he straightened and turned to Shundo. "There is no doubt. This is the head of Kanshusai, the son of Lord Sugawara."

"Finally." Shundo gestured at a soldier to take the head. "You have done well, Genzo. As a reward, you will be pardoned for hiding him." He turned to Matsuo. "Let's hurry and take the head to Lord Tokihira."

"Now that my task is done, may I be discharged on sick leave?" Matsuo asked.

"You certainly look like you need it. You may go," Shundo said. He gathered the soldiers and set out. Matsuo followed them some distance behind.

Takebe and Tonomi, exhausted from the ordeal, closed the gates behind them. They went inside and freed Sugawara from his hiding place and praised the gods for helping him survive.

"I almost shouted with joy when Matsuo was deceived," Tonomi said.

A knock at the gate froze them. The voice of Kotaro's mother floated to them. "Let me in! I'm the mother of the new student."

Takebe clamped his hand over Tonomi's mouth when she looked ready to scream. "Settle down. I will handle this."

He left her and let Chiyo in.

"I fear my naughty boy must be causing you trouble," she said. "Where is he?"

"He's playing with the other children. School is over today," Takebe said. "You must take him with you."

She started toward the house. Takebe drew his sword and tried to cut her down from behind, but Chiyo was the wife of a samurai and knew how to defend herself. She darted aside. He continued to come at her, but she dodged and used the wooden box she carried to parry his blows. She tried to say something, but Takebe kept attacking until he cut the box in half.

A scroll of paper fell out of the box. Takebe froze midstrike as he read what it said. *Namu Amida Butsu.* It was a prayer for the dead.

"Did my son take the place of our young lord or not?" Chiyo asked. She breathed hard and met his gaze. "Tell me the truth!"

Takebe lowered his blade, feeling confused. "What?"

"I know everything about young Sugiwara," Chiyo said.

"Whose wife are you?"

A voice outside the gate said a poem before she could answer:

> In my service,
> the plum blossom has fled.
> The cherry has withered.
> How then can the pine be
> heartless to me?

Matsuo entered the garden and gazed at his wife. "Our boy has done his duty."

Chiyo trembled and collapsed to the dirt, sobbing.

"What is the meaning of this?" Takebe asked. He gripped his sword.

"I'm certain it is confusing for you. Although you may think otherwise, I never betrayed our lord." Matsuo explained how he had entered the service of Tokihira to serve Lord Sugawara in his exile as a spy. It cost him his relationship with his father and his family. He explained his idea to substitute his son for Lord Sugawara's son.

When he finished, Chiyo gazed up at the sky. "Our Kotaro must be happy in the next world for all he did. But I wish he had been born ugly so he could still be with me." Tonomi knelt beside Chiyo and rubbed her shoulder and whispered to her.

"Don't cry, Chiyo," Matsuo said. He looked at Takebe. "Tell me, did he die like a samurai?"

"Without a word, he calmly readied his neck after I explained how he was going to save our young lord. He even smiled at the last moment."

Matsuo wiped his cheeks. "Our little Kotaro was always good and clever."

Sugawara entered the garden. "If I had known he was going to die, I wouldn't have allowed it." He sniffed.

Matsuo and Chiyo bowed to him. "I have brought a present for you," Matsuo said. He whistled.

A retainer led Lady Sugawara through the gate.

"Mother!"

The Sugawaras rushed to embrace each other.

Takebe and Tonomi exclaimed when they realized who the woman was. "I had tried to find you. Where did you take refuge all this time?" Takebe asked.

"I've protected her from Tokihira," Matsuo said. "You need to take her and Kanshusai to Kawachi and unite with our lord beyond the reach of our enemies."

He lifted Chiyo to her feet. "Let's take Kotaro's body home." He gestured for their retainer to go inside and retrieve the body.

Chiyo took a white shroud from another attendant and draped it over the body the retainer brought out.

"This isn't the body of my boy," Matsuo said. "We are going to bury our young lord."

The Vengeful Man

The execution was ordered to take place in a samurai's garden. The man was taken there and made to kneel down in the sandy space crossed by a line of stepping stones. His arms were bound behind him. Retainers brought a bucket of water and rice bags filled with pebbles. They packed the rice bags around the kneeling man, wedging him so he couldn't move. The samurai arrived and was pleased by the arrangements.

The condemned man cried out. "I didn't knowingly commit what I am accused of. My stupidity is alone at fault. I was born stupid. I can't help but to make mistakes. But to kill me for being merely stupid is wrong." The man's eyes narrowed, and his voice held an edge. "And I will repay that wrong if you go through with this. I will be avenged, and evil will be rendered for evil."

The retainers muttered among themselves at this. If anyone was killed while feeling strong resentment, the ghost of that person would seek revenge.

"Frighten us as much as you please," the samurai's voice was gentle. "After you are dead. But I can't believe that you mean what you say. Will you try to give us some sign of your great resentment after your head has been cut off? We would believe you then."

"Since you seem bent on making this mistake. I most certainly will."

"Very well." The samurai drew his sword. "You see the stepping stone directly in front of you. After I cut off your head, try to bite the stone. If your angry ghost can help you do that, some of us may be frightened, and we will believe your resentment. Will you try to bite the stone?"

"I will bite it." The man growled. He glared at the samurai. "I will bite it! I will bite—"

The samurai's sword flashed, and the bound man slumped to the rice sacks. Two long jets of blood pumped from the shorn neck, and the head rolled into the sand toward the stepping stone. As it neared, it suddenly bounded and caught the upper edge of the stepping stone between its teeth. It clung for a moment before dropping to its side.

No one spoke. The retainers stared in horror at their master, but he seemed unconcerned. He held out his sword to the nearest attendant, who took a wooden dipper in his shaking hand and poured water over the blade. He wiped the steel with several sheets of soft paper.

The samurai sheathed his sword and used the stepping stones to go back inside.

For months afterward, the retainers and servants lived in fear of the ghost. No one doubted the man's desire for vengeance. Their fear made them see things that didn't exist. The sound of the wind threading its way through the bamboos sounded like voices. The shadows of the garden felt threatening. Eventually, the retainers got together and decided to ask their master to have the home cleansed by a priest.

"Quite unnecessary," the samurai said when his chief retainer told him the wish. "I understand that the desire of a dying man can cause fear, but in this case you have nothing to worry about."

The retainer looked at his master, afraid to ask for the reason of the samurai's confidence.

The samurai read the man's face. "The reason is simple enough. Only the very last intention of the man could be dangerous. When I challenged him to give me a sign, I diverted his mind from the desire for revenge. He died with the purpose of biting the stepping stone. Which he accomplished. He must have forgotten the rest. So you don't need to worry."

And indeed the dead man's ghost never appeared.

Watanabe Cuts Off the Demon's Arm

Long ago, a brave man named Yorimitsu Minamoto served the Emperor in Kyoto. Yorimitsu was also called Raiko. Raiko had three guardsmen who guarded the gates of the Imperial Palace. One of these men was Watanabe Tsuna.

As it happened, the blossom capital became full of thieves and murderers because the gate guards neglected their duties. People feared to go out at night. Even the thieves and murderers feared the streets at night. Demons prowled, looking for victims to eat.

The south western gate, called Rashomon, became a favorite place for these horned demons. So Raiko sent Watanabe to the gate. Watanabe tied his helmet tight under his chin and secured all the laces of his armor. He knew he was in for a night. He made sure his sword's edge was razor sharp.

Watanabe reached the gate and began his watch just as a terrible storm struck. The brave warrior ignored the elements and the sounds of the temple bells that rang out each hour.

When the hour of the Tiger, 3 o'clock, rang, Watanabe felt terribly sleepy. He pinched himself, jangled his armor, and increased his pacing to fight against the drowsiness. Yet the feeling continued to suffocate him. He pulled his dagger from its wooden scabbard and stabbed his thigh with its point. But even that failed to keep him awake.

He leaned against the post and fell asleep on his feet.

While Watanabe struggled to remain awake, a demon watched, squatting at the top of the gate. Pleased the warrior was finally asleep, he slid down the red pillar like a monkey. He seized Watanabe by his helmet and lifted him in the air.

Watanabe's warrior instincts broke the sleep spell. He snatched the demon's wrist with his left hand and drew his sword with his right. In a smooth motion, he swept it around his head and sliced off the demon's arm. The creature howled and leaped up the post.

Watanabe waited with his sword drawn, but by the time the sun arose, the demon failed to show itself again. With his shift finished, Watanabe collected the severed arm and return to Raiko to report the incident. Raiko examined the arm and praised Watanabe and rewarded the warrior with a silk sash.

"Be sure you lock this arm up," Raiko told Watanabe. "If we keep it separated from the demon for a week, he won't be able to reattach it. The demon will certainly come for it, so guard it day and night."

Watanabe bought a stone box. The box had a lid that slid in a grove and only came out when someone touched a secret spring. He laid the arm in it and put the box in his bedroom. He locked himself in and waited for the week to pass.

Six days passed without incident, and Watanabe felt confident about his defenses. He set the box in the middle of the room and took off his armor to rest. That evening, a knock came from his door.

"Who's there?" Watanabe asked.

The voice of his old aunt fluttered through the door." Me. I've come to see you and praise you for your bravery. I heard you cut off a demon's arm."

Watanabe cracked open the door and saw his old aunt. She had her left shoulder covered, but he suspected it was because of the aches of her age, so he helped her inside and to his bedroom. She sat on the mats in front of the box and praised him until he felt pride swell inside.

"Please let me see it," she said.

"Oh, it's nothing you will want to see."

"I've seen much in my time, nephew. An arm won't shock me."

"Fine." He worked the hidden spring and slid the lid open a little.

"My arm!" In a burst of smoke and light, Watanabe's aunt transformed into the demon and retrieved the arm. It flew up to the ceiling and scrambled out of the smoke hole.

Watanabe grabbed his bow and arrows and rushed outside. The demon fanged a grin at him from its perch on a high cloud. The cloud flew off to the north west.

Watanabe went to Raiko, who called his other two retainers. After a brief discussion, they concluded the demon must have fled to the mountains of Oye. They set out to kill it and any other demon that lived there.

Yoshiteru Murakami's Faithfulness

Yoshiteru Murakami served Prince Morinaga, the third son of Emperor Godaigo. The Emperor was content to leave the running of Japan with his Regent, Takatoki Hojo. Prince Morinaga resented the Regent and felt frustrated with his family for their preference for quiet and comfort.

"The man has no business being the Regent," Prince Morinaga often said. This outspoken attitude caused trouble in the court.

Eventually, the prince grew tired of the situation and decided to leave. He and his followers disguised themselves as warrior priests and sneaked out of Kyoto. They traveled toward the borders of Yamato and the mountains in the region. Although the area was only thirty miles from Kyoto, there were no roads. He came to a small border village called Imogase midway through his fifth day of travel. The village had a wooden wall and a guard house staffed by militia.

The prince and his eighty followers approached the gate and the man who waited just outside it. The prince made sure his Imperial banner was raised to the wind.

"My name is Shoji," the man said. He crossed his arms and glowered. "If you want to pass through here, one of you will have to stay as a hostage. For mutual safety, you understand."

The prince frowned at the man's impertinence, but he didn't say anything. He wasn't going to stoop below his station and address a commoner. And Yoshiteru, his most trusted leader, wasn't around. Yoshiteru had stayed back to gather enough straw to make a new pair of sandals. The prince motioned his second to address the man.

Shoji remained unmoved. For twenty minutes he and the second bickered, until Shoji threw up his hands. "Anyone can say he is a prince these days. I'm a simple villager and don't know. You carry the Imperial flag, but you look like warrior priests to me. My orders require me to hold one of you hostage, and I'm not about to ignore those orders. Just give me that Imperial flag, and I will make that my hostage."

The prince gestured for the flag to be passed to Shoji. They had wasted enough time as it was. Shoji took the flag, and the prince continued into Yamato.

A half hour later, Yoshiteru arrived at the guard house. When he saw Shoji carrying the flag, his hand fell to his sword. "What is the meaning of this?" he shouted.

"Oh another warrior priest," Shoji said. "Your friends went on ahead of you." He explained the situation.

"You don't have the right to even look at the Imperial Flag of Japan, let alone touch it," Yoshiteru said. His sword flashed out, slicing into Shoji. Yoshiteru twisted and sliced into another man one-handed as he caught the flag with the other. He killed two more on his way through the village. He kept running through the rest of the day and into the evening when he finally came upon the prince. As he walked into their camp, brandishing the flag, they cheered him.

Two days later they reached Yoshino, and they built a fortress over the course of several months. Eventually, the Regent heard of their location and sent an army. The prince and his followers held out for two days, but the army smashed the gates on the morning of the third day. Two-thirds of the prince's men died in the fighting.

Yoshiteru took three terrible wounds as he tried to hold the gate. Knowing he was going to die from them, he hurried to the prince.

"Master, I am going to die from these wounds. There are few of us left, but we will hold them off while you disguise yourself and escape. Give me your armor, and let me pretend I am you. I will show our enemies how a prince can die."

The prince agreed, and Yoshiteru donned the armor. By the time they finished, he was weak from the loss of blood, but he returned to the innermost wall and struggled to where he could be seen by the enemy.

"I am Prince Morinaga," he shouted. "I am in the right, and sooner or later Heaven will punish you. Watch how a prince can die, and do the same, if you dare, when the reckoning comes!"

Yoshiteru drew his short sword and ripped open his stomach. He reached inside, seized his quivering entrails, and flung them at his enemies. He stood a moment longer before falling dead over the wall.

His head was taken to the Regent as the head of Prince Morinaga. As for the real prince, he lived to plot his revenge.

Objects and Talismans

The Bell of Miidera

On one of the hills that overlook the blue mirror of Lake Biwa, stood the ancient monastery of Miidera. Founded by the pious Emperor Tenchi, the monastery had stood for over 1,000 years.

Near the monastery's entrance stood a bronze bell five and a half feet high. It had once hung in the temple of Gihon Shoja in India. The Buddha had built the temple, and when he died, the Dragon King of the World under the Sea claimed it. The bell was among the treasures the hero Toda claimed after helping the Dragon King and Queen with a problem in the kingdom. Toda had presented it to the monks at Miidera.

A beautiful woman in Kyoto heard of how polished the bell was, and despite how she wasn't allowed to enter the monastery as a woman, she could think of nothing else but to see herself in the bell. She wanted to powder her face and dress her hair in the bell's pure reflection.

She waited until the priests were busy studying their sacred scriptures and sneaked up the hill and into the belfry. She gazed into the smooth surface. She saw her reflection as she had never seen in her small silver mirror. She studied her sparking eyes, her flushed cheeks, and her dimples. For the first time, she could see the reflection of her entire body.

Charmed by the brilliance of the reflection, she touched her fingertips to the bell and prayed aloud.

"Please let me possess a mirror of this size and brightness and purity."

Suddenly, she felt the cold metal move away from her. She opened her eyes and drew in a breath. As she watched, the bronze shrank away from her fingertips, leaving five pits. Seeing this, she remembered the story of how the gods would punish any woman who touched the bell. She fled.

Over time, her touch's impurity stole the bell's polish until it became dull and dark.

When the hero Benkei was a monk, he wanted to steal the great bell. So like the woman before him, he crept up Miidera hill and slipped into the belfry. He used his great strength to pull out the cross beam the bell hung from and shouldered the beam. Balancing the bell proved quite the challenge, but he managed to steal the bell away as the monks studied. He carried it seven miles to his home on Mount Hiyei and pulled it up his monastery's belfry.

The sound woke his fellow priests. When they saw him hanging the bell, they marveled at Benkei's strength. They wanted to strike the bell to sound their joy, but Benkei wouldn't have it.

"I won't ring the bell until you make me some soup. I'm terribly hungry," he sat down on the cross piece of the belfry and wiped his forehead.

The priests dug out their great iron pot, which was five feet in diameter, and made a hearty stew. Benkei ate the entire pot before he was satisfied.

"Now you may sound the bell," he said.

At the first strike, the bell quivered and rang out a mournful sound that softened into a murmur. To the priests, it sounded as if the bell said, "I want to go back to Miidera. I want to go back to Miidera."

"What a strange bell," one of the priests said. "It wants to go back."

"I know what troubles it," the old abbot said. "It needs sprinkled with holy water from Mount Hiyei. Then it will be happy with us. Bring me the water."

A young monk brought a pure white shell filled with water. The abbot took it and climbed to the belfry. "I dedicate you, oh bell, to Mount Hiyei." He brushed the water over the bell and then signaled the monks to ring it.

"I want to go back to Miidera," the bell rang.

The bell's mourning enraged Benkei. He pushed the monks away from the log striker. He dashed the striker hard into the bell, shattering the wood and cracking the bell. The bell's shriek stormed through the monastery.

"I want to go back the Miidera," the bell whispered at the end of its shriek.

The monks decided to let the cracked bell rest for a few days. But whenever they rang it, it said the same thing.

Finally, Benkei had had enough. He unhooked the bell, beam and all, and carried it up the mountain. Once he reached the peak, he kicked the bell down the slope toward Miidera and left it there. The Miidera monks heard the racket. They found the bell in a valley and returned it home. Since then, the battered bell has rung just like any other bell.

The Bell of Dojiji

Every day, Anchin read the Great Books of the Good Law. Though he was young, he had the knowledge and holiness of an ancient monk. He regularly fasted and meditated for long sessions. His skin was like ivory, and his eyes were as deep as a brown pool in autumn. He spoke like an angel and smiled like a Buddha. He lived in a monastery deep in the mountains.

One spring day, the Abbot sent for Anchin. "My son, quickly put on your sandals and take a few spares. You will need your hat, your rosary, and your begging bowl. You have far to go, over the mountain and across the great plain."

After Anchin readied to leave, the Abbot stopped him. "Remember, if any traveler does you a kindness, commend him to the gods for nine existences."

"I will remember." The young monk set off.

As he traveled, Anchin sang the sutras. Birds twittered about him. One of them chanted the Scripture of the Nicheten, the Praise of the Sutra of the Lotus, and other sacred sayings.

The monk smiled. "Sweet and happy bird."

"Oh, you of the Compassionate Mind," the bird replied.

When Anchin came to the great plain, the sun shined high overhead. The wild flowers languished in the heat, and Anchin also felt tired. He saw a marsh and stopped under a tree that grew near it to rest. He rested and watched the heat's haze glitter. Only the haze didn't move as it should. He squinted and saw a dazzling lady walking through it. She wore a robe of interwoven green and gold. Golden sandals clad her feet, and she carried a jewel in each hand. A scarlet ribbon held back her hair. She also wore a crown of matching flowers.

He stumbled to his feet as she neared.

She gazed into his eyes. "My name is Kiohime." Without waiting for his permission, she touched her right jewel to his forehead and his lips. With the jewel in her left hand, she touched his rice-straw hat, his staff, his rosary, and his begging bowl. The wind caught a lock of her hair and blew it across his face, making his heart thump.

Then she disappeared.

Anchin continued his journey in a daze. A rich traveler riding a horse threw a silver coin in his bowl. A woman gave him a piece of millet cake, and a little boy even tied the strap of Anchin's sandal. Through all of this, he didn't say a word of thanks, the encounter with the strange lady had left him in such a state. The birds didn't sing for him any longer, nor could he sing the sutras.

He completed his circuit and found himself back at the monastery. He tried to return to his prayers and studies, but he couldn't focus. His heart felt hot. All he could do was think of the lady of the green and gold robe. He murmured her name in his sleep and repeated it instead of his prayers.

His fellow monks wondered if he had gone mad.

When he couldn't handle it anymore, Anchin went to the Abbot and spoke about his encounter and his love for the woman. "What can I do?"

"My son, you are suffering for a sin from a former life. Karma has to be worked out."

"Then nothing can help it?" Anchin asked. "Are you angry with me? Please tell me what I need to do."

The Abbot shook his head. "Fast and pray. Stand in the ice-cold water of our mountain waterfall for an hour at sunrise and for an hour at sunset. This will purify you of our carnal affection and escape the perils of illusion."

So Anchin did what the Abbot told him. But his trouble refused to leave him. He couldn't be faithful to his vows and to his love.

One of his brothers asked the Abbot, "What bothers Anchin? Did a fox or badger possess him?"

"Just leave it be," the Abbot said.

The seasons gave way to summer, and Anchin still couldn't be freed from his passion. He paced his cell one hot night. He turned to see Kiohime standing in the moonlight streaming from his open window. She was dressed just as he had seen her.

"I waited a long time on the plains for you," she said.

Anchin trembled at the sight of her. "I couldn't come again and keep my vows."

She smiled and lifted him into her arms.

He tore away from her and ran. His bare feet slapped against the polished wood of the hall, and his white robe flew around him. He passed the statue of Amida resting on her lotus and dashed out of the monastery for the pine trees and down the mountain path.

Kiohime followed behind him no matter how hard he pushed himself. Her feet didn't touch the ground, and she spread her green sleeves like wings. Anchin realized he wasn't dealing with any normal creature.

He staggered into the temple of Dojoji at the plains that ringed the mountain. His knees gave out as he crossed the threshold. Kiohime's breath warmed the back of his neck, and he thought he was lost. But he saw the temple bell of Dojoji ahead of him. It hung a short distance from the ground. With the last of his strength, he crawled under it and crouched in its hollow.

Kiohime stopped and smiled. She didn't call for him as a lover would. She just stood there a moment. Then, she leaped on top of the large bronze bell and sliced the ropes with her sharp teeth. The bell clanged down, trapping Anchin inside.

Kiohime hugged the bell and crawled about it. Her green sleeves blanketed the metal. As she skittered around it, her body changed. Her green and gold robes changed to scales. Flames streamed from her lengthening lips and from her eyes. A dragon coiled around the bell where a woman once skittered.

She lashed at the bell with her tail until Anchin cried for mercy. But the Dragon Lady continued to strike the bell of Dojoji with her tail until dawn.

The Bell of Mugen

Long ago, the priests of Mount Mugen, in the province of Totomi, wanted a bell for their temple. So they asked the women of their region for old bronze mirrors.

A young wife of one of the farmers presented her mirror, but she soon regretted the donation. The women of her family had passed it down through many generations. Whenever she visited the temple, she saw it lying in the courtyard among the hundreds of other donated mirrors. The mirror had a relief of a pine tree, a bamboo tree, and a plum flower on its back. If she had money, she would've bought it back from the priests. She also considered stealing it, but the chance never arrived.

She grew increasingly unhappy about the situation. She had foolishly given away a part of her life. But she kept her pain to herself.

When the priests sent the mirrors to the foundry, one mirror refused to melt. They tried multiple times, but still it refused. The mirror kept coming out of the blazing hot furnace cold to the touch. News spread about the mirror, and the relief that decorated it. Everyone knew whose mirror it was.

The young woman felt ashamed and angry as people accused her of selfishness. After all, it was her cold, selfish heart that kept the mirror whole. She couldn't bear the shame of her revealed secret so she wrote the following letter:

When I am dead, it will not be difficult melt the mirror and cast the bell. But to the person who breaks that bell by ringing it, great wealth will be given by my ghost.

She drowned herself that day.

The foundry melted the mirror and cast the bronze bell without further difficulty. But the words of the woman's suicide letter circulated. As soon as the bell was suspended, people lined up to ring it. Each swung at it with all their might, but the bell was well made and withstood the pummeling. Each day, even into the night, people tried to break the bell. The priests protested the efforts, but everyone ignored them.

The priests finally grew tired of the constant interruptions and took the bell down. They rolled it downhill and into a deep swamp. The muck swallowed the entire bell so that no one has been able to find it. But the story remained. People took to breaking objects as substitutes for the bell, hoping for the ghost of the woman to appear.

A woman called Umegae traveled with the warrior Kajiwara Kagesue. They soon ran out of money, and Umegae remembered the story of the Bell of Mugen. She took a basin made of bronze, imagined it was the bell, and beat it until it broke, crying out for three hundred pieces of gold with each swing.

A guest staying at the same inn heard the racket and asked what was going on. When he learned of the traveler's story, he gave Umegae three hundred ryo. The inn's dancing girls made the event into a song:

If, by striking the wash basin of Umegae
I could make honorable money come to me,
Then I would negotiate for the freedom of all my girlfriends!

This story added to the fame of the Bell of Mugen, and many people began to emulate Umegae in the hopes of having her luck. Among these people was a poor farmer who lived near Mount Mugen, on the bank of the Oigawa. He had wasted his money with drinking, gambling, and carousing. In desperation, he made a mud and clay model of the bell in his field. He then beat the clay bell until it broke, crying out for great wealth with each swing.

Out of the ground ahead of him rose a white-robed woman with long, loose flowing hair. She held a covered jar. "I have come to answer your prayers as they deserve to be answered. Take this jar." She placed the jar in the farmer's hands and disappeared.

The happy man rushed into his house to tell his wife the good news. He sat the heavy jar in front of her, and they opened it. The jar was filled up to its brim with—

Sorry! I really can't tell you what filled it.

The Black Bowl

In a part of the country near Kyoto lived an honest couple. Their cottage stood lonely on the outskirts of a deep forest of pine trees. Many said the forest teemed with foxes and tengu. People thought the couple strange for willingly living where fairy children played hide and seek every morning. The woman was considered a wise woman; villagers whispered that the husband was a warlock. But the couple never hurt anyone and lived in poverty with their daughter. As for the daughter, she kept herself neat and had refined manners, but she could outwork any boy in the rice fields. She went barefoot and wore a gray, homespun gown. She tied back her long hair with a wisteria vine. The sun had browned her, and she was thin.

One season, sickness visited the family, claiming her father and afflicting her mother. As the mother lay dying, the girl cried.

"Child," her mother said with her faded voice. "Do you know you are as pretty as any princess?"

"What does that matter?"

"Do you know that you have the manners of one too?" the mother asked.

"It's not like they can help you." The girl continued to cry.

"Daughter, would you stop crying for a minute and listen?"

The tone of her mother's voice stopped the girl's tears. She lay beside her mother so she could better listen.

"Listen and remember. It's not good for a poor girl to be pretty. If she is pretty, lonely, and innocent, only the gods will help her. And they will, my child. Fetch me the black rice bowl from the shelf."

The girl fetched it.

Her mother sat up and placed the bowl on the girl's head.

202 The Black Bowl

"It's heavy, Mother." She lifted the bowl to look at her mother.

"What it will protect you from is heavier." Her mother held her gaze. "Promise me you won't take it off until the right time comes."

"I promise. But how will I know when the time comes?"

"You will know. Now help me outside. I want to see the fairy children play this morning."

The girl helped her mother out to a grassy spot in the morning sun. The fairy children soon appeared from the forest to play their games. Their bright clothes fluttered as they played and laughed. Her mother smiled.

A few moments later, she died.

The girl buried her mother beside her father near the edge of the forest. She stayed at home, mourning them until her store of rice ran out. She knew she had to move on, so she gathered her meager supplies, put on her sandals, and visited her parents one last time.

The black bowl shaded her face from everyone and also kept her face cooler than when she worked the fields. She soon came upon a village. Two women looked up from their washing and glared at her.

"Look at that whore," the first said. "She wanders with a bowl on her head so she can entice every passing man."

"She likely says something like 'Come and see what hides under this,'" the second woman said. "It would make any honest woman sick."

The girl hunched her shoulders and hurried through the village. As she passed, several children threw clods of mud and rocks at her.

She was almost clear of the village when a young man stepped in front of her. "Well, what do we have under here?"

"Please, sir. Just let me pass."

"Not without a look." The young man grabbed the edge of the bowl and tugged. The bowl remained in place, but he let out a howl as if someone stabbed him. He clutched his hand to his chest and staggered back. The girl hurried past.

A safe distance from the village, she sat on a stone and cried. Her tears slipped from her white chin and fell to her lap.

A wandering singer happened by. His *biwa* was strapped across his back. He saw the tears slip from the girl's chin—the only part of her face visible under the bowl's shadow. He stopped and leaned in. "Oh, girl with a black bowl on your head, what makes you cry so?"

"The world is hard. I'm hungry and tired. No one will give me work."

"If I had any money, I would give it to you," the singer said. "I feel sorry for you. The only thing I can offer is a song." He whipped his *biwa* around and strummed it.

> The white cherry blooms by the roadside,
> How black is the canopy of cloud!
> The wild cherry droops by the roadside.
> Beware the black canopy of cloud.

Hear the rain. Hear the rain!
From the black canopy of cloud.
Alas the wild cherry
Its sweet flowers marred.
Forlorn on the spray.

"I'm sorry," the girl said. "I don't understand your song."

"It's plain enough." The singer gazed at her a moment longer and went his way. He came to the house of a rich farmer and asked to sing. He sang the same song he had just composed for the girl.

"Tell us what your song means," the farmer said.

"The wild cherry is the face of a girl I met by the road. She wore a large black wooden bowl on her head—the black cloud in my song. From under it her tears flow like rain. I saw them on her white chin. She cried out of hunger because no one would give her work."

"I would like to help this poor girl," the farmer said.

"She sits not far from your gate," the singer said.

The rich farmer took the girl in and worked her in the fields. She worked hard each day, pleased to finally have food and a good place to sleep. She impressed the farmer with her diligence and gentle nature. After the harvest season ended, he took her into his home to care for his sick wife. The girl sang as she worked, to the delight of the family, and thanked the gods each night for her fortune. All through this she wore the black bowl.

New Year came around, and the wife had the girl clean the house to prepare for their son's arrival from Kyoto. When the handsome young man arrived, the family called their neighbors together for a feast. The girl with the bowl on her head worked her best in the kitchen.

When the rice wine finally ran out, the son went into the kitchen to fetch more. There he saw the girl fanning the kitchen fire with a split bamboo fan. "Who is this? I need to see what is under the black bowl," he said to himself.

After the holiday passed, the son remained home to court the girl. As the weeks passed, his curiosity became love for her gentle character. He decided to marry her and set up the wedding day.

When the day came, the young women of the village dressed the bride in a robe of white with scarlet *hakama*, a sleeveless jacket. They hung a cloak of blue and purple over her shoulders. Throughout this, the girl didn't say anything. She worried because she had brought her future husband nothing at all. His parents weren't pleased with his decision to marry her.

Tears glistened on her white chin.

"Let's take that ugly old bowl off," said the lead woman. "We need to do your hair." The women tried to lift the bowl, but it refused to move. They tried several times, all of them together, and still the bowl sat.

"Leave it be," the bride said. "You are giving me a headache."

So the women were forced to take her to the ceremony with the bowl on her head.

After she settled across from her husband-to-be, he smiled. "My love, I am not afraid of the wooden bowl."

The wine cups were brought for the ceremony. As soon as she drank from the first cup, the black bowl exploded into a thousand pieces. Among the pieces showered silver, gold, pearls, and all sorts of gems.

But her husband-to-be didn't spare the gems a glance. His gaze locked on her face. "My love, there are no jewels that shine like your eyes."

The Cape of the Woman's Sword

For two years into the Bunroku period, the villagers of Amakusa couldn't catch a single fish. The fishermen didn't see a single school. And they sometimes heard rumbling sounds coming from under the sea off Cape Fudo.

The villagers visited the village elder, an old fisherman, and asked him what was going on.

"I fear the noise we hear off Cape Fudo isn't an earthquake," the old man said. "The sound has to be the anger of the God of the Sea." When the villagers pressed for what to do, the old man couldn't offer any suggestions.

A few days after this meeting, Tarada anchored his junk for the night near the cape. After the sailors stowed their sails and checked the lines, they pulled their beds up to the deck to sleep. The night kept most of the day's heat. Toward the middle of the night, a rumbling sound woke the captain.

Tarada listened to the sound coming from the bottom of the sea. It seemed to come from the anchor. The anchor's rope trembled. Tarada had heard something similar in the Naruto Strait. He gazed into the night, listening closely, when he saw a beautiful young woman standing on the bow. She wore the finest white silk. A glittering haze surrounded her.

Tarada shouted to wake the men, and he crept toward the waiting woman.

"If only I could be back in this world. That is my only wish," the strange woman said. She attempted to say something else, but the sound of the sea roared over her words. A wave crashed over the bow like a hand and pulled the strange woman into the sea.

Tarada rushed to the rail, but the sea was calm. The woman had disappeared. The next morning, Tarada went on shore to ask the people of Amakusa if they had seen such a strange woman and to share what he had seen.

"Two years ago, we never heard the noises we hear now off the cape," the village elder said. "We also had plenty of fish to catch. But we've not seen such a girl. She has to be the ghost of a girl who drowned, and the noise is made by the God of the Sea. "The old man thought a moment. "The god might be angry because we haven't removed her body from his bay. Her body must have fouled the bottom of the sea."

The elder summoned the other fishermen and shared his thoughts. Everyone agreed to the possibility, but no one knew what to do. Finding the body would be dangerous. Bringing it up would be more dangerous still, not to mention unpleasant. No one volunteered, but the name of Sankichi came up in the discussion. Sankichi was the best swimmer in the village, but he was also a liability. Because he was mentally slow, no one wanted to marry him or care for him. He was also honest and religious. If he died, the village wouldn't suffer much loss, and he was spiritually ready should the worst happen.

The elder asked Sankichi for his help. The man listened as the elder repeated the story several times. Finally, he signed he would do the work or die trying. In fact, the man felt proud that he could do something to help his village despite how they had treated him.

The next day during low tide, all the villagers gathered on the beach to cheer Sankichi. One of the fishermen rowed him out to Tarada's junk. There he used the anchor's rope as a guide to dive. He swam until he reached the bottom, passing through hot and cold currents. He looked about, but he didn't see a corpse or bones or anything to suggest the girl was there. He swam a short distance from the anchor and came to a rock projecting from the shelf. On top of it sat a sword wrapped in old cloth. He untied the string and exposed the blade. It gleamed in the murk without a single speck of rust.

People say spirits live in swords, Sankichi thought. *It must be the Goddess of the Sword that makes the sound that scares the fishermen.*

He snatched the sword and made for the surface where Tarada's men hauled him aboard. From the beach, the villagers cheered. Sankichi couldn't enjoy himself, however. As soon as he hit the deck, he fainted from the cold.

Tarada ordered lanterns and torches brought over. The crew rubbed Sankichi's arms and legs until he came to. They returned him to shore, where he signed his adventure. The head official of the village, Naruse Tsushimanokami, examined the sword, but he wasn't able to find a name on the blade.

"Because the sword has been in the salty sea for years unknown, yet the blade is still beautiful, this has to be a holy relic," he said. "We need to build a shrine dedicated to Fudo and place the sword within it."

So the village did just as he suggested and enshrined the sword. They made Sankichi the shrine's caretaker. The day the sword was placed into the shrine, the fishermen brought home a catch that threatened to burst their nets. So the fish returned, and the village prospered. Sankichi was never called dumb or ridiculed by anyone again. He lived a long, happy, and respected life.

The Feather Robe

As the moon maiden flew to earth, she looked like a pearly white cloud in the sky. She had left her home behind, deciding to no longer serve the moon so she could enjoy the beauty of earth. Spring filled the air with the scent of plum blossoms. As she floated, she admired the lush new-green and the pine groves that fringed the strand near Cape Miwo.

She played her flute as she admired, filling the air with the sounds of her happiness. People wondered where the music came from, and as she floated by, flowers fell from her feather robes. She arrived over a beautiful spot on the shore and landed at the foot of a pine tree. She laid her flute on a rock nearby and took off her feather robe. She hung it on a branch and walked off to dip her feet into the sea.

Meanwhile, a fisherman sat on the shore, admiring the view. Spring birds sang from the pines. The sea danced and sparkled in the warm sunshine. Then sudden movement caught his gaze. White feathers fluttered from the branch of a pine tree. He squinted and saw the feathers were actually a beautiful white robe. He got off his rock and padded across the sand toward it.

As he was about to take down the feather robe, a lovely young woman approached him from the sea. "That is my robe," she said. "Will you please give it back?"

"I found this robe, and I plan to keep it. It's certainly a treasure no one has ever seen," he said.

The young woman's lower lip trembled. "I can't fly without my robe of feathers. If you keep it, I won't ever make it back to my heavenly home. Please give it back to me."

"The more you beg, the more determined I am to keep it."

"Don't say anything else," the young woman said. "You don't know who I'm looking for, yet you remain selfish. Fine then. I will ask the wild geese to take me back." She called out to the geese that fly across the face of the moon, but the geese overhead only screamed at her and flew off.

She called out to the gulls circling the ocean, but they too ignored her, flying in wider circles further out to sea. She pressed her hands together as she stared at them.

Her desperation touched the hard heart of the old fisherman. "Fine. I will give you back your feather robe if you will dance for me."

"I will show you the dance that makes the Palace of the Moon turn. But I cannot dance without my feathers."

The man clasped the robe tight. "Do you think I'm a fool? If I give you the robe, you will fly away before you dance for me."

The young woman glared at him. "Promises made by mortals can be broken, but heavenly beings do not break their word."

The fisherman felt ashamed. Reluctantly, he gave her the robe.

She put on the robe with a flourish and retrieved her flute. She began to dance and played a strange song from her home in the moon. She sang of the Palace of the Moon, where thirty kings ruled. Fifteen wore robes of white when the moon dulled, and fifteen wore robes of black when the moon waned.

The dance went on for only a short time. Her small feet soon danced on the air as she rose into the sky. The white feathers of her robe gleamed against the dark pine trees. She floated past the height of Mount Fuji and then still higher until she reached the Palace of the Moon.

The Flute

Long ago, a man lived in Edo. He and his wife lived honestly and gently, but they never had any sons. However, they had a daughter named Yone. When Yone was twelve years old, her mother died. Yone's father went wild with grief. Finally, he collapsed onto the floor and refused to move or to eat.

Eventually, he recovered enough to resume his winter work. Each day, no matter how deep the snow piled, father and daughter would visit the mother's grave. Yone's faint sandaled footprints glided next to his heavy impressions. When spring returned, he went to gaze at the cherry blossoms. He tied a poem on a branch to flutter in the wind. When he returned home, he planted an orange lily, the sign of forgetfulness. He had decided to move on.

But Yone still remembered her mother.

Before the year ended, he found a new wife. Yone's new stepmother despised her because of her close relationship with her father. Yone's patient and gentle ways only inflamed the woman against her more. Yone knew that the woman would try something terrible as soon as her father was away. She worried every night, yet she never said a word to her father.

One day, business called the father to Kyoto. He called Yone to him. "Come here, my dear little daughter. What gift should I bring home to you?"

She hung her head and didn't say anything. Fear welled in her. She couldn't be alone with her stepmother. She couldn't!

"Do you want a fan or a roll of silk? Maybe a red obi?"

Despite her best effort, she began to cry. He took her on his knees and soothed her. She hid her face in her sleeves and cried as if he was dying instead of just leaving. "Don't go. Please don't go, father."

"I have to. I wish I didn't have to leave you, but I will be back sooner than you'd think." He rubbed her back.

"Take me with you!"

He shook his head. "It's too far for you to walk with me. It's not like you will be alone while I'm away."

She shuddered and sobbed. "Father, if you go, you won't get to see me ever again."

He felt a chill at her words. *I'm just being foolish,* he thought. But he couldn't shake the dark feeling.

The morning he was supposed to leave arrived. Yone came to him before dawn with her little bamboo flute.

"Why, what's this?" the father asked.

"I made it myself from the bamboo that grows behind our garden. It's for you. If I can't go with you, at least you can play this flute and think of me." She wrapped it in a handkerchief of white silk and wound a scarlet cord around it.

He took it and put it into his sleeve. Then, he set off toward Kyoto. He looked back three times. Yone stood at the gate and watched him. Then the road turned, and he saw her no more.

The long journey to Kyoto proved easier than he had expected. The weather remained mostly fair. Once he reached the city, his business proved quite profitable. But the city enticed him with all of its entertainment. Before the father knew it, three months had passed and he barely thought of Yone waiting back home.

One evening, he was getting ready to go out with his friends when he found the little flute in the sleeve of his traveling clothes. When he saw it, a chill squeezed his heart. With trembling hands, he unwrapped the flute and put it to his lips.

A long wail sounded.

The flute fell from his nerveless fingers. He called for his servant. When the man appeared, he said, "Please tell my friends I am unwell. I won't be going out tonight."

After the servant left, the father sat for a long time, gazing at the flute. Finally, he picked it up and blew into it.

"Come back to Edo!" a quivering child's voice rose from the flute. "Come back, Father!" The voice cut off into a shriek and broke off suddenly.

The father held the flute out. A terrible feeling fell upon him. He stumbled to his feet and ran outside. He dashed out of the city. He traveled day and night, not even stopping to sleep or eat. Other travelers avoided him, whispering that he was a madman or afflicted by the gods. He didn't care. He only cared about the emptiness that he felt in his heart where his daughter should've been.

He arrived home, covered with dirt. His feet bled, and exhaustion made him wonder if he was only half alive.

His wife met him at the gate.

"Where is she?" the father asked.

"Who?"

"My daughter. Yone!"

The woman laughed. "How should I know. She is reading or in the garden. She might even be asleep or at a friend's house."

He stalked toward her. "Where. Is. My. Yone?"

The woman stepped back. Her eyes widened. "In the bamboo grove."

He ran, calling out Yone's name.

The grove stood empty. The wind rustled the dry leaves, and the small stream gurgled. He reached into his sleeve and pulled out the little flute. He gently placed it to his lips. Out of the flute came a thin, sad voice.

"Father. My wicked stepmother killed me three months ago. She buried me in the bamboo grove. There you will find my bones. But as for me, you will never see me again."

The father lowered the flute. He then saw the little mound of dirt. Tears slid down his face. He turned and stalked back to the house where his wife waited.

"You didn't find her?" she said. "She must be at her friend's—"

He drew his sword and cut off her head.

He went inside and dressed in coarse, white clothing and put on a rice straw hat. He found his trusty staff and his straw raincoat. *I will visit every holy place in Japan to atone for my stupidity*, he thought. He tucked the little flute next to his heart.

The Golden Hairpin

Hasunuma was a well-liked samurai who lived in the city of Sendai. The gods blessed him and his wife with a daughter called Hasuko. Saito, one of Hasunuma's friends, happened to have a son of the same age. The fathers decided to wed their children once they were of age.

Saito presented Hasunuma with a golden hairpin. "Take this hairpin as a token of betrothal from my son. His name will be Konojo. May they live long and happy lives together."

Hasunuma gave the hairpin to his wife to keep.

A few months later, Saito displeased his lord and was dismissed. This forced him to leave Sendai with his family. He didn't have a chance to even tell Hasunuma before he had to leave.

Seventeen years passed, and Hasuko grew to be the most beautiful girl in Sendai. She was second only to her younger sister, Kei. Suitors constantly approached Hasuko, but she refused to marry any of them. Her father had told her about her engagement when she was just a baby, and she wanted to remain faithful to her father's promise.

She worried that she would never find her betrothed. Hasunuma never did hear where his friend had gone. She worried so much that she grew sick and died three months later.

On the day of Hasuko's funeral, her mother placed the golden hairpin in her daughter's hair. "Dearest, this is the pin given to you by your betrothed, Konojo. Let it bind your spirits in death, as it would have in life. I pray you will enjoy endless happiness."

Two months after the funeral, Konojo visited the family at the request of his father.

"If only you had arrived three months ago," Hasunuma said. "Hasuko would still be alive if you had. Where did you all go when you left here? Tell me everything."

Although Konojo had never met Hasuko, his parents had raised him to love her. "I also kept to my father's promise. Father took us to Edo and then to Yezo Island. He lost all his money and died not long afterward. I've been working hard to earn enough to marry Hazuko, but I could only make enough to come here."

"Konojo," Hasunuma said. "I had wondered if you were an honest man. You seem to be just that, but you should have sent a letter. If you had, Hasuko would still be with us." He paused to gather himself. "You should go to Hasuko's tomb. She would like that."

Konojo prayed and burned incense before her tombstone. When he returned, Hasunuma waited for him.

"I want you to live here with us. It is the least I could do for my old friend. You can stay in the house in the garden," Hasunuma said.

Konojo gratefully accepted the offer and became a part of the family. Two weeks later, Hasunuma, his wife, and Kei were called to attend a religious ceremony. They left Konojo to watch over the house. He stood by the gate, watching them leave, when he heard a metallic clank beside him.

A golden hairpin lay on the cobblestones. He surmised it was Kei's and picked it up. He went back into the house and prepared for the evening. He had settled to sleep when a knock came at the door.

At first, he thought he was just hearing things, when a second knock, louder than before, jarred the door.

"I hope it's not some spirit coming to bother me," he muttered.

He opened the door and saw Kei. It took him a moment to collect himself enough to speak. "What are you doing back, Kei?"

"I had to see you," she said. "Since I first saw you, I loved you. I dropped my golden hairpin to give me an excuse to come back to you."

Konojo frowned and felt scandalized. "We would dishonor your father if we indulged in your love for me. We can't go through with your obvious intention."

Kei balled her small hands into fists. "If you don't love me as I love you, I will tell Father that you tricked me here and insulted my honor."

The young man swallowed. He didn't doubt she would do as she said. Feeling trapped, he gave into her intention. For the next month, she visited every night until Konojo began to love her as she loved him.

One evening, as she lay in his arms, he said, "My dearest, I don't like our love remaining a secret. We should run away together. If I asked your father to marry you, he would refuse me."

"Let us leave tonight," Kei said. "We can go to Ishinomaki and visit Kinzo."

He thought a moment. "Kinzo had remained loyal to Father." He hugged her close. "Let's go then."

They gathered a few clothes and set out. When they arrived, Kinzo was pleased to take in his late master's son and the beautiful lady.

A happy year passed.

Kei leaned on Konojo just as she had the night they fled and said, "We should return to my parents. They are likely over their anger by now. I don't want them to worry about me."

Konojo agreed. Although the year was the happiest he had lived, he felt he had dishonored Hasunuma's kindness.

The next day, they returned to Sendai. Konojo's stomach churned at the thought of seeing Hasunuma again. They stopped at the outer gate.

"I think it will be better if you go in first," she said. "If they get angry, show them the golden hairpin."

Konojo took a deep breath and walked to the door. He asked the servant that answered the door to let him see Hasunuma. Instead of the servant returning to fetch him, Hasunuma himself came to the door.

"My dear boy," said the old samurai. "I'm glad to see you again. I'm sorry you didn't find your life with us to be good enough, but you could've told us you had to go. But then, your father was the same way. Welcome back."

Konojo blinked with confusion. "I've come to ask your forgiveness."

"For what?" The old samurai straightened.

"For running away with Kei." Konojo told his story.

When he was finished, Hasunuma glowered at him. "Don't joke about my daughter. She has been in a coma for well over a year."

"A coma?" Konojo asked. "She's just in that palanquin." He gestured behind him.

Hasunuma squinted over him. "I don't see a palanquin or anyone else at the gate."

Hasunuma's wife came out to see what was going on.

"I'm not lying. Look!" Konojo pulled out the golden hairpin. "Kei told me to give this to you as poof."

"How did you get that?" Hasunuma's wife snatched the hairpin from his hand. "I put it into Hasuko's coffin just before it was closed."

Hasunuma and Konojo shared a look. Just then, Kei walked out. She showed no signs of her long illness.

"Kei!" Hasunuma said. "How?" He looked her up and down. "You've somehow dressed and even done your hair after not being able to eat or even recognize us for a year."

"I'm not Kei. I am the spirit of Hasuko. I was unhappy to die before marrying Konojo. My spirit possessed my sister's body and lived with Konojo for the last year. The Kei you thought in a coma was her soul." Hasuko's spirit regarded Konojo. "I am ready to rest, but Konojo, you must marry my sister. If you do this, I will be able to truly rest. Kei will also become well. Will you promise to marry her?"

Hasunuma recognized the voice and the mannerisms as Hasuko's. He didn't doubt that the links between the sisters allowed Hasuko to possess Kei. "But you've been dead for more than a year now. Why would you come to us now?"

"I had to live with Konojo as flesh and blood. I am satisfied with our one happy year." Hasuko looked through Kei's eyes at Konojo. "Will you promise to marry my sister?"

Hasunuma and Konojo shared a look. The old samurai nodded.

"I will," Konojo said. "My word."

Hasuko held out Kei's hand. "This will be the last time you will touch my hand." Konojo took it, and Hasuko smiled. "Goodbye, my love. Goodbye, Father. Mother."

Kei fainted, and Konojo caught her.

Kei roused a few minutes later and gazed about her. "How did I get out here?"

"Do you remember anything? Anything about your sister visiting you?" her mother asked.

Kei shook her head. She didn't remember anything about the previous year or know anything about Hasuko and the golden hairpin.

A week later, she and Konojo married. The family donated the golden hairpin to the shrine at Shiogami.

The Hosokawa's Bloody Document

Long ago, a widow and her daughter lived in the lands of the Hosokawa. The daughter's name was Kazuye. Her father had been murdered just six months before. Kazuye and her mother vowed to bring the murderers to justice. No one helped them in their search, and their substantial fortune didn't help them find the culprits.

They were reduced to begging for food in the streets, but they continued to pray each day in the temple for help. Kazuye decided that if she encountered a man to marry, she would make him join them in their quest.

Kazuye and her mother returned from their daily prayer when a group of rough men circled them. The men insulted and spat on them. A handsome young samurai named Okawa Jomoyemon happened to pass. He drew his sword and sent the scoundrels running in short order.

He sheathed his blade and bowed. "Who do I have the honor of serving?"

Kazuye gazed at Okawa, thinking that she had found the man she needed. "My name is Kazuye. Thank you for saving us." She smiled her best smile at him.

Over time, she managed to encounter him often enough that he began to fall for her. While she worked at this, an old friend of her father managed to get her a job in Prince Hosokawa's household as a maid. She worked hard and quickly won the lord's favor, much to the jealousy of the long-term servants.

One evening, Okawa and Kazuye arranged a secret meeting in the apartment Lord Hosokawa had given her. Okawa served a different lord, but his love for the girl made him throw caution aside. Kazuye used that evening to tell him of her father and of her mission.

"Please help me avenge my father," she whispered in his ear.

"I will speak no more of love until I have killed the murderers of your father," Okawa said.

Now one of the jealous maids who was listening at the door slipped and rustled the screen as she left to tell of the strange samurai. Kazuye caught a glimpse of the woman fleeing and grew anxious. If Okawa was found, they would both be put to death. She urged Okawa to hide in the armor chest, but when the lord's men arrived, they found Okawa.

They took the lovers before Lord Hosokawa who ordered Kazuye to be executed.

"She is not responsible," Okawa said. "The fault is all mine. Let me die in her place. But I also have to tell you her story." He told the lord everything about her father and his vow to avenge the murder.

Okawa's and Kazuye's honor impressed Lord Hosokawa. "Would you serve me as honorably?" he asked Okawa.

Okawa's eyes filled with tears. "I will sacrifice myself for you at the first chance."

So Okawa and Kazuye served the lord and continued Kazuye's search for her father's murderers.

A year passed, and a great fire broke out in the castle. The fire spread too fast for anyone to think of saving anything except themselves. When everyone was clear, Lord Hosokawa suddenly remembered that he had forgotten his title deeds. Without them, his family would have no claim to the land. His retainers had to restrain him from rushing back to the castle.

When Okawa heard this, he saw his chance to repay Lord Hosokawa's kindness. He rushed into the burning castle and broke open the iron safe. With the documents in hand, he turned to discover the fire had cut off his escape. As the flames reached for him, he thought that his body might be able to save the documents. He drew his sword, disemboweled himself, and thrust the papers into his stomach. He collapsed on the flaming floor and died.

When the fire ended, Lord Hosokawa found Okawa's charred body. Inside it were the bloody documents, untouched by the flames.

The Mallet

Cho and Kane worked as farmers. They worked hard to plant their rice and harvest it. Cho liked to save his earnings, and it showed. He owned a large farm that prospered each year. But he was a mean, sour man. He didn't offer tea or rice to travelers or anything to beggars. His children feared him, and the villagers pitied his wife.

Kane, despite his hard work, was poor. Unlike his brother, everything he touched went poorly. His silkworms died. His rice fields didn't prosper. In spite of this, he lived a happy bachelor life. He loved a good song and a good cup of saké. He treasured his small home, his pipe, and his humble dinner. He was always ready with a joke and gave what he could to those who needed it. But he was in a bad way, nonetheless.

"There's nothing for it but to pocket my pride and see my brother," Kane said to himself. He borrowed some clothes from a friend and went for a visit.

When he arrived, Kane saw a ragged-looking Cho waiting for him. "May I come in and talk a bit?" Kane asked.

"You can, but you won't find anything to eat this time of day."

"I didn't come for food anyway," Kane said.

After they settled inside, Cho gazed at his brother's fine clothes. "You must be doing well. I can't afford to go about muddy roads dressed like that. Times are very bad lately."

Kane chuckled. "These? I borrowed these. I couldn't come to you naked. My rice crop is ruined, and my silkworms are dead. I don't have even a penny to buy seed or worms. Honestly, I'm at my wits' end. I came to you as a beggar. Can you give me a handful of seeds and a few silkworm eggs?"

Cho made a face. "So you came to rob my wife and miserable children?" Cho made a fuss but eventually relented.

He gave Kane a handful of dead eggs and a handful of musty, moldy rice. "These are the best I have. I cannot afford to give you these, and may the gods forgive me for robbing my poor wife and children."

"Thank you, brother," Kane bowed to the floor. "Thank you!"

He left his brother, believing his luck had turned at last. When he returned home, he gathered a large store of green mulberry leaves. He waited for the silkworms to hatch. Strangely, the dead eggs hatched several lively, hungry silkworms. They ate the leaves and quickly weaved themselves into cocoons. Elated, Kane told his neighbors of his good fortune. He asked a peddler to tell his brother Cho what happened and to give him thanks again.

When Cho heard of his brother's luck, he wasn't pleased. He went off to visit. When he arrived, Kane wasn't there. He went to look at the silkworms and saw they were spinning excellent cocoons.

He cut all of them in two and returned home.

When Kane returned, he went to look at his silkworms. He scratched his head. "They look different from this morning. Like they've been cut in half." He went out to gather more mulberry leaves.

Those half-silkworms ate all the leaves and grew full size again. Now Kane had twice as many as before. When Cho heard of this, he chopped his own silkworms in half. Unlike his brother's silkworks, Cho only succeeded in killing them.

Kane sowed the moldy rice, and it came up as healthy as the best starts.

One day, a flock of swallows settled on Kane's field. He rushed out, clapping his hands to scare them off, but just moments later they returned. Each time he drove them away, they returned just two minutes later.

By the ninth time, Kane stopped to wipe his face. "This is becoming a habit." When they settled for the tenth time, Kane chased them over the hill and as far as he could drive them until at last, they continued to fly away. He fell back in the shade of several pine trees, breathing hard and sweating. He lay on the soft moss and decided to rest for just a moment. He fell asleep.

He dreamed of a group of children coming to his mossy glade. The children danced among the pine trees, as pretty as butterflies. They danced with bare feet. Their long black hair fluttered about them. Their white skin gleamed like plum blossoms.

"These have to be fairy children," Kane said to himself.

The children formed ring around Kane. "Leader! Fetch us the mallet."

A beautiful boy of about fourteen stood. He lifted a mossy stone. Under it rested a plain mallet made out of white wood. The boy lifted it and stood in the circle of children. "Now what will you have?"

"A kite," one of the children said.

The boy shook the mallet, and a kite fell out of it. The kite was far larger than the mallet and had a long tail and a good ball of twine.

"What else?"

"A shuttlecock and racket," a little girl said.

The boy shook the mallet, and out dropped the girl's request.

"Now what else?"

"A lot of candy!"

"You are greedy," the boy said. But he shook the mallet, and sweets appeared.

The children continued to request books, clothes, and other desires until every child in the ring had a treasure. Then, the boy replaced the mallet under the mossy rock. They went off to play with their new treasures. Their bright clothes and faces faded into the forest.

Kane awoke as the sun began to set. As he sat up, he felt a mossy stone under his hand. He lifted it. Nestled in the loamy soil was the mallet.

He looked around the forest. "I'm going to borrow this for a little while," he said.

He took it home and spent the evening shaking gold coins, saké, new clothes, farmer's tools, musical instruments, and everything else he had ever desired out of the mallet. He became the richest farmer in that area almost overnight. But his heart also grew kinder and more generous.

When Cho heard of his brother's sudden wealth and of the mallet, he decided to have one for himself. "Why does that idiot spendthrift Kane have all the good luck?"

He visited his brother and begged rice from him. Of course, Kane gave Cho a sackful. Cho planted it and waited for the swallows to arrive. When they finally did, he chased them just as his brother had done until he found the mossy glade with the pine trees.

"This should be it," he said. He lay down and feigned sleep.

The fairy children came to play, just as they had with Kane. They plopped into their circle and called out. "Leader! Fetch the mallet."

The leader stood and lifted the mossy stone.

No mallet.

The children stamped their feet and cried out in anger. They thrashed and raged at the plants.

"See this ugly old farmer?" the leader's voice cut across the din. "He must have taken our mallet. Let's pull his nose!"

The children set upon Cho with shrieks. They pinched, pulled, and beat him. They bit him with sharp teeth until he screamed. The leader pinched his nose and pulled. His nose grew longer and longer until it reached his waist. Still the leader pulled until Cho's nose reached his feet.

The children laughed and mocked him. They scampered away like leaves on the wind.

Cho groaned. He gathered his long, flaccid nose in his hands and went to his brother's house.

"Kane, I am very sick," he called.

Kane came out and tried to hide his shock. "So I see. How did you catch it?" Kane felt tears in his eyes at the sight of his brother's strange misfortune.

Cho shared what happened. As he spoke, his burdened heart opened. He spoke about how he had given Kane dead eggs and bad rice and about all the other bad things he had done.

"Please forgive me. Please help me," Cho said.

"Wait a minute." Kane went inside and retrieved the mallet. He rubbed it gently up and down Cho's long nose. As he did, it grew shorter and shorter until it returned to its natural size.

Kane gazed at him. "If I were you, I'd go home and try to be a different man."

Cho agreed to do just that. After he left, Kane sat in thought for a while. When the moon rose, he went out with the mallet. He walked to the mossy glade and returned the mallet to its place under the stone.

"I'm the last man in the world," Kane said, "to be unfriendly to the fairies' children."

The Mirror from Kyoto

Long ago, a man of simple mind and manners lived a day's walk from Kyoto. He had lost his wife years before. The man lived quietly with his only son. He avoided women. Even his servants were all men. Everyone lived happily in this male household. They spent their days working the rice fields, fishing, and viewing whatever nature's beauty was in season.

One night, as the man sat smoking and warming his hands over charcoal, he turned to his son. "It's about time you married."

The young man blinked at the suddenness of his father's proclamation. He chuckled until he noticed his father's straight face. "You must be joking."

"I'm not."

"But, Father. I'm afraid of women."

His father shook his head. "And you think I'm not? I'm sorry, but you have to marry."

"Why?"

"It's the way of nature. I will die eventually, and you will need a wife to take care of you."

"I can care for myself without a problem."

The father sighed. "Some things only a woman can do, as you will find out."

The father found a suitable woman named Fusa. During the wedding ceremony, the young man couldn't help but stare at her, but he had no idea what to say to a woman! He took a bit of her sleeve and stroked it. Fusa flushed and paled and flushed again. She began to cry.

"Please don't do that, for the gods' sake," the young man said.

"You don't like me. You don't even think I'm pretty."

"You are prettier than the bean flower. You are prettier than the hen in the barnyard and the carp in the pond. I want you to be happy."

She dried her eyes and laughed at his awkward helplessness. "Your *hakama* has holes in it. I will have to patch them."

Time passed. The couple grew used to each other, and the young man lost a little of his awkwardness around Fusa. About a year after the wedding, the father died and left his son all of his estate. The wealth did little to ease the son's grief. He refused to leave his father's grave. Fusa did what she could to help him. She brought him the best meals and sat with him. The son grew thin and pale despite her efforts.

She worried about her dear awkward husband. In desperation one afternoon she said, "How would you like to go to Kyoto for a little while?"

"And why would I want to do that?"

She wanted him to enjoy himself, but she knew he would refuse if she said that. "Think of it as a kind of duty. Every man who loves his country should see Kyoto. I want to know what the latest fashions are, so you would be doing me a favor too."

"I don't want to go." He gazed at his father's tombstone. "It's time to plant the rice anyway. There's no end to the work I should be doing."

It took Fusa two days of mentioning Kyoto for him to finally approached her. "I'm thinking of going to Kyoto."

"Well, what gave you that idea?" she asked.

"I've been thinking that it's a type of duty. That every man who loves his country should see it."

"Indeed, it is," Fusa said. She hid her smile. "I'll pack for you."

As the young man walked toward the city, he felt his spirits lift. He took his time, soaking up the gardens, temples, and other sights Kyoto offered. He saw shops selling the finest goods. Everything threatened to overwhelm him.

He came upon a shop full of metal mirrors glittering in the sunshine. "Such pretty silver moons," he said to himself. He lifted one of the mirrors and gazed into it.

He paled and fell back, still gazing into the mirror. "Father? How did you come here? Praise the gods, you aren't dead. Although you are still pale, you look far younger than I last saw you. Your lips are moving, but I can't hear what you are saying. Will you come home with me?"

"Fine mirrors, they are," said the shopkeeper. "No one can make better, as you already can see."

The young man clutched the mirror tight. "How much?" He worried the shop keeper would take his father away.

"The price is just a trifle. Two *bu*. I'm almost giving it away at that price."

"Praise the gods for their mercy." The young man smiled at the price and paid it.

The shopkeeper wished he would've asked for more, but he took the coins and packed the mirror in a fine white box. He tied it with green ribbons.

The young man left with the box under his arm. "Father, I need to buy Fusa something before we head home." He visited another shop and bought a pair of coral hairpins and a new silk *obi*.

When the young man returned home, Fusa was pleased to see him looking like his old self. The gifts also pleased her. The young man didn't mention the mirror. He placed it in their alcove's cupboard next to a prized vase. Each morning and evening, he spoke with his father in the mirror. They spoke at length and often laughed together. Of course, it wasn't long before she noticed how he left bed early each morning and came late to bed each night.

One night, as they prepared for bed, she asked, "Why do you go to the alcove so often?"

"My father came home, and it only cost me two *bu!*"

"I... see."

"That is so cheap to have my father back again, isn't it?"

"Indeed," Fusa said, wondering what he meant. "And why didn't you mention this?"

Her husband blushed. "I just didn't think about it."

She didn't press him. Instead, she waited until he fell asleep and then went to the alcove. She didn't see the old man, but she did find the white box and opened it.

"What a strange object," she murmured. She lifted it and saw a woman. The woman stared back at her with wide eyes. Anger flushed the woman's face.

"A woman! He keeps another woman. A dancing girl from Kyoto no doubt. Don't you frown at me, hussy." Fusa threw the mirror into the box. Despite herself, she began to cry.

Her crying woke her husband. "What is the matter, darling?"

"Don't darling me!" She sobbed. "I want to go home."

The young man blinked with confusion. "You are home with your husband."

"Some husband. You keep another woman in the alcove's cupboard. You even dress her in my clothes!"

"But, it's my father who stays in the cupboard," he said. He picked up the mirror. "See! It's him. I brought him home from Kyoto."

Whenever Fusa looked, however, all she saw was the other woman. The argument continued until one of the servants went out to ask the abbess of the nearby temple for help. The abbess returned with the servant to find the husband and wife not speaking with each other.

"Let me see the mirror," she said. She stared at it for a time. "This poor woman, and it is a woman. She is obviously troubled by what she had done to this happy household. In fact, she has shaved her head and become a nun."

The husband and wife looked at the abbess.

"I will take her with me and teach her," the abbess said. "Now take each other by the hand and forgive each other."

Fusa took her husband's hand. "So, I was right."

"Yes, you were, my dear." The young man pursed his lips. "Although I'm not sure how my father will do at the convent. He was never one for religion."

The Mirror of Matsuyama

Long ago, a man, his wife, and their daughter lived in a remote part of Echigo Province. One day, the father received a summons to visit the capital on business. The journey would prove long and dangerous. The roads were poor and poorly policed, so the wife felt understandably anxious. She wanted to go with him, but their daughter was far too young for such a journey. It also would leave their home abandoned. All she could do was help him prepare.

The moment soon arrived.

"Don't be anxious. I will be back soon," he said, "Take care of everything, especially our daughter."

"Take care of yourself, and come back immediately." She wiped her tears.

Beside her, their little daughter smiled. She thought this journey would be like her father's usual walks to the nearby village. "Father, I will be good while I wait for you. So please bring me a present!"

The father looked back, feeling his eyes warm with tears. He drank in the view of his home, his wife, and his daughter. "I will." He hurried away before he could lose his resolve.

The mother and daughter watched him until he disappeared into the morning's fog.

"You and I will have to take care of everything until he returns," the mother said.

"I will be good. Please tell father how good I was when he gets back. Maybe he will give me a present."

"Father is sure to bring you something. Be sure to think about him and pray for him every day until he returns."

With winter soon approaching, the mother and daughter set about preparing for it. They made three sets of clothes. Whenever they had a few moments between chores, the mother taught the girl how to read. The days passed quickly, and the busyness helped keep loneliness away throughout the winter.

When the father finally returned, the journey had left its mark. He was more weathered and sunburned, but his wife and daughter recognized him all the same. He came to the newly green spring garden. They helped him inside their home, where he sat gratefully down. He pulled around the bamboo basket he carried. He took out a beautiful doll and a lacquer box full of cakes.

He gave the girl the doll. "A present for taking care of your mother and the house while I was gone."

"Thank you." The little girl bowed her head to the tatami mats. She snapped her head up and held out her hands. She had never seen a doll or box so beautiful.

The father dipped into the basket again and brought out a square wooden box. Red and white string tied it. He handed it to his wife. "And this is for you."

Inside the box sat a metal disk with a handle. One side shined like a crystal. On the back of it were carved pine trees and storks. She had never seen anything of such craftsmanship. She gazed into the polished disk.

Her gaze snapped to her husband, and her eyes widened. "Somebody is looking at me. What have you given me?"

He laughed. "That's your own face you see. That is a mirror. Whoever looks into its clear surface will see her own face reflected there. They've used them in the capital for a long time. Every woman is expected to have one there. It's said that if a woman's mirror is bright and clear, her heart is pure and good. On the back is the Emperor's insignia, so you need to treasure it."

"If the mirror represents my soul, I will certainly treasure it. I won't use it carelessly." She carefully placed it back in its box.

Years passed, and the little girl grew to become a beautiful sixteen-year-old. On her birthday, the mother became sick. At first, they thought it was only a cold. But as the days went by without improvement, they called for a doctor. The doctor did what he could, but the mother continued to grow weak. Her family remained by her side, doing whatever they could to comfort her and heal her.

222 The Mirror of Matsuyama

One day, the girl sat near her mother's bed, trying to hide her worry behind a smile. Her mother took her by the hand and gazed lovingly into her eyes. The woman struggled to breathe.

"My daughter, nothing can save me now. When I am gone, promise to take care of your father and be a good and dutiful woman."

"Mother," Tears choked the girl's voice. "Don't say such things. All you have to do is get better. That will make us all happy."

"Don't look so sad. It is just my time. I have something to give you so you will remember me." She pulled a square wooden box close and untied its silken cord. "When you were still little, your father brought this back from the capital. It is called a mirror. Whenever you feel lonely and want to see me, look into it and I will be there. You will be able to see me whenever you want and tell me what's on your heart. I won't be able to speak, but I will always listen and understand no matter what happens to you in the future." She handed the mirror to her daughter. She sank back to her bed with a peaceful expression.

She died quietly later that day.

It took the father and daughter some time to heal from their grief. Their lives felt gray without her. The daughter found that her love for her mother only increased as time passed. Everything about daily life reminded her of her mother.

One day while her father was out, her sorrow and loneliness threatened to consume her. She went into her mother's room and cried. She wanted to see her mother again and feared that she would forget. Then she remembered her mother's last words.

She scrambled to the cupboard that held the mirror. Her heart beat with expectation. She took out the box and carefully lifted the mirror out of it. She gazed into its smooth face. Inside was her mother's face. Her mother appeared young and beautiful. She could hear her mother's voice in her mind, telling her again to grow up a good and dutiful woman.

"That has to be my mother's soul. She knows how much I've missed her and so came to comfort me." She felt her sorrow lighten.

Each night, she took out the mirror and gazed at what she believed was her mother's soul. She did all she could to grow up as her mother would've wanted.

A year passed, and her father remarried after his family pressured him. The daughter decided to do whatever she could to respect her new stepmother. At first, everything went well. But as the weeks turned to months, the stepmother tried to get between the father and the daughter.

She often complained about the daughter's behavior, but the father expected some tension, so he ignored her. In fact, the complaints drew the father and daughter even closer together. The stepmother began to watch the daughter closely, looking for a way to drive her out of the house. What she discovered struck her with fear.

One morning, she went to her husband. "Please let me leave you today."

The suddenness of the request took him by surprise. "Why do you ask me this? What is so disagreeable?"

"It's not you. But if I stay here, I am going to die. Let me go home." The woman began to cry.

"Tell me what you mean! How is your life in danger?"

"Your daughter dislikes me. She shuts herself into her room, and when I pass, I see she has made an image of me. She's trying to kill me through magic and curses. It's not safe for me to stay here."

The father doubted his gentle daughter was capable of such a thing. But he had also noticed how his daughter spent more time in her room alone. He didn't want to doubt his wife's fear.

"I will go and see for myself. You don't have anything to fear from her." He padded to his daughter's room.

He found his daughter peering into the mirror at what she thought was her mother's face. He opened the door the rest of the way, and she looked up in surprise. She slipped the mirror into her long sleeve.

"What are you hiding?" he asked.

She paled and gazed at him with shock. He had never spoke to her in such a way.

"Is it really true that you've been cursing your stepmother and praying for her death? What evil spirit has possessed your heart that you should be so wicked? What has made you so disobedient and unfaithful?"

She had never heard of such a thing from her father. She couldn't bear the idea of her father feeling angry toward her. "Don't say such dreadful things, Father. Please. I would never be able to curse anyone. Someone has been telling you lies. Or maybe an evil spirit has possessed your heart. I haven't done anything."

"Then what are you hiding? Why are you always alone in your room?"

She pulled out the mirror. "This is what you saw me looking at."

"This is your mother's mirror. I wondered what happened to it. Why do you spend so much time looking at it?"

She told him her mother's last words.

"I don't understand how you meet the soul of your mother by looking at the mirror," he said. He didn't understand how she didn't know she looked at herself in the mirror.

"It's true. Look for yourself," she held out the mirror and pointed at her reflection. "See!"

"Now I understand," the father said. "I'm an idiot. Your face is like your mother's when she was your age. What you've seen this whole time was your own face. You are truly a faithful daughter with an innocent heart. Living in constant memory of your mother has helped you grow to be like her." He smiled and shook his head. "She was always clever like that. I'm sorry I doubted you."

He thought about how his daughter must have suffered to turn toward the mirror so often for comfort. He thought about how she had kept to her mother's words.

And he cried.

While this went on, the stepmother listened outside the room. When she heard the father's apology, she pushed open the door and bowed to the mats.

"I'm so ashamed of myself. I didn't realize how faithful a child you are. I thought you hated me as I disliked you. I've misjudged you. Please forgive me and let me start over. I will think of you as the child I never had. I will make up for trying to separate you from your father. Just please send some of your love for your mother my way."

"I never hated you," the daughter said. "Let's start over." She paused. "Mother."

From that day on, the stepmother did all she could to make amends. And the three lived happily.

The Sword of Idé

Idé and his wife had only one child, a boy named Fugiwaka. As a samurai, Idé was often away at war. So Fugiwaka was raised by his mother and his nanny, Matsu.

The family owned a sword that an ancestor used to kill eighty-eight enemies in a single battle. They kept the sword in the family's shrine with the statues that represented the gods that had always watched over the family. Each morning and evening, Fugiwaka visited the shrine with this nanny. Each time, he had Matsu open the cabinet that protected the sword. She would take the sword from its pedestal and unwrap its red and gold cloth, revealing the unblemished steel.

At bedtime, Matsu sang him to sleep. Afterward, she would remind him of his responsibilities. "Remember, my lord. The sword is your treasure and your trust. It is your fortune. Cherish it, guard it, and keep it always."

So the days passed until Fugiwaka's mother suddenly became sick and died. After a time, Idé took another wife—Sadako— and had a son with her. He named the boy Goro. Soon after, Idé died in an ambush, making Fugiwaka the head of the family.

Sadako hadn't gotten along with Fugiwaka, and she quietly plotted for a way to have her son become the head of the family. When Fugiwaka turned fifteen, she arranged for him to be thrown out of the house in the middle of the night.

Sadako stood there when the boy was thrown outside in his sleeping robe. The boy didn't even have sandals.

"Why?" Fugiwaka asked. "Why do you take my birthright?"

"I don't know of any birthright. Go make your own fortune if you can. Your brother Goro is the head of the House of Idé." She shut the door in his face.

Fugiwaka stood a moment, hoping he was having a nightmare. But it was no nightmare. Unable to do anything else, he walked away. He had come upon a crossroads, when a voice called out to him.

His nanny Matsu appeared, ready for travel. She wore sturdy clothes and carried a staff and a sack of supplies. "My lord, I've come to follow you."

Fugiwaka embraced her and cried into her chest. "What of my father's sword? I've lost my trust."

"That isn't so, my lord. Take this gold. I will return and guard the sword. You don't have to worry."

Fugiwaka took the money and left for the nearest town. Matsu returned and took the sword from its shrine. She buried it until she had a chance to give it to Fugiwaka.

Soon Sadako learned the sacred sword was missing. She knew of Matsu's loyalty and surmised she had taken it. "Bring her to me!" she ordered.

Her men brought Matsu to Sadako, but no matter what the woman did, Matsu refused to speak. "We will see how long you remain stubborn," Sadako said.

She threw Matsu into the darkest dungeon cell and withheld food and water. Each day, Sadako went down to question the nanny. Matsu remained silent until the woman left.

Alone in the dark, Matsu allowed herself to despair. "I will die before I can bring my lord his sword. I have to find some way to get it to him."

Seven days passed. Sadako sat in the garden's house to cool herself with the evening breeze. Summer proved stifling. She saw a woman approach her, walking through the garden's flowers. The woman looked frail and thin. Her steps faltered and struggled.

Sadako sat up. "How did Matsu get out?"

Matsu stopped beneath a tree and clawed the ground. She cried as she dug. Stones cut at her hands, but she continued to dig until she pulled the sword from the soil. She clasped the sword against her chest with a cry.

"I have you now." Sadako vaulted from the garden house and ran toward the nanny. She reached to catch Matsu, but the woman and the sword vanished. Sadako was perplexed. She stared at the empty air. How had the woman escaped?

Sadako ran to the dungeon, collecting servants on her way. Inside the cell, Matsu lay dead.

"Send for the Wise Woman," Sadako said.

The Wise Woman came in short order. "How long has she been dead?" Sadako asked.

The woman examined the dead nanny. "She starved to death. Two days." She looked up. "You need to give her an honorable burial. She was a good soul."

Sadako had the cell searched, but the sword didn't show up.

***

Fukigwaka tossed and turned on his bed in the wayside inn as he dreamed. In his dream, Matsu knelt beside him.

"Will you sleep now, my Lord Fugiwaka?"

The sound of her voice calmed him. "I will sleep now, Matsu."

"Remember, my lord. The sword is your treasure and your trust. It is your fortune. Cherish it, guard it, and keep it always."

She laid the sword by his side. He turned over and clasped the handle.

"I will remember."

"Goodbye, my lord."

When he awoke, the sword remained in his hands, and he realized it hadn't been a dream.

The Theft and Recovery of a Golden Kannon

Mumashima Iganosuke served the Lord of Kii as a samurai. One night as he stood guard, a skilled thief named Yayegumo slipped into the castle and stole the lord's prized golden Kannon statue. That morning, the lord called Iganosuke as soon as he learned that statue was stolen.

"What excuse do you have?" the Lord of Kii asked.

Iganosuke bowed. "None. I fell asleep at my post. I will commit suicide to atone for my foolishness."

"And how would that benefit me?" the lord asked.

"My lord?"

"Dying won't return the statue. Someone saw the thief Yayegumo escaping with it. If you return with the statue, your sin will be forgiven."

Iganosuke bowed low. "I won't return without it."

He immediately set out to find the thief, but the wily thief knew how to disappear. For four months, he searched until he heard reports of robberies in Chugoku. He hurried down from Izumo to Okayama, where he boarded a ship to make for the town. Iganosuke felt hopeful as he heard more. Yayegumo had to be behind the difficult robberies. As he sailed, he kept to himself although his fellow passengers proved quite sociable.

One of them, a young, handsome samurai smoked from a gold pipe while chatting with his neighbor. Another samurai, about sixty years old, came up to the young man and said, "Sir, I've lost my pipe and tobacco. May I borrow yours for a moment?"

The young man proffered his pipe and pouch. "Certainly."

The old samurai took three puffs. As he emptied the pipe over the rail, the pipe fell out of his hand and disappeared into the sea. The old samurai spluttered. "I'm sorry."

The young man looked annoyed, but he was too refined to disrespect his elders. "The pipe was a gift from the lord of my clan. I don't know how I will face his anger." He paled.

"It looks like the only way is for me to die," the old samurai said. "I was a samurai of some importance when I was young. I know how to conduct myself. It was my carelessness." The old man drew his right arm and shoulder from under his kimono and reached for his short sword.

The young man seized the old samurai's sword hand. "That won't help. Then I would also have to explain your death. I lost the pipe by lending it to you. I am the one who should die as an apology."

Iganosuke stepped forward. "Don't be so quick to die. I am a good diver and swimmer. And the water isn't deep. If you would allow me, I will try to find the pipe."

Neither of the samurai could swim, so the thought had never occurred to them. "Please try," said the young man.

Iganosuke stripped and dived into the sea. He swam to the stony bottom. Luckily the water was clear. He quickly found the pipe gleaming between smoothed stones. At the same time, he saw something else shining next to the pipe. He thrust the pipe between his teeth and seized the other object. To his astonishment, he pulled out the golden statue of Kannon he was searching for.

Iganosuke made for the surface and scrambled back onboard. He handed the pipe to the grateful young samurai. Both samurai bowed to the ship's planks. As Iganosuke dressed, he said, "I am a retainer of the Lord of Kii. I came to hunt for the thief Yayegumo that stole this very statue." He gestured at the statue sitting beside him. "As fortune had it, your pipe landed right next to it."

"And my name is Matsure Fujiye of Takamatsu," the old samurai said. "Only a month ago the same Yayegumo tried to steal a great treasure from my lord's bedroom. He managed to escape me, but I chased him to the shore just before a storm arose. I caught a few glimpses of something golden stuffed in his kimono. I watched him try to escape on a boat only to wreck. We found his body some days later, but he had nothing on him. Your Kannon must have been what I saw."

Iganosuke returned to the Lord of Kii and accounted of his good fortune. Pleased to have his family's statue returned, the lord rewarded Iganosuke.

White Saké

On the night Lake Biwa and Mount Fuji were born, Yurine became sick. Yurine was a poor man who loved his rice wine. He became so weak that he thought he was dying and wanted to drink one last cup before he did.

"Koyuri!" he called.

His son of fourteen years came in.

"Fetch me some saké," Yurine said.

Koyuri frowned. They had run out of rice wine a while ago, and he had spent their last coin on medicine. He didn't tell his father any of this. Not knowing what else to do, he took his father's wine gourd and went down to the beach to think.

"Koyuri!" an unfamiliar voice called his name.

He stopped and looked around. He gazed up at the pine trees that fringed the shore. Beneath them sat a man and a woman. Their red hair shimmered in the sunlight. Even their skin was the same bright red. They wore clothes made of green seaweed. Koyuri froze, feeling his heart thump. He had never seen such strange people.

"Koyuri, my boy. Please come over here," the man said as he gestured.

Koyuri clutched the gourd and crept closer. The couple drank saké from large flat cups. Beside them sat an immense rice wine jar. The saké was whiter than any he had seen before. Thinking of his father, he lifted his gourd.

"Could I have a little of your saké?" Koyuri told them about his father's illness.

The red man smiled. "Certainly." He took the gourd and filled it. "That's why we called you over here in the first place."

"Thank you. Thank you!" Koyuri bowed to the ground.

He dashed home and burst through the door. "Father! I've got you some saké, the best I have ever seen. I'm sure it tastes as good as it looks."

The old man struggled to sit up. He drank from the gourd. After a long pull, he grinned. "That is indeed the best I've ever tasted."

The next day, he asked Koyuri for more. The boy returned to his two red friends, who were happy to refill the gourd. This continued for the next five days. Each day, his father grew stronger.

Throughout this time, Yurine's neighbor, Mamikiko, watched. He too was fond of saké but couldn't afford it. As he saw Koyuri bring a fresh gourd each day, he grew jealous.

"Koyuri! Come here, boy," Mamikiko said.

"What can I do for you?" Koyuri had just returned from his red friends.

"Give me your gourd." Mamikiko snatched it from the boy. "Do you think your father is the only man good enough for saké?" He took a long drink and spat it out. His face twisted, and he wiped at his mouth with the back of his hand. "What filth is this? Do you dare give me this while saving the best for your father"? He dumped the gourd.

He punched Koyuri in the ribs. The boy doubled over with a gasp. Mamikiko drove another fist into the boy's ribs. "I'll keep beating you if I don't get some good saké."

"I'll take you," Koyuri managed. "I'll take you."

The boy led the way, trying not to cry from pain and from losing his father's drink. Koyuri's friends were still drinking when they came to them.

"Koyuri, why are you crying and why are you back so soon?" the red man asked. "Did you father drink it already? He must like it as much as we do."

"No, my father hasn't—"

"I am as fond of saké as anyone," Mamikiko said. "Will you give me some?"

"Help yourself," the red man gestured at the jar.

Mamikiko filled the largest of the cups and smelled it. He smiled at the scent. He took a long pull and spat it out in a cloud. "What is the meaning of this?" He spluttered and wiped his mouth.

"So you don't know who I am," the red man said. "I serve the Dragon King of the Sea and live on the bottom of the ocean in the Sea Dragon's Palace. We heard that a sacred mountain had appeared, so I came to see it." He smiled at Koyuri. "That's when Koyuri came to me with a sad tale. You see, the saké you drank and spat everywhere is sacred. It tastes good if you are righteous. It tastes terrible to the wicked. It's a poison to them."

The red man skewered Mamikiko with his gaze. "And you are indeed a greedy, selfish man." He and his friend laughed.

"Poison?" Mamikiko grabbed his throat. He fell to the ground and bowed to them. "Please give me the remedy. I don't want to die. Please forgive me. I will change."

The red man pulled out a case and pinched a small amount of powder from it. "Take this with some saké. It's better to repent and change even in your old age than not at all."

Mamikiko drank the white saké this time and found the powder had made it sweet. He felt stronger and well. "Koyuri, I'm sorry. Please take me to your father so I may apologize to him too."

"Koyuri." The red man held out a slip of paper. "This is the recipe for our saké. Give this to your father."

Some years later, Mamikiko and Yurine built a hut on the southern base of Mount Fuji. There they brewed white saké from the recipe Koyuri received. Mamikiko and Yurine lived for 300 years, making their saké for everyone who wanted it.

Personal Stories

How an Old Man Lost His Growth

Long ago lived a man with a lump the size of a tennis ball growing out of his right cheek. He did everything he could to get rid of it, but not a single doctor or treatment helped. The lump grew until it was nearly as large as his face. He resigned himself to carrying it for the rest of his life.

One day, his family ran out of firewood, so his wife sent him out to chop more. Autumn colored the mountain, and the air smelled fresh. He took his time, enjoying the pleasant weather. The afternoon passed as he chopped wood.

After gathering his pile, he hadn't trudged far when a storm suddenly blew in. The wind and rain grew fierce. He took shelter in the hollow trunk of a tree. The thunder shook the forest floor, and the heavens seemed to be on fire from the lightning. The old man wondered if perhaps the end of everything had come, but the sky soon cleared. The red of the setting sun painted the damp and battered forest.

He was about to leave his shelter when he heard footsteps. He thought his friends had come looking for him. He gazed around the tree only to see hundreds of demons approaching him. Some were as large as giants. Others had eyes that were larger than any part of their bodies. Some had absurdly long noses, and still others had mouths that extended from ear to ear. Horns grew out of their foreheads.

The old man lost his balance and fell out of the hollow. He lunged back into the tree, praying that they hadn't seen him. He was wondering what he was going to do and how he was going to get home . Suddenly, the demons began to sing.

Curiosity overwhelmed the old man's fear. "Just what are they doing?" He whispered and gazed around the tree.

The leader of the demons sat just beside the tree's opening. The other demons sat just a short distance away drinking, dancing, and eating. Despite his earlier fear, the old man found the demons' antics amusing.

He laughed. *I've never seen anything so strange.* He became so entranced by the sight that he stepped out of the tree to watch.

The demon leader drank from his large rice-wine cup and watched one of the demons dance. "Your dance is getting boring. Isn't there anyone who can dance better?"

The old man didn't entirely understand what possessed him, but he had been an expert dancer in his youth. It had been decades since he had had a chance to dance. Before he could think about it any further, he found himself dancing among the demons. When he realized what he had done, he knew his life depended on how well he pleased the demon leader. He poured his skill into his dance and forced his old limbs to move.

"He dances well," the demon leader said. "I've never seen such a skilled dancer."

When the old man finished, the leader said, "Thank you for such an amusing dance. Please drink a cup of rice wine with us." He pushed his large cup at the old man.

The old man bowed. "Thank you for your kindness, my lord. I fear I have only disturbed your party with my unskillful dancing."

"Nonsense. You must visit us again and dance for us."

"Thank you. I will," the old man said.

"Then you will come tomorrow?" the leader asked.

"I will."

"You must leave us something as a pledge," a large demon said.

The old man felt a chill. His enthusiasm disappeared. "Whatever you like." What else could he say?

The leader looked at his fellow demons. "What should he leave us?"

"It should be his most important possession," a demon with a huge mouth said. "Humans believe a growth like he has on his cheek is good fortune. Let's take that from him so he will be certain to come back for it."

"Clever." The leader nodded. He stretched out his hairy, clawed hand and took the lump from the old man's cheek. The growth came off as if the demon had plucked a plum from the tree. The old man didn't feel anything except a small tug.

The demons vanished.

The old man touched his smooth right cheek and smiled.

The moon shined like a slice out of the night sky. The old man used its light to hurry home, patting and rubbing his cheek all the while. He danced and leaped as he worked his way down from the mountain.

He burst through his front door. His wife paced and wrung her hands. "I was so worried. Where were you?" She turned to him. "What took—" She stared.

"Handsome, aren't I?" The old man grinned at her shocked expression. He told her about his adventure.

The next day, their wicked neighbor called on the old man. Their neighbor also suffered from a growth on his left cheek. When the old man arrived, the neighbor blinked. "It is really gone! I had heard the rumors but...how did you do it?"

The old man accounted his adventure and described where the neighbor could find the hollow tree. The neighbor went up into the mountain soon after. He found the tree and settled in to wait until twilight. Just as he had been told, the demons appeared and held a feast.

After a little while, the demon leader gazed around the forest. "It's time for the old man to come as he promised. So where is he?"

The disagreeable neighbor ran from his hiding place and kneeled before the demon. "I've been waiting for you to speak."

"Ah, you are the old man from yesterday. Thank you for coming, you must dance for us soon."

The neighbor had never danced before, but this didn't trouble him. After all, they were only demons. What could they know of dancing? So he hopped about, waving his arms and stamping his feet, imitating every dance he had seen.

"What happened? He dances worse than any of us," one demon said.

"Enough," the demon leader said. "Your dance is quite different from yesterday. I don't want to see such dancing again. Take your pledge back and go away."

The leader took out the old man's lump and threw it at the neighbor's right cheek. The lump attached itself as if it had grown there all the while. The wicked neighbor tugged at it whirling around as he did, but he might as well have tried to tug off his foot. Exhausted and hurting, he realized the demons were gone, but the lumps remained on both his cheeks.

How Masakuni Regained His Sight

Awanokami Masakuni was a swordsmith that lived in Kyoto. He lived with his beautiful little daughter, Ai. Ai was fourteen and thought of no one except her father.

Masakuni became renowned for his skill, making the other swordsmiths jealous. One night, Ai awoke to a terrible cry from her father. She found him writhing on the floor in agony, clutching his right eye. One of his rivals had slipped into the house and stabbed it out. Ai went to find the local doctor, but nothing could save her father's eye.

"Who did this to you, Father?" she asked as the doctor worked.

Masakuni gritted his teeth. "It happened before I could see who it was. It was dark." He laid his massive hand on Ai's petite hand. "We will have to return to our village now."

"But you can still make your blades, can't you?"

"Not with just one eye. At least, not with the quality for which people know me."

Several days later, they returned to his native village, Ohara in Awa Province. They had barely been there for a week when Masakuni's left eye became inflamed. His sight began to fade.

Ai sorrowed. For her father to lose both his eyes was terrible. She didn't know what she could do. He had already lost his art. She waited on him day and night: she cooked and made sure he had everything he needed. But frustration still boiled in her. His left eye grew worse.

In January, she started going up the rocky mountain of Shiratake to the shrine dedicated to Fudo to pray for knowledge that would cure her father. After she prayed, she stripped and went to the icy waterfall to meditate.

For three months she did this every day, yet her prayers remained unanswered. However, she didn't lose heart. One day, she went to the waterfall in a terrible freeze. Ice coated all the rocks, and even the great waterfall had reduced to a trickle. She stripped and slipped under the trickle, but after just a few moments she passed out, fell into the basin, and hit her head.

Just then, an old man and his servant were climbing the mountain to look at the iced waterfall. He saw Ai rolling in the half-frozen water. They pulled her out and rubbed her limbs until some heat returned. Blood flowed from the wound on her head. The servant lit a fire. They warmed her clothes and piled them on her. After about twenty minutes, Ai opened her eyes.

"Did you try to kill yourself?" the old man asked.

"No." Ai whispered. "I was praying under the waterfall to save the eyesight of my father. This is the hundredth day I've done this. And I will keep coming here until my father is healed." She told the story of how her father was blinded.

"Today might be the answer to your prayer," the old man said. "I am Dr. Uozumi, the chief doctor of Kyoto. I am the only one who has a full degree in the Medical Sciences of the Dutch. I will see what I can do for your father. Put on the rest of your clothes, and let's pay him a visit."

Ai wanted to run down the mountain to her father. She often had to stop and wait for the old man despite the wound on her head.

After they arrived at the house, Uozumi examined Masakuni. Luckily, he had the Dutch medicines he needed. Each day, the doctor tended Ai's father until on the tenth day Masakuni's eye was cured.

"Thank you," Masakuni said. "And thanks to the mercy of Fudo-sama." Masakuni decided to make two swords as a tribute to Fudo and to Dr. Uozumi. He purified himself by eating a vegan diet and bathing in cold water for ten days before he got to work.

Despite Masakuni losing his right eye, the swords impressed Dr. Uozumi with their quality and artistry. "You need to come back with me to Kyoto."

"I can't. My days of smithing are over," Masakuni said.

"Nonsense. This is proof your blacksmith skills remain," Uozumi lifted the sword. "Besides, do you want Ai to waste her beauty away here? She could thrive in Kyoto." He thought a moment. "She would do well as a maid for the Lord of Karasumaru."

"Whatever you think is best, Father," Ai said.

Masakuni thought a long moment. "All right. We will go."

Ai entered the service of the Lord of Karasumaru and was happy. Five years later, Masakuni died and was buried in the cemetery of Toribeyama.

Little Silver's Dream of the Shoji

Little Silver didn't care for strange animal stories. Whenever her nurse told her ghost stories at night, she feared the creatures would come for her.

"You don't have to be afraid," the nurse said one night. "Draw pictures of a tapir and lay it on your pillow. It will keep you from having bad dreams. The tapir will eat them!"

Little Silver did just that and settled to sleep.

She dreamed she was in Osaka. There she boarded a ship and sailed to the southwest. She gazed over the rail and saw ghosts of men and women shimmering in the sea. They didn't seem aware of her or of being water-ghosts. They ran and played. Others talked with each other. Once in a while, the ship would slice over a ghost, but it would join back together as if nothing had happened.

One ghost neared the ship. "Please give me a water dipper," it said in a squeaky voice.

Little Silver wondered why a ghost needed a dipper when one of the sailors on the ship appeared with one in hand. The dipper had no bottom! The sailor handed it to the ghost without a word. This happened several times. Then the ghosts began to use the dippers to bail water into the ship!

"If those dippers had bottoms," Little Silver said, "We'd be in trouble."

When dawn arrived, the ghosts disappeared.

The ship passed an island lined with large rocks of red coral. A large ceramic jar stood on the beach. Long-handled ladles surrounded it. Piles of red-lacquered wine cups also rested on the sand. Little Silver saw a group of wizen people walking from the hills. Some of the people stooped with age and had crooked, dark faces that made Little Silver think of hickory. They all had long red hair that cascaded down their backs. Their faces had the permanent flush of hard drinking. They arrived at the jar and began using the ladles to fill the cups. The scent of the rice wine burned Little Silver's nose.

After drinking for a time, the strange people began to dance. The eldest twirled their hair and pirouetted around the jar. The younger people clapped and waved their ladles. Their red hair streamed in the wind. This continued for a while, with breaks for more drinks between.

Finally, they threw down their cups and ladles. "Now to work!" shouted the oldest creature.

They scattered across the beach. Some gathered shells and burned them to make lime. Others made mortar, and still others made glue by boiling fish skin. A few younger creatures dived into the sea and returned with red coral. Little Silver soon realized that they were building up the red coral cliffs, and that the cliffs were actually some sort of house.

"What is that house for?" she asked one of the sailors.

"Oh that? That's the storehouse for the King of the Shoji. He stores the treasures of life, health, happiness, and property that men throw away or trade for saké."

Little Silver remembered her father talking about a neighbor drinking like a Shoji. Mr. Matsu had once been rich but had all his property "go to the Shoji."

Suddenly, the ship struck a rock. The sudden lurch in her dream jerked her awake. "Tapir, come eat!" She cried out, still half asleep. She fell back to her pillow and back to her peaceful sailing dream.

The next morning, she laughed at how the ghosts dipped water for nothing and at her nurse for thinking a tapir drawing could keep dreams away.

Scents and Jingles

A rich merchant named Kisaburo lived in Edo. He lived as a miser and moved next door to Kichibei's shop. Kichibei caught and cooked eels for a living. During the night, he caught them. During the day, he cooked them. He cut the eels into pieces three to four inches long and laid them on an iron grill over hot charcoal that remained warm by his constant fanning.

Kisaburo wanted to save money, so he took his seat at meal time close to his neighbor's door. He ate his boiled rice and smelled the grilling eels. He figured he could imagine he was eating the eel. Sometimes he could even taste them from the scent. The amount of money he saved doing this pleased him.

Kichibei learned of this and wondered if he could charge his stingy neighbor for the smell of his eels. He made out a bill and presented it to Kisaburo. Strangely, Kisaburo seemed pleased with this. He called to his wife to bring his iron money box.

He pulled several coins from the box and jingled them. Then he touched the bill with his fan and bowed.

He smiled. "There we go, Kichibei. We're even."

"What? You need to pay me!"

"I just did. You charged me for the scent of your eels. I've paid you with the sound of my money."

Shiragiku, the White Chrysanthemum

On the outskirts of a remote village nestled next to Mount Aso, a temple bell rang. Not far from the temple stood a small cottage where a fifteen-year-old girl called Shiragiku lived. She wrung her hands and gazed down a road festooned with fallen leaves. Her slender figure quivered with her worry.

Some days ago, her father had gone out to hunt. It wasn't like him to be gone for so long without a word. After all, he was all she had. She watched and listened carefully for any sign of her father. But everything remained the same. She heard the steady flow of water in the bamboo pipes that brought it to her house. The wind rustled the fading leaves. As she waited, mist rolled in, and a quiet rain began to fall.

"What if he is hurt and alone somewhere?" she whispered to herself. "I need to go find him."

She hesitated only a moment longer before gathering her things. She put on her straw rain hat and picked up her walking stick. She stuffed a small bag with food and set out down the mountain road her father had taken. As she trudged, the rain stopped. The moon soon shone through the clouds.

She had walked for two hours when she came upon an old Buddhist temple illuminated by the moonlight. Chanting slipped between the pines and cryptomerias. She wondered who would be chanting in such a remote place so deep in the night, so she crept closer. The temple sagged. Weeds grew throughout the garden and between the paving stones. Even the posts of the torii gate shook in the wind.

Shiragiku knocked on the battered wooden door. The shuttered window beside the door opened, and a young monk poked his head out. His eyes widened, but he said nothing. He only stared. The girl grew self-conscious, not realizing that her beauty captivated him. Her skin shone like snow, and her black hair, disheveled as it was by the wind, tantalized.

"I'm looking for my father. He went hunting and hasn't returned. Has anyone come to this temple in the last few days?" Shiragiku asked.

Her sad eyes made him wonder if she was an angel. "Who are you? Where did you come from?" he asked.

The wind rattled the temple, and the girl pulled her clothes closer. "I'm the daughter of a samurai from Kumamoto. My house was once rich and happy, but when the war broke out, that changed." She closed her eyes against the memories. "Even the grass of my old home smelled of blood. My father went to war. Mother and I escaped here while Father fought with the rebels. Mother hoped father would return, but she died from her grief before he did. I was left alone."

She opened her eyes and smiled sadly. "Father came back last spring, but he never got over Mother's death. The other day he went out to hunt and hadn't returned. So I went out to find him."

"And what is your family's name? What is yours?" the monk asked.

"Honda is my family's name. Shiragiku is mine, and my father is Aki-toshi."

"Do you have any brothers you could go to for help?" the monk asked.

"I had an adopted brother named Akihide, but he left us so long ago I don't remember him. Mother had me memorize her messages for him in case I met him."

The young monk looked sympathetic. "Poor girl, your story is a sad one. Why don't you rest here for the night? Another storm is coming." He disappeared, and the door opened.

The monk's voice seemed familiar to Shiragiku. As he settled her into the temple and brought her food, his movements made him seem even more familiar. Her runaway brother would be about the same age as the monk.

"Can I do anything else for you?" the monk asked.

She bowed to the floor. "Thank you, but I'm fine now. Please forgive me for causing you trouble."

"It's no trouble. Good night."

After the monk left, Shiragiku knelt at the shrine at the end of the room. Statues of Amida Buddha and Kannon stood there. She prayed for help to find her father and for her brother to return. After she finished, she went to sleep.

She dreamed of her father.

"Shiragiku, I've fallen over a cliff. I'm trapped in a chasm. The brambles and bamboo grow too think for me to climb out, and I fear I won't live for much longer. So I came to see you one last time."

She awoke screaming for her father. Morning's light streamed through the cracks of the temple. She found a simple breakfast of rice and bean soup waiting for her. She gulped it down and left before she saw the monk. The vivid dream pushed her deeper into the forest. She shivered with the cold, and she trusted that her connection with her father would guide her.

At last, she reached the top of the mountain. She sat down on a boulder to catch her breath just as the mist began to clear. She gazed about, hoping to see some trace of her father. The mountains didn't offer any help.

A sudden noise startled her. She twisted just in time to see a group of thieves rush at her. Their callused hands gripped her. Her cries for help echoed, but she knew no one would hear her so far out. The thieves cuffed her and dragged her down the mountain toward a house. Moss covered the walls, but the house was otherwise built so tight that not a single slip of light invaded it.

The chief of the thieves leaned against the house. "You've brought quite a prize this time."

The thieves untied Shiragiku's hands and led her into the house. A meal of rice and fish and wine waited for them. They sat down and ate. The leader passed some food to her. Hungry from the long walk, she ate.

After she finished, he turned to her. "It must have been fate for you to come to me. So now you should consider me your husband and serve me all your life. I have a good *koto*. You will play it to show your gratitude for our marriage. I like music. But if you disobey me, I will make your life as hard as climbing a mountain of swords."

One of the men brought her the *koto*. Tears fell as she played and sang of her pain. Several of the thieves whispered in wonder at what sort of life she had lived to play something so sad.

Outside the house in the shadow of a tree stood a young man listening to the music. He recognized the voice. As soon as the music ended, he rushed into the house with a short sword. In a few moments, the leader lay dead. Two more lay dying, and the rest had fled before the young man's anger. He took Shiragiku by the hand and led her to the moonlit window.

The young man was the priest of the temple she had visited the night before.

"I am your brother, Akihide," he said. "You obviously remember how I ran away when you were three. I had angered Father, so I ran away to the capital. I reached it as the cherry blossoms fell from the trees. I studied under a priest and repented of my foolishness. I remembered our parents' love and regretted what I had done to them. Eventually, homesickness and that regret drove me to return here. I had planned to beg for forgiveness, but the war had changed everything. When I finally made it home, it was as you remember. Ruined and bloodied. I thought everyone had died, so I traveled until I came to the temple you found me within. I wanted to be alone with my regret and prayers."

He smiled. "I was praying when you arrived. I planned to tell you who I was that morning, but you had left, so I followed you." He paused. "If I had been a better son, I would've spared Mother, Father, and you all that you suffered." His grip tightened on his sword.

Shiragiku grabbed his hands to keep him from stabbing himself. "Father forgave you. He always hoped you would return. So did I. Mother hoped you would keep the family shrine and continue the house." Her mother's dying words about her adopted brother bubbled up in her memory, but she forced them away.

The sword fell from his hands. "You're right, sister. I can still be the son I should've been."

They left the house, hand in hand. They hadn't gone far when they heard footsteps behind them. Three of the men who had escaped confronted them.

Akihide stepped in front of his sister. "Run, Shiragiku."

"But—"

"Run!"

She ran. She swept past the trees and down the ragged hills. When she stopped, her heart thrummed. She gazed back from where she came, hoping to see her brother. Instead, she only saw a small shrine. She rushed toward it and fell to her knees.

"Please, help my brother and father. Keep them safe."

An old man cutting wood saw her crying at the ruined shrine. "What's the matter?"

"Oh, good sir. My brother...." Between sobs Shiragiku accounted her story.

"It will be okay. Why don't you stay with me and my wife?" the old man asked.

Shiragiku had nowhere else to go, so she accepted his kind offer. The old couple quickly grew to love her as a daughter. Shiragiku did what she could to show her gratitude for their kindness, but she never stopped thinking of her brother and father. Every so often she asked the old man to let her go look for them. He refused because of the risk and all the bandits still about.

"It's wiser to wait for them to come to you," he told her.

During those quiet years, she bloomed into a beautiful woman. She was like a chrysanthemum among wild flowers.

One day, the village chief offered to marry her, and the old man consented. When he told her, Shiragiku begged him to reconsider. "I first have to find my father," she said.

"It's been several years, child. You need to settle into life," he said.

That night she cried. As her mother lay dying, she had shared her intent for Shiragiku to marry her adopted brother Akihide. "I can't disobey her dying wish, nor can I disobey my new adopted family," she said to herself.

The days passed, and the marriage gifts began to arrive. The old couple felt pleased that they had done the right thing for her, but Shiragiku remained torn between her duties.

One night, she decided that her mother's dying wish mattered more. She decided that she would die before she broke that wish. She slipped out of the cottage and into the rain, looking back at the cottage and silently thanking the old couple for their kindness. She padded down the empty streets of the village and out into the rice fields. Then, she ran until she reached the pine forest and looked for a place to die. The roar of the river drew her.

When she reached the river, she stopped and gazed at the white ribbon gleaming in the moonlight. "I will die now. Father, brother, please forgive me. I will wait for you beside Mother."

She walked toward the river's edge.

"Stop! Tell me who you are and why you want to kill yourself," a voice said behind her.

She turned and saw Akihide standing on the knoll. Their eyes widened as they met each other's gazes. They both rushed toward each other and clasped arms. As they touched, the rain stopped. Akihide led Shiragiku to a boulder. They sat and shared what had happened since they had last seen each other.

The Beautiful Dancer of Edo

Sakura-ko was a samurai's daughter who had become a geisha to feed her mother after her father died. She lived on a narrow street. Sounds of geisha practicing their shamisen filled the air at all hours. Sakura-ko proved gifted with the shamisen. She also played the *koto* and the *biwa*.

Sakura-ko's liquid eyes and ivory skin attracted many teahouse appointments. Her conversation skills and charm could melt the hardest man. She spent her days looking down on the street from the gallery of her geisha home.

People would point and exclaim, "There's Sakura-ko, the Flower of the Cherry. The most beautiful dancer of Edo."

But as she looked down at them, she often said to herself, "The narrow street is paved with bitterness and broken hearts. The houses are full of vain hopes and regrets. The flowers in the gardens are watered with tears, yet these people don't realize this."

If you watched her dance, you'd never guess she had such a sorrowful heart. Gentlemen compared her to the rainbow-winged dragonfly and to the morning mist dancing in the new sunlight. She danced like the shadow of a willow tree on the river. They would never guess the resentment she carried from her three lovers.

The first was a middle-aged, rich and great man. When he first tried to win her, he sent a servant with a lot of money.

"You're obviously lost," she told the servant. "You should have gone to the merchant street and bought your master a doll. Let him know he won't find a doll here." She shut the door in the servant's face.

After the servant accounted this, the master visited her. "Come to me, Flower of the Cherry," he said. "I must have you."

"Must?" She raised her eyebrow.

"Must is the only word for how I feel."

"And what will you give me?"

He didn't hesitate. "You will have the finest kimono. I will give you a house with servants. Gold hairpins—whatever you want."

"And what do I give you in return?" She narrowed her eyes.

"Just yourself, Flower of the Cherry."

"Body and soul?"

"Body and soul." He licked his lips.

"Goodbye. I plan on remaining a geisha. It's a fun life." She laughed and shut the door in his face.

The second lover was old. He hired Sakura-ko to dance at a feast he had scheduled, but he remained attached to her throughout it instead of being a proper host. "Sakura-ko, I am madly in love with you!"

"I can easily believe it," she said.

"I'm not as old as you may think."

"If the gods are compassionate, you might have some time to prepare for your end. You'd best go home and study your scriptures." Sakura-ko adjusted a hairpin. "It is time for me to dance."

After her dance, he made her sit beside him and called for wine. Her geisha sister, Silver Wave, served them. After making her drink with him he pulled her close. "Come, my love. My bride! There was poison in that cup, but you don't have to be afraid. We will die together as lovers."

"Please. My sister and I aren't children. Nor are we foolish. I didn't drink the saké. Silver Wave poured me fresh tea. But I feel sorry for you. I will stay with you until you die."

He died in her arms.

The third lover was a young, courageous man. He happened to see Sakura-ko one day during a festival and went out of his way to find her. He finally found her watching the street from the railing of her gallery. He stopped in the shadows to listen to her softly sing:

> My mother made me spin fine thread
> Out of the yellow sea sand.
> A hard task. A hard task.
> May the dear gods speed me!
> My father gave me a basket of reeds.
> He said, 'Draw water from the spring and carry it a mile.'
> A hard task. A hard task.
> May the dear gods speed me!
> My heart would remember.
> My heart must forget.
> A hard task. A hard task.

May the dear gods speed me!

When she looked down, her gaze met his. He wiped a tear from his eyes and called out, "Do you remember me, Flower of the Cherry? I saw you last night."

"I remember you well."

"I am not as young as I look. And I love you. Please be my wife."

Sakura-ko blushed.

"My dear," the young man said. "Now you are a flower of the cherry indeed."

She shook her head. "Child, go home and don't think of me. I'm too old for you."

"Old? There's barely a year between us!"

At this point, people stopped and watched the two, tittering behind their hands.

"No, not a year, but an eternity. Don't think anymore of me." Sakura-ko went inside.

Of course, the young man could think of nothing else. He couldn't drink or eat or sleep. After several days, he finally went out to the geisha street, fainting with weakness. Sakura-ko came home at dawn and found him slumping near her home. Without saying a word, she helped him to his house outside Edo and stayed with him until his health returned. Three months passed.

One evening, they sat together admiring the stars. Sakura-ko smiled at them. Happiness filled her heart.

"My dear," the young man said. "fetch your shamisen and let me hear you sing."

The spell broken, she did as he asked. "I will sing a song you already know."

> My mother made me spin fine threat
> Out of the yellow sea sand.
> A hard task. A hard task.
> May the dear gods speed me!
> My father gave me a basket of reeds.
> He said, 'Draw water from the spring and carry it a mile.'
> A hard task. A hard task.
> May the dear gods speed me!
> My heart would remember.
> My heart must forget.
> A hard task. A hard task.
> May the dear gods speed me!

"What does the song mean? Why do you sing it? It is so sad." He frowned.

"It means it's time for me to leave you. I must forget you. You must forget me."

He grabbed her hand. "I will never forget you. Stay."

She smiled. "I will pray for you to find a sweet wife and have many children."

"I don't want any wife except you. I want your children, Flower of the Cherry!"

She pulled her hand away. "That can't happen."

The next day she was gone. The young lover looked all over for her, but she had disappeared. Eventually, his family found him a wife, and they had a son together. When the boy was five years old, he sat at the gate of his father's house. A wandering nun came by, begging for alms. The servants brought her rice.

"Let me give it to her," the boy said.

As he filled the begging bowl and patted the rice down with the wooden spoon, the nun caught his sleeve and gazed into his eyes.

"Why do you look at me like that?" he asked.

"I once had a boy like you, and I had to leave him."

"The poor boy! Why?"

"It was better for him. Far better." She turned away and continued down the road.

The Birth of Riki

People called him Riki the Simple and Riki the Fool because he was forever a child. But those same people were kind to him, even when he set a house on fire by putting a lit match to a mosquito net. At sixteen, he was tall and strong, However, his mind remained that of a two-year-old. He continued to play with the smallest children. The older children didn't want anything to do with him because he couldn't learn their games and songs. His favorite toy was a broomstick, which he rode as a pretend horse. He would ride on his broomstick for hours, up and down the front of the scholar Hearn's house, laughing. Hearn eventually had to send him on his way when the scholar had to work.

He bowed his head and went off, his broomstick trailing behind him. Despite his strength, he remained harmless as long as he didn't play with fire. He seldom gave anyone a reason to complain. When he disappeared, Hearn didn't notice for several months.

"What happened to Riki?" Hearn asked an old woodcutter. Riki used to help him carry his bundles of wood.

"Riki? He died nearly a year ago. Apparently, he had some brain disease. When he died, his mother wrote his name in the palm of his left hand. She wrote Riki with the Chinese character and *baka*—stupid—in kana. She prayed over him, asking that he be reborn in a better condition."

The woodcutter shook his head. "About three months ago, a boy was born in Kojimachi to the Nanigashi family. The boy had the same characters on his left hand! Well, the family knew that the birth must have been because of a prayer. One of their men came here, and that's how I heard about it. The vegetable merchant told him the story."

"The family sent two servants to look after Riki's mother," the woodcutter said. "She was glad to hear it. After all, the Nanigashi have money, as you know. But they were upset about the word *baka*. The servants asked where Riki was buried and asked for dirt from his grave."

Hearn frowned. "What did they want with that?"

"I'm getting to that," The woodcutter offered the scholar a drink from his gourd. "She went with them to Zendoji Temple. They paid her ten yen for helping them. I wish I had that type of money."

"And the dirt?"

"Apparently, you can remove the characters on the boy's hand by rubbing them with the dirt taken from his previous grave."

The Boy Who Drew Cats

Long ago in a small country village lived a poor farmer and his wife. They had a number of children and struggled to feed them. The eldest son, despite being only fourteen, helped his father with everything. The little girls helped their mother as soon as they learned how to walk.

But the youngest child, a little boy, was too weak and small to do any work. His parents decided the boy should become a priest—he was a clever boy for his age. They took him to the village's temple.

"Will you make our son your acolyte?" the father asked the priest.

"That depends on him," the priest said. He bent to the boy. "Should a little boy accept anything told to him?"

He shook his head. "No. You have to use common sense and understand things for yourself."

The priest's eyebrows raised. "What is the best way to teach the Dharma?"

The little boy didn't hesitate. "With kindness."

The priest looked at the parents. "I will make him my acolyte. He has the mind for it."

The boy proved a quick study and absorbed all the priest's lessons. He also proved obedient except for a single stubborn habit. The boy liked to draw cats instead of studying. Whenever he was alone, he would draw his cats: in the dirt, in the margins of the priest's books, on the temple screens. Everywhere he could. No matter how the priest chided and punished, the boy persisted.

"Why do you draw cats everywhere?" the priest asked one day as he stared at the latest drawings on a screen.

"I don't know. I just can't help it."

"You can't be my acolyte." The priest sighed. "Get ready to go home today."

The boy choked. He didn't want to go, but he had already caused the priest too much grief. He turned away to pack, but the priest stopped him. "Let me give you some advice," the priest said. "Avoid large places at night. Keep to small places."

"What do you mean?" the boy asked. But the priest didn't say anything else. The boy thought it over as he packed.

He left the temple and started home. He felt certain that his father would punish him for not becoming the priest's acolyte, so he turned toward the village instead. The village stood a twelve-mile walk away. He had heard there were other priests in the temple there. He decided to ask them to take him in.

The boy didn't know that a demon had driven the priests out of the temple and used it as his den. The demon had also killed several warriors sent to drive it out.

The boy arrived at the village that night. The villagers were all in bed, but a light burned in the temple on the hill. He walked to the temple and knocked. After several more tries without a response, he pushed the door open.

He sat down inside to wait for a priest to arrive. Dust coated everything in the temple, and cobwebs hung from the corners.

"The priests would certainly like an acolyte to clean for them," he said to himself. "But why would they let everything get so dusty?"

Several large white screens caught his gaze. Although he was tired, they beckoned to him. He pulled out his writing box and started painting his cats on them. He painted for some time, but exhaustion soon made it hard for him to lift his brush. He was about to lay down when he remembered the priest's advice.

The interior of the temple was quite large, and he began to feel afraid. He found a cabinet and closed himself within it to sleep.

He awoke to screams and fighting. It sounded as if giant cats were having a scuffle. He held his breath and listened, feeling his heart thump. The temple shook, and the sounds grew louder.

Then, silence.

The boy waited, afraid to move. After some time, morning light slipped through the small opening of his cabinet door. He opened the door a little and peered out. Blood covered the temple floor. In the middle of the great hall lay a monstrous rat. Something had clawed gouges out of the rat's body. Its lifeless red eyes seemed to follow him, but it didn't move.

"What could have killed it?" the boy asked.

Then he noticed the screens. All the cats he had drawn the night before had red mouths. The blood glistened. He knew somehow his drawings had killed the demon rat.

After this event, the boy became an artist famed for his lifelike and powerful cat drawings.

The Contest Between Women of Extraordinary Strength

During the rule of Emperor Shoumu, a woman of extraordinary strength lived in Ogawa market. Mino no Kitsune stood taller than most men, and her strength equaled one hundred men. She took pride in her abilities that no man possessed, but she didn't use them for good. Instead, she robbed any merchant who passed the market.

At the same time, another woman of great strength lived in the village of Katawa. Unlike Mino, this woman was short. One day, she heard of Mino's robbery and wanted to see just how strong this woman was. She loaded two-hundred and fifty bushels of clams on a boat and also loaded twenty vine whips.

Mino came upon the boat and quickly stole the clams away. After selling them, she returned to the boat and asked the woman where she found her clams. But the Katawa woman remained silent. Mino continued to pester, growing increasingly angry with the woman.

Finally, the Katawa woman had enough. "Does it matter where I come from? At least I don't smell of rotting fish and of the fishermen."

Mino's eyes widened at the insult and made to strike down the woman. The woman snatched one of the vine whips, grabbed Mino's hands, and whipped her. Mino struggled against the woman, but the woman's grip wouldn't budge. The woman used ten of the twenty vine whips to cut deep into Mino's skin.

"I give up!" Mino said. "I'm sorry for what I have done."

"From now on you will not live in this market or bother the sellers. If you bother anyone here again, I will beat you to death."

Mino sagged against the woman's grip and nodded. As soon as the woman released her, she fled the area and never stole from anyone again. She realized that no matter how strong a person was, someone in the world would always prove stronger.

The Diving Girl of Oiso Bay

Long ago, a samurai named Jiro Takadai lived in Kamakura. He became sick and was ordered to spend August at Oiso to rest in peace and quiet. He settled on a small inn that faced the sea. He looked forward to gazing at the waves and writing poems.

After he arrived at Oiso and checked into his room, he went to the sea for a swim. He swam about half a mile when a sudden leg cramp struck him. A diving girl and her father happened to sail by. As soon as they saw Takadai's struggle, they went to the rescue. When they arrived, he had lost consciousness and sunk.

The girl jumped overboard and dived to the bottom of the seabed. She snatched him and brought him back to the surface. Her father hauled Takadai into the boat.

Before they reached the shore, Takadai came around enough to realize that he had been saved by a beautiful *ama* of just seventeen. As he watched her, her beauty struck him. Not even a samurai girl looked as her. Nor did samurai girls show such bravery. By the time they reached the shore, he had recovered enough to help them haul their boat up the steep beach and carry their fish to their thatched cottage.

"Thank you for saving me," he said. He turned to the father. "You have a jewel for a daughter."

She waved her hand, apparently too embarrassed to say anything.

"I'm glad Kinu saw you in time," the father said.

"Well, I should go rest. Thank you again." The samurai turned toward the inn, which stood just a few hundred yards away.

He didn't sleep that night. The memory of the beautiful girl plagued him. He saw her face when he closed his eyes. When day finally broke, he spent it looking for her, but all he saw was the silhouette of her and her father when they returned from fishing at dusk. He met them at the shore.

"Hello, Kinu!" he called.

She didn't react. She gathered the nets and their catch and followed her father to their cottage. Although she hadn't said anything, the sight of his savior inflamed his love for her even more. He pulled his servant aside and handed him a letter asking for her hand in marriage.

"Take this to the cottage, and give it to the diving girl Kinu."

The servant did as he was ordered. The girl took the letter and bowed. "Thank your master for me. Tell him also that no good would come of a union between one of so high a birth as he and one as lowly as me. Such a badly matched pair will never make a happy home."

When the servant told Takadai her words, he was astonished. He never thought a fisher girl would refuse an offer from someone as high a rank as him. "Maybe she is being coy and shy," he said. "I will wait a few days. She knows of my love for her now. She will think of me and be anxious to see me."

Takadai stayed in his room for the next three days. On the evening of the fourth, he wrote another letter and sent his servant to deliver it.

When the servant handed Kinu the letter, she laughed. "You are a funny old man, bringing me these letters. This is the second in four days, and until four days ago I had never had a letter sent to me. What is this one about?"

She read it and turned to the servant. "I don't understand. You told him my message, right? We would never do because of our differences in position. Is your master right in his head?"

"He is. Except for his love for you," the servant said. "He talks and thinks only of you. Even I'm tired of hearing it. I pray to Kannon each day for the weather to cool off so we can return to Kamakura. He's read me his love poems for the last three days. I hoped we would go fishing instead."

The servant sighed. "Why don't you just marry him? Then we could all be happy and fish every day and stop this foolishness."

Kinu crossed her arms. "Selfish old man. I should marry him so you can fish? Go and tell him I said no. Our positions are too different, and we would never be happy."

When the servant told Takadai her words, he grew despondent. He wrote one more letter and even spoke to her father when he came to the inn.

Kinu's father shook his head. "She's all I have. Besides, all our diving girls are strong minded as well as strong bodied. They are in constant danger, and they are not weak like farmers' girls. Their minds are stronger than those of us men. Take my advice: give up. I agree with my daughter on this. As great an honor as you offer, she would be unwise to marry someone of your station."

Takadai felt his heart crack, but he realized the fisherman was right. He bowed and retired to his room. He remained there, growing thinner. The day they had set to leave quickly approached, but instead of recuperating, his stay at Oiso proved worse for his health. He felt as if life had no meaning.

He resolved to end his life in the sea. At least that way his spirit could occasionally see Kinu.

That evening he wrote one last letter to her. He waited until everyone was asleep and slipped the letter under her cottage door. Then he went to the beach. He tied a large stone to a rope around his neck and climbed into a boat. He rowed himself a hundred yards from the shore and jumped overboard.

The next morning, Kinu found the letter. She read that he was going to kill himself out of love for her. She rushed to the beach and saw the empty fishing boat bobbing several hundred yards from the shore. Without hesitating, she swam to it. Inside the boat she found Takadai's tobacco box and his medicine box.

"He has to be here somewhere," she said. She dived overboard.

She found his body a short distance from the boat. Despite the weight of the rock that his arms still grasped, she managed to bring his body to the surface. With some effort, she got him onto the boat and rowed to shore.

Takadai's old servant stood on the beach, wringing his hands when she arrived. "I feared it would come to this," he said.

Kinu looked down at the dead samurai. "I didn't love him. But he loved me and died for me. To make sure his spirit will be at peace, I won't marry anyone."

The servant nodded. "I'm sure my master will rest well with such a promise."

He took Takadai's body back to Kamakura where it was buried.

Not long after the servant left, seagulls began to circle where Takadai had drowned. They would rest and take flight again. Some would leave, but other seagulls replaced them. The village fisherman marveled at such a strange sight. But Kinu knew that Takadai's spirit must have passed to the seagulls. She prayed for him to find peace and saved enough money to build a small shrine to him on the shore.

By the time she turned twenty, the news of her beauty had spread. Many offered to marry her, but she refused them all. During her entire life, the seagulls were always where Takadai drowned. When she drowned nine years later in a typhoon, the seagulls also disappeared. Apparently, his spirit no longer feared Kinu would marry.

The Faithful Servant

During the reign of Emperor Engi, there lived a man celebrated for his poems and other writing. Because of his talents, he won the favor of the Emperor. Sugawara Michizane quickly became the head of the government. Affairs went well for a while, but soon his ideas clashed with other powerful Imperial Court officials. A man named Tokihira soon looked for a way to oust Michizane. Tokihira served in a position just under Michizane, but no matter how hard Tokihira searched, he couldn't find a fatal flaw in Michizane's character.

One day, one of Tokihira's spies learned that Prince Toki had fallen in love with Michizane's daughter. The lovers had been meeting in secret. Tokihira took the news to the Emperor.

"Your Majesty," Tokihira said. "This news grieves me, but it is a serious plot you need to know about. Sugawara Michizane arranged for your younger brother, Prince Toki, to fall in love with his daughter. They often meet in secret. What's more, I learned Michizane plans for your assassination, or at least to dethrone you in favor of Prince Toki. Michizane plans for Prince Toki to marry his daughter soon."

Emperor Engi had viewed Michizane as a friend, so this news troubled him. But he had to hear Michizane's side of the story. After Michizane responded to the summons, the Emperor shared the accusations. Tokihira stood beside the Emperor.

"I am innocent of this," Michizane said. "In fact, I hadn't known until this moment of Prince Toki and my daughter's meetings."

"It is your word against Tokihira's."

Michizane bowed to the ground. "It is a plot by him. I would never want to hurt you, my Lord."

"Your Majesty, you can't believe any word this man says," Tokihira said. "What father wouldn't know about his daughter meeting with an Imperial Prince? And if he didn't, what other things does he neglect?"

No matter what Michizane said, Tokihira had a counter. Emperor Engi grew increasingly hurt and furious with his former friend until he finally had enough. "Enough of this. Michizane, you are banished to Tsukushi on the island of Kyushu. Get out of my sight."

Michizane bowed and left the room. He gathered his family and dismissed all of his vassals. Among his vassals was a man named Takebayashi Genzo. Genzo took Michizane's wife and son, Kanshusai, and fled to a small town. There he changed everyone's names and established a small school to support his master's family. Michizane went into exile with only his faithful servant Matsuo.

Soon after they settled in Tsukushi, Matsuo heard of a plot to have Michizane's son killed. Matsuo thought long on how to prevent this but could only come up with the idea of offering his own son instead.

Matsuo traveled back to Kyoto and offered to become Tokihira's servant and the hunter of Kanshusai. Tokihira readily accepted the offer, pleased that someone stepped up to kill the boy. Tokihira had taken Michizane's position, and he couldn't well be enmeshed in a plot to kill a young boy.

Matsuo served his new master well. Tokihira began to trust him and gave him critical assignments. During this period, Tokihira discovered where Genzo had hidden Kanshusai. He ordered Genzo to send back the boy's head. As soon as he heard of the order, Matsuo sent his son Kotaro to Genzo's school and visited Genzo in a disguise.

"It's me, Genzo," he said.

"Matsuo! What—"

"I have a plan to save our Master's son." Matsuo explained it.

"I can't kill an innocent boy like that!" Genzo said.

"It's either that or Kanshusai will die."

Genzo thought a long moment.

"If you don't do it, I will," Matsuo said.

"I can't have a father kill his own son. I will do it."

When Tokihira's officials arrived, Genzo offered Kotaro's head in a wooden box. They carried it back to Tokihira and said, "Now you don't have to fear anything from Michizane's son. The schoolmaster Takebayashi Genzo did the work."

Tokihira knew Matsuo once served Michizane, so he sent for him. "Tell me if this is Kanshusai's head or not," Tokihira said.

Matsuo did what he could to hide his sorrow. He pulled his son's head out of the box by its hair. "Indeed, my lord. This is the head of Kanshusai."

The Old Woman Who Lost Her Dumpling

Long ago, lived an old woman who loved to laugh and make rice dumplings. One day while she made dumplings for dinner, one fell and rolled into a hole in the earthen floor. The old woman reached into the hole.

Suddenly, the floor collapsed, and the old woman fell in.

She tumbled and rolled for a long time. Finally, she came to a stop on a road just like the road outside her house. She gazed about. Rice fields surrounded her, but no one worked in them. "Odd that underground would be so bright," she said.

The road sloped ahead of her. "My dumpling has to be someplace ahead. It couldn't have rolled too far." She ran down the slope. "Where is that dumpling of mine?"

She came across a statue of Jizo standing by the roadside. She stopped and asked, "Lord Jizo, have you seen my dumpling?"

"I did," the statue said. "I saw your dumpling rolling down the road. But don't go any further. There's a wicked demon living down that hill. It eats people."

The old woman laughed. "As long as he doesn't eat my dumpling!" She ran down the road, shouting, "My dumpling. My dumpling! Where is my dumpling?"

She came to another Jizo statue. "Did you see my dumpling?"

"A dumpling rolled past just a few moments ago," the statue said. "But don't go any further. There's a demon—"

She laughed and ran on.

She came across a third statue. "Lord Jizo, have you seen my dumpling?"

"Don't talk about your dumpling right now. The demon is coming. Hide behind my sleeve and keep quiet," the statue said.

The old woman did as the statue advised. A few moments later, a demon approached. It bowed to the statue. "Good day, Jizo."

"Good day," the statue said.

The demon sniffed the air with its large nostrils. "Jizo, I smell a human nearby. Don't you smell it?"

"I think you are mistaken."

"No. I certainly smell one." The demon gazed at the statue.

The old woman couldn't help herself. The demon's twitching nose struck her as funny, and she laughed.

The demon reached around the Jizo statue and plucked the old woman up. She continued to laugh.

"I thought so," the demon said.

"Don't hurt that old woman," the statue said.

The demon made a face. "I won't. I want her to cook for me. You don't need to worry, Jizo. She will only have to do a little work every day. Goodbye."

The demon took the old woman down the road until they came to a wide river. He put her into the boat that waited there, and they crossed the river, angling toward an enormous house. The old woman had never seen a house so large. The demon took her into the kitchen.

"Cook some dinner for me and the other demons who live here." He handed her a wooden rice paddle. "You must always put only one grain of rice into the pot. When you stir it with this paddle, the grain will multiply until it fills the pot."

The old woman did as the demon told her. As she stirred the rice grain, it kept multiplying until the large pot was full. The old woman stayed with the demon for a long time, cooking for him and his friends. The demon remained true to his word. He never hurt or scared her, and her work was quite easy. But she felt lonely and wanted to go back to her own small house and back to her dumplings.

One day while the demons were away, she slipped the magic paddle under her clothes and went to the river. The boat waited for her. She climbed in and set off. She had rowed only about a quarter of the river's width when all the demons saw her. Fortunately, the demons couldn't swim, nor did they have an extra boat.

"We need to get our cook and our magic paddle back," the demon said.

"Let's drink the water of the river. That will stop her," said one of his friends.

They knelt and drank as fast as they could. Before the old woman made it halfway across the river, the water ran quite low. But the old woman kept rowing. The water grew shallow enough that the demons waded into it.

The old woman dropped her oars and pulled out the magic paddle. She shook it at the demons and made faces until they burst out laughing. As soon as they did, they couldn't hold their massive amounts of water anymore. They threw it up, filling the river once again. The demons barely made it back to their side of the shore. The old woman grinned and rowed to the other shore and ran back up the road.

She didn't stop running until she found the hole she fell down and climbed back out.

After she patched the floor of her house, she felt happy. She could make rice dumplings whenever she pleased. She had the magic paddle that let her make as much rice as she wanted. She sold her dumplings and quickly became rich.

The Story of Princess Hase

Prince Toyonari Fujiwara lived in the ancient capital of Japan, Nara, and worked as a State Minister. His wife, Princess Murasaki, was a noble woman. They had married young, but they didn't have children. After a long discussion, the couple decided to travel to the temple of Kannon at Hase to pray for a child. They stayed at the temple for some time, daily offering incense. During their stay, the goddess answered their prayers.

Princess Murasaki gave birth to a healthy daughter. The couple named the baby Hase-hime, or the Princess of Hase, because she was a gift from the goddess.

When Princess Hase was five years old, her mother became sick. Toyonari called in the best doctors and paid for the best medicine, but nothing could be done. Knowing that she was dying, Princess Murasaki called little Hase to her side.

"Honey, I'm dying. You must grow up to be a good girl. Do your best not to trouble anyone, even if your father marries again. I want you to obey whomever he finds as if she were me. Be submissive to your superiors. Be kind to those under you. Become a model woman."

"I will, Mother."

Not long after the death of Murasaki, Prince Toyonari married Princess Terute. Although little Hase did her best to view Terute as her mother, her stepmother resented the girl. She couldn't see Hase as her daughter despite Princess Hase giving her no reason to complain.

Princess Hase studied hard, growing to like music and poetry more than any other subjects. She learned the koto, and when she was twelve, she could play so well that the Emperor summoned her and her stepmother to play for him.

They arrived during the Festival of the Cherry Blossoms. The Emperor ordered Princess Hase to play the koto and her stepmother to accompany her on the flute. The Emperor listened through his curtain. Although Hase and Terute were nobles, no one was allowed to see the Emperor.

So they played. Hase's skill astonished everyone who listened. However, her stepmother wasn't one for study and neglected her daily practice. She played so poorly that one of the Court ladies had to take her place. Of course, this humiliation only made her resent her stepdaughter further. The Emperor's gifts to Princess Hase only salted her wounded pride more.

"If only Hase wasn't here. My son would have all the love of his father," Princess Teruta said to herself. As she left the Imperial Palace, she resolved to kill her stepdaughter.

She plotted until the Boys' Festival arrived on May fifth. She took two bottles of sweet wine, mixing poison into one of them, and collected several cakes. She marked the poisoned bottle.

When she entered the room, Princess Hase was playing with her little brother. His toy warriors stood around him in sharp ranks while she told stories about each of them.

"You are both such good children." She smiled. "I brought you some sweet wine and cakes as a reward for being such good children."

She filled two cups from the different bottles. She watched Princess Hase closely as she did, looking for any signs of suspicion.

Princess Hase took one of the cups and gave her little brother the other. Teruta watched Hase expectantly. Suddenly, her little boy screamed. He collapsed on the floor, doubled in pain.

"No, dear gods, no!" She gathered him in her arms.

One of the attendants ran to fetch a doctor, but by the time he arrived, the boy was dead.

Teruta's hate for Hase only increased. She blamed the girl for somehow knowing which cup had the poison and giving it to her brother. She vowed revenge.

When Hase was thirteen, the rainy season threatened to flood Nara. Tatsuta River, which flowed through the Imperial Palace grounds, swelled its banks. The Emperor ordered all the temples in the area to pray for the rain to stop. But the prayers failed. Someone in the Court remembered how the poet Ono-no-Komachi once brought rain during a drought by praying in verse. Princess Hase was known, despite her young age, for her poetry, so the Emperor sent an order to Prince Toyonari.

"Hase," her father said. "The Emperor has ordered you to write a poem to pray for this rain to stop. The Emperor's health also declines. His life depends on it. The entire palace will be flooded soon."

Hase didn't feel up to the challenge. Fear threatened to freeze her ability to write, but she gave the task her best. Her deadline came quickly, but she managed to finish her poem in time. She had written it on paper flecked with gold. With her father and her attendants and a few Court officials, she went to the bank of the angry river. She lifted the paper toward the sky and read in her loudest voice.

As she read, the river quieted. The rain lessened and stopped. Soon after, the Emperor's health recovered.

The Emperor awarded Hase with the rank of Lieutenant-General, Chinjo. And people began to call her Chinjo-hime, the Lieutenant-General Princess. Everyone loved and respected her. Everyone except her stepmother.

She burned with jealousy toward Hase and did whatever she could to separate Hase and her father. But Toyonari ignored her.

One day, while Toyonari was away, she ordered her servants to take Hase to the Hibari Mountains and kill her. She invented a story about the girl dishonoring the family as justification and appointed her vassal Katoda as the one responsible for the deed.

Katoda wasn't a fool, however. He knew the story was false, so he feigned obedience and took Hase into the mountains. With the help of local villagers, he built a cottage and sent for his wife to come stay with them. Princess Hase knew her father would set everything right when he returned, so she settled in with the loyal retainer's family.

When Prince Toyonari returned, his wicked wife claimed Hase had done something wrong and ran away. He called his retainers together and ordered a search. They rode out into the Hibari Mountains.

He found himself in a valley and saw a tiny house. A beautiful, clear voice reading Buddhist scriptures aloud drifted toward him. Recognizing the voice, he rushed toward the cottage.

"Hase!"

The beautiful girl jumped to her feet. "Father!" She ran toward him and buried her face into his chest.

He stroked her dark hair. "Tell me what happened."

Katoda emerged from the cottage and bowed before his master. He told Prince Toyonari everything that had happened. As his servant spoke, Toyonari's anger flared.

"You have done well, Katoda," he said. "You will be promoted to my chief retainer. Let's go home, Hase."

When Princess Terute heard Toyonari had found Hase, she fled and returned to her father.

Prince Toyonari adopted a son from one of the Court nobles to be his heir and to marry Hase. Princess Hase lived to a good old age and birthed several healthy children. Everyone said she was the wisest and most beautiful woman to have reigned in Prince Toyonari's ancient house.

Tsubosaka

In a village nestled in Yamato province, close to Tsubo mountain, there lived a blind man named Sawaichi and his wife Sato. Sawaichi earned a meager living giving koto and shamisen lessons and was known as an honest man. Sato handled the daily household chores and earned a little money sewing and washing. But despite their hard work, they continued to grow poorer.

One morning Sawaichi played on his shamisen.

"I'm glad you feel in better spirits today," Sato said as she listened. "It's been awhile since you've played your shamisen."

"I'm not playing this for fun. I'm so depressed I feel like I could die from it," Sawaichi said. "Please sit down. I've had something troubling me for a long time now."

She sat near him, trying to figure out what he meant. Now that she watched him, she could see something deeply troubled him.

He cleared his throat. "Time really does fly like an arrow. We've been married for three years already, and I've wanted to ask you this so many times, Sato. Why do you still hide your secret from me? We've known each other since we were kids. So why don't you tell me?"

"What are you talking about? I haven't kept a secret from you. If I've done something to make you upset, please tell me. I don't want you to be unhappy." She got closer to her blind husband.

"Every night between three and four, I wake and stretch my arms to you. But I've never been able to find you." Sawaichi shook his head. "But I understand. I'm blind. I know I'm not much to look upon either with how smallpox disfigured me. I don't need to see to know that much." He touched his face. "While you are a beautiful woman. I'm resigned to my fate and won't be jealous. Please, just tell me." Tears slid from his eyes.

"How can you suspect me of that? Do you think I'm the kind of woman who would leave you for another man? We are united until death, and I've always hoped to find a way to cure your blindness. That's why I rise every dawn. I climb to the top of Tsubosaka every morning to pray to Kannon for your sight to be restored. But after three years, my prayers still haven't been answered. And now you accuse me of an affair!"

"I'm such a fool. Please forgive me." He pressed his palms together and raised them. "Forgive me. Although you pray for me, I know I will never see again."

"What are you saying?" Sato rubbed her bare foot, thinking of all the times she had walked in the snow to the shrine.

"There's no way Kannon will answer your prayers since I held such suspicions of you."

"Let's pray together, and we will see." She grasped his hand and helped him up. She helped him dress in his best clothes, and together they climbed Tsubosaka.

When they reached the temple, they both gasped for breath from the hard climb. No matter how many times Sato trudged that path, it never got any easier.

"Here we are, Sawaichi," Sato said. "Before we pray, why don't you sing a song to cheer you mind?"

"You're right. It wouldn't do to pray with distracted thoughts." Sawaichi thumped his walking stick on the ground to measure the rhythm. He began to sing as they entered the temple.

"Is suffering the cause of love?
Or love the cause of suffering?
My love must vanish like the dew.
I—"

Sawaichi tripped on a stone. Sato managed to catch him just before he fell.

Sawaichi laughed. "I've forgotten the rest of the song. What does it matter now?"

Sato led him to the altar where statues of Amida Buddha and Kannon rested. Incense scented the air. She positioned him in front of the statues. "We're here," she said. "Let us stay together and pray all night."

They settled before the statues and began to chant their prayers in the quiet. The priests of the temple were used to Sato's visits and left her alone to do their other tasks. Several hours crept by when Sawaichi suddenly clutched her arm.

"Sato. I came here because you wanted to, but I know I will never recover my sight."

"Why do you keep saying that? Emperor Kammu was blind too, but when he prayed to Kannon he was healed. Kannon sees emperors and people like us as the same. You have to be patient and trust in Kannon's mercy."

Sawaichi was quiet for a time. "All right. I will fast here for the next three days," Sawaichi said. "Return home and come back in three days."

"I'm glad you will give this a chance. Just please be careful. The mountain is steep, and there is a deep precipice on the top of it. Don't leave the temple." Sato touched his shoulder and left.

Sawaichi waited until he could no longer hear her footsteps or the sounds of the priests. Then, he fell to the floor and cried. "Sato, you will never know how grateful I am for you. You loved a blind, poor, ugly wretch. And I even doubted your fidelity. Forgive me, Sato."

He writhed on the floor, venting all of his miseries until he was exhausted. "What's the use of living any longer when Kannon ignores three years of Sato's prayers? The only thing I can do to show Sato my gratitude is to die and free her from our marriage. May she have a happy second marriage. Maybe if I die in this holy place, I can be saved in the next world."

He stood and left the temple. He followed the sound of flowing water up the mountain until he came to the peak. He felt the wind whip at him. Before he could think twice about his decision, he dropped his staff and jumped.

Three days later, Sato stumbled up the familiar path to the temple. Only her husband was nowhere to be seen. She found one of the priests. "What happened to my husband?"

The man shook his head, unable to speak past the grief he felt for her. He pointed to the peak above the temple. She rushed past him and up to the peak. She gazed down the sheer cliff and saw Sawaichi's body stretched on the ground, far beyond the reach of anyone.

She stepped back from the edge and collapsed. "Why, Sawaichi? I only wanted to heal your blindness. If I had known..." She looked up at the sky. "I will join you in death, Sawaichi." She said a final prayer to Kannon and Amida Buddha and leaped off the cliff.

***

The morning mist retreated as the sun rose. Above the bodies of Sawaichi and Sato, Kannon shined brighter than the dawn on the horizon.

"Sawaichi," Kannon said. "Your blindness was because of sin in your former life. Because of your wife's faith and prayers, I will prolong your lives. Devote your lives to prayer and make a pilgrimage to the thirty-three holy places. Awake, Sato. Awake, Sawaichi."

The temple's bell rang the hour of the morning prayer.

Sato and Sawaichi found themselves back on the peak. They stared at each other with the memories of the past three days fading like dreams.

"Sawaichi, your eyes!" Sato touched her husband's cheek.

"I see you, Sato. I see you!"

Sato smiled. "It is due to Kannon's mercy."

"You really are beautiful." He gazed over the peak at the lightening sky. "You remember everything too don't you?"

Sato nodded. "I do."

Sawaichi smiled. "My gratitude for Kannon is deeper than the sea." He took his wife by the hand and went down to the temple. They prayed prayed their gratitude to Kannon and asked for protection as they began their pilgrimage.

Places

Horaizan

Jofuku was the Wise Man of China. He was well-read and understood the secrets of birds, beasts, plants, and the earth. He wrote poetry and philosophy as well as practicing magic. All of China honored him, but he wasn't happy. *Mutability* was written on his heart. Both the word and the tyrant that ruled China troubled him.

"Jofuku," the tyrant said. "Teach the nightingales of my woods to sing the songs of the Chinese poets."

Of course, this task was impossible. "My liege," Jofuku said. "Ask me something else, and I will give it to you."

"You should be careful," the Emperor said. "Wise Men are cheap. Am I the one to be dishonored?"

"Ask me something else."

"Well, change the scent of the peony with that of a jasmine. The peony is brilliant, imperial, but the scent of the foolish jasmine flower is better."

Jofuku remained silent and looked at his feet.

"By the gods, you are worthless!" The Emperor looked at his bodyguard. "Someone cut off his head."

"Liege," Jofuku said. "Spare my life, and I will sail for Horaizan. You've heard of the herb of immortality that grows there. I will bring it back to you so you can live forever."

The Emperor held up his hand to this guards as he considered. "Go on then." He skewered Jofuku with his gaze. "And leave immediately."

Jofuku bowed and left. He gathered several brave companions and chartered a ship captained by the most famous sailors. By the time he gathered the supplies and money he needed it was the full moon of the seventh month.

Much to his surprise, the Emperor came down to the seashore to see him off. "Make speed, Wise Man. Bring me the herb of immortality. If you return without it, you and everyone with you will be executed."

"Farewell, liege," Jofuku called from the ship.

They sailed east. The sea proved wild. The days proved hot and the nights cold. Several of the men died from sickness. A few more died to pirates. Finally, a typhoon caught them. Waves larger than mountains threw the ship. Masts snapped, and many men were swept overboard.

Jofuku was among them.

He awoke on a shore. A gray dawn broke behind a distant, pearly mountain. When he squinted, he saw a great tree growing on the top of the mountain. Closer to him stood trees loaded with citrons, persimmons, and pomegranates. Birds with blue and gold feathers filled the air.

"Somehow I must have been swept to Horaizan." His voice scraped his dry throat. "And that must be Fusan and the tree whose branches hide the Mysteries of Life."

He tried to get up but failed. Just then, several young men and women approached. They offered him water and food. He found his strength return immediately. The young men and women smelled sweet and spicy.

"How strange," he said. "I don't feel my old age anymore."

"What is old age?" a young woman asked.

Jofuku stood and tested his joints. "I don't feel any more pain either."

"What is this pain?"

Jofuku gazed inward for a moment. "I don't feel mutability on my heart."

"What does mutability mean?" the young woman asked.

"Did I die?" Jofuku asked.

The young woman of Horaizan cocked her head. "What is death?"

***

Wasobiobe was the Wise Man of Japan. He rivaled Jofuku for wisdom despite his young age. Wasobiobe enjoyed sailing. He would often venture far from the shore and meditate among the waves. Once he fell asleep. As he slept, his boat drifted east. He awoke the next morning in the shadow of Fusan, the Wonder Mountain. His boat had somehow ventured into a river of Horaizan. He steered her among the flowering irises and lotuses until he reached the shore.

Young women and men greeted him. Among them was Jofuku, who had become young again.

"Welcome, brother," one of the young men said. "Welcome to the Island of Eternal Youth."

They offered him the fruit of the island. After he ate and sat with them for a time, they took him into the woods. Wasobiobe hunted with them and bathed with them in the warm sea. Night never touched the island. No matter what Wasobiobe did, he never felt the need to sleep. Nor did he feel pain.

After several days, Wasobiobe approached Jofuku. "I can't find my boat."

"Why do you want a boat here?" Jofuku asked.

"I want to return home."

Jofuku frowned. "Aren't you happy here?"

Wasobiobe shook his head. "I have a word written on my heart that troubles me. Even here, I can't find peace. The word is *humanity.*"

"Strange." Jofuku stroked his smooth chin. "I once had a word on my heart too—mutability. But I've forgotten what it means. Do you also forget your word?"

"I can never forget it."

Wasobiobe left the Wise Man of China and looked for the Crane, who was a great traveler. "I want you to take me home," he told the Crane.

"If I did, you would die," the Crane said. "This is the Island of Eternal Youth, and you've been here one hundred years already. If you leave now, old age, pain, and weariness will strike you. You will die."

"It doesn't matter. Take me home, please."

He climbed onto the Crane's back. They flew day and night without rest. At last, she said," Do you see the shore?"

"I do. Praise the gods."

"Where do you want to go? You have only a little time to live."

"Good Crane, just set me down on the sand of my country under that pine tree. Take me to that poor fisherman mending his net. I will die in his arms."

So the Crane laid Wasobiobe at the fisherman's feet. The fisherman took the Wise Man into his arms, and Wasobiobe rested his head against the fisherman's chest. Pain wracked him.

"I might have lived forever," Wasobiobe whispered. "But for the word written on my heart."

"What word?"

"Humanity." Wasobiobe smiled and died.

"So it is with everything that lives," the fisherman said.

How Saigyo Rock was Named

Some twelve miles south of Shodo Island lies Naoshima. The ex-Emperor Shutoku was banished to Naoshima for leading a rebellion. Stranded with only the clothes he wore, Shutoku walked the beach, wondering what he should do. He wondered if he should kill himself or try to make a living on the lonely place. Night came on him before he could make a shelter, so he settled in to listen to the sad waves.

The next morning, he had decided to live. He set off along the shore to find a place to set up his new life. He walked a short distance and came upon footprints. He followed them and saw smoke coming from a rocky area. Feeling curious, he climbed and came to a hut. A fisherman named Sobei and his wife Oyone worked outside.

The ex-Emperor strode up to them. "I am Emperor Shutoku. I was exiled here." He followed with many questions about the island.

"Sir, my wife and I are humble folk," Sobei said. He could tell the man was of high station by his bearing and speech. "We live peacefully and happily here. You're welcome to share our humble food with us. Our house is small, but you can stay with us while we build a better one for you. Let us be your servants."

The ex-Emperor was relieved and quickly became one of the family. He helped them build a house for himself. He helped the old couple with their fishing and gardening.

That autumn he fell sick with a fever. Oyone made medicine from the herbs of the island and nursed him through the winter. One day, as he was healing, he went out to sit by the sea and became absorbed in a flock of seagulls that followed a school of sardines. He failed to notice fourteen armored men surrounding him.

A gray haired, kind-looking old warrior stepped up and bowed. "My beloved Lord. We've found you at last. My name is Iga Furuzuka. I was sent by the Emperor to take your head. He worries that even banished you will threaten the peace of our country. Please don't fight us. I don't want to do this."

Without a word, the ex-Emperor arranged himself and stretched his neck.

Iga was touched by this. "What an example of a samurai." He struck off the ex-Emperor's head with a single blow.

One of the samurai respectfully placed the head in a silken bag. They buried the body with due honor.

"Go back to the ship and take Shutoku's head to the Emperor. I will remain here for a time to mourn what I had to do."

This surprised the samurai, but they left Iga to his grief.

Sobei and his wife went out to find the ex-Emperor. They knew of his favorite spot to gaze at the sea. They found Iga there crying.

"What happened?" Sobei asked. He saw the blood on the sand. "Who are you, and where is Shutoku?"

Iga stood and explained his mission. As he finished, fury struck the old couple. They drew their fishing knives and attacked the warrior. Sobei came from the front and his wife attacked from behind. But they weren't warriors, and Iga had long experience in war. In seconds, he had them both by the wrists. Their knives dropped to the sand.

"I know you are good people. Please listen. The man you knew wasn't the real ex-Emperor. He was my son Taro Furuzuka."

The old couple froze. "What do you mean?" Sobei asked.

"The Emperor believed ex-Emperor Shutoku remained a threat and was exiled to this island. He was meant to die here. I was charged with taking him here. Although I am of the Imperial Court, I dislike the Emperor. So I left my son here. He looked much like Shutoku, and he was glad to take his place. Unfortunately, the Emperor wasn't satisfied with banishment. So I was sent to bring back the ex-Emperor's head."

He took a shuddering breath. "You have lost your friend. I lost my son. But the ex-Emperor still lives. He is on his way here in disguise to meet with me. I will have you know how deeply grateful I am of how you treated my son."

The old samurai bowed to the couple. The old couple remained silent, not knowing what to do. They cried tears in sympathy. They spent the next half hour that way, waiting for the tide to take away the stained sand.

The ethereal sounds of the biwa touched their ears. Iga stood, drying his eyes. "The real ex-Emperor is coming. He doesn't go anywhere without his biwa, and he uses it to send coded signals. He asks if it is safe to come forward."

The old couple had never heard such music. The sounds tugged at their sorrow. The music came nearer until they saw a man walking along the beach. The man dressed in poor clothing and looked exactly like their lost friend.

Iga bowed and led the stranger to the old couple. "These people took care of my son, thinking he was you."

"I am grateful to you," the ex-Emperor said. "You also saved my life. I count you among my most loyal followers."

As he spoke, a ship carrying away Taro's head passed in the distance. The ex-Emperor, Iga, and the old couple knelt on the sand near the blood stains and prayed for the spirit of Taro.

The next day, the ex-Emperor announced his decision to stay on the island of Naoshima with Sobei and Oyone. Sobei took Iga to the mainland.

The ex-Emperor lived a year on the island, playing his biwa and praying for Taro's spirit. At the end of the year, he died from sorrow. Sobei and his wife decided to build a small shrine to him. Many years later, the eccentric priest and poet Saigyo visited the island to pray. He sat on the favorite rock of Taro and the ex-Emperor. The rock is still known as Saigyo's Rock.

The Legends of Lake Biwa

Long ago, Akechi Mitsuhide built a castle at the southern side of Mount Hiyei. The castle frustrated Toyotomi's efforts, holding out despite Toyotomi's superior forces. As time went on, Toyotomi called on a fisherman from Magisa village to show him where Akechi's water supply originated. Soon after the fisherman showed the origin of the water, Toyotomi cut off the supply, and Akechi and most of his men killed themselves rather than surrender.

Since that day, whenever rain or snow falls, a fireball leaps from the castle ruins and attacks any fisherman on Lake Biwa. Sometimes the light leads them off course. Once a fisherman struck it with a bamboo pole and the fireball burst into many small flares that swept out and engulfed all of the boats in the area. The fisherman called the fireball the Spider Fire of the Spirit of the Dead Akechi.

***

Long ago, a beautiful girl named Tani lived in the village of Komatsu. She was the daughter of a wealthy farmer and loved to learn. She wanted to learn things that common women couldn't learn. She found a talented young monk who was the chief priest of one of the smaller temples at the foot of Mount Hiyei. She convinced him to teach her and took a boat across the lake to visit him whenever she could.

She soon fell in love with him and crossed the lake more frequently despite her parent's protests. She sailed even when the waves were too high for even a hardy fisherman to dare. Finally, she told the priest of her love for him and attempted to get him to renounce his vows.

The monk didn't know what to say to dissuade her. He thought to give her an impossible task, knowing that Lake Biwa became impossible to navigate in February.

"Tani, if you cross the lake on the evening of February 25 in a washtub, I might cast off my robes and forget my vows."

Blinded by her young love, she went home determined to do exactly as tasked. At last, the twenty-fifth arrived. Tani selected the best and largest washtub. After dark, she set out without the least bit of fear. When she was halfway across the lake, a storm broke over Hiyei Mountain. The waves rose, and the wind slashed, blowing out the light the monk always kept burning for her. Despite her best efforts, Tani lost her way in the darkness, and her washtub capsized.

Some people say the monk had blown out the lantern instead of the wind. But in either case, Tani was never seen again.

Since that night, every February 25th sees a storm. People say it is because of Tani's spirit.

The washtub drifted to Kinohama village where it was picked up by the match-maker Gensuke. He split it and made it into matches. When he learned of Tani's story, he declared the 25th a holiday.

***

On Shibaya Street, a teahouse called Kagiya once sat. A beautiful geisha named Tagahana used to work there. Although she was barely seventeen, her heart already belonged to Denbei and his heart to her. Denbei worked as a clerk for a rice merchant in Otsu, but he had little money to spend on a geisha at such an expensive teahouse. He became jealous and unhappy toward all those who could hear her sing and watch her dance during their dinners. He eventually began to embezzle from his master and adjust the ledgers to hide it. When Tagahana asked him how he could afford to see her so often, he told her.

"My dearest," she said. "what you've done out of love for me will be discovered. You can't hide it forever. We have only one way to be happy. We have to die together. If I ran away with you, I would be captured. If you are discovered...."

"Will you leave with me tonight?" he asked.

"Two in the morning, while everyone sleeps. You know that pine tree near the east end of town? From there we will go to Ishiyama temple and pray to Kannon. Then we will die in Firefly Valley. Our souls will depart together."

The lovers met as planned and fled. They stopped at a teahouse at Ishiyama to spend their last hours together before going to the temple to pray. Then they went to the valley. They hugged once last time and wrote a prayer on a slip of paper. They each shoved their prayer into the soft black rock that festooned the valley.

The lovers died at each other's hands.

People continue to tie pieces of paper to the black rocks of the valley to pray for their love and the spirits of Denbei and Tagahana.

The Lake of the Lute and the Matchless Mountain

When heaven and earth were first created, Lake Biwa and Mount Fuji didn't exist. Suruga and Omi were both plains. Men planted rice where the lake and mountain now exist.

But one night, a terrible earthquake shook the foundations of creation. Clouds fell to the earth. Floods poured from the sky, and the sound of dragons fighting filled the air. When morning finally arrived, everything was calm again. The sky and earth were as bright as when Amaterasu had come out of her cave.

The people of Omi awoke to a great sheet of blue where they had tilled land the day before. They wondered if the blue field of heaven had fallen. They came near the waters and tasted it to discover the water was as fresh as a mountain stream. They climbed the hills nearby to get a better look. The outline resembled a music instrument, so they called it "the lake of the four-stringed lute." Others called it the Lake of Omi.

The surprise of the Suruga people was still greater that morning. Sailors far out at sea rubbed their eyes and wondered if the Iwakura, the eternal throne of heaven, had fallen. Some thought they had lost their way and found an unknown island, but they soon recognized the familiar shore. Many of the villagers awoke to find their homes on the side of a slope. They saw distant villages from their windows and far above them the snowy head of a mountain disappearing into the clouds.

"What will we call this newborn of the gods?" the villagers asked. Many offered their thoughts.

"No other mountain is so beautiful," one villager said. "There's no equal anywhere. Call it Fuji (no two such), the peerless, the matchless mountain."

"It is so tall and grand," another said. "Call it Fuji, the rich scholar, the lordly mountain."

"Call it Fuji, the never dying mountain."

"Call it after the flower of joy, Fuji, the wisteria mountain. It looks blue and purple in the distance, just like the flower."

So everyone agreed to call the mountain Fuji while still choosing their own meanings. Stories of the pearly mountain that offered immortality to whoever climbed it quickly circulated. People believed the elixir of immortality could be found somewhere on it.

In one of the far-off kingdoms of China, a rich old king heard of these stories. He feared death and spent his days studying alchemy in the search of the philosopher's stone and the elixir of life. Among the king's sages was an old, wise man who concluded that Japan contained the Fortunate Isles that hid the true elixir of life. The king sailed out with five hundred of the most beautiful young men and women of his kingdom.

Unfortunately for the king, the rough seas and severe storms had weakened him. When he finally landed near Mount Fuji, the ascent proved too much for him. He died halfway from the peak.

His collection of people gave up their search and buried their master in Kii Province. Instead of returning to China, the young men and women paired off and married. They settled into the eastern part of Japan.

Long afterward, when Buddhists came to Japan, one noticed Fuji had eight peaks around its caldera. The peaks resembled the petals of a sacred lotus flower. It seemed Buddha had honored Japan with the sacred symbol of Nirvana. So they named the mountain Fuji, the sacred mountain. Many believed that the earth scooped out to form Lake Biwa had been piled up to make Mount Fuji.

White Bone Mountain

At the base of Mount Shumongatake, in the northwestern province in Echigo, stood a temple that marked the burial ground of Lord Yamana's ancestors. The temple was called Fumonji, and many important priests kept it. One such priest was Ajari Joan, an adopted son of the Otomo family.

Ajari was an educated man with many followers, but even a priest of his renown was still only human. He fell in love with an attractive eighteen-year-old girl named Kiku.

"I will give up my priesthood and my reputation if you will only marry me," he told her one day.

She refused and kept refusing.

A year later she died of a fever. Rumors quickly spread that Ajari had cursed her with his jealousy. The rumors weren't without merit. Ajari lost his mind when she died. He neglected his duties and ran through the temple each night, shrieking and scaring everyone. Finally, one night he dug up Kiku's body and ate one of her breasts.

After he was discovered in the act, people believed he had turned into a demon and refused to go near the temple. All of his followers left, and the temple soon began to fall into ruin with no one to tend it. Thorn bushes grew on its roof. Moss grew across the once-polished floors. Bird roosted, and forest creatures made it their home.

Seven months later, an old woman who owned a tea house was about to close her shutters when she saw a priest approaching. "Demon priest!" she cried and slammed the last shutter in his face. "Stay away."

"What do you mean by Demon Priest?" he asked loud enough for the woman inside to hear. "I'm a traveling priest, not a thief. I need a place to rest."

The old woman peered through a crack in the shutters and realized the priest really wasn't Ajari. She opened the door. "I'm sorry. I thought you were the Demon Priest from the temple near the mountain." She explained the situation. "One day the mad priest will come out and kill all of us."

"So this priest has broken his vows and the teachings of the Buddha," the priest said. "He has become a slave to worldly passions?"

"I don't know about worldly passions, but our priest turned into a demon. He even dug up and ate the flesh of the poor girl he cursed."

The pilgrim priest stroked his chin. "People have turned into demons, but they are usually commoners, not priests. Besides, I had heard Ajari Joan was a virtuous and clever man. In fact, I'm here to meet him tomorrow."

The old woman grabbed his arm. "Don't think of going. Stay here and rest all day and then go on. I will offer you my best tea."

The pilgrim sighed. "I will go no matter what you say."

The next afternoon, the pilgrim left for Fumonji Temple. The old woman accompanied him to the path that led up to the temple.

"I ask you to reconsider," she said.

The pilgrim only smiled and went on his way. He reached the temple at dusk. The gates screeched on their broken hinges, and leaves piled thick on the path. He crunched over them and struck a small temple bell with his staff. Birds and bats flew out of the temple at the sound. He struck the bell again and waited.

At last, a wizen priest came out. He gazed at the pilgrim with wild, unfocused eyes. "Who are you, and why do you bother me? For some reason everyone left me. If you want a place to stay, go to the village. You won't find food or a bed here."

"I am a priest from Wakasa Province. I've come a long way, and it is too late for me to go to the village. Let me remain here for the night."

"I can't order you away. You can stay if you like, but I don't have anything to offer you." Ajari sat on the corner of a rock. The other priest sat nearby without saying anything else.

Darkness fell, and a wane moon rose.

Ajari stood. "Find a place to sleep wherever you can." He disappeared into the ruined temple.

After a moment, the pilgrim went into the temple, tripping over the shattered furniture, statues, and beams Ajari had destroyed in his madness. He began to believe the old woman's story. After searching for several moments, he found a place between a fallen statue and the wall and settled to sleep. He supposed it was a safe enough place, but he couldn't tell for certain in the darkness.

He tried to focus on the pleasant gurgling of a mountain stream somewhere in the night. But the sounds of rats fighting and of the bats kept intruding. He didn't hear anything from Ajari.

Just as he was about the drift off, the temple shook with the sounds of statues and furniture being smashed. Between the crashes, he heard the pattering of the mad priest's bare feet.

"Oh, where is the beautiful Kiku?" Ajari shouted from somewhere in the darkness. "Where is she? The gods and the demons have joined forces to keep us apart. But I will defy them. Kiku. Kiku! Come to me."

The pilgrim listened as the man's ravings grew distant and made his escape. He fumbled in the blackness and had to hide several times when Ajari neared. As the morning's first light sliced the darkness, the pilgrim priest managed to find his way out of the temple. He sat on the rock he had occupied the previous evening and waited. Despite the harrowing night, he wanted to confront the sick man and read him a lesson of the Buddha's teachings.

Toward midday, he heard sounds inside the temple, and Ajari came out, looking dazed. But the pilgrim felt relief. The man wasn't raving.

He stood and approached Ajari. "My friend, my name is Ungai. I am a fellow priest from the Temple of Daigoji in Wakasa Province. I heard of your great wisdom, but I've also heard you've broken your vows and lost your heart to a young girl. Your love has turned you into a demon, so I've made it my duty to help you. Stop and listen to the Buddha's teachings, and tell me if I can help you."

"Please tell me how I can forget the past. I want to become a holy and virtuous priest again."

"Come and sit on this rock," Ungai said. "Now you will sit on that rock until you can explain this teaching. 'The moon on the lake shines on the winds between the pine trees, and a long night grows quiet at midnight.'" Ungai stood, bowed, and left the mad priest on the rock.

For a month, Ungai wandered from temple to temple, teaching. His circuit took him back to the teahouse near Fumonji Temple.

"Have you heard or seen your Demon Priest?" he asked the old woman.

"I haven't. Some people say he left, but no one knows for sure. No one dares to go look."

"Well," Ungai said. "I will go tomorrow and find out."

The next morning he found Ajari still sitting on the rock, muttering the words he had left. Ajari's hair and beard had grown long, and he had somehow grown even thinner.

Ungai felt tears in his eyes when he saw Ajari's determination. "Get up. You are indeed a holy and determined man."

Ajari didn't move. Ungai poked him with his staff, but to his horror, Ajari crumbled as if he was made of sand and disappeared on the wind.

Ungai stayed at the temple for three days to pray for Ajari's soul. When Ungai returned to the village and accounted what happened, the villagers asked him to become their priest. Under his guidance, they rebuilt the temple and renamed it Hakkotsuzan, White Bone Mountain.

Yoro Waterfall

Long, long ago there lived an aged woodcutter and his son on the slopes of Mount Tagi. They cut brushwood and sold it on their backs for a living. They could only afford rice and radishes. Only once or twice a year, usually on New Year's or the Emperor's Birthday, they treated themselves to fresh fish. But the old man loved rice wine and bought a gourd of it each week.

As the years passed, the woodcutter grew so stiff that he could no longer climb the mountains. His son managed to cut double the amount of wood and kept everyone fed. The old man made sure to welcome his son back when he returned at dusk. He felt proud of his son's strength and sense of responsibility.

One winter, the snow fell thick. Bamboo bent, and the branches of pine trees snapped under the weight. The son struggled to trudge through the snow and cut enough wood so he could buy food. He often quietly went hungry so his father could have his warm rice wine.

He went up a different path one morning in the hopes to find better luck when he came across the faint scent of warm rice wine on the breeze.

He followed the scent and came upon a waterfall foaming over the rocks of the hillside. As he walked closer, the spray fell into his mouth.

Saké!

He filled the empty gourd he carried and returned home to his father. Each day, he visited the waterfall of rice wine and refilled his father's gourd. His father's stiffness receded, and he regained a portion of his old strength.

Soon news of the fountain spread until the Emperor heard of it, and he personally made the journey to see the mysterious waterfall. To this day, young and old enjoy picnics at the foot of the waterfall. Sadly, only pure water flows now.

Romances

Choyo and the Recluse

Choyo lived in a village called Teiheigun that nestled at the foot of Kanzanrei Mountain in Korea. When she was sixteen, her father died and left her the fortune he had made as a merchant.

At the foot of the same mountain lived a woodcutter. The woodcutter lived a simple and frugal life alone in his dilapidated hut. Most people knew him as a morose and standoffish man. They nicknamed him The Recluse and often wondered why he kept to himself. After all, he was strong and handsome for a thirty-year-old. The local villagers also wondered about what his true name was.

One evening, the Recluse traveled down the rough mountain path with a load of firewood on his back. He had stopped to rest in a pass shaded by huge pine trees when a rustling sound startled him. He tensed and gazed around the area. Just recently, people had been killed by tigers on the mountain.

A pheasant flew from the bushes, imitating the sound of a wounded bird to try to draw his attention from her nest.

He relaxed. "It is odd, though," he said to himself. "She should've done that as soon as I approached." He listened closer and caught the sounds of people talking. Not knowing who approached, he hid behind the trunk of a large tree. His hand tightened on his axe.

Three men came into view, shoving and dragging a beautiful, disheveled girl. The Recluse waited until they neared and sprang out to block their way.

"What are you doing with that girl? Let her go, or you will suffer," he said as loudly as he could.

The bandits looked at each other and smirked. The largest pointed at the Recluse. "It's three of us to one of you. Get out of our way, you fool, and we will forget we saw you. If not..." His smirk turned dangerous.

The woodcutter wasn't afraid of them. He hefted his axe and planted his feet. The bandits drew their swords with a show of confidence. In a flash, the Recluse was on them, moving faster than they could react. His axe almost cleaved the biggest man in half at the waist. At the same time, he kicked the second hard enough to send him into the nearby ravine. The third released the girl, threw down his sword, and ran.

The Recluse bent to the girl. He pulled out his water skin and offered it to her. "Who are you? And how did those men get hold of you?"

She sobbed and drank from the skin. "I'm Chiyo Choka from Teiheigun village. Today is the anniversary of my father's death, so I went to pray at his grave at the foot of Gando Mountain. I was taking the long way back when those men caught me. Thank you for saving me! Please, tell me your name."

"Ah, so you are the famous beauty of Teiheigun. You might know me as The Recluse. If you will come with me, you can rest at my hut for a bit. Then, I will take you home."

"I'd like that."

He helped her down the mountain path and to his hut. He offered her tea and a small meal. Then he took her to the outskirts of her village. "You should be safe now." He bowed and left her before she could say anything else.

That night, Choyo couldn't get the woodcutter out of her mind. The next day she told her friends of how The Recluse had saved her.

"You are in love with him," one of her friends told her. "All you've done is talk about him this past week."

She shook her head. "I should go thank him. I will bring him fish and some other food."

Her friends smiled at her.

Choyo found The Recluse at home sharpening his axes. He stopped and looked up at her with some surprise.

"I wanted to thank you for saving me the other day," Choyo proffered the food she had carefully wrapped.

"You don't have to thank me. Any man would've done the same." He paused a moment. "But it is an honor to hear it from lips such as yours. I can't accept your gift. If I did, I would be in your debt."

"It is no debt to me. Please take it."

He shook his head and returned to sharpening his axe.

"Do the different trees require different axes?" she asked.

He looked at her but didn't say anything.

"I had heard different woods smoke foods differently. I'm sure you could tell me more."

His whetstone worked.

She huffed. "Well you've beaten me today, but I will come back. I will eventually beat you and make you accept a gift from me."

The Recluse regarded her with a knit brow. "You are welcome to come back. I'll always be glad to see you, but I won't be under your obligation by accepting a gift."

Choyo frowned at the strange answer. On her way back home, she listened to her heart beating far faster than the walk warranted. Excitement filled her, and she smiled. "We will see who wins in the end."

For the next two, months she revisited The Recluse whenever she could. She gradually forced him into conversation. He brought her wildflowers and berries from the highest point on the mountain, but he otherwise made no motion toward her. By then, Choyo had decided that she was in love and that she had to win their game. She suspected he also loved her but something was holding him back from declaring it.

During the third month, Choyo went to see The Recluse. He wasn't home, so she sat and waited. It struck her how such a noble man would live in such a wretched hut. With her wealth, she could easily lift him to a state of life more on par with his character. As she mused, the woodcutter returned, but instead of his usual rags, he was dressed in curious, foreign-looking clothes.

"I see you are surprised to see me dressed this way," he said. "Today we have to say goodbye. I have to leave."

"Leave? Take me with you! It's not for a woman to say it, but I love you! I will go with you wherever you go. I will follow you even to the cave where the demons of hell live. I can't be happy without you." She fell on her knees.

The Recluse shook his head. "It's impossible. I also love you, but it cannot be." He straightened. "My name is Sawada Shigeoki. I am a samurai from Kurume, Japan. Ten years ago, I committed a political offense that forced me to flee my country. I came to Korea disguised as a woodcutter. Now that our government has changed, I can return home. I have told no one of my true identity."

He took a deep breath. "Forgive me for leaving you. I do it with tears in my eyes and sorrow in my heart." He turned and left the hut.

Choyo cried until night fell. She stayed the rest of the night in the samurai's hut. When her servants found her that morning, she had a fever. They carried her home where she lay for three months. When she finally recovered, she gave most of her money to the nearby temples and charities and sold her house. She kept only enough money to buy rice and settled into the samurai's hut.

She was found dead in that hut just a few years later. The villagers said she died of a broken heart. She was twenty-one.

How Kinu Returned from the Grave

Once a rich merchant lived in Osaka. Fortune smiled upon him with every business venture he tried until he had all the world offered. His daughter, Kinu, rivaled the angels in beauty. However, next door lived a humble tobacco seller. Although his home was little more than a shack, he was blessed with a handsome boy named Kunizo.

Kinu and Kunizo played together most days. They developed a deep affection for each other at a young age and impressed everyone with how well suited they were for one another. Although he was poor, Kunizo received the best education and soon developed the same tastes in literature as Kinu. But as they grew older, the rich merchant and his wife discouraged their daughter from playing with a boy obviously inferior to her. Although the two could rarely play together, their bond remained strong. Both cherished their memories of each other's company.

When Kinu turned seventeen, her beauty and charm became so cele-brated that a son of a great nobleman asked for her hand. Her parents immediately gave their consent, pleased with the status such a marriage would give them. They began to prepare for the wedding.

The same day her parents accepted the offer, Kinu was out with her friends and her old nurse. They visited a theatre. Kinu always wore the most resplendent clothing her family could buy. During her visit, the audience gazed at her more than at the play.

As fate likes to work, Kunizo happened to be at the play too. Wonder-ing what distracted everyone from the play, he followed their gaze and saw his old playmate. He wanted to talk with her, but he didn't dare. Not with his station. So he gazed at her as a moth would gaze upon a star.

It wasn't long before Kinu spied him among the sea of faces. Her memories rushed out to fan the love for him that had never faded. They shared a smile meant only for each other.

That night, Kunizo returned to his humble home, feeling depressed. His memories couldn't deny the gulf that existed between them.

"It would be easier to pass from hell into heaven," he muttered.

Meanwhile, Kinu returned to her home with an equally troubled heart. Kunizo's hopeless look tore at her. Both Kinu and Kunizo fell sick from their intertwined emotions. Kinu felt trapped. The looming marriage made her shiver and toss harder in her fever. She prayed for some means to escape.

"Everything will be fine," her old nurse said. "Just focus on healing."

"You don't understand," Kinu said. "I saw Kunizo for the first time in ages. My heart stirs for him." She began to cry. "I'm trapped."

Her nurse couldn't bear to see her dear child in such pain. Against her better judgment, she made a promise, "I will carry a message to Kunizo for you."

At this, Kinu perked up enough to write a poem while she played her koto. The song brought her some comfort, so she kept singing it.

Her nurse eventually found the chance to share the love song with Kunizo. The thought that Kinu still loved him restored his health enough that he could return to his life. When the nurse returned to tell of her success, Kinu's illness grew worse. Her parents sent for the best doctors, but nothing could keep her from wilting like a fading flower.

When news of her declining health reached Kunizo, he wrote his own poem and gave it to the nurse:

> To my Kinu:
>> So near, beloved, yet long leagues apart.
>> The ladder to your heaven so far and dim.
>> Its steps I dare not climb!
>> One night my soul became a butterfly.
>> Straight to your sweet presence

It fluttered softly through the starlit dusk.
Behind your purple tasseled blinds
What ecstasy.

Kunizo's poem comforted Kinu. It confirmed what she had only guessed: that he loved her. She gave her nurse a response:

To my Kunizo:

What does it matter that our tired feet
Tread on thorny paths and forlorn wastes
If only we climb together?
What does it matter if only a hermit's hut
Shelters us from the wind's cold blast?
Beyond the mists is one shining star,
The true guide for our hearts beckons!
We shake off Earth's dust, and hand in hand
We set out in faith to Love's lonely peak!

The two lovers continued to exchange their poems with the help of the old nurse. With each poem, Kinu's health improved. However, this encouraged her parents to select an auspicious day for the marriage and finish their preparations.

When Kinu realized her destiny was carved, she became frantic.

"I can't disobey my parents," she said to herself. "But neither can I marry any man except Kunizo!"

The days passed too quickly as she tried to find some solution. All she could come up with was to isolate herself in her room once she arrived at her future husband's house. If he would insist on seeing her, she would die.

She wrote her goodbye letter to Kunizo in her own blood, explaining her plan and her resolve to remain true to him. She tied the letter closed with a long lock of her own black hair.

Finally, the wedding day arrived. Kinu didn't resist the dressing or preparation, but neither did she react. Although her family praised her beauty and her expensive wedding clothes, they could see she was dead inside. As she climbed into the palanquin to be carried off to her husband, Kinu steeled her heart to do whatever she had to do to escape the marriage.

Her husband happened to already have a lover, a famous dancer and singer. She agreed to live with him as an in-house lover in the hopes that he would name her his wife. When she heard of his marriage to Kinu, she prayed for the wedding to be canceled. When she saw Kinu's procession near in the falling darkness, she couldn't contain her anger and hurt. She rushed into the garden with a dagger. She stabbed herself in the heart and threw herself down the well.

At the same moment she plunged, the gates opened to allow Kinu's procession inside. An unearthly gust of cold wind whirled around the mansion, extinguishing all of the lights. The wind stopped in front of the procession and coalesced into the dancer who had just killed herself. Pale blue mist swirled around her. Blood ran from the wound in her chest, and her disheveled long hair whipped around her.

She pointed at the bride and shrieked.

The nobleman and his attendants saw this from the house's entrance. In a rage, he drew his sword and rushed at the wraith. He swung, and as soon as his blade connected, the shade disappeared.

The attendants relit their lanterns. Kinu's parents opened the door of the palanquin to check on their daughter. Kinu lay back on her cushion, as pale as a white lily. She didn't appear to breathe.

"Doctors!" the nobleman bellowed. "Someone get the doctors!"

The doctors could only confirm that the young bride was dead.

Kinu's parents took her lifeless body home with them. Their hopes for a bright future was dashed. Their pride and joy was gone.

Two days later, her parents laid Kinu to rest. When Kunizo heard the news—that his beloved's darkest decision had come true—he decided to join her in death. But first he had to see her face one last time. That night he went into the cemetery and easily disinterred the coffin. He took a deep breath and wrenched open the lid.

Kinu blinked at him. The flush of life sat on her cheeks.

She sat up. "What happened?"

Kunizo could only shake his head. "Somehow you are alive." He smiled. "You're alive!" He forgot himself and hugged her tight.

"I remember seeing a wraith," Kinu said. "Then nothing. I feel like I've been sleeping."

Kunizo laughed. "What matters is you are back to me. I have a relative that can keep us safe."

They fled that night, stopping at Kunizo's aunt's house to rest. After she heard their story, she decided that it was the will of Heaven for them to remain together. She arranged for them to cross the sea and to stay with her brother on the island of Shikoku. When they arrived at Marugame, Kunizo's uncle, who was an innkeeper, received them warmly and helped them settle into the town. The lovers spent the next several years happily. But the fear that the nobleman might learn Kinu was alive remained a troubling specter on their happiness.

Kinu's parents had spent the years mourning her. They decided to take a pilgrimage to pray for the soul of their little girl. Over the course of their journey, they arrived at Marugame to visit. When they were shown their room, they saw a beautiful screen with a poem written on it. The handwriting reminded them of Kinu's and the poem was one of her favorites. They called the uncle to ask him how he came upon such a thing.

That was when they learned Kinu was alive.

When the parents met Kinu and Kunizo, they cried for joy and for sorrow for how they had almost caused their daughter's death. They insisted on taking the couple back to Osaka. There, they lived happily together, and the entire town never stopped wondering about how Kinu returned from the grave.

Kiyo and the Monk

Kojima's teahouse sat in a quiet and shady valley near the banks of the Hidaka River. The mountains, deep forests, and waterfalls attracted poets and monks and picnickers. The teahouse's garden was the first thing people saw as they emerged from the forested hill called the Dragon's Claw. The garden mimicked the mountains, forests, and other features in miniature. It even had small irrigated rice fields. A two-foot waterfall completed the scene with its white-sanded stream. The garden drew many visitors who enjoyed the mountain trout and other local food the teahouse served. A pagoda and monastery stood close to the teahouse.

Kojima also had an eighteen-year-old daughter named Kiyo. Her grace, like that of bamboo swaying in the moonlit breeze, attracted still more visitors to the teahouse. The visitors enjoyed watching her tend the garden or go about the teahouse's business. For the youngest of the nearby monks, she proved to be quite a distraction.

One such monk, named Lift-the-Kettle after a passage in the Sanskrit classics, studied hard. He learned ten new Chinese characters each day. He knew the name of every statue in the temple of the 3,333 images in Kyoto. He had visited the temple and prayed "Glory be to the sacred lotus of the law" five-hundred thousand times.

One day, he returned from visiting a shrine and caught sight of Kiyo working in the garden. Passion like he had never known kindled. He hurried to the monastery to meditate until it passed. But days later he couldn't help himself. He had to see her again, so he made an excuse to pass by the teahouse. When he saw Kiyo wasn't in the garden, he found himself going inside.

"Could I have tea?" he asked.

Kiyo peered out at him. "Just a moment!"

Kiyo returned with the tea, and they fell into an easy conversation. After that day, the monk visited every day, often staying late. As the weeks passed, even that wasn't enough. At Kiyo's bidding, he began to steal out of the monastery at night to cross the river and spend time with her.

The months passed, and the monk's conscience began to trouble him for breaking his vows. His love for Kiyo warred with his conscience, back and forth like a shuttlecock. But his conscience proved stronger. He decided that he had to break off his connection with the girl. He didn't want to hurt her with a sudden break. It would also bring scandal to her family and his fellow monks. He decided to gradually break off their relationship. He began to spend less time with her, claiming his duties as an excuse.

However, Kiyo had other thoughts. She decided to win him over or destroy him in the process. One night she stayed up until two in the morning. Then, dressed in only a thin, white robe, she went out to a secluded part of the mountain where a lonely shrine dedicated to Fudo stood. The scowling statue held the sword of vengeance.

"Honored, Fudo," Kiyo prayed. "Please change my lover's heart. Bring him back to me or destroy him if his heart can't be changed."

After she finished, anger at her situation flared in her. She hurried to the shrine of Kampira, whose long-nosed servants were said to teach sorcery. The devotees to the god had hung votive tablets, locks of hair, and other marks of their pledges around the shrine.

She fell to her knees outside the small structure. "Kampira, please teach me how to transform myself into a serpent dragon."

Each night she went into the mountains to pray. One night, the long-nosed servants of Kampira appeared and told her that the god had heard her prayers. They started to train her in sorcery, and they were surprised at how quickly she learned. She learned how to transform into a serpent dragon with the power to melt iron and with the strength to crack stones.

The monk continued to reduce his visits, no matter how much Kiyo pleaded with him to stay with her. Tears proved useless. The distance continued to grow.

"Kiyo," the monk said one night. "This will be my last visit."

She grabbed his robes. "No! Stay with me! What is so sinful about our love that you have to go!"

"I have to." He took a deep breath. "This isn't an easy sacrifice for me. But I—"

Kiyo's dark gaze silenced and frightened him. He wrenched himself away from her and ran toward the river. He dashed into the temple and hid under the temple bell.

Kiyo watched him go, giving him one last chance to see his mistake and return to her. When he disappeared into the temple's grounds, she muttered the incantation she had learned and raised her T-shaped wand. Her lovely face, limbs, and body lengthened. Scales sprouted along her skin until she became a fearsome serpent. She slithered toward the temple, following the scent of her former-love. She found him cowering under the great bronze bell. She went up into the belfry, snapping the thick timbers and sending the bell—and the hapless monk—plunging to the earth. She coiled around it, her scales sparking against the metal, and squeezed.

The bell groaned under the pressure and heated under the friction of her coils. Trapped in the bell, the monk shouted his prayers. The noise drew out the rest of his monks, but all they could do was pray and watch as the bell grew hotter and melted. The bronze melted over the serpent and the monk until only a pool of molten bronze and a few white ashes from the former lovers remained.

Same's Kimono

Enshu Hikoyemon lived in Edo with his sixteen-year-old daughter Same. He loved Same dearly and gave her everything she could want. Same and her maid often went to the Temple of Homyoji to pray.

And to see a certain young priest.

One day, she and the young priest lit the same incense stick, and her hand brushed against his. A thrill like she had never felt coursed through her, leaving her dizzy and shaken. When she returned home, she went straight to her room.

The next morning, she told her maid, "Tell my father I will remain in bed. I don't feel well."

Days passed with her remaining in her room. Concerned, Hikoyemon knocked on her door. "Why don't we take a trip to the sea?"

"I'd rather not."

"What about the Temple of Ise or to Kompira?" he asked.

"I can't."

Hikoyemon called his doctor, but he couldn't find anything wrong with her physically. "She has something on her mind. She will be fine once she gets over it," the doctor said.

"I do have something on my mind," Same said.

Her father leaned closer. "What can I do to help?"

She looked away. "I love a young priest in Hommyoji Temple. Don't be angry. I don't know him, but my heart is heavy for him. Please, tell him I love him. I will die without him."

"It will pass. This is just an infatuation. Give it a few more days."

The days passed, and Same's health declined. She grew thinner and paler.

"Let's go find your priest," Hikoyemon said. He couldn't bear to see her suffering so.

They failed to find him on that visit and on the second. Same shut herself in her room and refused to leave again. Hikoyemon discovered that the priest his daughter loved was a member of the most strict sect and wasn't going to give up his vows for her. But he decided to make an effort anyway.

When the priest returned from a pilgrimage, Hikoyemon approached him. "You know the girl named Same who often comes to this temple? I came to tell you that she loves you and has become sick from it. Would you consider marrying her?"

The young priest gestured at his robes. "I've devoted myself to Buddha. Nor will I tolerate anyone insulting my vows like you just have."

Hikoyemon stepped back. "I didn't mean...." He bowed. "My apologies."

When he told Same of the priest's dedication, she fell into a deep depression. At a loss for how to help, Hikoyemon had an expensive kimono made for her, hoping it might make her want to show it off. She put it on and showed it off to him, just for his sake, but she immediately took it off and returned to her bed.

She died two days later of a broken heart.

After her lavish funeral, Hikoyemon donated the kimono to the temple so the priests might pray for her. Unfortunately, the head of the temple wasn't a pious man. Knowing the value of the kimono, he sold it.

A year later, the kimono returned to the temple. This time it was donated by a father whose daughter died in a love-affair. She happened to have died on the same day as Same. The head priest sold the kimono again.

One year later, the priests heard of yet another girl who died on the same day as Same. The same kimono also returned to the temple. This third event made the honest priests wonder, until the head priest decided he had best confess. He assembled all the priests and asked for advice.

"The spirit of Same is in the kimono," a priest said. "It must be purified and burned to appease her spirit. "

The priests set up a time for the ceremony. They went through the purification rituals and set the kimono alight. Although the weather was calm, a sudden gust of wind fanned the fire. The wind swirled around the fire until it formed a fire whirl that reached the ceiling of the temple. The fire engulfed the old timbers. The priests and onlookers barely had time to escape before the entire temple blazed. The fire whirl expanded to encompass the entire area. Embers cascaded to the nearby wooden houses. Moments later, the entire area surrounding the temple blazed.

For seven days and seven nights, Same's despair burned across Edo, claiming 188,000 people.

The Blind Beauty

Kichijiro was born in the village of Tai, but when his father died, he went to live with his elder brother Kichisuke in the town of Maidzuru. When Kichijiro turned fifteen, he decided he couldn't depend on his brother any longer and set out to make his own way.

After looking for several weeks, he found a job with Shiwoya Hachiyemon, a merchant. Kichijiro worked hard and soon impressed his new master. Hachiyemon favored his apprentice over his older assistants, finally trusting Kichijiro with the keys to his safe.

Hachiyemon had a daughter Kichijiro's age named Ima. She fell in love with Kichijiro, but he wasn't aware of her affection. He remained too busy trying to build his life's foundation to think of marriage or love. In the six months he served his master, Kichijiro earned the jealousy of the older clerks, especially the jealousy of Kanshichi. Kanshichi also loved Ima, but Ima rejected him.

One day, Hachiyemon sent Kichijiro to Kasumi in Tajima Province to buy a ship. While he was away, Kanshichi broke into his room, where the safe was kept, and stole two bags of gold from it. After Kichijiro returned, he discovered the 200 ryo was missing. He immediately reported this to Hachiyemon.

After several hours of searching, the money was found in an incense-burner that belonged to Kichijiro. Of course, Kanshichi found it, but he didn't accuse Kichijiro of stealing it. Hachiyemon called both young men to him.

"The money was in the safe when I left," Kichijiro said.

Hachiyemon didn't say anything. He believed Kichijiro, but he also knew he had to prove Kichijiro's innocence to his disgruntled assistants.

Kanshichi saw his master's reluctance. "Evidence seems to point to Kichijiro's guilt. If he isn't punished, I and your other clerks will have to leave your service. And that would be the end of your business. It would be best to send *him* away."

Hachiyemon frowned. "Kichijiro, he is right. I have to send you away. I don't believe you are guilty, but I can't lose all my clerks." He paused for a long moment. "Ima loves you, you know. If you can prove your innocence, I would love to have you as a son-in-law. Think about how you can. My best wishes are with you."

Kichijiro felt tears in his eyes as he realized he might not see Ima again. He straightened. "I will prove my innocence and return to marry your daughter."

As he left, he came across Ima waiting outside. "I heard everything," she said. "I won't rest until I find out who did it. I won't marry anyone else except you."

"Oh, Ima. I wish I had realized your love for me before now," Kichijiro said. "But I will return."

Kichijiro packed and returned to his brother Kichisuke. He worked with his brother and uncle for the next four years. Kichijiro managed to purchase land and earned a share in the business.

While Kichijiro worked to rebuild his reputation, Kanshichi hounded Ima. She ignored him until one night he attacked her and tried to kidnap her. Fortunately, her father heard the scuffle. He threw Kanshichi out. This only inflamed Kanshichi more; his love became hatred for Ima and her father.

Late one night, Kanshichi set Hachiyemon's house and warehouses on fire. He was caught and executed, but not before Hachiyemon lost everything. Hachiyemon took Ima to a small fishing cottage he owned on the backs of the river. Three years later, he died.

Ima's friends urged her to marry instead of living alone.

"It's better to live alone," she told them, "than to marry someone you don't care about. I can love no one but Kichijiro."

That same year, Ima contracted an eye infection that struck her blind.

Meanwhile, Kichijiro traveled to Maidzuru to show off his improved reputation and ask Hachiyemon for Ima's hand. When he arrived and found the house he remembered was gone, he chanced upon Ima's friends who filled him in about Hachiyemon's misfortune and of Ima's blindness. They led him to the cottage and called out.

"Ima!"

She came out of the cottage and cocked her head. "You have someone different with you."

"Oh, Ima!" Kichijiro said.

Ima's milky eyes widened. "Kichijiro?"

"It is me, my love." He stepped forward and embraced her. "I've finally come to marry you."

Ima cried and tried to push him away. "You can't marry me now. I'm blind."

He stroked her black hair and chuckled. "Nonsense. I can and will marry you. I kept thinking of you as I worked these last four years. I have property in Kyoto, but if you would rather live here, I will live with you. I want to restart your father's old business. After we marry tomorrow, we will visit my uncle and ask for his advice on how to do that. He has long wanted to see you."

After a humble, heartfelt marriage ceremony, they set out to Kyoto. Kichijiro's brother and uncle welcomed Ima. Kichijiro's uncle agreed to help fund his idea to revive Hachiyemon's business. Kichijiro returned to Maidzuru and built the new office right where the old one stood. In the garden, he erected a tombstone dedicated to Hachiyemon. At the foot of the nearby mountain, he also set up a memorial to Kanshichi, in the hopes that his spirit might be touched by Kichijiro's kindness.

The Cherry-Blossom Idyll

Taira Shunko lived in the old capital of Kyoto. In his spare time, he enjoyed writing poems. His father decided he needed to finish his education in Edo where Shunko proved an apt scholar. Some months after his arrival, he stayed at his uncle's house to recover from an illness. He didn't fully recover until spring, and to celebrate he decided to visit Koganei to see the cherry blossoms. The cherry trees lined the Tama River. Various tea houses enjoyed the shade and the view. Between the tea houses were various shelters. Shunko picked one at which to enjoy his picnic lunch.

Once he finished his lunch—and enjoyed a little too much rice wine—he sauntered under the trees and sang praise to the cherry blossoms. As he enjoyed the soft pinks and whites, he lost track of time. The sun began to set, and a wind scattered the blossoms like scented snow. He realized he was alone except for the birds that sang from the trees.

He sat in the moss beneath an ancient cherry tree and wrote a few poems as the light faded:

> Throughout the land, Spring holds its high court.
> Obedient to its call, I come
> To lay my tribute at your matchless shrine.
> And to vow allegiance to the Queen of Flowers.
> How can I praise your sweet perfume?
> The heavenly pureness of your blossom's snow?
> I linger, spellbound, in your fair kingdom
> I'm riveted, a prisoner to love!
> Take this poor verse to your fragrant breast,
> Let it hang as a symbol of my true homage
> Your perfection cannot be acclaimed
> nor can your infinite beauty.
> Your fragile petals flutter on my robes
> and pluck at my heart, binding me to your realm
> with fairy fetters. I can never leave your bowers
> I will worship you evermore, my Queen of Flowers.

He tied the poem to a branch of the tree that shaded him. When he stood to leave, he realized twilight had fallen. The crescent moon shined overhead. He also realized that he didn't know where he was. He walked for a time but failed to get his bearings. He had started to worry when a young girl appeared with a lantern.

She bowed to him. "My mistress waits for you. Please follow me."

Shunko felt perplexed, but he was also grateful for help escaping the cherry-tree labyrinth. He followed the girl for a time in silence.

"Who is your mistress?" he asked.

"You will understand when you see her. My lady told me you had lost your way."

Shunko rubbed his chin as he thought. He hadn't spoken to anyone all day. Likely it was one of his friends living in Koganei.

The girl set a quick pace. She led him into a valley cut by a mountain stream. They walked along a narrow path that wound to a tiny house nestled among several ancient, blooming cherry trees. The girl opened the bamboo gate and smiled.

"This is my mistress's house. Please enter."

Shunko strolled through a miniature garden where he encountered another girl with a lit candle. She didn't say anything. Instead, she gestured and led him inside the house. They passed several rooms until they reached a large guest room. The walls and screens were painted with cherry blossoms and mountains. Lanterns lit the room, and cushions were arranged as if he was expected. Incense, mingled with the scent of cherry blossoms, filled the room. Tired from walking all day, Shunko sank to the cushions. The girl left.

He heard the rustle of silk, and the screens of the room slid open. A young woman entered. Her kimono gleamed azure, and the cherry blossom petals that scattered across it appeared to be lit by the moon. Her face was the beauty of stories.

She laughed behind her hand as she noticed his fluster. She bowed. "I've long lived alone here, so your arrival fills me with joy. I wanted to prepare a feast for you, but there's nothing worthy of you in this valley. Please enjoy our poor entertainment."

A servant appeared with trays of food and a golden wine jar with a crystal cup. The woman's presence eased Shunko's anxiety and weariness. She filled the crystal cup with amber wine and proffered it to him. Shunko had never tasted anything so sweet. She refilled his cup until the wine jar was empty. Shunko felt a strange gladness fill his heart as he drank and ate and spoke with his mysterious host.

She played the koto for him. As she played, he realized she strummed the same poem he had written earlier in the evening. He savored the sounds and wished he could stay in the woman's presence forever, but he knew he would have to leave soon.

After she finished playing, she said. "It's too late for you to return home. Everything is prepared in the next room. Please stay and rest. Please forgive me for not being able to do more for you."

Servants entered as she spoke, and they led him into the next room. Shunko sank into the silk quilts and slept.

A cold wind across his face forced him awake. A rosy dawn flushed on the horizon. Shunko found himself lying on the ground under the same cherry tree that had inspired his poem. His memory of last night felt too vivid for a dream. He gazed into the branches of the cherry tree as he thought. Could the woman from last night be the spirit of the cherry tree? Unable to reach an answer, he stood, stretched, and left. He wandered for a time before coming across the main road.

Three days passed. Shunko couldn't forget his experience that night or the young woman's beauty. Unable to deal with his feelings, he returned to Koganei. But during those three days, all of the cherry blossoms fell. The wind scattered the blushing-snow as if it hadn't existed. Shunko felt disappointed, but he also accepted that was the way of cherry blossoms. He searched for the valley without luck. Nor did the servant girl appear to guide him.

Each year, Shunko returned to the same spot in the hopes of finding the valley and the mysterious woman. Despite his lack of success, his love for the woman remained strong. He decided not to marry anyone but her. Five years he searched until news from Kyoto arrived. His father had fallen sick.

As Shunko journeyed home, he grew depressed about both his father's situation and his inability to find his cherry blossom love. As he walked, he sang:

> Cold as the early spring wind,
> chilling the sheathed buds
> with its sting.
> The bare branches wither
> so too the human heart.
> Cold as the March wind's bitterness
> I am alone. No one comes to see
> or cheer me in these days of stress.

A passing old man heard Shunko and felt pity for him. "Please excuse me for bothering you, but if you are tired, you can rest at my house tonight. It's just in that valley."

Shunko bowed. "Thank you. I will take you up on your offer."

After a hearty meal and a long talk with the old man, Shunko went to bed. He dreamed of Koganei and the beautiful woman. He smelled the cherry-blossom wind. He noticed a cloud of cherry blossoms fluttering like white butterflies. Then, he saw a strip of paper hanging from a nearby tree branch. He untied it:

> The memory lingers in your mind,
> Walk east of the temple
> and there wait for your destiny.

He awoke to find himself reciting the lines. He knew it wasn't just a normal dream and suspected it was linked with his cherry blossom woman, but he first had to tend to his father. He left the next day and continued home. He found his father in the last stages of his illness. The doctors had given up. His father lasted a few weeks longer, just long enough to get his estate in order. When he died, Shunko became the head of the household. He and his mother spent the winter secluded and mourning.

By the time April arrived, Shunko itched to see his cherry blossoms. An old friend joined him. Shunko had been too occupied to think much on his mysterious dream, but he also hadn't forgotten it. They traveled to the Eastern Mountain and past Chionin Temple. When they reached Koganei, a bloom of cherry blossoms blew over them like a cloud. Encouraged by it, Shunko hurried to his cherry tree. Sitting on its roots was a golden ring, engraved with the character for flower, *hana*. Shunko and his friend wandered until they came across a teahouse in the late afternoon.

While they rested, Shunko listened to several girls speaking and laughing in the next room.

"The day has been perfect except for Hana's ring."

"It's not a big deal. But the ring has my name on it. I don't like the idea of a stranger finding my name."

Shunko stood and went into the next room. "Excuse me, but is this your ring?" He held it out.

The youngest of the trio bowed and murmured her thanks while an elderly woman took the ring from him. As the young girl raised her head, Shunko froze.

It was the cherry blossom girl!

The girls stared at him as he tried to recover. The elderly woman spoke up. "Why don't you join us for some wine and tell us where you found the ring."

Shunko shook his head, unable to speak, and left them. He and his friend returned home for Shunko to recover from his shock.

The next day, a servant woke him. A visitor had arrived to speak with him. Shunko readied and found the elderly woman from the day before. Gifts of silk lay on the mats.

"My charge's parents sent me to thank you for your kindness yesterday," she said.

"Please, tell me about your charge. Hana," he said.

The elderly woman smiled. "She is the youngest child of a samurai family. At seventeen, she is renowned for her beauty as you've seen. Many have wanted to marry her, but she devotes herself to study and doesn't care for worldly things."

"Why does she refuse to marry?"

The woman looked around as if someone was watching. "Several years ago," the woman whispered. "her mother and I took her to visit Kyomidzu Temple in spring to see the cherry blossoms. As you know, Kannon protects all lovers who pray to her for a happy union. Hana's mother prayed for her daughter's future happiness in marriage."

She took a breath. "While we walked near the waterfall, we lost sight of Hana. She had strayed while admiring the blossoms and listening to the falling water. Suddenly, a cold wind blew. You can imagine our worry when we noticed she was missing. I ran everywhere and found her lying on the ground near the waterfall, pale and senseless. We carried her to the nearest teahouse and tried to wake her, but she refused to wake. Night fell and still she didn't wake, but an old priest appeared and knelt beside her. He prayed over her."

"What happened next?" Shunko whispered.

"We waited with her throughout the night. As did the priest. Around dawn, she came back to us." The elderly woman wiped a tear. "The old priest handed Hana's mother a card and said, 'This was written by your daughter's future husband. In a few years he will come for her.' Then he disappeared as mysteriously as he came. "

"What was on the card?" Shunko asked.

"A poem. Hana had changed too. She started studying with serious-ness when she had ignored her studies before." The old woman gazed at him. "It seemed fate directed you to my foster-child. When I told Hana's mother about you, she said: 'Thanks be to Heaven! At last he's arrived.'"

Shunko swallowed. Kannon had to be behind everything. "Please tell your mistress this poem." He recited the poem he had composed under the cherry tree so long ago.

The poem started a whirlwind. Hana's family accepted him as Hana's predicted husband. Shunko found himself at the bridal feast in just a few short weeks. Hana wore an azure wedding kimono with scattered cherry blossoms embroidered across it—the same one Shunko saw all those years ago.

Shunko caressed his bride's hair. "I've loved and waited for you ever since your spirit came to me from Kyomidzu Temple."

The young lovers pledged their love to each other for all their lives to come and lived blissfully to the end of their days.

Sagami Bay

On Hatsushima Island, a beautiful girl named Cho became known for her charm and refinement. By the time she turned eighteen, every young man on the island had fallen in love with her, but few dared to ask for marriage. Among them was a handsome twenty-year-old fisher-man named Shinsaku.

Shinsaku approached Cho's brother Gisuke about his prospects. Gisuke rather liked Shinsaku and didn't have a problem with Shinsaku marrying his sister. In fact, he suspected their mother would also ap-prove of Shinsaku if she were still alive.

So Gisuke went to speak with his sister. "You know, you really should marry soon. You are eighteen, and we don't want spinsters on Hat-sushima or girls brought from the mainland to marry our men. Shin-saku would be a good match."

She rolled her eyes. "Please spare me the talk about being a spinster again. I don't intend to remain single. Out of all the men of the island, I'd rather marry Shinsaku."

This delighted Gisuke. He and Shinsaku decided to hold the wedding in three days. As news of this spread, the other men of the island grew angry at Shinsaku. The men ignored their fishing as they debated about a way to thwart Shinsaku and give each of them a fair chance at winning Cho's hand. Some disagreements even broke into fistfights.

The news of the fights and grumbling reached Gisuke and Shinsaku. They consulted with Cho and agreed to break off the marriage for the island's peace. But this did little to take the kettle off the fire. Each day, fights broke out among the thirty bachelors of the island. Depressed that her happiness and life could cause such hardship in the village, Cho decided she had only one recourse. She wrote two letters, one for Gisuke and one for Shinsaku.

"For over three hundred years our people have lived happily and peacefully. Now because of me, all we have is fighting and anger. It would be better if I hadn't been born. So I've decided to die to bring everyone back to their senses. Please tell them this. Farewell."

After leaving the letters next to the sleeping Gisuke, she slipped out of the house and into a stormy night. She climbed the rocks near their cottage and leaped into the sea.

The next morning, Gisuke found the letters. He rushed out to find Shinsaku. After they read the letters, they went out to search for her, knowing that they were already too late. They found her straw sandals on the rocks near her home, and Gisuke knew she had jumped into the sea. He and Shinsaku dived and found her body on the seabed. They brought it back to the surface and buried it near the outcropping from which she had leaped.

From that day, Shinsaku couldn't sleep. He kept Cho's letter and straw sandals near his bed, surrounded by flowers. Each day he visited her tomb. As time passed and his grief increased, Shinsaku decided his only recourse was to join her. He went to her tomb to say goodbye. He happened to look up on the rocks and saw her standing there.

"Cho!" he shouted and ran toward her.

Shinsaku's shout woke Gisuke, and he rushed out of the house. "What's going on?" he asked.

"I saw her," Shinsaku said. "I was going to jump into the sea so I could find her, but then she showed herself."

Gisuke made a noise deep in his throat as he thought. "She did that to stop you. She wouldn't want you to die. Rather, you should dedicate your life to something. Tell you what, I will help you build a shrine to her. She will wait for you to die naturally. You can please her by never marrying anyone else."

Shinsaku nodded. "How could I marry another woman?"

Cho's death had shaken the other bachelors of the island. When they learned Shinsaku and Gisuke started building a shrine to Cho, they joined them. The shrine was called "The Shrine of O Cho-san of Hatsushima." On the anniversary of her death, each June 10th, the islanders held a ceremony in her memory. And every June 10th, it rained. The fisherman wrote a song in her honor:

> Today is the tenth of June. May the rain fall in torrents!
> For I long to see my dearest O Cho-san.
> Hi, Hi, Ya-re-ko-no-sa! Ya-re-ko-no-sa!

The Lady of the Drawing

Toshika lived in Edo. Born to a samurai family, his father served the Tokugawa Shogunate as a high official. This allowed Toshika to live a life of a scholar. He wasn't interested in social events and rarely left home. He preferred to spend his days reading, tending his flowers, practicing the tea ceremony, writing poetry, and playing his flute.

One day, a friend Toshika hadn't seen for a while stopped in. He had returned from his visit to Nagasaki and brought a Chinese drawing of a beautiful woman. The souvenir pleased Toshika. He examined it carefully but failed to find the signature of the artist. The drawing seemed to be a portrait of an actual woman instead of an idealized drawing. The longer he gazed at her face, the more he felt pulled to it. He hung the drawing in the alcove of his room.

Whenever he felt lonely, he sat and stared at the drawing, sometimes even talking to it. As days passed, Toshika began to think of it as a person. He envied the artist who had the luck to draw the woman. Each day, the figure seemed more alive and the face more exquisite. The wistfulness of her soft, dark eyes pulled at his heart. He started placing fresh flowers in front of the drawing each day. He arranged his bed so he could look at the drawing before he fell asleep. He had read many stories of the supernatural power of great artists and knew the best could inject life into their work.

He began to believe the spirit of the woman lived inside the picture. He could almost see her breast rising and falling with her breathing. Her scarlet lips appeared to move as if she spoke to him. One evening, he dedicated a poem to her:

> Your sweet beauty is like the sunflower
> The crescent moon, your arched brows
> Your lips, the cherry's dewy petals flushed with dawn
> Your hands, twin flakes of freshly fallen snow
> Blue-black, like a raven's wing, your hair.
> As the sun peers through rifts in the clouds
> your body gleams through your robes.
> Your cheeks bewilder me,

so pure, so delicate, rose-misted ivory.
Like a sword, you pierce my breast
with the messages of your dark eyes.

As I gaze on your drawn form,
I feel like your spirit is enshrined.
Surely you live and know my love for you!
The one who gifted you to me
was the gods' own messenger,
sent by Heaven to link our souls

It's sad that you were born in a distant land
far from me
Your heart must be like a lonely pine
You need someone to love and cherish you.

But don't sorrow, my love,
For Time's care-laden wings will never dim your beauty
You are immune to Fate's poisoned darts.
Anguish and grief will never corrode your heart,
And your beauty will never change.
While earthly beings wither and decay,
sickness and concern will pass you by.
Art can grant where love is impotent,
it lavished you with immortality.

If only the high gods could grant the prayer
of my wild heart and passionate desire.
Step down from your niche
Step down from your picture on the wall!
My soul thirsts for your presence
to crown my days with rapture—be my wife!
How swift the hours would then pass away
In complete bliss and lovers' ecstasy,
My life, my love, I dedicate to you.
Please make it a thousand lifetimes for me!

He smiled at the thought. He supposed the original woman had died long ago, but the drawing would protect her soul. He placed the poem above the drawing and read it aloud. Then, he sat with the sliding screens open to the newly blooming garden. The fragrance of peach blossoms wafted on the breeze. As the day faded into soft twilight, the crescent moon shed her tender radiance.

Toshika felt strangely happy as he read and thought deep into the night.

In the stillness of midnight, a soft rustling made him turn around. The beautiful woman detached herself from the paper and stepped down. She glided toward him—he didn't dare breathe. She knelt opposite of his desk and bowed. He tried to say something, but his voice failed him. All he could do was stare.

Her voice reminded him of a nightingale. "I wanted to thank you for your love and devotion. Your poem moved me. If you really think of me as you wrote, please let me stay with you always."

He grasped her hand, her warm hand. "I have loved you since you arrived. Be my wife, and we will be happy evermore. Please tell me your name. Where do you come from?"

She smiled, and tears slid down her cheeks. "My name is Shorei. My father's name is Sai. He descended from Kinkei, and we lived in China at a place called Kinyo. One day, when I was eighteen, bandits came and carried me away with the other women of our village. They sold me into slavery. I longed for some news of my parents everyday. One day, an artist came to where I was kept and chose me to paint. The drawing made me famous, and men came to see me. But I couldn't bear my life. I became sick and died. The gods must have decided to have mercy upon me for me to be here now."

Toshika wanted to make up for her wretched life. "Let me comfort you with some poetry."

"I also enjoy writing poems," Shorei said.

Shorei's poetry impressed him along with the beauty of her calligraphy. They took turns reading their poems aloud, comparing and critiquing each other. While Toshika recited a poem, he suddenly awoke.

He immediately gazed at the alcove. Shorei's drawing hung there as it had before he dozed off. As he gazed at the drawing, the red lips quipped into a smile.

He impatiently waited for the day to pass and for the chance for sleep to bring Shorei back to him. And return she did. Each night, she stepped down from the drawing and into his dreams. He didn't tell anyone of this. He believed the power of poetry linked him with the spirit of the portrait. Although he enjoyed the nightly visits, Toshika wanted nothing more than for Shorei to be his wife during the day and during the night.

One night, Shorei came to him.

"What's the matter, my love?" he asked.

She began to cry.

"What is the matter? Are you not happy with me?" he asked.

She shook her head and hid her face in her sleeve. "I've never dreamed of the happiness you've given me. But now I must leave you."

"Why? Why do you have to go?" He snatched her hand. "You are my wife, and I will never marry another woman."

"Tomorrow you will understand. I won't be able to come to you, but if you don't forget me, I may see you again." She slipped from his grasp and walked to the alcove. She smiled sadly at him as she vanished.

He shot awake. Sparrows twittered on the roof. Feeling empty inside, he opened the wooden doors. Afternoon sunlight streamed inside. He went through the motions of the day. His servants watched him, worried that he was sick.

Later that day, one of his friends visited. "You know, you really should marry," he said after they had settled into conversation. "I know of a lovely girl who suits you."

"Don't trouble yourself. I don't intend to marry anyone right now."

His friend saw that Toshika wasn't going to relent, so he changed the subject. Soon after he left, Toshika's mother arrived with her usual gifts. He tried to appear cheerful for her, but all he could think of was the loss of Shorei.

"Toshika," his mother said. "Your father and I think you need to marry. You are our eldest son, and you need to carry on the family's name. We know of a beautiful girl who will make a perfect wife for you. She's the daughter of an old friend, and her parents are willing. We just need your consent."

Toshika frowned. Is this what Shorei meant? He felt as if fate had come upon him. "Fine. I will marry her," he said.

As his mother took care of the marriage arrangements, Toshika watched Shorei's drawing. Without her nightly visits, he struggled to eat or find joy in anything. He didn't think about his marriage. He trusted she would find some way to keep her promise to him. As the days passed, the drawing lost its vitality. The tinted inks faded, and the liveliness disappeared. But he had no time to dwell on it. His family called him home to prepare for the marriage.

When the day of the ceremony arrived, he knelt in front of his bride, feeling forlorn at breaking his vow to Shorei. When he looked up, his breath caught.

Shorei smiled at him.

When they returned to his home, Toshika compared her with the portrait. The drawing didn't do her justice.

The Reincarnation of Tama

A rich timber merchant once lived in Edo with his wife. Although their business flourished, by the time they were middle aged, they still lacked children. They decided to make a pilgrimage to pray for a child. After their journey, they rested in a resort seated in the hills. The wife spent her stay in the mineral springs, hoping the medicinal waters would help.

A year passed, and she finally gave birth to a daughter. They named her Tama, the jewel. Tama grew into a beautiful girl, and people compared her to a morning glory, sprinkled with dew, that glowed in the summer dawn. Her only blemish was a mole on the side of her snowy neck. She also proved to be a gifted child. She learned her letters and literature with little effort. She learned how to dance, sing, and play the koto. She took to flower arranging and the tea ceremony.

When she reached sixteen, her parents decided it was time for her to marry.

One day, a pale, handsome young man passed by Tama's house playing the flute. Although he dressed like a poor man, he carried himself with dignity. He had dark eyes and the creamy complexion of an aristocrat.

"Can you tell me about that young man?" Tama asked her nurse.

"That's Hayashi. Poor young man didn't have a mother, and now he's lost his father too. He and his samurai father were well known as scholars and skillful musicians as you can hear."

Tama's heart went out to the young man for his loss. "I want to play my koto with him. Can you please speak with Mother and arrange this?"

Her mother thought it was a good idea, and the young samurai became a regular visitor. Hayashi and her father often played *go* together. Over time, Hayashi became like a member of the family. Tama and Hayashi gradually fell in love. They used their instruments to express their feelings to each other. The harmonies blended with their hearts. Hayashi's flute spoke of his consuming love for Tama. Her koto offered an ardent, gentle response.

Although Tama's parents remained unaware of their growing love, her nurse saw the signs. She helped the lovers meet in secret, where they pledged to always remain together. They discussed how to get Tama's parents to consent to their marriage. Hayashi knew that her merchant father had ambitions for his daughter and doubted he would ever consent for a man like himself.

The next day, Tama's father came to her. "A rich man I've long favored asked for your hand. I gave my blessing. Preparations for your wedding are underway." He smiled. "The man will be able to take excellent care of you."

Tama cried. Despair enveloped her, and she fled to her room to tell her nurse of the news.

Hayashi had promised to play *go* with her father that day. The nurse had arranged for the lovers to meet earlier.

"Your nurse wouldn't tell me what is going on," Hayashi said.

Tama couldn't contain her tears. "Oh, Hayashi! My parents gave their consent."

He blinked. "I didn't—" His heart clenched as he realized what the news meant.

"The only thing we can do is run away and elope," she said.

He hugged her and stroked her hair. "We will run away tonight."

"I would rather die than be apart from you," Tama said.

"What is this?" Tama's mother stormed into the room and snatched Tama from him. "After how well we treated you, you dare to thank us like this?"

"Mother, it's—" Tama said.

"Get out and never come back!" Tama's mother said to Hayashi. "And I will tell your father about this, Tama."

Her parents shut her into the innermost rooms, and her Mother kept a close eye on her. Hayashi fled the house and went to live in another part of the city.

Tama was inconsolable and soon became so sick that the wedding had to be postponed. As days passed, her health grew worse until she couldn't leave her bed. Her parents tried to distract her by taking her to theatres and gardens, but it didn't help. They took her to the mineral springs of Hakone and Atami, but even those waters didn't help. Finally, they called a doctor.

"It's love-sickness," the doctor said after his examination. "if she doesn't unite with the man she loves, she will die."

The mother turned toward her husband. "We have to let her marry Hayashi. Although he isn't your choice, she loves him."

The father consented, and they sent out a search for the young man. Only no one knew where he had gone.

A year passed. Her father's consent brightened Tama's health for a time, but the months dragged on, and her health declined again. The disappointment of the search proved too much for her.

She died on her seventeenth birthday.

On the same spring morning, Hayashi fished on Sumida River. As usual, his thoughts turned to Tama. He longed for news of her, but he feared her father would kill him if he returned.

He sighed. "She has probably forgotten about me by now. She will be with her new, rich husband."

Evening soon fell. As he walked home, he saw a girl coming toward him. She glided under the arches of the blossoming cherry trees. The oranges, golds, and reds of the sunset flamed behind her. The sound of the river sounded like the strings of a koto.

"Tama?" he asked. "Tama!" He wanted to run to her, but he resisted the urge.

She stopped in front of him, more beautiful than ever. She seemed to glow.

"What happened since we were forced apart?" he asked. "I'm so glad to see you."

"After you left, my parents dismissed my nurse for helping us meet in secret. She returned to her old home."

"Then you didn't marry?"

Tama shook her head and narrowed her eyes. "Do you think I would forget you? You are my love forever, even after death. My parents broke the marriage and tried to find you. But you had disappeared. So I went out to find you with the help of my nurse." She smiled. "I'm so happy to see you. Why don't you show me where you live and tell me what you've been doing?"

Hayashi shared his anxieties about her and how he had thought of her everyday along with the other trials he faced. "I vowed to myself never to marry any other woman," he said.

They entered his house together. Her nearness thrilled him to his fingertips. He turned away to light his lamp. He turned around. "You know, Tama. I—"

Tama was gone.

He rushed outside. "Tama!" He called her name and searched around his home and down the road. She had vanished as suddenly as she appeared. A sense of foreboding made him shiver. His memories of their time together crowded in on him and drove him to the house of an old friend. He asked the friend to ask about Tama and her family for him. His friend returned late that night with the news of Tama's death.

"She died because of her love for you," Hayashi's friend said.

Hayashi slumped home, "Oh, Tama," he kept saying. "If had I known of your sickness, I would have come to you. Please send your spirit to me again. Please!"

For weeks he was sick with grief. He felt responsible for the death of the girl. Finally, he decided that he had to atone for her. He decided to enter a Buddhist monastery and joined the order of itinerant monks called Komuso.

Before he left Edo, he visited the temple where his lost love was buried and knelt before her tomb. "I will dedicate my life to praying for your peace and a happier rebirth," he said. He took out a piece of paper and rubbed her name from the tombstone. He folded it and placed it in the fold of his robes, against his heart.

After becoming a monk, Hayashi rested from his wandering on the anniversary of Tama's death. He set up the rubbing of her name and burned incense and played his flute throughout the night as an offering to her sweet, tender spirit. He lost himself in his memories.

Over the years, the burden on his soul lifted until finally peace and serenity filled him.

His wanderings brought him to Koshu province. Exhausted and lost, he spent several hours looking for a place to take shelter for the night. Finally, he came across a cottage. As he approached, a ferocious looking man appeared.

"I'm looking for shelter for the night," Hayashi said.

The man didn't say anything. He just walked inside and left the door open. Hayashi followed him. Inside was a single room with a small kitchen. The room didn't have any furnishings. Only a sword and a gun stood in one corner. The man clapped his hands, and a girl of about fifteen appeared from the side room.

"Bring our guest food and the brazier." The man picked up the sword and gun and left.

The girl knelt beside him. Tears scrubbed clean ruts across her face. "Get out while you can. The man is a thief and will kill you for whatever you carry."

The girl waited on Hayashi. Although she was filthy and fearful, he could see she was not fitted for her surroundings. "How did you get here?" he asked.

"My home is in the next province." She smeared her face with her sleeve. "After my father died, the man you saw demanded money of my mother. She didn't have any, so he carried me away to sell me as a slave. But he was wounded and has been recovering for the past month. Please take me with you!"

Although he was a monk, Hayashi still had the heart of a samurai. He picked her up and fled into the night. He ran for some time before he had to finally set her down. They continued on and by dawn had reached the neighboring province. Once on the high road, the girl recognized where she was and led the way to her house.

Hayashi politely waited outside during the reunion of mother and daughter. When the girl finally reappeared, she had taken time to wash and put on better clothing. Her mother joined her.

Hayashi stared at her. The girl looked exactly like his lost Tama so many years ago. She even had the same mole on her neck! His memories overwhelmed him for a long moment.

"Do you have some relatives in Edo?" Hayashi finally managed to ask. He looked at her mother. "Your daughter looks exactly like a girl I knew years ago."

The mother studied him. "Is your name Hayashi? Did you live in Kuagawa fifteen years ago?"

"How could you know that?"

"I thought I recognized your voice," the mother said. "Fifteen years ago, I served the house of a rich timber merchant as a nurse. I helped you and Tama meet in secret. After I was dismissed for that, I returned here and married. Within a year I gave birth to a daughter who looked so much like Tama that I began to wonder if she hadn't been reincarnated."

"What day was she born?" Hayashi asked.

The mother told him, and Hayashi marveled. It was the exact day that Tama's spirit appeared to him. He told her of his encounter. "You are right. She has been reincarnated. Tama herself even told me she was on her way to you."

The mother smiled. "if that is the case, you should finally marry."

He shook his head. "I'm too old now. I could never keep such a young woman happy as the sad man I am now. But I will stay with you a little while and help you."

Several months passed. The Meiji Restoration changed Japan until the changes reached even the little village Hayashi stayed in. The villagers begged him to remain as a teacher in the new school the government set up because of his classical education. The mayor of the town also learned of Hayashi's past and pushed for him to marry Tama, the reincarnation of his first love.

Hayashi eventually relented when the young Tama also expressed marriage as her wish. The marriage proved a blessed one. The couple lived happily and had many children together.

The Story of O-Tei

Long ago, in the town of Niigata, lived a man named Nagao Chosei. Nagao was the son of a doctor and followed his father into the profession. At an early age, his parents betrothed him to a girl named O-Tei, the daughter of his father's friend. They had planned for the wedding to follow Nagao's studies, but O-Tei's health proved to be weak. When she turned fifteen, she became sick with tuberculosis.

As Nagao, knelt at her bedside, holding her hand, she said, "The gods know what is best for us. I wouldn't have made a good wife for you, and I would've only caused you trouble with my poor health. Please don't grieve for me. Something in me says we will meet again."

Nagao squeezed her hand. "We will meet again in the Pure Land. There we won't be separated again."

She shook her head, a soft rustle on her pillow. "We will meet again in this world." She smiled. "I will see you again if you want me to. But you will have to wait for fifteen or sixteen years."

"To wait for you would be a joy." He stroked her forehead. "We are pledged to each other for the next seven existences, after all."

"But you doubt."

"I doubt I will be able to know you in another body and with another name, unless you can give me some sign."

"I can't. Only the gods and the Buddha know how and where we will meet. But I am certain I will be able to come back to you." Her voice faded, and her breath rasped. A few moments later, she died.

Nagao had a mortuary tablet made with her death name inscribed on it. Each day he set offerings around it and thought about her strange last words. He wrote a promise to marry her if she could return to him in another body. He placed the promise next to her mortuary tablet.

As the only son in his family, Nagao's family pestered him to marry. Eventually, he relented and accepted a wife his father selected. But he continued to set his daily offerings to O-Tei. As the years passed, his memory of her faded, even if his affection for her did not. During those years, misfortunes fell on him. His parents died. Shortly after he also lost his wife and child. To heal his heart, he decided to go on a long journey.

He came upon a mountain-village called Ikao, famed for its hot springs. He stopped at the inn, and a young girl came to wait on him. His heart spasmed as he looked at her. She resembled O-Tei. He pinched himself to make sure he wasn't dreaming. As he studied her, his memories resurfaced. The way she walked, and even down to the mole on the back of her hand, matched.

"You look like a person I knew long ago," he told her. "Please, tell me, what is your name? Where are you from?"

She spoke with her familiar voice. "My name is O-Tei. And you are Nagao Chosei of Echigo, my promised husband." She smiled at his stricken expression. "I remember everything. Seventeen years ago, I died in Niigata. You wrote a promise to marry me if I ever returned to this world in the body of a woman." When she finished speaking, she fainted.

When she came-to, she couldn't remember the answer she gave him, nor could she remember anything from her previous life. But she loved him nonetheless. In a short time, they married and lived a happy life together.

Urasato, Midori, Tokijiro, and the *Kakemono*

Urasato sat in her rooms waiting for to night arrive. A gentle wind sighed through the pine trees, followed by the hush of the day's promise of rest. Snow fluttered from the black sky. Despite the peace of her surroundings, Urasato felt unhappy. With a sigh, she stood and left. A little serving girl named Midori followed her upstairs. As Urasato slumped to the mats of her bedroom, Midori fetched the tobacco tray with its tiny lacquer chest.

Urasato lit her dainty pipe and sighed. She puffed. Then, she tapped her pipe on the tray to empty its ashes. Only her sighs and the tap of her pipe broke the quiet.

Outside her home, Tokijiro waited in the cold. He kept to the shadows, hoping for a chance to see Urasato. He didn't want to think about what would happen if his secret visits were discovered. After all, tonight would be the last night he would see her in this life. He couldn't risk her anymore.

"Life is like a running stream," he whispered to himself. He shook his head. "If only I hadn't lost my lord's treasure, I wouldn't be skulking around like this." He regretted telling Urasato about how he had lost his lord's valuable painting to her master. He had to keep piling up his dishonor, but tonight he wouldn't have a chance to add more to the ledger. Tonight—after he saw Urasato—he would atone.

While Tokijiro hoped to see her, Urasato spoke with Midori. "Are you sure no one saw my letter to Toki?"

Midori nodded. "I gave it to him myself."

"Shh. Don't talk so loudly! Someone might hear you. Go see if Toki has arrived yet."

The little girl went out to the balcony and gazed into the garden. She spotted Tokijiro standing outside the fence. "He's here! Just outside the fence."

Urasato smiled. She rushed to the balcony and leaned out so she could see him. "Oh Toki! You're finally here."

Below, Tokijiro heard her voice. He looked up and hooked her gaze. His heart leaped as he saw her love for him in her smile.

"If only we weren't so far apart," Urasato said. "I have more to tell you than the number of teeth in my comb. I want to have your arm as my pillow instead of crying on my hand." She leaned further out, her figure supple as a willow branch. Her hair streamed.

Tokijiro couldn't tear his gaze off her. "Oh, Urasato. The longer I stay the worse it will be for you. If they discover us, both you and Midori would be punished."

"Don't speak like that." Urasato drew Midori to her and embraced her.

Footsteps thumped outside Urasato's room. Midori balled a piece of paper and threw it at Tokijiro—their signal for him to hide. A moment later the door opened and Urasato's hairdresser, Tatsu, stepped in.

"I'm sorry I kept you waiting. I wanted to come earlier but the customers—" Tatsu saw Urasato clutching her chest. "What's the matter? Why have you been crying?" She planted her fists on her hips. "Did you do anything, Midori?"

"I-I just don't feel well today," Urasato said. "I don't really want to have my hair done right now."

"Your hair is messy. It might help you feel better. I will also loosen it so it doesn't make you uncomfortable."

Urasato looked toward the balcony. "Fine." She settled in front of her mirror.

Tatsu began her work. "Listen to me. People cannot understand the feelings of others unless they've experienced the same."

Urasato gripped her kimono at what Tatsu implicated.

"When I was younger and unmarried, my future husband once borrowed money from me." She chuckled. "He used me as his money-box, but I loved him so I didn't let it bother me. I even sold all my clothes to help him. Well, things got so bad that we both considered committing suicide together. But a friend stopped us. Now, when we have the least taste of trouble, my husband threatens to divorce me." Her fingers worked at Urasato's hair. "Now I hate working for him. There's a proverb that says 'the love of a thousand years can grow cold.' Well, it's true."

"I don't have anyone to love me like you loved your husband," Urasato said.

Tatsu adjusted a few hairpins and met Urasato's gaze through the mirror. "You cannot commit suicide and leave Midori."

Urasato swallowed. In the mirror, she watched Midori wipe at her cheeks.

"Finished." Tatsu said. "Just remember what I've said." She bowed. Just before she left, she turned to Midori. "Oh, Midori. I'm going out by the side gate. Will you please fasten it behind me?"

Midori followed Tatsu down the stairs and to the side door. Tatsu opened it, almost hitting Tokijiro with it. Before he could move, she seized him and pushed him inside. Tatsu winked at Midori, opened her umbrella against the falling snow, and left.

Midori led Tokijiro up the stairs. He burst into Urasato's room and caught her hand. "I can't bear to live away from you. No, just listen. I want to die with you so we can be together forever."

Urasato shook her head. "I can't leave Midori. You can't leave me behind either."

Just then a harsh voice called out. "Come downstairs, Urasato." Footsteps approached.

"Quickly! Get under the *kotatsu,*" Urasato said.

Midori threw a quilt over the *kotatsu.* A moment later, Kaya entered. "The master sent for you and Midori. Follow me."

Kaya led them across the garden to another part of the house. The cold of the winter night mingled with Urasato's anxiety. Midori's feet pattered softly behind her. Kaya stopped in front of a screen and opened it to reveal their lord, Kambei, sitting beside a charcoal brazier. He glowered at them. Urasato and Midori entered and bowed to him, with hands on the floor.

"Has Tokijiro asked you for anything out of this house?" Kambei asked.

"I don't remember anyone asking me for anything," Urasato said.

"I figured you wouldn't talk. Kaya, tie her to the tree in the garden and beat her until she confesses."

Kaya seized Urasato and dragged her into the snowy garden. She tied her to a rough-barked pine tree and lifted a bamboo broom. "Just confess. We know all know you meet with him. I've had to constantly ask our master to forgive you. He's lost all his patience now."

Urasato cried.

"Have it your way." Kaya raised the broom.

Midori rushed forward to try to stop her, but Kaya flung the girl away. She beat Urasato until her clothing and hair were disheveled.

"Stop! Please stop." Midori hugged Kaya's legs. "Forgive her."

Kaya grabbed Midori and tied her hands behind her back. "I'm sure you know something. Confess or I will punish you too."

Tokijiro watched all of this from Urasato's balcony. He was about to leap from the balcony when Urasato looked up. She shook her head at him. Tokijiro caught her meaning and backed away from the railing. He realized he would only make matters worse if he tried to rescue her, so he went back under the *kotatsu* to wrestle with his helplessness.

Back in the garden, Kambei stood in front of Urasato. "You have to know Tokijiro came for my *kakemono*. You look surprised. Look at my room. That is the painting he is after. I know he asked you to get it for him."

"I've never been asked to steal anything," Urasato said.

Kambei's jaw tightened. "Midori! Where is Tokijiro?"

"I don't know."

"Midori doesn't know anything," Urasato said.

"She's always with you. She must know." He backhanded Midori. The girl fell to the snow. "Where is Tokijiro hiding?"

Kambei pulled out an iron knuckle. "Answer my question."

Midori squirmed away until she pushed against Urasato's legs. Midori's breath came fast.

"She doesn't know anything!" Urasato shouted.

Kambei lifted Midori and drove his iron-knuckled fist into her. Midori gasped and collapsed to the snow. She didn't move.

"What have you done to my daughter!" Urasato struggled against her ropes. "Midori, please forgive me. Although you don't know it, I'm your mother. I should have told you. I should have..." She broke down. If it wasn't for the ropes, she would've fallen across Midori's body.

"If you hadn't been so stubborn, this wouldn't have happened," Kaya said. She raised her bamboo broom. "Confess!"

Just then Hikoroku, the clerk of the house, ran out and pushed Kaya away. "This punishment is my work." He turned to Kambei and bowed. "Please forgive me, master. I know Urasato and Midori. They are goodhearted. Leave the punishment to me, and I will make them confess."

Kambei rubbed his forehead with a shaking hand. "Fine. I just want this over with." He saw he still wore the iron-knuckle and grimaced. "I need to rest." He retired to his room, closing the screen behind him.

Hikoroku turned to Urasato. "If you had listened to me, it wouldn't have come to this. I would have helped you. Please, just tell me what our master wants to know." He slapped his palms together and bowed to her in supplication.

"What are you saying, Hikoroku?" Kaya asked. "Whenever you see Urasato you always act like this. She won't confess to you like this. Just leave it to me."

"You won't hurt her!" He gestured at Kaya. "Just go away. I need to untie her."

Kaya pushed Hikoroku, but he snatched her boom and beat her with it until she collapsed senseless. He untied Urasato and Midori. Urasato scooped up Midori and brushed the snow from the girl's face.

Midori opened her eyes and groaned. "Are you okay, Mother?"

Urasato's eyes widened. Midori must have heard her. She hugged her daughter close. "I am. I'm sorry I didn't tell you sooner. I'm so sorry."

"You need to run away with me," Hikoroku said. "I just need to get my money. Please wait here until I return." He ran into the house.

Mother and daughter clung to each other under the pine tree. They shivered with cold and pain. Suddenly, snow showered them, and Tokijiro dropped down from the pine tree.

"I've seen everything that happened," Tokijiro said. "I creeped downstairs after what Kambei said and found my lord's *kakemono*." He pulled a rolled paper from his kimono. "With this, my lord will return me to his service. And I owe it all to you." He straightened. "Someone's coming." He slipped behind the pine tree.

Hikoroku stumbled through the snow. "Now we can go. Oh! I will get that painting for you." He returned to the house.

Tokijiro reappeared and snatched Urasato's and Midori's hands. "Let's get away from here." He tugged them through the garden and outside the gate. Tokijiro bent for Midori to climb onto his back. Together, they fled.

Sea Legends

The Earthquake Fish

Long, long ago when the gods came down from heaven to subdue creation, earthquakes often rocked the world. Human houses and lives were never safe, and even the gods could do little to stop them.

Kashima and Katori were charged with subduing the northeastern part of the world. They did their work well and traveled to the province of Hitachi. To help quiet the earthquakes, Kashima thrust his sword into the earth so the tip of the blade came out the other side. The hilt that stuck out of Hitachi turned to stone, and people called it the Rock of Kaname. Kashima's great sword acted as a rivet in a fan, holding all the sticks together.

Despite Kashima's efforts, the earth still quivered. The shaking was caused whenever the great earthquake fish would grow restless or angry. All of Japan rested on top of his back. His tail reached to the north, and Kyoto sat on hiss head. Attached to his mouth were huge twirling feeders. When the feeders moved, it was a sign of the fish's looming anger. When angry, he flapped his tail or bumped his head, causing an earthquake. When he floundered, he destroyed life and property.

In order to keep the earthquake fish quiet, the gods appointed Kashima to watch him. Kashima stood nearby the fish. When the fish grew violent, Kashima straddled him, took hold of his gills, and put his foot on the fish's fin. He held the fish down with his great weight. Sometimes Kashima needed to also free the great rock of Kaname, to lend him extra weight. So the fish quieted and the earthquake stopped. That was why people sing the following verses:

> No monster can move the Kaname rock
> Though he tugs at it ever so hard
> For over it stands, resisting the shock,
> The God Kashima on guard.
> These are things
> An earthquake brings;
> At nine of the bell, they sickness foretell,
> At five and seven, rain shows up
> At four, the sky clears
> At six and eight, the wind comes again.

The Jewels of the Ebbing and Flowing Tide

Chuai was the fourteenth emperor of Japan. He ruled with his wise and discreet wife, Jingu. When a rebellion broke out on Kyushu, the empress went when the emperor and his army. One night, as she slept in her tent, she dreamed of a heavenly being. The being told her of a land in the west that teemed with gold, silver, silks, and jewels. The messenger told her that she would succeed if she invaded the country.

"Conquer Korea," the messenger said as she floated away on a purple cloud.

In the morning, she told her husband of the dream and advised him to invade the country. But he didn't pay attention to her. When she insisted, he climbed a mountain and looked toward the west. He didn't see any land, not even mountain peaks. Not believing there was a country in that direction, he refused her request.

The same day, he was killed by an arrow as he fought the rebels.

This left Jingu the sole ruler of Japan. Determined to invade Korea, she prayed to all the gods for their advice and help. The gods of the mountains gave her timber and iron for her ships. The gods of the fields presented rice and grain. The grass gods gave her hemp for ropes, and the god of the wind promised to open his bag and let his wind fill her sails toward Korea. Only Isora, the god of the beach, failed to come. While her generals worked to finish the rebellion, she continued to call on Isora every night.

When Isora finally appeared, he rose out of the sea, covered with mud and slime. Shells stuck to him and seaweed clung to his hair. "What do you want?"

"Go to his majesty Kai Riu O, the Dragon King of the World Under the Sea, and ask him for the two jewels of the tides."

Isora dived and presented himself to the Dragon King in the name of the empress and begged for the two tide jewels. The Dragon King agreed and produced the two jewels. They seemed to be made of crystal and burned with inner light like white-hot steel. Each was as large as an apple but shaped like an apricot. The Jewel of the Flood Tide controlled how high and strong waves crashed. The Jewel of the Ebb Tide could pull the sea back to make dry land appear even to the bottom of the ocean.

When Isora returned with the jewels, Jingu's generals had put down the rebellion and now prepared the fleet for the Korean invasion. They had built three thousand barges, and two old gods with streaming gray hair acted as admirals. One was called Suwa Daimyo Jin, the Spirit of Suwa. The other was called Sumiyoshi Daimyo, who lived under an old pine tree at Takasago and presided over weddings.

The fleet sailed in October. They immediately encountered a storm that threatened to turn the expedition back. But then the Dragon King sent sea monsters and whales to lead the ships. They grabbed the ship's cables in their mouths and towed them forward until the storm stopped and the ocean calmed. Then the creatures left the ships to continue their journey alone.

Finally, the mountains of Korea rose in their sight. But Jingu could see the Korean army waited on the shore. Their war galleys sailed out to engage the Japanese fleet. The empress posted her archers in the bows of the ships and waited for the enemy to approach. When they were within range, she pulled out the Jewel of the Ebbing Tide and cast it into the sea. As soon as it touched the water, the sea receded from under the ships, leaving them stranded on dry land. The Korean soldiers leaped from their ships and raced toward the Japanese. The soldiers waiting on the shore also rushed toward the stranded Japanese fleet in the hopes to overwhelm them. The empress's archers opened fire.

The empress took out the Flood Tide Jewel and cast it into the shallow water. The ocean surged in and engulfed the entire Korean army. The water cast them to the shore like logs, and warriors in their iron armor sank in the waves. Only a few of the ten thousand survived.

The Japanese army landed safely and easily conquered the country. The king of Korea surrendered and gave silk, jewels, mirrors, books, pictures, robes, tiger skins, and treasures of silver and gold to the empress. She loaded the loot on eighty ships, and the Japanese army returned home in triumph.

Hachiman and the Dragon King of the Sea

Ojin, the son of Empress Jingu, was one of the fairest children born to an imperial mother. He was wise for his age and became the favorite of Takénouchi, the prime minister of the empress. Takénouchi had been the counselor of five emperors and was said to be three-hundred and sixty years old. Despite his age, he stood arrow straight. He served as a general in war and as a civil officer in peace. He wore his armor under his court robes. His white beard cascaded like a waterfall.

He wanted Ojin to live a long life as a wise ruler and mighty warrior. His mother once had control over the tides of the ocean, and she wanted Ojin to also have this power. So they had to get back the Tide Jewels. The Tide Jewels had the power to control the flow of the sea.

Takénouchi took Ojin on his shoulders and sailed out on the imperial ship. Once out to sea, he called on the Dragon King Kai Riu O to appear and give the Tide Jewels to Ojin. At first, the Dragon King didn't seem to hear. The green sea flowed as normal in the sunlight. Takénouchi listened and waited, gazing through the sparkling waves. Finally, he saw the head and the fiery eyes of the dragon below. He clutched Ojin tight to his shoulder and braced himself.

The waves surged upward, foaming and hooking as the Dragon King rose. Long mustaches graced the dragon's snout. His green, iridescent scales caught the sunlight. The king wore the jeweled robes of a true monarch embroidered with all the creatures of his ocean realm. He reclined on a huge abalone shell. A small lacquered chest rested between his claws.

"Take this chest. I can't stay long in this upper world of mortals," the Dragon King said. "With these jewels, I endow the imperial prince of the heavenly line of emperors. He will be invulnerable in battle. He will live a long life. I give him power over sea and land."

Takénouchi reached out and took the chest reverently. As soon as he pulled the chest onboard, the Dragon King plunged into the sea with a splash that rocked the ship.

Ojin grew up to become a great warrior as the Dragon King promised. He lived to be one hundred and eleven years old. Japanese soldiers honored him as the patron of war. When Buddhist priests came to Japan, they changed Ojin's name to Hachiman Dai Bosatsu, the Great Buddha of the Eight Banners.

The Abalone

Nanao was a small fishing village nestled in Noto Province. One night, a terrible storm and earthquake struck, leveling most of the village and killing nearly half the villagers. When the survivors emerged, they saw a rocky island in the distance that wasn't there the night before. The sea churned muddy and yellow.

It took some time before anyone in the village was ready to venture to the island. The other villages affected by the island's appearance happened to decide to explore the island on the same day. They wanted to see how the island affected the fish in the sea.

The island looked like a rock that some giant had dropped. Rock fish had already gathered around it, and it was too soon to tell if the island would support a lot of shellfish. Beyond the island, the villagers' old tai fishing area seemed unaffected. Each of the fishermen stayed out until dusk fishing. When they turned back home, they discovered a strange light shining from the bottom of the sea between the new island and the mainland. A storm also threatened them.

Each fisherman managed to make it home before the storm hit. The storm blasted the shore for two days. When they looked out on the third day, rays of light streamed from the bottom of the sea as if a sun sat on the ocean bed. None of the fishermen dared go out.

None except Kansuke and his son Matakichi.

Kansuke and Matakichi set sail from Nanao to fish. They spent the night at the tai fishing area. Toward dawn, they turned toward the new island to fish. Suddenly, the sea rose, and Kansuke fell overboard. Normally, it would be an easy matter for him to return to the boat, but when his head didn't appear, Matakichi dived in to rescue him.

As soon as he entered the water, the light illuminating the sea dazzled him. His father was nowhere to be seen. Wondering if somehow his father had grown confused and swum toward the rays, he dived toward them. It took several minutes for Matakichi to reach the bottom. A colony of abalone rose to meet him, forming an underwater city. In the center was the largest abalone he had ever seen. Rays of light streamed from it. Matakichi wondered at what sort of pearls he would find, but he still couldn't see his father, so he swam onward. He was a stronger diver than his father, but his lungs burned for air. Feeling despair, he made for the surface.

He emerged to a bucking sea and a boat that had shattered while he dived. He seized a bit of floating wreckage and swam toward the shore. He met the villagers on the shore and explained what he had seen and the loss of his father. But the other fishermen doubted him. abalone were too rare for so many to cluster together, but Matakichi wasn't known to lie.

Matakichi went to the village priest to explain what happened. "Please make me one of your disciples so I can pray for my father," he said.

"I would be glad to have a good young man like you. I will also pray for your father's spirit. On the twenty-first day from his death, we will take a boat and pray over where he drowned."

When the day came, the son and priest set out and prayed and returned without incident. That night, the priest awoke at midnight, feeling uneasy. He gazed around his room and saw an old man standing near his bed.

The man bowed. "I am the spirit of the great abalone laying on the bottom of the sea near the Rocky Island. Some days ago, a fisherman fell from his boat. I killed and ate him. This morning, I heard your prayers and that of his son. I felt ashamed for what I did. To atone for my action, I ordered my followers to scatter. And I will kill myself so the pearls of my shell can be given to Matakichi. Please pray for my spirit." The ghost vanished.

That morning, when Matakichi went outside, he saw a large abalone —the same one he saw when he dived—on the shore. He told the priest, who shared his nighttime visit with the young man. Inside the shell, they found the body of Kansuke and an immense pearl. They buried Kansuke.

Matakichi changed his name to Nichige so he could start a new dynasty and lived well on the wealth the pearl gave him.

The Awabi Festival

One day in June, a nobleman visited the Bay of Manazuru to relax. Unfortunately, he wasn't much of a swimmer and drowned on his first day. The fishermen attempted to find his body but failed. Two years passed, and the fishermen caught fewer fish until it became difficult to find enough fish to eat.

Several of the eldest fishermen linked the decline with the stranger who drowned.

"It is his unrecovered body," the eldest of them said. "The uncleanness offends Princess Gu-gun. We have to hold a festival at the temple of Kibune to appease her."

The fishermen went to Iwata, the head priest of the temple, and set a date. When the day arrived, hundreds of fishermen gathered with their torches and formed a procession. They advanced toward the temple, beating drums and gongs in rhythm. At the temple, Iwata read from the sacred books and prayed to the goddess, beseeching her not to abandon them and vowing that they would search for the body by every means available in order to cleanse the bay.

While the priest prayed, a light flashed out of the sea and blinded everyone. A rumbling noise rose from the bottom of the sea. The waves settled until they were as still as water in a bucket. A beautiful goddess rose out of the stillness. At first all the fishermen were afraid. When the fishermen noticed the goddess gazed at their ceremony, they put everything they had into the rituals. Even Iwata's voice deepened as he chanted. This went on a full hour with the goddess looking on. Without warning, another flash of light blinded everyone, and the goddess was gone.

The waves returned to their crashing.

The priest and the elder fishermen concluded the goddess was pleased with their ceremony. They surmised that the goddess was showing them the location of the body at the bottom of the bay. The fishermen selected two virgins to dive to the bottom of the bay to see if they were right. They sent Saotome and Tamajo, their best divers.

The pair dived to the bottom, but instead of finding the body, they found hundreds of lights reflected from the shells of abalone fastened to a large rock. The rock stood six feet high and twenty-five feet long. The young women caught glimpses of pearls in the shellfish. They each took an abalone with them to show to the priest.

When the fishermen saw the abalone, which normally didn't live in the bay, they decided that impurity didn't keep the fish away. Rather, it had to be the lights from the abalone shells. The fishermen and diving women went to the stone and removed all the abalone. Soon after they did this, the fish returned to the bay in large numbers.

At the suggestion of Iwata, the villages decided to hold a festival every 24th of June to express their gratitude to the goddess for showing them the problem. This festival came to be called the Awabi Festival or Abalone Festival.

The Jellyfish and the Monkey

Long ago, the Kingdom of the Sea was ruled by a king called Rin Jin, the Dragon King of the Sea. He ruled all the creatures of the sea, and he was entrusted with the Jewels of the Ebb and Flow of the Tide. The Jewel of the Ebbing Tide caused the sea to recede from land when thrown into the sea. The Jewel of the Flowing Tide made the waves rise as high as mountains.

Rin Jin's palace sat at the bottom of the sea. The walls were made of coral, and the roof was made of jade and chrysoprase. The finest mother-of-pearl tiled the floors. But for all his power and splendor, the Dragon King wasn't happy. He thought a wife would bring him that happiness. He sent his ambassadors throughout the kingdom to seek a young Dragon Princess to be his bride.

At last, they found a lovely young dragon. Her scales glittered green like the wings of summer beetles. Intelligence shone in her eyes, and all the jewels of the sea embroidered her robes. Rin Jin fell in love with her at once. Every living thing of the sea, from the great whales down to the smallest shrimp attended the wedding. Never had the Kingdom of the Sea seen such a gathering. The bride's procession to her new home extended from one end of the ocean to another. Each fish carried a phosphorescent lantern that gleamed blue and pink and silver. The light shone through the waves and into the night sky.

The Dragon King and his Queen loved each other dearly, but in two months' time she fell sick almost to her death. Rin Jin called for the best doctors in the kingdom. He ordered the servants to nurse her carefully and with all diligence. But despite the best attention by doctor and servant, she grew worse.

The Dragon King blamed the doctor for failing to cure the Queen. The alarmed doctor replied that he knew of the right medicine, but it was impossible to find in the sea.

"What is this medicine?" Rin Jin asked.

"I need the liver of a live monkey. If we can get that, Her Majesty will recover."

"That decides it. We must get it no matter what it takes. But where are we to find a monkey?" asked the King.

The doctor wrung his six arms. "On Monkey Island."

"And can any of my people capture a monkey?" asked the Dragon King. "Monkeys live on dry land, where we cannot go."

"That has been my problem too, but I'm sure one of your servants can go on shore."

The Dragon King called his chief steward on the matter. The steward thought for a time and finally came upon a solution. "I will send the jellyfish. He may be ugly, but he can walk on land with his four legs much like a turtle can."

So the jellyfish was summoned and told of his mission. The quest troubled the jellyfish. He had never been to Monkey Island, nor did he have experience capturing monkeys.

"I don't know how to trick a monkey," he told the chief steward.

"This is what you need to do. Make friends with one, and tell him that you are a servant of the Dragon King. Invite him to come and visit the palace. Describe its riches and all the wonders of the sea to grab his curiosity. "

"How am I to get him here? Monkeys can't swim."

The chief steward shrugged. "Carry him on your back. Put that shell of yours to use!"

With the plan set, the jellyfish left for Monkey Island. He reached the island in just a few hours, and soon after he landed, he saw a big pine tree with a monkey hanging from its drooping branches.

"I am one of the servants of the Dragon King," the jellyfish said. "I have heard much about your island and came to see it. Have you seen the Dragon King's Palace in the Sea?"

"I have heard of it, but I've never seen it," the monkey said.

"Then you should come with me. The beauty of the palace goes beyond description."

The monkey squinted at the hard-shelled jellyfish. "Is it really that beautiful?"

The jellyfish saw his chance and did his best to describe the palace and the coral gardens and the other curious aspects of the sea. As he spoke, the monkey grew more interested and came down from the tree so he wouldn't miss a word of the story.

"I have to go back now, Mr. Monkey. Do you want to come with me? I can be your guide and show you all the wonderful sights."

"I want to go," the monkey said. "But I can't swim."

The jellyfish waved the monkey off. "I can carry you on my back. I am stronger than I look, so don't worry."

The monkey took the jellyfish at his word and climbed onto his hard-shelled back. They went into the sea, and about halfway there the jelly-fish wondered if the monkey had remembered to bring his liver.

"Do you have such a thing as a liver with you?" the jellyfish asked.

The monkey frowned at such a strange question. "What do you want with a liver?"

"You will learn the reason later," said the jellyfish.

As they continued their journey, the monkey grew suspicious and pestered the jellyfish for the reason behind the strange question. The jellyfish felt sorry for the increasingly anxious monkey and told him everything. He spoke of the Queen's illness and the need for a live monkey's liver to cure her.

The monkey was horrified to learn of his fate. He also grew angry at how he was tricked. He hid his fear and began planning his escape. Soon an idea struck him.

"What a shame, Mr. Jellyfish," the monkey said. "That you didn't mention this before we left."

"If I told you, you would've refused to come with me."

"You're mistaken." The monkey leaned forward. "Monkeys can spare a liver or two, especially for someone as great as your Queen. If I had known I would've given one to you right off. But you didn't tell me, so I left all my livers hanging on the pine tree."

"So you don't have a liver on you?"

The monkey shook his head. "During the day, I usually hang my liver on the branch of a tree. As I listened to your story, I had forgotten about it or I would've brought it with me."

The jellyfish believed the monkey's story and felt disappointed at his mistake. The monkey was worthless without a liver. He told the monkey as much.

"We can fix that problem. I am sorry for the trouble I've caused you. Just take me back, and I will get my liver."

The jellyfish didn't like the idea of returning to the island, but the monkey assured him that he would bring back his best liver. The jelly-fish relented and returned to Monkey Island.

As soon as the jellyfish landed on the shore, the monkey shot off for his pine tree. He chattered and bounced on the branches for a moment before turning to the jellyfish. "Thanks for your trouble, and give my regards to the Dragon King on your return."

The jellyfish wondered at the monkey's mocking tone and asked about the monkey's intention. The monkey laughed and told the jelly-fish that his liver was too important to lose.

"But you promised," the jellyfish said.

The monkey jeered at him. "I will also tell my friends. You won't trick any of us again. None of us will let you kill us for our livers."

The jellyfish couldn't do anything but regret his stupidity and confess his failure to the Dragon King. As he returned to the sea, the monkey's laughter followed him.

When the Dragon King, the doctor, and the chief steward saw the jellyfish approach, they hailed him with delight. They thanked him for going to Monkey Island and asked him where the monkey was.

The jellyfish quivered with fear and told the story of his failure. As he spoke, the Dragon King grew angry. When the jellyfish finished, the Dragon King pronounced his judgment and called for his servants to carry it out immediately.

All of the jellyfish's bones were to be removed and he was to be beaten with sticks.

The humiliated and terrified jellyfish pleaded for mercy, but the Dragon King refused to relent. The servants of the Palace brought sticks and surrounded the jellyfish. They tore his bones from his body and beat him into a flat pulp. They dragged him beyond the palace gates and threw him out, leaving him to suffer the guilt of his foolishness and to suffer his lack of bones.

So it happened that the jellyfish lost his bones and shell. Since that day, all of his descendants have been soft and boneless and without shells.

The Cuttlefish Gives a Concert

Despite the monkey's escape, the Queen of the World Under the Sea recovered from her illness. The news of her recovery spread, and her kingdom celebrated. Music wafted throughout the land. While the Queen readied for her first public appearance since her illness, she listened to the singing of the commoners through her window.

The commoners didn't mention the monkeys or the jellyfish, but they poked fun at the jellyfish using puns. Of course, the Queen remained above such performances until one night.

She sat in her pink drawing room, biding time until her scheduled public appearance that evening. Everything in the room, except for a single green vase with its sponge-plant, was pink. Instead of flowers, her servants cultivated sea anemones. Stripes of shell, bordered in pink coral, covered the floor. The walls were made of the same material, and pink shells arranged into flowers lined the ceiling. Everything in the room was of the finest materials the kingdom could produce.

The Queen ignored the splendor around her and gazed out the window into the gardens below. Her maids sat at her feet. Music wafted through the window, quite different from the music the commoners had played earlier that day.

"What strange music is this?" the Queen asked. It seemed to be a mix of guitar, drum, singing, and everything at once. It sounded as if a band played to a large choir. The music drifted from the Cuttlefish's mansion.

The Queen debated about going to see what was happening. It wasn't proper for her to be seen in public before the evening's ceremony. She couldn't visit the Cuttlefish's mansion with a proper retinue.

"No, it is beneath my dignity," the Queen said. She went over to touch her anemones while her maids fanned her, but the music continued to pull at her.

Finally, she gave in. "If the concert is outside, I can watch it from the great green rock that overlooks the mansion. My husband doesn't need to know."

She set off with her maids, avoiding the white-coral high road for the path trimmed with fan coral. The sounds of drums and voices grew louder as she neared the top of the green rock. The concert below made her laugh as soon as she saw it. She had to cover her mouth to keep from giving herself away.

Lord Cuttlefish sat on a small, barnacle-covered rock in his garden. His wart-speckled head bent forward to read his music book. A wax candle, stuck on the feelers of a lobster, lit the book. Cuttlefish's six arms each resembled the trunk of an elephant, and he put them all to use. One of Cuttlefish's arms fingered the edges of the book. He played the guitar with two arms. One grasped the handle and pinched the strings. Another used an ivory stick to strum. A small drum perched on his shoulder while still another arm curled into a bunch and hit the drum like a fist. A bass drum sat on the ground in front of him, and he thumped it with a heavy drum-stick. Boom. Boom. Boom. His head bobbed the rhythm as he screeched out the same song the commoners sang earlier, all six of his arms moving as if they belonged to a separate creature instead of one.

In front of Cuttlefish, an orchestra worked. Fish sang through their gills. A long-nosed fish broke the high notes. A frog croaked bass and led the choir with his webbed fingers. A turtle sang while he gazed at the servants readying food. On one side, a mackerel refused to join in. The choir broke down when the servants brought over the trays of food and tea.

The dwindling music ended when the Cuttlefish kicked over his drum and put his instruments away. He slipped from his rock toward the refreshments. He flopped on his head and twirled his six arms around to the amusement of his guests.

The mackerel grimaced at the Cuttlefish and whispered under her fan to the fish next to her. "How undignified! What would the Queen say?"

Kappa kept the saké, tea, and cherry blossom water flowing. The guests ate dishes of radishes, rice noodles, flies, worms, bugs, and all sorts of bait for the young fish. The mackerel watched the Cuttlefish with disgust. He ate and drank like an entire school of fish. At one point, Cuttlefish climbed into a tub of rice and used all six of his arms to stuff himself.

While the feast wasn't up to the standard of the palace, the sight of it and the antics of the guests delighted the Queen. But she couldn't wait to see the end and returned to the palace.

The next morning, the Cuttlefish had a hangover.

The King of Torijima

Long ago, a lord named Tarao lived in Osumi province. Kume Shuzen served him as a retainer. One day, Kume traveled to the capital, Kyoto, on business for his master when Lord Toshiro of Hyuga and Lord Tarao argued over land. The two clans fought each other at the foot of Mount Kitamata. Lord Tarao was killed along with most of his men. Lord Toshiro also took the castle.

When Kume heard of this, he decided the only honorable course of action was to gather what samurai he could and fight on his dead master's behalf. Unfortunately, only fifty men came to his call. Kume and the men took to the mountain until they could recruit more, but Toshiro eventually discovered their hideout and staged a surprised attack. Only Kume managed to escape.

Kume made it to Hizaki and hid until he had a chance to steal a boat. But Kume wasn't a sailor. When he finally found a boat, he had no idea how to use the oars, and the little vessel didn't have a sail. Kume, at least, knew how to use that! The ocean's current swept him out to sea.

Kume lay in the bottom of the boat, stretching his provisions as far as he could, but by the second day, he had already run out of water.

On the morning of the fifth day, Kume felt something bump the boat. He forced himself upright and saw he had landed on a rocky island. He mustered what strength he had left and dragged his boat up the shore.

"I have to find water," his voice rasped. Sea birds watched him from the rocks. They sat on eggs and fished in the lagoon.

"At least I won't starve while they are nesting," he said.

As he stumbled across the beach looking for fresh water, fish churned the sea. Shoals of flying fish leaped into the air to escape a large albacore. Shellfish clung to the coral and rocks. He soon found a stream that held clean, fresh water, and he drank until he thought he'd drown.

Encouraged by the plenty he saw around him, he returned to his boat and dragged it further inland to avoid the tide. He ate fruit he found growing on the trees further inland and went to sleep in his boat.

When morning woke Kume, eight turtles surrounded him. He considered killing one for food but stopped. "Maybe my kindness to these turtles will save me like Urashima's kindness did. They might be messengers of the Dragon King."

After he ate more fruit and shellfish, he dragged his boat to sea so he could practice rowing and steering it. In the afternoon, he visited the highest point of the island, but he wasn't able to see land in any direction. He decided to stay on the island for a time. He had plenty to eat and fresh water to drink. To amuse himself and rebuild his strength, he decided to dive. He soon found the water teemed with pearl oysters and collected sixty pearls as he exercised. He made a bag and filled it. He hoped the pearls would allow him to avenge his master when he finally returned to the mainland. The next day, he made a sail out of his clothes and other materials he found around his island.

He spent the next six weeks practicing his sailing and collecting pearls. One day he saw a distant sail, but it didn't seem to come toward him or move at all.

"It has to be a stationary fishing boat. There has to be land somewhere that way. Tomorrow I will set out and see for myself. I might find some Chinese, but either way, I will be ready."

He filled his boat with fruit, shellfish, and eggs. He tied his bag of pearls around his waist and set sail. Little wind pushed against his makeshift sail, but he stayed up all night and steered the best he could. When morning broke, he found himself about four miles from an island. Elated by the sight of land, Kume rowed with his remaining strength.

At least one hundred angry natives waited for him on the beach. They brandished their spears, but Kume wasn't about to be stopped. His boat had barely reached the sand when he drew his sword and leaped into them. In short order, he knocked out several. He went out of his way to avoid killing them, knowing that he needed their goodwill. As the remainder fled, Kume managed to snatch one of them.

"Whose island is this? What people are you?" he asked. He gestured the best he could that he didn't want to fight them.

The man he had seized relaxed and seemed to understand. When Kume released him, he gestured at his fellows who came out from the jungle and stuck their spears into the sand. Kume revived the men he struck down, which awed the rest of the natives. Only two had died in the scuffle.

They took him to the village, and the chief of the village took him to a hut. As the days passed, Kume found the people kind and agreeable. He started to learn their language. Three months passed, and Kume had learned enough of their language to communicate well, and the chief had given him a wife. The villagers fished and grew sugar, yams, and rice.

One day while Kume told of his adventures, an idea struck him. "Why don't you come with me to Torijima? You can dive better than me for the pearls there."

"It's bewitched," Kume's wife said. "It's impossible to go there because a giant bird comes twice a year and kills all men who come close."

"I'm not afraid of a bird," Kume said. "I'd like to repay your kindness by showing you my Torijima. It's better than your island for fishing. Some of you, please come with me."

Thirty men decided to go with him, and the next evening they sailed. They reached the island just as the sun rose. Kume arrived first and alone, determined to face down the bird if it existed. As soon as he landed, an immense eagle swept down on him. The body of the bird was as large as a man's with a wing span many times that. But Kume had seen worse in his time on the battlefield and cut the monster in half as it swooped down on him.

From that day on, the natives made Kume the king of both their island and Torijima. He never made it back to Japan to avenge his master. He lived fifteen years on the two islands and was buried on the natives' home island. They named it Kumijima in his honor.

The Sazae and the Red Sea Bream

One day, a red sea bream and a herring watched the thick shell of the sazae. The sea bream wished he could also live in such a shell.

"What a mighty castle you live in, Sazae. When you shut your shell, no one could ever hurt you."

Sazae smiled at the flattery but shook his head to pretend at humility. "Thank you for saying so, but my little hut is just a shell. Although it's true I don't worry when I shut my door. I feel sorry for fellows like you who don't have a shell."

A great splash surprised them. The herring and sea bream darted away. Sazae retreated into his shell, keeping as quiet as possible. He wondered what caused the noise. Was it a net, a stone, or a fish hook?

"They must've gotten caught," he said. "But I'm safe thanks to my shell." He tightened his door and took a nap.

When he awoke, he peeped out. He saw piles of fish, clams, prawns, and lobsters lying around him.

"What is this? Am I dreaming?"

A great black-nosed dog poked his muzzle toward him. He shut himself inside his castle in a blink.

The shellfish lay in a fishmonger's shop with a slip of paper marked ten cents on his back. A few hours later, a laborer's wife took him home and stewed him in his own juices. The castle he prided himself within made a good saucer and was later thrown into a heap to be burned into lime.

Urashima

Each night Urashima sailed out to the Inland Sea to fish. On one such night, the moon shined bright. Urashima leaned with his right hand deep in the water. The moon's light had grabbed his mind. He ignored his nets and the list of his boat as it wandered toward a haunted part of the sea.

When he reached a certain point, the Daughter of the Deep Sea arose and wrapped her arms around him. She pulled him from his boat and sank with him to her cave on the sea bed. She laid him on her bed and sang to him.

Finally, Urashima awoke from his moon daze. "Who are you?"

"The Daughter of the Deep Sea." Her hair floated around her.

"Let me go home. I have children waiting for me."

"Oh, Urashima," she said. "Forget about your home, and stay with me. Your long hair has twisted around my heart."

"Please let me go home."

"You will be the King of the Deep Sea if you stay."

Urashima shook his head. "My children—"

"Fisherman of the Inland Sea," she sang. "Don't fear the Deep Sea tempest or of the drowned dead. You won't die."

"Let me go."

"Stay with me. Just one night."

"No," Urashima said.

At that, the Daughter of the Deep Sea began to cry. Her sobs tugged at Urashima.

"Fine. I will stay with you. Just one night."

The Daughter of the Deep Sea shared her love with him and returned him to shore that morning. She snatched his hand.

"I want you to take this," she pressed something into his hand. "To remember me." She smiled sadly.

Urashima held a small box made of pearl. Rainbows shimmered as it caught the light. The box's clasps were made of jade and coral.

"Don't open it," she said. She gazed at him for a long moment before turning away and disappearing into the sea.

Urashima slipped the box into his clothes and dashed for home. The scent of the pine forests made him laugh with joy. As he neared his home, he called for his children.

But something wasn't right. "They must still be asleep," he said to himself.

When he came to his house, he found four crumbling walls, overgrown with moss. Nightshade grew in the ruined doorway, and death lilies grew in the hearth. Ferns and other plants covered what was left of his home.

"Have I lost my wits? This is my house, isn't it?"

He sat down on the grassy floor and gazed around. It was his home, or what was left of it. "Where are my wife and children? What happened? Someone at the village will know."

When he reached the village, he didn't recognize anyone. He didn't find his children playing with the others in the village, nor did he see a familiar face anywhere. No one seemed to know him. He spent the day searching the village, so familiar yet so strange, for any hint he could.

At sunset he stood in the village square. A man hurried past and Urashima caught his sleeve. "Do you know a fisherman called Urashima?"

"I don't. Sorry."

People from the mountains passed by along with pilgrims and tradesmen. Urashima didn't recognize anyone.

Finally, an old man, stooped with age, passed.

"Old man," Urashima called out. "Have you heard of the fisherman Urashima? He was born in this village."

"No one of that name lives here. But there was a fisherman called Urashima who drowned a long time ago. My grandfather could barely remember him when I was a boy. It was that long ago."

"So he is dead." Urashima felt as if he were a fish nailed to a cutting board.

"Even his sons and grandsons by now. Good evening, stranger."

Urashima decided to go to the village cemetery and see for himself what the old man said. Night had settled in with its chill wind. The moon shined overhead by the time he reached the tombstones. It didn't take him long to find the markers of his family.

Urashima collapsed in front of the stones, and the box fell out of his clothes. He stared at, feeling numb, as the wind blew and the sound of the sea just beyond the cemetery filled the night. On a whim, he opened the box.

Faint white smoke rose from the box and floated out to sea.

Suddenly, Urashima felt exhausted. His hair turned white and his body shriveled. He felt his strength leave him. He reached out to close the box's lid with a wizened, spotted hand but stopped.

"The smoke is gone. What does it matter?" His voice faltered in his dim hearing. "I'm so tired."

He lay down in front of the graves of his family and died.

Supernatural Beings

Chin Chin Kobakama

Once there lived a pretty little girl who was also lazy. Her rich parents had a great many servants that did everything for her. They dressed and undressed her. They arranged her hair and even cut her food for her. She grew to be a lazy young woman.

At last, she married a brave warrior and lived with him. But he had few servants, and she had to do much for herself. Dressing gave her trouble, and it took a lot of effort to look as neat and pretty as her servants had made her look. But her husband often had to go to war, so should could sometimes be as lazy as she wanted.

One night while her husband was away, strange noises awoke her. Her paper lantern cast odd, moving shadows throughout her room. Hundreds of little men, dressed in samurai armor, danced around her. Each stood about one inch tall. They carried tiny swords and gazed at her as they danced, laughed, and sang:

We are the Chin Chin Kobakama,
The hour is late;
Sleep, honorable noble darling!

The little men made ugly faces at her. She tried to catch them as they passed, but they leaped away. She tried to drive them away, but they kept returning to their marching circle. They never stopped singing and laughing at her.

She cowered under her blankets. The men danced and sang throughout the night. The next morning, she didn't tell anyone what had happened. She was the wife of a samurai. She too was expected to be brave.

Each night, the little men returned at the same hour and marched around her. She quickly grew sick from the strain of their pestering. She lay in her bed when her husband returned. He sat at her side, accounting of his adventure and asking after her. At first, she didn't want to tell him anything. She worried he would laugh at her. But his kindness finally coaxed her.

He didn't laugh as she spoke. He sat straight and serious. "What time do they come?"

"At the Hour of the Ox."

"Tonight I will hide and watch for them. Don't be afraid."

That night he hid in the closet and peered through a crack between the sliding doors. When the hour came, he saw the little men climb up through the tatami mats. They began their dance and song as his wife accounted. They looked so strange and danced in such a funny way that the warrior struggled not to laugh. But when he saw how frightened his wife was of them, his mirth faded. He drew his short sword and burst out of the closet. He struck at the dancers.

The men all turned into toothpicks.

The samurai studied them for a long moment. "I see what is going on now. Whenever you are finished with your toothpick, I've watched you stick it between the floor mats. You've angered the fairies that take care of the tatami mats with your laziness."

She hid her face. "What can I do?"

The samurai called for his servant to burn the toothpicks. After that, the little men never returned.

Daikoku and the Demon

Long ago when the Buddha's disciples came to Japan, they grew upset with the people because they continued to worship Daikoku was the patron of wealth. The disciples decided to be rid of him, so they called Yemma, the judge of the lower regions, to destroy Daikoku.

Yemma commanded a legion of demons. The demons came in all sorts of colors: green, black, blue, and vermilion. But for such an important assignment, he called Shino, a cunning and old demon, to kill or remove Daikoku.

Daikoku proved difficult to find. Shino had to travel all over asking questions and often only finding clues that led to dead ends. One day he met a sparrow who happened to know where Daikoku's palace sat.

"He sits among his treasure," the sparrow said "and eats daikon radishes which are piled to the ceiling. His favorite pets are rats. He likes to store his rice in straw bags and considers rice more precious than money."

Shino thanked the sparrow for the information and set off. When he entered the palace gate, no one was around. He continued on until he came to a large storehouse built in the shape of a huge rice-measure. He didn't see a door or window, so he climbed up a narrow board leaning against the top. He peered over the opening and saw Daikoku sitting in a garden nestled inside the gigantic enclosure. Lucky for Shino, Daikoku faced away from him. Without hesitating, he dropped into the garden.

As soon as he landed, Daikoku began to squeak. His rat entourage looked at him.

"Mr. Rat, I feel some strange creature nearby. Chase him away."

The largest rat plucked a sprig of holly with thorns all over it and raced toward Shino with speed that surprised the old demon. The rat whacked him and chased him. Shino found a ladder and scrambled up it with the rat right behind him. Shino ran back to Yemma's palace as fast as he could. His skin burned where the rat struck him with the thorns.

He collapsed in front of his master. "Please don't send me against Daikoku again." He accounted the misadventure between gasps for breath.

The Buddhist disciplines soon learned they couldn't banish or kill Daikoku. They agreed to recognize him and make peace with him. When people heard how a rat drove away Shino with a sprig of holly, they started using the same technique. On New Year's Eve, they started placing sprigs of holly near their doorways to keep away demons and evil spirits.

Don't Throw Useful Things Away

Once, a little boy befriended a divine boy and girl who would come to play each day. His parents couldn't see these friends. The little boy grew sick, and during this illness the friends didn't come. When they finally visited, the boy was near death.

"We know what made you sick," the girl said. "Your grandfather owned a beautiful axe. I am a small tray that he made with it. And my brother is a pestle that was also made with the axe. But your father has been bad. He threw away the axe. It now rusts under the floor, so the axe made you sick to punish your father. We came to warn you. If you want to live, you must tell your father to find the axe, polish it, and make a new handle for it. Then you will be cured, and the axe will visit you in a human shape."

So the boy told his father of this. His father searched under the floor of the house and found the axe. He polished it and made a new handle for it. And his son immediately felt better.

After that, the axe appeared to the boy as a handsome man. The tray and the pestle also visited and became the boy's sister and brother. As a god, the axe knew everything that happened and their causes. So the boy learned everything the axe had to say. He knew why people became sick and how to treat them. Soon, people in the village saw the boy as a great healer and prophet.

For this reason, you should never throw away anything that belonged to your ancestors. You will be punished by the gods if you do.

Rokuro Kubi

One evening, the priest Kwairyo traveled through the mountains of Kai province. As night descended, he decided to spend it outside. He found a grassy spot by the roadside and lay down. He didn't mind the discomfort of the hard ground, and the root of a pine tree made an excellent pillow. His body was iron, and weather had never bothered him.

He had just settled when a man came down the road carrying an axe and a bundle of chopped wood. He stopped and watched Kwairyo for a moment. "What kind of man can you be to lie down in such a place? There are foxes, badgers, and more haunting these mountains."

"I'm just a wandering priest," Kwairyo said. "I'm not worried about foxes or anything like that. As for places like this, I rather like them. They are good for meditating."

"You must be a brave man," the woodcutter said. "This area has a bad reputation, and I can confirm it is dangerous to sleep here. I have a hut a little way from here. Please stay with me, or I will worry all night about you."

Kwairyo accepted the man's offer. The woodcutter led him along a narrow path that wound from the main road through the forest. It skirted cliffs and sometimes offered nothing but slippery roots to walk on.

The full moon shone by the time they cleared the path. The man's hut stood on top of a hill. The man led Kwairyo to a building behind the house. There, bamboo pipes carried water from the stream. As they washed their feet, Kwairyo enjoyed the smell of the cedar trees and the sound of some waterfall beyond them.

Four people sat inside the cottage, warming their hands at the fire. They bowed low to Kwairyo and spoke in ways that betrayed them as no mere peasants.

Kwairyo turned to the woodcutter. "Judging by your speech and manners, I imagine you haven't always been a woodcutter."

The woodcutter smiled. "You aren't mistaken. I used to be a person of distinction, but my actions ruined that. I used to serve a lord, but I loved women and wine too much. I now pray for a way to make some atonement for what I did. I try to help those who are unfortunate whenever I can."

"My friend, men are often foolish in their youth. According to the sutras, the strongest in wrong doing can become the strongest in right doing with good resolve. I don't doubt you have a good heart. Tonight I will recite sutras for your sake and pray you might be able to overcome the karma of your mistakes."

Kwairyo bade them good night, and the woodcutter showed him to a small side room. The others went to sleep. Kwairyo remained awake and quietly read the sutras by the light of a paper lantern. He read and prayed late into the night. Finished, he opened the room's small window to look at the night before going to sleep. The night thrummed with the songs of crickets and other insects mingling with the hushed waterfall beyond. Kwairyo felt thirsty and remembered the bamboo pipes at the rear of the house. He didn't want to disturb the sleeping household, so he decided to get a drink there.

He pushed open the sliding screen that separated his room from the main apartment and saw the five people laying beyond.

None of them had a head.

He stood stunned, imagining some crime had happened. Then he noticed there was no blood. The headless necks didn't look cut. *This is either an illusion,* he thought, *or I was lured into the house of a* Rokuro Kubi. He recalled reading about them in a book. If you removed the body and the head couldn't find the body, it would panic and dash itself on the floor like a ball until it died.

He grabbed the foot of the woodcutter and pulled it to the window. He pushed it outside. Then he went to the back door and found it barred.

"The heads must have left through the smoke hole in the roof," he muttered to himself. He unbarred the door. He stalked through the garden and to the cedars beyond it. He heard voices talking in the grove. He followed them until he caught sight of five heads flitting about and chatting. They ate worms and insects they found on the ground or among the trees.

The head of the woodcutter spoke. "Isn't that priest nicely fat? I look forward to eating him. I was foolish to talk to him as I did. It only made him recite those sutras, keeping me from going near him. Perhaps he is asleep now. Someone needs to go and see if he is."

The head of the young woman floated toward the house. After a few moments, it returned, alarmed. "The priest is gone! What's worse, he's taken your body and hidden it."

The woodcutter's eyes widened, and his hair bristled. "Without my body I will..." Tears fell. "I will eat him before I do. I—" The head glanced around and stopped. "There he is! Behind the that tree."

The heads flew toward Kwairyo, but the strong priest tore a sapling from the ground and struck them as they came. Four heads flew away. The head of the woodcutter continued to attack the priest no matter how often Kwairyo knocked it away. It latched onto Kwairyo's sleeve with its teeth. The priest grabbed the head's topknot and punched it, but the head held fast.

It shuddered and moaned between its teeth and then stopped moving. Despite his strength, Kwairyo couldn't force the jaws open.

With the head hanging from his sleeve, Kwairyo returned to the house and caught the four Rokuro Kubi squatting together. Their bruised heads had returned to their bodies. As soon as they saw him, they screamed and fled into the woods.

Dawn's light filtered through the trees. Kwairyo knew that demons could only act at night. He glanced down at the head. Blood and dirt covered it. He laughed. "What a trophy, the head of a demon." He gathered his few possessions and continued his journey.

He came to Suwa and walked the main street with the head still dangling from his sleeve. The sight drew a crowd. The police arrived and took Kwairyo to prison, surmising the head belonged to a murdered man. As they questioned him, Kwairyo said nothing. He only smiled.

The next day, the police brought him in front of the magistrates.

"Explain why you have a head fastened to your sleeve," one of the magistrates ordered. "And why you parade your crime so shamelessly."

Kwairyo chuckled. "I didn't fasten the head to my sleeve. It did that itself. Much against my will, I might add. It's the head of a Rokuro Kubi." He told them the story.

The magistrates didn't find the story as funny as the priest did. They thought he was a hardened criminal who insulted their intelligence with such an outlandish tale. They all ordered his execution, except for a very old man. Throughout the trial, he didn't say anything, but after hearing the opinion of his fellow magistrates, he stood up.

"Let me examine the head. If the priest has spoken the truth, the head will be his witness. Bring the head here."

The police couldn't remove the head, so they took off Kwairyo's clothes and brought it to the judges. The old man examined it thoroughly. He found several strange, red characters on the nape of its neck.

"Look at these," he said. "Also notice how the neck doesn't show any evidence of being cut." He gave them a moment to look. "I'm quite sure the priest has spoken the truth. This is the head of a Rokuro Kubi. You will always find these characters on the neck of one. As you can see, they are not painted. It's also well known that they live on the mountains of Kai province."

He regarded Kwairyo. "What sort of priest are you? You are more courageous than priests I know. You have the look of a soldier. Perhaps you were once a samurai?"

Kwairyo nodded. "Before becoming a priest, I went by the name of Isogai Heidazaemon Takatsuru of Kyushu. Some of you may remember that name."

Murmurs of admiration swept the courtroom. The magistrates dismissed the charges and escorted him to the local lord's castle. There they offered a feast in Kwairyo's honor and made him take a gift before they allowed him to leave. When Kwairyo left Suwa, he felt happy. He also took the head with him.

A day or two after he left, Kwairyo met a thief.

"Strip," the thief ordered, brandishing his weapon.

Kwairyo removed his clothes and offered them to the thief. The man then saw the head dangling from the sleeve. He cried out and dropped the clothing.

"What kind of priest are you? You are worse than me. I've killed people, but even I wouldn't walk around with a head fastened to my sleeve." He recovered himself and frowned in thought. "That head would be useful. I could frighten people with it. Will you sell it to me? You can have my robe, and I will give you five ryo for the head."

"I will let you have the head and robe if you insist," Kwairyo said. "But that isn't the head of a man. It's a demon's head. If you buy it and have problems, please remember that I was honest with you."

"What a nice priest. You kill men and then joke about it. Here is my robe and the money. I will take the head."

"I wasn't joking. The only joke, if you can call it one, is paying good money for a demon's head." Kwairyo chuckled and went on his way.

The thief used the head to pose as a demon priest for a time. When he reached Suwa, he learned the true story of the head. He worried that the spirit of the Rokuro Kubi would give him trouble and decided to take it to its body and bury them together. He found his way to the lonely cottage in the mountains of Kai. However, he couldn't find the body, so he buried the head by itself in the cedar grove behind the cottage and set up a tombstone. He brought a Shinto priest to consecrate the area. The Tombstone of the Rokuro Kubi can still be seen today.

The Bamboo Cutter and the Moon Child

Long ago lived an old bamboo woodcutter. He and his wife lived a poor, hardworking life. Unfortunately, the gods hadn't blessed them with children. Each day, he went out to cut bamboo, which he used to make furniture and other household items to sell.

One morning, he went out as he always did to the bamboo forest. As he entered a thick grove, soft white light filled the area. He gazed at the sky to be certain the full moon hadn't settled over the clearing. He noticed the light streamed not from the sky but from a single bamboo stalk. He dropped his axe and approached the strange sight.

In the center of the stalk stood a tiny human, only three inches in height.

The man stared at the beautiful, tiny girl. "The gods must have sent you to be my child. They would've known I come here every day." He gently picked up the girl—she hugged his thumb tight—and carried her home.

His wife was astonished at the little girl. But she also immediately took to her. The wife gently placed their new daughter in a basket to keep her safe. The old couple lavished their love on the tiny girl, praising the gods for their generosity every time they prayed together.

The next day, the old man went up to the grove to work. As he cut down the bamboo, he noticed something glistening inside. He looked closer and found gold and jewels hidden inside every stalk he felled. He used the money to build a fine house. He became known as one of the wealthiest men in the area.

Three months passed. The bamboo child grew quickly, from three inches to a full-grown young woman. Her foster parents dressed her with the best kimono. Her beauty was so striking that the old couple placed her behind screens. They let no one else see her and waited on her themselves. Any room she entered filled with a soft light, as if she were the moon itself. The old couple named her Princess Moonlight.

They held a festival to celebrate her naming. Everyone who saw her through the screen marveled at her beauty. Word quickly spread, and suitors soon came to their home. They made holes in the fence surrounding the house, hoping to see her as she went from room to room. Many stayed day and night for a chance to glimpse her. The old man and his wife did what they could to keep their daughter safe from them. Eventually, the suitors realized how hopeless their desires were and went home.

Except for five samurai.

The men stood outside the fence in all weather. They wrote letters and poems about their love. But Princess Moonlight never replied. Winter settled in, and still they didn't give up. Spring came, and finally the five asked the old bamboo cutter to show Princess Moonlight to them.

"I can't," he told them. "I'm not her real father, so I can't make her obey me. If she doesn't want to be seen by you, she won't be seen by you."

At this, the five samurai returned to their homes to ponder the best way of touching the Princess's heart. Each of them prayed for a chance. After several days, seeming of one mind, the five returned to the house.

The old man went out to them. "The Princess has decided to never see any man."

"Please speak to her for us," one of the five said. "Tell her that each one of us bursts with love for her. That we have gone without food and sleep in all sorts of weather just to see her once."

The old man felt sorry for the young men. He also admired their dedication and decided any one of them would be an honor to his daughter. He went to Princess Moonlight and said, "Although you are a heavenly being, I've raised you the best I can. Could you listen to my request?"

"Father, there's nothing I wouldn't do for you. You call me a heavenly being, but I don't remember anything before I met you and Mother."

The old man smiled. He felt his eyes fill with tears. "I'd like to see you happily married before I die. I'm over seventy, after all. You should see these five suitors and choose one of them to be your husband."

"Why? I don't want to marry right now."

The old man hung his head. "Who will take care of you when I die? When your Mother dies?"

She looked away. "I'm nowhere near as beautiful as everyone says I am. They will be disappointed. If whomever I choose doesn't know me, he will change his mind once he does."

"What kind of men would you want to see? These men have endured a lot for just a chance to see you in the last five months. What else do you want from them?"

She looked up. "They need to prove their love for me. They need to bring me something from a distant country."

That evening when the suitors arrived to sing of their love, the bamboo cutter met them. "She has agreed to see you. If—"

The men cheered.

The old man raised his voice. "If you can prove your love." He pointed at the first samurai. "Bring Princess Moonlight the stone bowl that belonged to Buddha. It is in India."

He pointed at the second samurai. "Go to the Mountain of Horai. Bring back a branch of the tree that grows on its summit. The roots of the tree are like silver; the trunk is gold. It bears fruit like white jewels."

The old man moved on to the third man. "Go to China and bring back the skin of the fire rat."

"And you, search for the dragon with the stone that radiates five colors. Bring back the stone."

The fifth samurai stepped forward. The old man nodded at him. "Find the swallow that carried a shell in its stomach. Return with the shell."

The men shared a look. They knew the tasks the Princess had given them seemed impossible, and they each returned home in despair. Over the next few days, each man thought more of his love for Princess Moonlight and resolved to try his best.

The first samurai sent word to the Princess that he was starting his journey. But he didn't have the courage to travel all the way to India. He traveled as far as Kyoto where he bought a stone bowl from one of the temples. He wrapped it in a gold cloth and waited. Three years later, he returned to the bamboo cutter with the bowl.

Princess Moonlight wondered about the samurai returning so quickly. When her father presented the bowl, she expected it to fill the room with light. When she unwrapped it, she turned to her foster father. "This is a fake. It doesn't fill the room with light. I won't see him."

The samurai threw the returned bowl away and went home to give up all hope of winning the Princess.

The second samurai sent word that he was setting out for Mount Horai. He set off east until he came to an island. On his journey, he learned that the mountain only existed in fables. So he found six skilled jewelers and had them make a gold and silver branch like what was said to grow from the fabled tree. He placed the branch in a lacquered box and traveled to the bamboo cutter. He made sure to rip his clothes and cover himself in dirt so it looked like he traveled far and hard.

"You should see him," the old man said to his daughter, presenting the box. "He traveled hard and found what you wanted." He opened the box and pulled out the branch. "I've never seen such a treasure."

Princess Moonlight remained silent. She took the branch and examined it. "This is fake. No one can fetch a branch from the tree this quickly."

The old man went out to the samurai. "Where did you find the branch?"

"Two years ago, I took a ship to search for the mountain," the samurai said. "A great storm arose and tossed me to an unknown island. There I found demons who tried to kill me, but I managed to befriend them. They helped the sailors repair my ship. As we sailed, food gave out and everyone got sick. But finally, on the five hundredth day, I saw the peak of the mountain. I landed and found a shining being that told me I had found Mount Horai. It was a hard climb, but I—"

"There he is!" Four craftsman approached the samurai. "You still haven't paid us!"

The old bamboo cutter frowned. "For this, I presume?" He lifted the branch.

"Yes!" they exclaimed.

"Take it," the old man said. He glared at the samurai. "Never come back here."

In a rage, the samurai rounded on the craftsman and attacked them. They fled, and the warrior beat them all the way.

The third samurai had a friend in China. He wrote this man to send him the skin of the fire rat, promising any amount of money. Eventually, his friend sent word that he had arrived with the requested skin. The samurai met him at the port city and paid a large amount of money for the pelt. He placed it carefully in a box and sent it to the Princess.

When the Princess received the box, she tossed the skin into the fire. The real skin of a fire rat wouldn't burn, but this one burned immediately.

The fourth samurai had sent his servants throughout Japan and China to find the dragon Princess Moonlight wanted. No one was allowed to return until they found it. But the servants knew the request was impossible, so they used the time to take a protracted vacation on the samurai's coin. Meanwhile, the samurai got his house ready for the

Princess. After a year, his servants still hadn't returned. The samurai grew desperate. He took two men with him and hired a ship. He ordered the captain to search for the dragon. Of course, the captain was more sensible than that; he refused. But the samurai forced the captain and crew out to sea anyway.

They encountered a terrible storm that lasted so long that the samurai decided to give up the hunt. When they finally landed, the samurai was sick. He suspected the Princess wanted him dead. His servants finally arrived, surprised that he praised them despite their failure.

"I'm sick of adventure," he said. "I don't want anything else to do with that woman."

The fifth samurai also failed to find the swallow's shell.

By this time, Princess Moonlight's fame had reached the ears of the Emperor. He sent one of the Court women to see if she was as beautiful as stories said. If so, he would summon her to the Palace and make her one of the ladies-in-waiting.

Princess Moonlight refused to see the Court lady.

"You have to," the old man said. "It's an order from the Emperor himself." He wrung his hands.

"If I am forced to go to the Emperor's Palace on his order, I will vanish from the earth," she said.

When the lady returned and accounted the Princess's words, the Emperor decided to go and see her. He planned a hunting trip near the bamboo cutter's house. The next day, he went out and rode ahead of his entourage. He came to the house and went to the Princess's room.

He had never seen anyone so beautiful. She really did emit a soft light from her skin. When the Princess noticed him peering at her, she tried to run. The Emperor caught her arm.

"Please, listen to me."

She hid her face in her sleeves. "Say it quickly and get out."

"Please come back with me. I will give you a position of honor and everything you want. A beauty like you shouldn't be hidden. I'll call my palanquin—"

"No." She looked up at him. She seemed to grow transparent. "If I go with you, I will vanish." She faded further as he watched.

"I will let you remain free if you don't vanish," he said.

She regained some of her solidity.

The sound of horses filtered through the window. He sighed. "I have to go." He gazed at her for several moments before turning away.

He thought of her long after he returned to the Imperial Palace. He wrote poems dedicated to her and sent them. She replied with poetry of her own. Her poems gently told him how she could never marry anyone on earth.

The old man and his wife noticed how Princess Moonlight would gaze at the moon and cry. One such night, he approached her. "Tell me why you cry at the moon."

"It's my true home." She gazed at him with damp eyes. "It's not that I don't love you and Mother, but my time with you is nearing its end. On the fifteenth day of this month, my friends from the moon will take me home."

"So you remember now."

She nodded. "I don't want to leave you. You've made me so happy."

The Emperor soon heard about this and sent messengers to confirm the story. The old man cried when he confirmed it.

"But I will capture them," he said. "I won't let them take her."

The messengers returned and told the Emperor the old man's words. On the fifteenth, the Emperor sent two thousand warriors to watch the house. One thousand of them were stationed on the roof. All of them were well-trained archers. The bamboo cutter and his wife hid Princess Moonlight with them in the innermost room.

"No one is to sleep tonight," the old man told all his servants. "Protect Princess Moonlight."

"It's not going to matter," Princess Moonlight said. "You won't be able to stop them. Father, Mother. I'm sorry. I would've liked to stay with you and give you a little in return for all the love you've given me."

Toward dawn, just when everyone thought the danger had passed, a cloud fogged the house. In the middle of the cloud stood a chariot with a band of glowing beings. One wore the clothing of a king. He stepped out of the chariot.

"Come out, bamboo cutter."

The old man confronted the glowing king.

"It's time for Princess Moonlight to return home to the moon. She was sent here as punishment for a crime. We know you've taken good care of her. We rewarded you for this with the wealth you enjoy. The wealth you collected from the bamboo."

"I've raised the Princess for twenty years," the old man said. "She has never once done anything wrong. You are looking for a different woman." The old man gestured. "Look elsewhere for your sinful woman."

The glowing being ignored him. "Come out, Princess Moonlight."

The doors to the innermost room opened on their own, revealing Princess Moonlight shining brighter than the being. A messenger was suddenly beside her and led her to the chariot. She looked back to see her earthly father with a helpless expression.

"I will be fine." She forced a brave smile for him. "I don't want to leave you. Whenever you look at the moon, I will be looking back."

"Let us go with you," the wife said.

Princess Moonlight took off her outer kimono and handed it to the old man. "Keep this to remember me. Thank you."

One of the moon beings in the chariot held a coat of wings. Another held a phial that glimmered with the Elixir of Life. She swallowed a little of the elixir and tried to give it to the old man. Before she could, the Moon King tried to snatch the elixir from her.

Princess Moonlight clutched the phial to her chest. "Wait! I cannot forget my good friend, the Emperor. I must write him to say goodbye while I remain a human."

She ignored the king's impatience and wrote her letter. She slipped the phial into the letter and pressed the letter to the old man. "Give this to the Emperor."

She climbed into the chariot. It lifted into the breaking dawn until it disappeared into the clouds.

Princess Moonlight's letter arrived at the Palace, but the Emperor feared to touch the Elixir of Life. He sent the letter and the elixir to the top of Mount Fuji. His vassals burned it on the summit at sunrise. To this day, people see the smoke rising from Mount Fuji.

The Demon of Adachigahara

Long ago, a demon in the form of an old woman lived on a large plain called Adachigahara. People whispered about how missing travelers and villagers were lured into the old woman's cottage where she ate them. No one ventured near the plain after sunset, and everyone tried to avoid the place during daytime.

One day at dusk, a Buddhist priest wandered into the plain. He was on a pilgrimage to various shrines and had lost his way. After a day of traveling, he was tired and hungry. Already, the autumn evening promised to be cold, so he felt anxious to find someplace to stay. After several more hours of wandering, he came upon a clump of trees and a ray of light gleaming among them.

"That has to be a cottage where I can stay."

The cottage looked as if no one had cared for it in decades. The roof sagged, and vines grew throughout its walls. Holes riddled it. Yet within the open door, an old woman sat spinning by the light of an old lantern.

"Good evening. Please excuse me for interrupting you at such a late hour, but I'm a traveler in need of a place to rest. Please let me stay the night."

The old woman stopped spinning and approached the priest. "You must be tired to have lost your way out here. Sadly, I don't have a bed to offer you."

"I'm more than happy to sleep on the floor. I just need shelter for the night. I'm too tired to walk further. It is also a cold night. Please allow me to stay," the priest said.

She hesitated. "Very well. You can stay. Come in, and I will make a fire."

The priest took off his sandals and entered the hut. The old woman busied herself with the fire and cooked a meal of rice. After they finished their meal, they talked together for some time. The pilgrim felt grateful that he had come across such a kind, hospitable old woman. The fire soon died, and the pilgrim began to shiver again.

"I will gather more wood," the old woman said. "Please watch the house while I'm gone."

"Let me go instead. You are too old to be getting wood on this cold a night." He started to stand.

The old woman shook her head. "You're my guest. Just sit there and don't move. Whatever happens don't go near or look into the inner room."

"I won't." The priest frowned in confusion.

The old woman left. The priest sat next to the dim lantern, rubbing his arms. An unsettled feeling blanketed him as he listened to the silence. He should've heard the usual night birds and animals, but not even the trees rustled. He paced to keep warm and to work off some of his anxiety. He found himself close to the door to the innermost room.

What could be in there?

He shook his head. He didn't want the old woman to be angry with him for disobeying her, so he returned to his place by the fire. Time passed. The woman still hadn't returned. The unsettled feeling soon grew into fear.

Something was wrong.

And it had to do with the secret in the inner room.

"She will not know I've looked unless I tell her," he whispered to himself. "Just a glance."

He crept toward the door and slid it open with a trembling hand. His blood froze. Piles of human bones filled the room. Layers of blood blackened the walls and the floor. In one corner, a tower of human skulls stared at him. In another corner, a lattice of arm bones stood. The scent made him feel faint. He fell backward with horror.

"What is this place? May Buddha help me! This old woman has to be the demon I heard about. When she returns, she will try to eat me too." He snatched up his hat and his staff and rushed out of the house and into the night.

He hadn't gotten far when a voice yelled for him to stop. He ignored the call and ran faster. Footsteps thumped behind him.

"Stop, you wicked man." The old woman's voice sounded close. "Why did you look into my room?"

Fear pushed away the priest's exhaustion. He knew if she caught him, he would become her next meal. While he ran, he chanted, "Namu Amida Butsu."

Behind him the old hag raced. Her hair streamed behind her, and her face contoured with rage. She brandished a long, blood-stained knife.

Just when the priest could run no further, dawn broke. As the sunlight touched the demon, she vanished. The priest collapsed to the grass, breathing hard and feeling grateful for the sun. He knew the Buddha's protection had saved him. He took out his rosary and bowed toward the sun. His thankful prayers rang out across the plain. Then he set out toward another part of the country, only too glad to leave the haunted plain behind him.

The Demon Spider

In a lonely part of the country, a temple stood. Demons had claimed the temple, and many samurai had disappeared in an effort to destroy them.

One night, a brave samurai approached the temple. He stopped and turned to his companions. "If I'm still alive by morning, I will hit the temple's bell." He took the lantern and left his companions.

Inside the temple stood a large, dusty statue of Buddha. The samurai settled against its base and waited with his sword close at hand. Time passed. The natural sounds of a summer night—cicadas chirruped and other night creatures called—filtered into the temple.

Around midnight, a demon appeared. It appeared to be human, except it had half a body and only one eye. It sniffed the air. "I smell a man."

The samurai remained still.

The demon smelled the air a bit longer and then left. Then, a priest entered the temple. He played the shamisen as he walked. When the priest came close, the samurai drew his blade and leaped up. The priest didn't startle.

Instead, he laughed. "Did you think I was a demon or something? I'm the only priest of this temple." He lifted the instrument. "This keeps the demons away. Why don't you play a little?" He extended the shamisen to the samurai.

The warrior grasped it. Instantly the shamisen changed into a thick tendril of a spider web. The priest grinned at him. The priest's face extended, and eyes popped from its forehead. Its body distended. Legs burst from its body as it morphed into a giant spider.

The samurai tried to free his left hand, but the spiderweb held fast. He managed to draw his sword, slashing at the head of the spider as it lunged at him. Dark blood sprayed. The creature squealed and backed away. The samurai struggled against the web, but his sword got stuck in its stickiness. Soon he could only hang helpless.

Dawn broke, and the samurai's companions entered the temple to find the samurai alive but trapped. After they freed him, they followed the dark blood of the spider out of the temple. The drops led them to a hole in the temple's forgotten garden. A pained, hissing groan came from the hole.

The spider had trapped itself in its desire for safety. It took some time for the samurai and his companions to dig up the demon spider. But they kept at it until at last the samurai killed it. With the temple finally safe, the nearby villagers restored the grounds.

The Faceless Ghost

Late one night, a merchant hurried up a steep slope on Akasaka Road when he came upon a woman crouching by the moat. She cried, and afraid she intended to drown herself, he stopped to help her. She dressed well and had her hair arranged like a young noblewoman.

"Please don't cry like that," he said. "Tell me what the trouble is. I'd be happy to help you."

She hid her face in her long sleeves and kept crying.

"A lady like you shouldn't be here at night. Please tell me what I can do to help you."

She turned toward the moat and away from him.

He laid his hand on her shoulder. "Nothing is so bad that you need to kill herself."

The girl turned and dropped her sleeve. She had no face! Where her nose, eyes, and mouth should've been was nothing but smooth skin, like the white shell of an egg. The merchant screamed and fled.

He ran up the slope as fast as he could. A lantern shined in the distance, and he made for it. The lantern illuminated the stand of a noodle seller. Pleased to find light and another human, the merchant collapsed at the noodle-seller's feet.

"What happened?" the man asked. "Did something hurt you?"

The merchant shook his head while he panted.

"Are thieves after you?"

"Not thieves," the merchant gulped air. "I saw a woman by the moat. She...I can't tell you what she showed me!"

"Did she show you something like this?" The noodle seller stroked his face. As he did, his nose flattened, and his eyes and mouth disappeared until he had no face.

The lantern went out.

The Ghost of the Flute's Tomb

Long ago, a blind man named Yoichi lived near Lake Kumeda. The villagers of Kumedamura liked him for his honesty and kindness. He worked as a masseur, and he carried an iron cane and a flute. The flute told people he was nearby and ready to work, and work he did! He earned enough to have a little house and a single servant to help him.

One spring evening, Yoichi walked home from working all day in the village when he heard a girl crying. She sounded familiar. He followed the sobs toward the lake shore when he heard the splash. He rushed into the water and managed to drag her out.

"Who are you, and why do you want to die?" he asked.

"I'm Asayo, the teahouse girl," she said. "I can't live on what I'm paid, and I haven't eaten for two days. I can't continue with this kind of life."

"That's no reason to kill yourself. I will take you to my house and do what I can to help you. If I remember right, you are only twenty-five, and I'm told you are still fair. Have you thought of marriage?" He reached out and touched her shoulder. "I will see you are fed and given dry clothes."

Asayo stayed with Yoichi for the next few months, and they married. Although Yoichi treated her kindly, Asayo proved selfish and even unfaithful to him as a wife.

That August, a troop of actors arrived in the village. Among them was Sawamura Tamataro. Asayo went to see the plays and fell in love with Tamataro. They began an affair, and she lent him any sum of money he wanted and often visited him at indecent hours of the night. Soon everyone in the village knew of their affair. Everyone except Yoichi. But no one wanted to tell him of his wife's infidelity.

Several times Tamataro stayed with Asayo at Yoichi's house, but the actor remained so quiet that Yoichi didn't know he was just a room away.

Finally, one of Yoichi's neighbors couldn't take it anymore. "Yoichi, your wife has been cheating on you with the actor Tamataro."

Yoichi frowned. "Why would you say such a thing?"

"Everyone knows it. In fact, he is at your house with your wife right now. He visits nearly every day. Many of us would be glad to help you punish her."

He shook his head. "I will take care of it." He left and rushed home as fast and as quietly as he could.

When he arrived, the front door was locked. He went around back to find the back door was locked as well. Yoichi heard Asayo and Tamataro inside. Rage filled him and gave him strength. Using a rope, he pulled himself to the roof, intending to climb down through the smoke hole in the roof. He tied a second straw rope and cast it into the hole, but as he slid down it, the rope snapped. He plunged inside and cracked his head on a hard wooden block used for stretching cloth.

Asayo and the actor rushed out at the sound and found Yoichi dead. They waited until the next day to tell everyone that Yoichi had died by falling down a flight of stairs. They buried him quickly and without the proper rites. All of his property went to Asayo.

A few months later, Asayo and Tamataro married. The village shunned them for what they had done to Yoichi. The villagers suspected something had happened to Yoichi because of them. For their part, Asayo and Tamataro kept to themselves.

Although Yoichi didn't have children, he had a friend named Okuda Ichibei who lived in the village of Minato. One night, he awoke to see the Yoichi standing over him.

"Yoichi! I'm glad to see you, but why did you arrive so late at night? Why didn't you let me know you were coming? I would've stayed up for you and had a meal ready. Never mind, I will call a servant. Please sit down and let's talk."

Yoichi shook his head. The movement didn't look natural to Ichibei, but he couldn't say why. "I'm no longer alive," Yoichi said.

"Well, you would be tired after such a long journey. I—" Ichibei cut off as he noticed he could see the wall through his friend. "Oh, Yoichi! What happened?"

"I need to be avenged so I can rest in peace."

Ichibei shed a tear for his friend after the spirit finished. "My old friend, you don't even have to ask. I would've avenged you as soon as I heard what happened."

Yoichi smiled and faded into the night.

Ichibei awoke that morning, wandering if he had dreamed up Yoichi. He turned to get up and saw Yoichi's wooden flute. Ichibei had carved Yoichi's name into it and given it to him. He snatched it and prepared to leave.

When he arrived at Yoichi's house, Asayo opened the door. "I heard my friend Yoichi had died," Ichibei said.

"It was terrible. He fell down the stairs and smashed his head," Asayo said, feigning sorrow. "He mistook the staircase for a door. Now I'm married to his friend, an actor called Tamataro." She gestured at the man standing beside her.

"Please come in, and let's talk about our mutual friend," Tamataro said.

Ichibei entered and listened to their lies. The stories the two told had just enough truth to fool someone who didn't know Yoichi as well as Ichibei did. He kept a careful mask over his anger and wondered how best to avenge his friend.

Time passed, and a wind storm arose outside. In the midst of it, the unmistakable sound of a flute played.

Asayo's eyes widened. As the playing grew louder, she screamed and clutched Tamataro. "It's Yoichi!"

"And why would you be afraid of your husband and friend visiting, even as a spirit?" Ichibei asked.

The sound of the flute seemed in the room with them. Suddenly, an icy gale rushed into the ceiling's smoke hole. And the ghost of Yoichi floated down. He glimmered and looked sad.

Asayo and Tamataro stood up to run, but their legs gave out from fear. Tamataro seized a lamp and flung it at the ghost. It passed through him and shattered on the wall beyond. Flames licked up the paper and wood, aided by the wind.

Ichibei fled. As he looked back, Asayo and her husband sat frozen, captured by Yoichi's sad spirit. The flames spread fast, driving Ichibei back. He listened to the screams of Asayo and Tamataro as the flames engulfed them.

When the fire finally burned itself out, Ichibei swept up all the ashes and placed them in a tomb. He buried the flute where the house stood and had a monument built commemorate his memories of Yoichi. He called the monument "The Flute Ghost's Tomb."

The Ghost of the Violet Well

Shinge, a beautiful seventeen-year-old girl, walked through the valley of Shimizutani with her four servants, looking for the perfect spot for their picnic. Each spring, she visited the valley to search for her favorite flower, the violet.

The girls collected various flowers into their bamboo baskets. Each tried to outdo the other with the prettiest basket of flowers. But Shinge didn't find as many violets as she usually did.

"Let's go to the northern end of the valley where the Violet Well is," she said. Without waiting for her servants, she dashed off. The other girls laughed and chased after her.

Shinge arrived first and came across a cluster of violets. The sweet smell enticed her, and they were the most luscious purple she had seen. She reached out to plunk the entire cluster at once when a mountain snake raised its head. Surprise and fear struck her as if they were clubs, and she fainted.

The other girls walked and giggled among themselves, thinking it would please their mistress to arrive first. They took their time plucking flowers and chasing butterflies.

Three of the girls dropped their baskets and screamed when they saw Shinge laying in the grass with the green snake coiled near her head.

However, the fourth girl, Matsu, kept her wits enough to throw her basket of flowers at the snake. It uncoiled and slid away to find a quieter spot. She rushed forward and bent over Shinge, fearing the worst. The other girls joined her, but nothing they could do would revive Shinge. She grew paler, and her lips turned purple.

The girls didn't know what to do, nor could they carry her all the way home in time to save her.

"Don't be so sad. I can help your young lady if you let me," a man said behind them.

They turned and saw a handsome young man. "A snake bit her," Matsu said, recognizing him. "Doctor Yoshisawa."

He approached Shinge and took her hand in his. He felt her pulse and examined her carefully. Then he took out a small case of medicine and poured a little white powder onto a slip of paper.

"It's fortunate I came this way after visiting a patient. Give her this medicine while I hunt the snake."

Matsu mixed the medicine with a little water and made Shinge drink. Miraculously, color returned to Shinge's lips and cheeks.

The doctor returned a few minutes later, carrying a dead snake on a stick. "Is this the snake you saw?"

"That's the one."

"It quite poisonous. If I had been even a little later, your mistress would've died."

As he spoke, Shinge sat up and gazed up at him. In that moment, Matsu saw love blossom in that gaze.

"So you are the one who brought me back to life? Please tell me your name," Shinge said.

The doctor smiled and bowed. Without saying another word, he turned and left.

The girls helped their mistress home, but the medicine had done its work, and she didn't need help at all. Shinge's parents were grateful when they heard the story. However, five days later, Shinge became sick. She couldn't sleep and didn't want to talk to anyone. Her parents sent for doctors, but none of them found anything wrong with her. Yet as each day passed, she became weaker.

Matsu asked for an audience with Shinge's mother and father, Asano Zembei. As a great lord, he wasn't usually inclined to listen to servants, but he knew Matsu loved his daughter as much as he did. He was also desperate for some solution.

"Master, if you will let me find a doctor, I can promise to find one who will cure her," Matsu said.

"Where would you find such a doctor? We've already called the best in the province."

"My mistress isn't suffering from an illness that medicines can cure. She is sick at heart. She loves the doctor I know. Her heart's suffered from the day he saved her from the snakebite."

"What is the name of this doctor?"

"Doctor Yoshisawa. He is a handsome young man of courtly manners, but he is of low birth. The only cure for your daughter is to let her marry him."

Shinge's mother looked at Zembei. "I don't want to see our daughter die of heartache as we almost did. Let us at least see if he can make a good son-in-law. "

Zembei agreed, and Matsu promised not to say anything about the plan.

After Shinge's parents shared their desire for an engagement, she began to eat and recover. Ten days later she was called before her father and mother.

"My sweet daughter," Zembei said. "I've made careful inquiries about Dr. Yoshisawa. Sadly, I cannot consent to your marriage to one of so low a family."

Shinge knew her father's decision was final no matter how she would protest, so she bowed and went to her room where she cried bitterly. Matsu did her best to comfort Shinge.

The next day, Shinge was gone.

Matsu and the entire Asano household searched for her. Even Dr. Yoshisawa joined them. On the third day, Matsu went out to the valley, thinking Shinge might have hidden there. She found Shinge floating in the Violet Well.

Two days later, the Asano family buried their daughter. On the day, Yoshisawa drowned himself in the well.

A month later, people who visited the valley during stormy nights claimed to see a ghost floating over the well. Others claimed to hear a young man crying in the Valley of Shimizutani.

The Ghost of the Wall Hanging

Sawara studied under the artist Tenko. Tenko's niece, Kimi, managed the household. As time passed, Kimi fell in love with Sawara. He also secretly loved her, but he had his work. And that came first. For Kimi, love mattered more.

One day, while Tenko was away, Kimi came to Sawara, carrying a tray of tea.

"I can't hide it any longer," she said. "I love you." She served him tea with trembling hands. "Would you like to marry me?" She sat back and looked at her hands.

Sawara took a sip of the tea—excellent as always—to steady himself. "I would be delighted to marry you."

Kimi looked up. A smile played across her lips.

"But not yet," Sawara continued. "I need three years to establish myself as an artist in my own right."

"But you promise?" she asked.

"I am going to study with Myokei. Everything has already been arranged." Sawara sipped his tea. "But I will return as soon as I've made a name for myself."

He left a hopeful Kimi behind the next morning.

Two years passed without word from Sawara. Admirers came to ask her uncle for Kimi's hand in marriage. Tenko debated what to do when a letter from Myokei arrived. Myokei praised Sawara and wrote that he wanted Sawara to marry his daughter.

"I suppose Sawara has forgotten about Kimi," Tenko said to himself. "Yorozuya would make a good husband for Kimi." He wrote a letter expressing his approval and sent it.

Then, he went to Kimi. "I received a letter from Myokei and have sad news. Myokei wants Sawara to marry his daughter, and I have told him I approve of the union. I want you to marry Yorozuya. He will take good care of you as a rich merchant."

As Kimi listened, tears welled in her eyes. Without a word, she went into her room.

"She will come around and see it is for the best," Tenko said.

The next morning, Kimi was gone. Tenko sent his students to find her, but no one did.

When Myokei received Tenko's letter, he told Sawara of the arrangement.

"I'm honored, but I can't," Sawara said. "I'm already engaged to Tenko's niece."

Sawara sent a letter to Kimi. After a week of waiting for a response, he left for his old home. When he reached Tenko's house, he learned that Kimi had run away. He held out hope for her return, but as the months passed, he gave up. He married the daughter of a wealthy farmer. Her name was Kiku.

Soon after his marriage, the Lord of Aki commissioned him to paint seven scenes of the Islands of Kabakarijima. Sawara traveled to the islands and made a number of sketches. As he worked, a woman wearing a red cloth about her waist gathered shells from the beach. Her hair hung loose and flowed about her shoulders.

When she saw him, she dropped her basket of shells. "Sawara?"

He looked up. "Kimi? It is you!"

"Oh, Sawara. When I heard you were to marry Myokei's daughter, I couldn't bear it. It isn't true, is it?" She saw his expression shift. "Nothing prevents our marriage now."

He shook his head. "I can't. I thought you had deserted your uncle and forgotten me. I'm married."

Kimi's hope shattered. She fled from him toward her hut standing just off the shore. Sawara chased her. He burst into her hut. "Kimi!"

She looked at him—tears streaked her cheeks—and thrust a knife into her neck.

Sawara rushed to her and tried to stop the bleeding. She gazed at him, and her lips moved as she breathed her last. Sawara gently laid her down. Her dark hair fanned around her. Not knowing why, he took out his pad and sketched the woman who loved him.

He buried her in a quiet, shady spot.

When he returned home, he painted a hanging scroll from the sketch he made of her. When he finished, he hung it on his wall as his way to honor her.

That night, he snapped awake. By the light of the moon, he saw a ripple shake the painting he had made of Kimi. The ink moved, and a pale hand reached out of it and grasped the edge as if it was a door frame. A black-haired head emerged. The figure's disheveled hair flowed around as if blown by a sea breeze.

Sawara couldn't move. He could barely breath.

Kimi pulled herself out of the painting. The knife wound gaped at her throat. She glided toward Sawara.

He could only clench his blanket. Beside him, Kiku rolled over in her sleep.

Once beside him, Kimi stopped and stared down. Darkness obscured her face. She didn't move any closer to him. She just stood there. An hour passed. Then two. Exhausted from his terror, Sawara passed out.

The next morning, he awoke to find everything normal. Kiku slept peacefully beside him. He rubbed his forehead. "It was just a nightmare."

The next night Kimi came again. She came each night and stood beside him while Kiku slept on. By the fourth day, Sawara knew it had to be more than a nightmare. He rolled up the wall hanging and took it to Korinji Temple.

"Please pray for the soul of this woman," Sawara told the head priest. "I wronged her. To make amends, I will also send my wife back to her parents."

Kimi didn't appear that night or any other night.

The Ghost Procession

A priest passed by Shozenji Temple just as a deluge settled in. The temple stood dark and forgotten against the rain, but he didn't want to risk catching a chill, so he went inside. The temple sagged, and nature had stretched her green fingers into the building. But he found a small room off of the main building that was still in reasonable repair. The rain beat at the remnants of the roof, and the wind howled through cracks in the temple's walls. He attempted to sleep, but the cold settled into him.

Sometime near midnight, strange unnatural noises came from the main building. Curious about the noise, he went to see the cause. He peeped through a battered door. Inside the main chamber, a company of one hundred ghosts danced and wrestled and played. At first, the priest felt alarmed, but his curiosity kept him watching.

After close to an hour, darker, more threatening spirits appeared. Whereas the original ghosts flitted about like children at play, these ghosts moved with sinister purpose. Their bones showed through their ragged clothes. They absorbed the light of the moon and the other playful ghosts.

The priest backed away and fled to his small room. He barred the door. His hands shook as he settled in to pray for the souls of the dead.

At dawn, it continued to rain, but he didn't care. He departed and came upon a village where he told them what he had seen. News spread until the painter Tosa Mitsunobu heard it. He had always wanted to paint a ghost procession. Pleased that he might finally have a good reference, he set out for the temple.

When he arrived, he stayed up all night, but he didn't see any ghosts or hear any noises. The next morning, he opened all the windows and doors and flooded the temple with light. Complex drawings of ghosts lined the walls everywhere he looked. He counted more than two hundred drawings.

"If only I could remember all of them," he said. He took his notebook and spent the day recording every detail.

While he worked, he noticed how the cracks in the damp walls sheltered mildew and various mushrooms that lent the drawings color and a sense of movement. Mitsunobu felt grateful for the imaginative priest. Without the priest's stories, he wouldn't have found such a treasure of reference material for his future paintings.

A Haunted Temple in Inaba Province

An old temple stood on a wild mountain near Kisaichi village. The trees grew thick around it, blocking the daylight. Many priests had tried to live in the temple, but all had died. No one who spent the night in the temple lived.

During the winter of 1701, a priest named Jogen arrived in the village. He had come to see the haunted temple. He was fond of studying haunted places despite the fact that he didn't believe in ghosts. Yet, he hoped to see one. He asked the villagers what they knew about the place. Afterward, he stopped at the inn.

"Don't go to the temple," the innkeeper said. "Many good priests have tried to spend the night there. Every one of them was found dead the next morning. Don't try to defy the evil spirit that lives in the temple. We want a temple here, but not at the price of so many priests. We've considered burning it down and building a new one."

"Thank you for your concern." Jogen said. "But I want to see the ghost and try to put it to rest. The temple must have hidden books and histories. Of course, I also want to become the head priest."

The innkeeper sighed. "At least let my son guide you to the temple. It isn't easy to find if you don't know where to look."

The next morning, Jogen and Kosa, the innkeeper's twenty-year-old son, gathered provisions and set out. Kosa planned to guide Jogen to the temple and leave him there for the night. He promised to return the next morning with his father to see Jogen—and likely give him a decent funeral.

The temple sat on a steep ledge. Large moss-covered rocks jutted out of the forest soil. When Jogen and Kosa had made it halfway, they sat to rest and eat. They took their time, and soon voices drifted toward them from below.

The innkeeper and eight village elders appeared from the pines.

"I came to ask you one more time to reconsider," the innkeeper said. "We don't want the temple open if it costs another life."

Jogen shook his head and shouldered the provisions Kosa carried. "I should be able to find the temple now. I'd appreciate it if you would return tomorrow with carpenters. The temple is likely needing repairs. Don't worry about me. I will see you tomorrow." He started up the path.

The villagers watched him go. Kosa felt relief that he wouldn't have to travel from the temple alone as night fell.

Jogen took some time to reach the temple. Grass and mushrooms grew tall in the courtyard. Creepers curled around sodden, rotting posts. The air smelled of damp decay. The sight made Jogen worry more about the temple falling in on him than ghosts attacking him. Inside the temple stood a large gilded figure of Buddha along with smaller statues of saints. Fine vases, incense-burners, and iron stands stood around the great chamber. Behind the temple, Jogen found the living quarters of the priests. It looked as if six priests had tended the temple in the distant past.

Night closed in as he wandered about the grounds. He pulled out a lantern and lit it. He also found several candles and placed them on each side of the Buddha. Then he prayed for two hours. After he finished, he hid behind an old column to listen and watch.

He heard nothing but the wind and the night life outside until sometime near midnight. The air buzzed around Jogen as if he had neared a hive of bees. It vibrated his chest. When he peered around the column, he saw the glowing skeleton of a man. Tattered, loose priest's clothes draped over it. Red flames glared out of the eye sockets of a skull covered with stretched, parchment skin. Around the skeletal priest floated a strange ghost that reminded Jogen of a tadpole. As the spirit priest floated upward, the tadpole ghost followed. The skeletal priest flew up to the base of the Buddha statue.

The priest sat and faced Jogen.

Jogen broke out in a cold sweat. He trembled so hard he could barely stand, and he bit his tongue to keep from screaming. He forced himself to peep around the column. The strange tadpole ghost had disappeared. But the priest still sat on the base, turning only its head right, left, and upward. Jogen watched this for an hour. While he watched, he recorded everything he saw in his journal.

The air buzzed, and the other ghost reappeared. It circled around the skeletal priest several times. The priest then disappeared. The tadpole ghost swirled around the Buddha and the statues of the saints three times and then shot out of the temple.

That morning, Kosa and five villagers came up to the temple. They found Jogen alive but paralyzed and unable to speak. They carried him and his journal to the village, but halfway there, he died. The villagers kept his journal and used it to warn others away from the temple.

Two years later, lightning struck the ruin, and it burned down. The villagers searched the charred remains for any of the statues and artifacts that may have survived. They came upon a buried skeleton in the bushes not far from where Jogen had died. The villagers gave the bones a proper funeral.

Since that day, no one saw the ghosts again.

The Peony Lantern

Hagiwara was a high-ranked samurai who lived in Edo. The women of the city loved him, but his young thoughts focused on pleasure rather than love. He spent his time with other young men, seeking new adventures and fun.

One bright New Year's Day, he joined several young men and women in a game of badminton. He played with skill and grace, catching the gilded shuttlecock and tossing it lightly in the air. He smirked as a sudden impulse hit him. When the shuttlecock returned to him, he smashed it high into the air and over the bamboo fence of the nearby garden. He went to get it.

"Don't worry about it, Hagiwara," a young man said. "We have more than a dozen of them."

"But this one was gilded and looked like a dove."

His friend laughed. "We have six more like that one."

Hagiwara ignored him and climbed the fence. He dropped into the garden where the shuttlecock should've been, but he didn't see it. He looked around the garden, checking bushes with his racket.

"Look all you want," his friend called from over the wall. "We are going home now."

The light began to fade as Hagiwara looked. He refused to give up his search. His pride wouldn't allow it. Movement caught his gaze, and he looked up. A girl stood a short distance away with the gilded shuttlecock in her hand. She gestured at him.

He ran toward her, but she dashed away then stopped and beckoned at him again. He followed her until they came to a house nestled deep in the garden. Three stone terraces led up to the house. Plum trees blossomed on the lowest step. On the highest stood a young woman. She wore a kimono of water-blue silk with sleeves so long they touched the ground. Gold lined her obi. Pins of gold and coral and tortoiseshell gleamed in her long hair.

Hagiwara knelt and bowed his forehead to the ground.

"Come into my house, Hagiwara," the woman said. "I am O'Tsuyu, the Lady of the Morning Dew. You followed my handmaiden O'Yoné. Please come in. I am glad to see you."

So the samurai went in. The Lady of the Morning Dew danced while O'Yoné played a scarlet tasseled drum. Afterward, they served him a dish of red rice and offered sweet rice wine.

It was dark when Hagiwara made to leave. O'Yoné and the Lady escorted him out of the house. "Please come again," she said.

"Yes, you need to come again," said O'Tsuyu.

The samurai laughed. "And if I don't? What would you do?"

The lady stiffened at the joke. She laid her hand on his shoulder. "Death will come for you and for me."

O'Yoné shuddered and hid her eyes behind her sleeve.

Hagiwara felt his hairs raise at the tone of O'Tsuyu's voice. His joke had gotten darker than he had expected. He went into the night, feeling afraid. He wandered toward his home but found himself going around in circles throughout the city. When he finally found his home, dawn broke. He stumbled to his bed and fell into it.

He chuckled. "After all of that, I left the shuttlecock behind."

The next day, Hagiwara sat alone in his house, thinking. "It had to have been a joke a couple of geisha played on me." Evening arrived. He dressed in his best and went out to join his friends. He spent the next week gallivanting and trying to forget his encounter with the woman who called herself O'Tsuyu.

But he couldn't enjoy himself. On the last day of the week, he slapped his table. "By the gods, I am tired of this. I will find that garden and confront them." He set off into the city. He wandered through streets and alleys and covered every bit of the city. But he didn't find the garden or the Lady of the Morning Dew.

He continued this each night until he became sick. He still couldn't eat or sleep. He grew thin and lost his strength. Yet he still pushed himself to find the garden. It had to be somewhere he had missed. For three months he did this.

His servant tried to stop him. "You have a fever. You need to rest and see a doctor."

"Leave me alone," Hagiwara said. He left his house on his quest. He soon came to a quiet suburb and to a bamboo fence that looked familiar. He laughed and shook his head. The fence wasn't far at all from his home! He clambered over it and into the garden.

The garden was overgrown and looked far different from his first encounter. Moss covered the three terraces, and the plum tree looked forlorn. The house stood still with its shutters closed.

A cold rain began to fall.

An old man came up to Hagiwara as the samurai stood wondering what to do. "What are you looking for?"

"The white flower has fallen from the plum tree," Hagiwara said. "Where is the Lady of the Morning Dew?"

"She died five or six moons ago. She suddenly grew sick. She's in the graveyard on the hill. O'Yoné lies next to her. She couldn't allow her lady to go on alone." He gestured at the garden. "I tend the garden, but I'm old and can't do what I used to do."

Hagiwara returned home. He wrote O'Tsuyu's name on a piece of white wood and burned incense in front of it. He made various offerings to her memory, praying that she had found peace.

The Festival of *Bon* came. The people of Edo took lanterns and visited the graves of their loved ones. They brought flowers and food as offerings. Hagiwara walked in his garden that night, savoring the reprieve from the summer heat. Cicada chirruped. Now and then, a carp splashed in his pond.

Hagiwara heard footsteps on the lane beyond his garden hedge. He listened to the hollow sound, recognizing it as the sound a woman's *geta* made as she walked. He looked over the hedge.

Two slender women walked hand in hand. One of them carried a lantern with a bunch of peony flowers tied to the handle. The lantern swung as they walked. Hagiwara supposed the woman must be observing the festival. As they passed him, they looked at him.

He knew them and cried out in shock.

The girl with the peony lantern held it up so its light fell on him. "Hagiwara! We were told you were dead. We even prayed for you every day."

"O'Yoné, is that really O'Tsuyu?" He opened the garden's gate and rushed out to them.

"Who else could it be?"

"How was it that I lost you?" Hagiwara asked.

"We moved to a little house in a quarter called the Green Hill," O'Yoné said. "We couldn't take anything with us and have grown poor."

The Lady of the Morning Dew hid her face behind her sleeve.

Hagiwara gently pulled her arm away from her face. Her tears glistened in the peony lantern's light. "You won't love me," she said. "I've lost my beauty because of my hardships."

As he gazed at her, he felt his love for her consume him until he couldn't say anything,

She drooped. "Can I go now?"

"Stay. I want you to stay."

Despite his best effort to spend every moment with her, Hagiwara fell asleep. When he awoke, she and O'Yoné were gone. He immediately made his way to the Green Hill. He asked the residents where he might find the Lady of the Morning Dew, but no one had heard of her. He searched the quarter. It seemed as if he had lost his love for a second time.

He turned toward home in despair. He passed a temple and saw two graves. One was little and obscure, but the other had a tombstone. Before the tombstone hung a lantern with a bunch of peony flowers tied to its handle.

He stared at the tombstone and lantern for some time. He smiled and said, "'We have moved to a little house...a very little house....upon the Green Hill. We couldn't take anything with us, and we've grown poor. With grief and want my mistress has become pale.' A little house, a dark house. Yet you will make room for me, oh my beloved." He gazed at the graves a little while longer before returning home.

His servant met him. "Master, what bothers you?"

Hagiwara forced a smile. "Nothing at all."

The servant saw that death had marked Hagiwara.

Every night for the next week, the maidens of the peony lantern visited Hagiwara. They came at the same hour regardless of the weather. On the seventh night, the servant awoke. Fear and sudden sadness tangled in him. He went to his master's room and peered inside.

Hagiwara hugged a fearsome creature that defied the servant's ability to describe. His master seemed unaware of the fearsome thing. He smiled at its hideous, ruined face and stoked its dank green robe. The servant backed away and fled to find a priest. He accounted everything he saw to his friend. "Is there any hope for him?"

"Who can defy karma?" the priest asked. "But there is a little hope. Before night falls, you need to set a sacred text above every door and window of the house. Roll the golden emblem of the Tathagata into your master's sash."

The servant did as his friend suggested.

When the usual hour came, the servant crouched in the garden.

"What is this, O'Yoné?" O'Tsuyu asked. "I don't see my lord?"

"We should go home," O'Yoné said. "Hagiwara's heart has changed."

"I won't. You must find a way to bring him to me."

O'Yoné shook her head. "We can't go in. See the sacred writing over every door and window? We can't pass them."

O'Tsuyu wailed. "I had loved you through ten existences," she said.

The two walked away.

The next night repeated with the servant watching while Hagiwara slept. The wraiths came and left.

On the third day, Hagiwara went to the public bath, and a thief stole his talisman. That night, he lay awake. The servant, exhausted from the previous nights' vigils, slept. A heavy rain fell, tearing all the sacred texts from the windows and doors.

The sounds of women's footsteps sounded at the usual time. The two stopped at the garden hedge. The sound of their voices drifted into Hagiwara's room through the open window.

"This is the last time, O'Yoné," O'Tsuyu said. "Bring me to my lord."

Hagiwara tried to stand, but his legs refused to move. "Come, my love," Hagiwara called out.

"I cannot!" O'Tsuyu said. "Though I want to."

"Come, my love," Hagiwara said.

O'Yoné noticed Hagiwara's open window and led her mistress to it. They floated upward and passed through the window like mist.

"I'm here," O'Tsuyu said as she solidified.

That morning, Hagiwara's servant found his master dead. At his feet stood a peony lantern burning with a strange yellow flame. The servant shuddered, lifted the lantern, and blew it out.

The Secret

Long ago in Tamba Province there lived a rich merchant named Ina-muraya Gensuke. He had a daughter called O-Sono. O-Sono was clever and pretty. Gensuke didn't want her to only have the education country teachers could give her, so he sent her to Kyoto. After she finished her education, she married a merchant named Nagaraya, a friend of her father. She lived happily with him for four years and had a child. Sadly, O-Sono grew sick and died.

On the night of her funeral, her little son sat with his father. "I saw Momma. She's in the room upstairs and smiled at me."

"Your mother is gone."

"She isn't! She wouldn't talk to me, so I became afraid and came to tell you."

Nagaraya went upstairs with his other family members. By the light of a small lamp, he saw her. She sat in front of her clothing chest. Her head and shoulders appeared solid, but from her waist down, she grew transparent and disappeared. Stunned, Nagaraya and his family went downstairs.

His mother shivered. "A woman is fond of her things. O-Sono was quite attached to hers. Perhaps she came back to look at them. Dead people do that, I heard, unless the things are donated to a temple. If we present her clothes, her spirit will find probably find rest."

The following morning, they emptied her clothing chest and took all of O-Sono's possessions to the temple. But she came back that night and looked at the chest. She didn't try to open its drawers. She just stared at it.

Nagaraya's mother went to the temple and told the chief priest, Daigen Osho, what was happening.

"There must be something that worries her in or near that chest," Daigen said.

"But it's empty."

"Tonight I will watch that room and see what needs to be done," the priest said. "Make sure no one enters the room unless I call for them."

That night, Daigen settled into the room. Nothing happened at first, but after the Hour of the Rat, O-Sono appeared in front of the chest. She looked wistful and didn't seem aware of Daigen.

He said a sacred chant and then said to O-Sono: "I've come to help you. Something in that chest is making you anxious. Do you want me to help you find it?"

O-Sono's shade nodded.

Daigen opened the top drawer. It was empty. As were the second, third, and fourth. He carefully searched behind them and under them. He examined the interior of the chest. Again, nothing. The shade continued to watch. Daigen wondered if perhaps something was in the lining of the drawers. He removed the paper lining from the first drawer. Nothing! The second and third also had nothing. But under the lining of the fourth drawer he found a letter.

"It this what concerns you?" he asked the shade.

O-Sono turned toward him, her gaze fixing on the letter.

"Shall I burn it for you?"

She bowed to him.

"I will burn it in the temple this morning. No one will read it, except me. "

O-Sono's shade smiled and vanished.

At dawn, the priest found the family waiting. "Don't worry. She will not appear again."

He burned the letter as soon as he returned to the temple. It was a love letter O-Sono had written when she studied in Kyoto. Only the priest knew what she wrote, and that secret died with him.

The Secret of Iidamachi Pond

Yehara Keisuke lived in Kasumigaseki. As a vassal of the Shogun, he was due respect, but people also liked him for his kindness and fairness. In Iidamachi lived another vassal named Hayashi Hayato. He and Yehara's sister were married for five years and had a daughter. Their cottage had seen better days, but it was theirs. They also enjoyed the pond in front of it. Hayashi owned about two hundred acres of farmland with half of it producing at any one time. So they were able to live without working too hard. In the summer he enjoyed fishing for carp, and in the winter he wrote poetry.

One day Yehara's sister Kome visited.

"I need your help in divorcing Hayashi," she said.

"Divorce! Why do you want a divorce? Didn't you say you were happy? Hayashi has treated you well."

She shook her head. "Hayashi has always been kind, and we love each other. But Hayashi's family has owned their farms for three hundred years. Nothing will make him move, and I didn't want to either until twelve days ago."

"What happened?" Yehara suspected the worst as he studied his sister.

Kome hesitated. "I was sitting outside watching the clouds passing over the moon while talking with my daughter. Suddenly, a white figure appeared as if it walked on the lilies of the pond! It approached us slowly, dripping water as if it had drowned. My daughter grabbed me and cried out: 'Mother, do you know Sumi?'"

She trembled and hugged herself. "It was terrible to look at. It looked like a girl of eighteen. Before I could respond, it started shrieking 'Help me!' over and over again. I could only cover my eyes and scream for Hayashi. He came out to find us in terror, but he had seen nothing."

"'Perhaps you saw the kappa that was said to live in the pond.' He smiled at me as if I were younger than my daughter. But the next night the figure returned, and every night since." Kome sobbed. "I can't stay there. My husband doesn't see the ghost and only laughs at me."

"I will talk to him," Yehara said.

The next day, Yehara spoke with Hayashi about what Kome had said.

Hayashi frowned. "I've lived in this house my entire life but haven't seen anything. I asked my servants and neighbors, and they hadn't seen anything either."

"How could the little girl know the figure's name?" Yehara asked.

"I don't know." Hayashi crossed his arms and thought for several moments. "There's only one thing to do. Drain the pond and see what lurks inside."

That day, he had his servants cut the bank of the pond and drain it. Because the pond was old and deep, it took until the next day to fully drain. Hayashi ordered his men to dig into the mud at the base of the pond.

Just as he made the order, his grandmother arrived. "You don't need to do that. I can tell you about the ghost. It's my fault Sumi can't rest."

"Your fault?" Hayashi asked.

"When your grandfather was alive, we had a beautiful servant girl, seventeen years old, named Sumi. As you can guess, your grandfather had eyes for her and she for him." Her mouth twisted. "I was thirty by then and had already lost my better looks. So I was jealous of her. While your grandfather was out, I took Sumi to the pond and beat her. I wanted to ruin her beauty. She fell into the pond and got entangled by the weeds. I left her there, honestly believing the water was shallow enough for her to get out on her own."

"But she drowned," Hayashi said.

His grandmother sighed. "Your grandfather found her when he returned. He buried her himself. Fourteen days ago was the fiftieth anniversary of her death. I suppose that is why Sumi's ghost decided to appear." She gazed at her grandson. "We need to say prayers at Sumi's tomb to put her to rest."

The entire household did as the grandmother wanted, and the ghost stopped appearing to Kome. From that day on, Hayashi believed in ghosts.

The Snow Lady

An old man and a young man traveled together toward a distant province. They soon got lost in a wild, lonely country. By nightfall, they came upon a swift river with no bridge or ferry in sight. As they pondered what to do, snow began to fall. The white flakes fell on the dark water.

"The snowflakes are so white against the water," the young man said.

The old man shivered and sat on the ground. He pulled his cloak around him. The young man walked up and down the bank, blowing on his hands to warm them. A short distance away, he spotted a small hut. He rushed back to the old man.

"The gods have provided us a shelter for tonight." He pointed toward the hut.

"I can't move any further," the old man said.

The young man scooped him up and carried him into the shelter. A pile of leaves stood in the corner, but they didn't see any firewood. The young man laid the old man down and covered him with the leaves. Then he settled against him and covered them both with their straw raincoats. Despite the cold, they soon fell asleep.

Icy air against his cheek snapped the young man awake. The door of the hut stood open, and a snow storm swirled outside. He sat up.

A woman knelt beside the old man. She bent over him so close they their faces almost touched. Her white skin blended with her white clothes. Even her long hair shown white in the snow-lit darkness. She stretched her hands toward the sleeping man, and bright icicles hung from her fingertips. Her breath misted.

As she stood, snow fell from her in a gentle shower.

"That was easy," she murmured. She glided toward the stricken young man and sinking down beside him, took his hand in hers. Her touch stole whatever warmth he had left. A deadly sleep overpowered him.

"This is only a pretty boy," he heard as his consciousness faded. He felt the woman stroke his hair. "I can't kill him." He felt cold breath on his ear. "You must never speak of me or of this night. Don't tell your family or even your wife. Don't speak of me to the sun, the moon, or to the fire, water, wind, rain or snow. Swear to me."

"I swear," he managed just before his awareness fell into darkness.

He awoke to a man making him drink from a steaming cup.

"By the mercy of the gods, I came upon you in time," the man said. "But your old companion is past anyone's help."

The young man cried for the old man. When he had recovered, he thanked the man for his help. Together, they buried the old man. The next day, the young man left the hut and returned to his village.

Years passed. The young man didn't say anything about the Snow Lady. One summer, he was returning from a trip when he came upon a girl walking the same road. She carried a heavy bundle, staggering from the weight of it and with apparent exhaustion.

"Where are you going?" he asked.

"To Edo. I have a sister there who will help me find work."

"And your name?"

"My name is Yuki. I—" She swayed and dropped to her knees. "I'm sorry. This heat...."

"Let me help you." The young man scooped her into his arms and carried her toward his mother's house. She laid her head against his chest. As he looked at her face, he shivered.

"These summer days tend to get chilly about sundown," he said.

When they arrived at his mother's house, they gave Yuki cool water. She recovered and went her way, thanking the young man for his kindness. She started staying with them on her regular travels. The young man spent many hours conversing with her, and he soon fell in love with her. Her skin shown as white as jasmine despite all her time traveling in the sun. Eventually, they married and had seven children together. Each of the children were blessed with their mother's fairness and grew up strong.

Despite the pains of childbirth and the passing of the years, Yuki remained slender and youthful. Women wondered how she remained young while they aged, but Yuki's husband was the happiest man for miles around. He often prayed to the gods to express his gratitude.

One winter evening, after Yuki had put her children to bed, she sat with her husband. Outside, a snow storm raged. As Yuki sewed a new set of clothes for their daughter, her husband watched her.

"Dear, as I watch you tonight, I remember another snowy night that happened years ago."

Yuki didn't say anything.

"I'm still not sure if it was a dream. I saw a woman as beautiful as you. Indeed, she was much like you."

"Tell me about her," Yuki said, continuing to sew.

"I've not spoken of her to anyone." He told of his journey and the meeting with the Snow Lady. "Afterward she made me swear not—"

"You must never speak of me or of this night," Yuki said. "Don't tell your family or even your wife. Don't speak of me to the sun, the moon, or to the fire, water, wind, rain or snow. Swear to me."

Her husband stared.

"All this you swore to me, my husband. You were not even to speak of it to me. Yet you've broken your oath." She folded the clothes and set them aside. She left her stricken husband and went to her children's room.

She bent close to the eldest. He turned away from her in his sleep. "Cold," he shuddered.

She drew the quilt over his shoulder and went to their daughter. The little girl awoke and threw out her arms. "Mother."

"I've grown too cold to cry anymore," Yuki said.

She returned to her husband. He looked up at her with wide eyes. The knowledge of what he had done glistened in them.

"Even now I can't kill you. Take care of my children," the Snow Lady said. "Goodbye."

Her body burst into fine snow. A wind rushed through the smoke hole in the ceiling and caught the glittering flakes. It rushed back out, taking the snow with it.

The Spirit of the Lantern

Koharu Tomosaburo lived in the town of Aoyagi in Kai province. His grandfather served Ota Dokan, the founder of Edo. Tomosaburo lived with this wife and ten-year-old son. One day his wife became sick and suffered from spasms of pain. Nothing the doctors could do helped her, and Tomosaburo spent most of his time tending her and doing whatever he could to help her.

One evening he dozed, worn out from his anxiety for her. The lantern next to him flushed a brilliant red and flared into a pillar. The light snapped him awake, and he saw the figure of a woman standing in the pillar of fire.

"I know of your anxiety for your wife," the figure said above the crackling flames, "Her illness is a punishment for her faults. A demon has possessed her. If you worship me as a god, I will cast out the demon."

Tomosaburo glared at the figure and drew his sword. "I don't know if you are the demon or not."

The figure laughed. "I came here only out of kindness, and you show me your sword? Your wife will pay for your actions." Just as suddenly as the flames appeared, they died back down, and the figure disappeared.

Tomosaburo's wife convulsed with pain. She writhed and groaned, and nothing Tomosaburo could do helped. He realized he had made a mistake. He went to his family's shrine and prayed to the Spirit of the Lantern, asking for forgiveness for his thoughtless behavior.

When he emerged, his wife no longer suffered. As the hours passed, she improved, and a few days later her normal health had returned.

One evening, they sat together speaking of her miraculous return to health when the nearby lantern flared. A column of fire erupted and the spirit appeared.

"Despite how you treated me last time, I drove out the demon and saved your wife's life. In return, I ask a favor of you, Tomosaburo," the spirit said. "I have a daughter now of marriageable age. I want you to find a suitable husband for her."

Tomosaburo frowned. "But I'm a human and you are a spirit. We belong to different worlds. How am I to find a husband for your daughter?"

"It's easier than you think." The flames fanned around the spirit. "All have you to do is take blocks of foxglove wood and carve several little men. When you finish, I will give one of them to my daughter."

"If that is all you want, I will do it."

The spirit vanished. For the next several days, Tomosaburo carved several detailed miniatures using all of his skill. When he completed them, he stood them in a row on his desk, and the next morning, all of the wooden figures had disappeared. He surmised the spirit liked his work and hoped he had seen the last of it.

But that night the spirit again appeared. "Thanks to your help, my daughter's future is settled. We would like you and your wife to attend the marriage feast."

Tomosaburo didn't want anything else to do with the spirit. However, he was aware of what it could do to him and his wife. He tried to think of some way to avoid the invitation, but before he could, the spirit vanished.

The spirit visited the next night. "Everything is ready for the feast. The wedding ceremony has already finished, but we would like you to attend the after-ceremony. Please follow me." The spirit gestured at Tomosaburo and his wife to follow. The spirit stepped out of the lantern's flame, becoming full-size, and glided out of the room. Unable to do anything else, Tomosaburo and his wife followed the spirit.

Despite his reservation, Tomosaburo didn't want to appear ungrateful for the spirit's help with his wife's illness. The spirit led them outside where a gold and lacquer palanquin with a train of bearers waited for them.

A tall man dressed in ceremonial robes bowed to Tomosaburo. "Honored sir, please allow us to take you to your destination."

Tomosaburo and his wife gaped at each other. They had never seen such richly dressed servants. Tomosaburo worried about what consequences might await them, but they couldn't turn back now. So they climbed into the palanquin, and the procession set off.

Clouds darkened the night sky, hiding the moon and the stars. Tomosaburo couldn't see anything beyond the bamboo blinds. The palanquin felt like it floated instead of being carried on men's shoulders. Some time passed. Then the ghostly illuminated outline of a mansion appeared. It cast enough light for the couple to make out a wooded park and a great gate. The bearers passed through the gate and through the garden to lower the couple at the entrance of the house. A group of servants and retainers already waited in the gloom.

Tomosaburo and his wife were ushered into a large, well-lit reception room and seated in the place of honor near the alcove. Maids dressed in ceremonial costumes brought refreshments. Tomosaburo didn't lower his guard as he rested, and he tensed when another usher arrived to take them to the feast. They followed the usher through the mansion. Despite his caution, Tomosaburo marveled at the rich woodwork and art they passed. The floors of the halls held a mirror polish. The ceiling was inlaid with decorative carvings. The support pillars were even made of rare petrified wood.

When they entered the feast-hall, Tomosaburo recognized the faces of the guests. He saw several friends and family who had died years ago. As he and his wife entered, the guests greeted them, but no one seemed to recognize him. He saw the newlyweds dressed in traditional wedding clothes. The groom resembled one of the figures he had carved. After everyone settled to eat, servants paraded with lacquered trays shaped like large shells. All sorts of delicacies sat on them, and wine flowed freely. Conversation and laughter rang. The normalcy of it eased some of Tomosaburo's apprehension. Soon, he laughed and join in the conversations around him.

He lost track of time until he looked up to notice dawn inched above the window. He blinked and found he and his wife back in their own room. Shaken by the experience, Tomosaburo hoped he had finally seen the last of the lantern spirit. Days passed without any sign of the spirit returning, and he began to relax.

But on that same night, the lantern flared and the lurid glow of the spirit filled his room.

Tomosaburo had had enough. He grabbed a wooden cup and flung it at the spirit. It struck it on the forehead, overturning the lantern, and plunging the room into darkness. The spirit wailed. Its glow faded and disappeared into a luminous trail of vanishing blue smoke. Beside him, his wife screamed with pain and collapsed, spasming.

Again, Tomosaburo could do nothing to help. Two days later, she died.

Tomosaburo regretted his actions and prayed to the spirit, apologizing for what he had done. But this time, the spirit didn't answer his prayers. It never appeared again. Tomosaburo decided he couldn't live in the house where his wife had died. He also feared the house itself was haunted. When the movers arrived, they were unable to move a single piece of furniture. It was as if every piece was nailed to the floor. Nothing they did could move even a vase or a book.

Tomosaburo was ready to just leave everything behind when his son in the next room cried out. He dashed inside to find his son spasming on the floor. He died a few days later, ending the revenge of the Spirit of the Lantern.

The Story of Mimi Nashi Hoichi

Centuries ago, a blind man named Hoichi lived at Akamagaseki. People marveled at his ability to play the biwa and recite stories from memory. He had trained since childhood and had surpassed his teachers at a young age. He was particularly known for his renditions of the history of the Heike and Genji. At the beginning of his career, he was poor, but he managed to find a friend to help him. The priest of Amidaji enjoyed poetry and music and often invited Hoichi to the temple. He eventually offered Hoichi a room in return for entertaining him on certain evenings.

One summer night, the priest and his acolyte left to hold a funeral service, leaving Hoichi alone. It was a hot night, so the blind man sat outside in the veranda. The veranda overlooked a small garden at the rear of the temple. Hoichi practiced his biwa until midnight, but the night still proved too warm to sleep indoors.

He heard footsteps at the back gate. Someone crossed the garden and stopped in front of him. A deep voice boomed, startling him. He was expecting the priest.

"Hoichi!" the voice had the command of a samurai.

"Yes! I'm sorry, I don't know who calls. I'm blind."

"Don't be afraid. I was sent with a message for you. My lord is of exceedingly high rank and is staying in Akamagaseki and wants to view where the battle of Dan-no-ura happened. He has heard of your skill in storytelling and wants to hear you tell the story."

Hoichi couldn't disobey the summons from a samurai, so he put on his sandals, gathered his biwa, and went with the messenger. The messenger grabbed him with a hand so hard it could've been warm iron. He guided Hoichi along at a fast pace. The messenger clanked, apparently wearing his armor and weapons.

They stopped, and Hoichi sensed a large gateway ahead. He couldn't remember any gate in the town except the main gate of the temple.

"Kaimon," the samurai called. "I've brought Hoichi."

A bar scraped at the other side of the gate. Hoichi heard the sound of hurrying feet and the voices of women further inside. The samurai helped him climb several stone steps. At the last step, he was told to leave his sandals. Then a woman's hand replaced the samurai's and led him deeper inside. He felt the polished wooden floor under his feet as she led him into what seemed to be a maze. They entered a room full of voices and silk rustling.

The woman led him to a cushion. "Please sit here."

Hoichi settled in and tuned his biwa.

An older woman's voice rang out. "It's time to hear the history of the Heike to the accompaniment of the biwa."

Hoichi knew the entire history would take many nights to recite. "What portion do you want me to recite?" he asked.

"Recite the story of the battle at Dan-no-ura," the woman said.

Hoichi strummed the biwa and began to tell the story. The battle happened on the sea. He used his instrument to emulate the straining of the oars and the rush of the ships. He mimicked the hiss of the arrows and the shouts of the men. The biwa sang of the steel clashing as Hoichi told the story. Whenever he paused, he heard comments from his audience.

"I've never heard playing like this."

"Not in all of Japan is there another singer like Hoichi."

He drew encouragement from the comments and sang with all the skill he had. But when he came to the part of the story where women and children had died and the suicide of Nii no Ama with her imperial baby in her arms, the crowd's mood changed. Some cried. Others wailed. The din frightened Hoichi. He had never heard of such a reaction. A few tears here and there, sure, but nothing like this. He continued with the story. Gradually, the listeners settled as he neared the end. When he finished, the silence hung for a long moment.

"Although I was told you are a skillful biwa player and storyteller, we didn't know anyone could be as good as you proved to be tonight," the older woman said. "Your lord intends to reward you, but he wants you to perform once every night for the next six nights until he leaves. Come here tomorrow at the same hour. You are to speak to no one of your visits here. Our lord doesn't want attention. You may return to your temple."

Hoichi returned at dawn. The priest had also arrived, but he supposed Hoichi was asleep. Hoichi rested during the day, not saying anything about his visit the night before. That night, the samurai came for him again and led him.

However, this time the priest learned Hoichi was missing. That morning he summoned him. "We've been worried about you! It's dangerous for you to go out blind and alone at night. Why did you go without telling us? I could've sent someone with you. Where have you been?"

"Please excuse me, my friend. I had some private business, and I couldn't arrange the matter at any other time."

The priest frowned. It wasn't like Hoichi to dodge a question like that. He suspected something was wrong, but he didn't ask anything else. However, he quietly ordered the temple's servants to watch Hoichi and follow him if he left the temple after dark again.

That night, the servants followed Hoichi as he left to perform. But it was a rainy night, and they lost track of him. The men went into the town, asking if anyone had seen Hoichi. No one had. As they returned to the temple by the seaside road, they heard the sound of a biwa from the Amidaji cemetery. They followed the sound and discovered Hoichi sitting alone in the rain in front of the tomb of Antoku Tenno. All around him burned the blue flames of the dead above the tombs.

"Hoichi!" they called out.

The blind man didn't seem to hear them. He kept playing his biwa and reciting the battle of Dan-no-ura. The men rushed toward him and grabbed his arm.

"Hoichi!" one of the shouted in his hear. "Come home with us!"

Hoichi turned his head. "I can't tolerate you interrupting me in front of this august assembly."

The men were certain he was bewitched, so they grabbed him under his arms and dragged him back to the temple. The priest met them and made sure Hoichi changed into dry clothes. After his friend was settled, the priest confronted him.

"Just what were you doing in the cemetery?"

Hoichi realized his friend was truly worried. After a moment of thought, he decided to tell him everything.

"You should've told me earlier," the priest said. "You are now in danger. You've been spending the night in the cemetery among the tombs of the Heike. Everything you've been imaging is an illusion except for the calling of the dead. If you keep obeying them, they will tear you apart." The priest sighed. "I have to leave for another service, but I will make sure you are protected."

The priest and his acolyte stripped Hoichi and wrote the text of a holy sutra called Hannya-Shin-Kyo all over him, even down to the soles of his feet.

"After I leave," the priest said. "Sit on the veranda and wait for them to call you. But whatever happens, don't answer or move. Say nothing and sit still. If you stir or make any noise, they will tear you apart. Don't be afraid or even call for help. I've done everything I can do for you. Just sit still, and the danger will pass."

That night, Hoichi sat his biwa ahead of him and sat still. He barely even breathed. Then, as he expected, he heard the steps approach him.

"Hoichi!" the samurai called.

Hoichi remained still.

The samurai called a second and a third time. "Still no answer," he muttered. "I have to find him."

The samurai rattled, and Hoichi sensed the man beside him. Hoichi remained silent, wondering if the samurai could hear his heart.

"Here is the biwa," the samurai said. "I also see two ears. That's why he didn't answer. He doesn't have a mouth or anything else to answer with. I will take the ears to my lord to prove I've obeyed him the best I could."

Hoichi felt his ears gripped by iron fingers. The samurai tore them off as if plucking a pair of leaves from a tree. Pain shattered Hoichi, but he managed to remain silent somehow. The footsteps left the veranda and disappeared into the distance. Hoichi remained still.

Before sunrise, the priest returned and hurried to the veranda. He stopped and cried out in horror when he saw the blood. But his lantern's light also revealed Hoichi, sitting still with blood oozing from where his ears should've been.

"My poor Hoichi! What happened!"

At the sound of his friend's voice, Hoichi felt safe and started crying. He accounted what happened.

"It's all my fault," the priest said. "I wrote everywhere except on your ears. I had trusted my acolyte to do that part. I should have made sure..." The priest's voice broke, and he took a deep breath. "There's nothing for it now. We can only try to heal your wounds, but at least the danger is over. They won't visit you again."

With the help of a good doctor, Hoichi healed. The story of his adventure drew people to hear him play and recite. He soon became a wealthy man, but from then on he was known as Mimi-nashi-Hoichi, Hoichi the Earless.

The Tomb of the Priest

When Muso Kokushi, a Zen priest, traveled through Mino province, he got lost in the mountains. He wandered until nightfall when he came upon a ruined hermitage. Inside, he found an old priest.

"May I spend the night with you?" Muso asked.

"No. But there is a hamlet in the valley below. Follow the path, and you will find it."

About a dozen farm cottages made up the village. He went to the largest where the eldest son of the village headman received him. Forty people were already in the main room when Muso arrived. They took him to a small separate room and gave him food. Exhausted from his travel, Muso fell asleep immediately after he ate.

He awoke a little before midnight by the sound of crying. The sliding door opened, and the eldest son, carrying a lantern, entered.

"A few hours ago, my father died. Everyone you saw earlier was holding a vigil for his recovery. Now they pay their respects before they leave the village."

"Leave the village at this hour?" Muso asked.

"It is our custom to leave the village whenever anyone dies. There's another village three miles away. After we pray, we leave the body alone. Strange things always happen when we do this, so I wanted you to come with us. I will find you a place to sleep in the next village. But I suppose as a priest you don't have to worry about demons and spirits like we do. If you aren't afraid of staying with my father's body, you can stay here. Everyone else will be leaving."

"Thank you for your hospitality. I'm sorry you didn't tell me about your father when I arrived. Although I was tired, I would've done my priestly duty. I will stay here and perform the service after you leave. I don't understand why you leave, but I'm not afraid of ghosts or demons. So don't worry about me."

The young man smiled. "Thank you. It eases my mind that you will look after my father tonight." He looked over his shoulder. "It's time for us to go. Please tell me if anything happens when we return in the morning."

After they left, Muso went to where the father's body lay. The usual offerings were set out. The priest performed the traditional funeral and then settled to meditate and keep vigil. The village remained silent.

When the deepest hour of the night came, Muso sensed a Shape, vague and vast. Muso wasn't able to move or speak as the Shape passed him. It lifted the corpse and devoured it, shroud and all, beginning with the head. Then the Shape ate the offerings and left.

When the villagers returned that morning, they found the priest waiting for them at the headman's house. No one seemed surprised to see the body had disappeared.

The young man took Muso aside. "I was worried about you. I'm glad to see you are alive and well. As I expected, my father's body is gone. Did you see anything?"

"I did." Muso did his best to describe the Shape.

When he finished, the young man nodded. "Your description matches our oldest stories."

"Does the old priest on the hill sometimes perform the funeral rites for your dead?" Muso asked.

"What priest? We haven't had a priest in our village since my great-great-grandfather's time."

"I see." Muso didn't say anything else, keeping his suspicions to himself. He had to be certain before he said anything. He stayed with the villagers a little longer before heading out for the hermitage on the hill.

He found it without any difficulty. This time, the old hermit invited him in. "I'm ashamed," the old hermit said.

"You don't need to be ashamed for refusing me shelter last night. You directed me to the village, and they treated me well. Thank you for that," Muso said.

"I can't give any man shelter," the hermit said. "I'm not ashamed for that. I'm ashamed you saw my true form. I was the one who ate the corpse and the offerings. I am a *jikininki*, an eater of human flesh. Please, listen to how I came to be this way."

Muso nodded. "I'm listening."

"Long ago, I was the priest of this desolate region. All the mountain people used to bring their dead loved ones to me—sometimes from great distances—so I could perform the funeral rites. But I only did the service as a matter of business. I thought only of the food, clothing, and the importance my profession lent. Because of my selfishness, I was re-born immediately after I died as a *jikininki*." The hermit bowed to the dirt floor. "Please perform a Segaki service for me. Help me so I can escape this horrible existence."

As soon as he finished his petition, he disappeared. The hermitage itself disappeared too, and Muso found himself kneeling alone in the tall grass beside an ancient, moss-grown tomb.

Tsunu's Vision

A man named Tsunu once lived in a remote cottage surrounded by deep pine forests and Mount Fuji. He supported his family as a woodsman. He spent his days from dawn to dusk in the forests, cutting trees and taking the wood to the distant village to sell. He made up for his time away from his family each evening by sharing folklore and legends. He loved speaking of Mount Fuji. He had seen the great mountain rise out of the plain he had played in as a child.

"A mighty roar awoke me," Tsunu said. "I left this same cottage and there it was! The Mountain of the Gods." He mesmerized his family late into the night with the story.

The next morning, he went into the forest as usual with last night's story playing on his mind. He came upon a lonely clearing. The air smelled sweet. The sky shone so blue that he stopped, and joy filled him.

Movement caught his gaze. A little fox watched him from the bushes. It darted away as soon as it noticed Tsunu watched it. It was a nice, happy day so Tsunu decided to follow the fox and see where it went.

He came to a bamboo thicket. Morning dew still clung to the leaves despite being late afternoon. On the mossy grass sat two young women. Their otherworldly beauty stunned him. The shadows of the waving bamboos fanned their faces. Although they didn't say anything, Tsunu knew their voices would have to resemble the soft coos of doves. The women's movements reminded him of the swaying of a willow. Tsunu barely breathed, afraid he would disturb them and break the lovely scene. The breeze caught their hair.

I really need to go home, he thought. *I need to tell my family this story.* He noticed his knees felt stiff. He must have stood watching for longer than he thought. He leaned on his axe for support and it turned to dust. He looked down and saw a white beard flowing from his chin. Stunned, he turned and made for home. He walked for hours until he at last came to a hut. Although it seemed to be in the right place, he didn't recognize it. People he didn't recognize gazed out the windows at him.

"Where are my wife and children?" he asked them.

They spoke, but he couldn't understand what they said.

Gradually, he realized that several generations had passed in the hours he spent watching the fairy women. His wife, his children, and his children's children had lived and died. His body had aged too.

"There's nothing for it now," he said. He looked up at Mount Fuji. "But I still can spend time with my beloved mountain."

He spent his remaining years as a pilgrim that traveled Mount Fuji. As his story spread, people regarded him as a saint who brought them prosperity.

Yenoki's Ghost

Yenoki lived at the temple dedicated to Fudo on Okiyama. He worked as a priest and caretaker for twenty years, yet he had never seen the statue of Fudo the shrine housed. One morning, he saw that the head priest had left the shrine's door ajar. Yenoki's curiosity finally got the better of him. He peered through the crack with his right eye.

But he saw nothing.

He turned away from the door and found he could no longer see out of his right eye.

"I shouldn't have looked," he said. "I deserve this punishment. I have to purify myself to ease the god's anger."

For the next one hundred days, Yenoki fasted in the mountain. When he finally emerged from his fast, his old friends didn't recognize him.

"Tengu!" they shouted as they fled.

Despondent, Yenoki went back into the mountain. He called himself the One-eyed Priest despite how the gods had changed him during those one hundred days. As the years passed, Yenoki took to meditating under an enormous cryptomeria tree on the east side of the mountain. At the base of the tree, he died.

Sailors used the enormous tree as a marker and began to pray to the one-eyed priest whenever a storm threatened them. If a light blazed from the top of the tree, the sailors knew the priest answered their prayers for safety.

At the base of the mountain sat a village. Each year, the villagers held a festival for the spirits of the dead. During those three days, the spirits would return to earth to visit their family shrines. However, during these nightly festivals, the young men and women of the village would indulge themselves in all sorts of immorality. Kimi, the daughter of Kurashi Yozaemon, promised to meet her lover, Kurosuke, during the first evening of the festival. Kimi was on her way when she came to a thick grove of trees. Standing on the edge of the grove was a man she thought was Kurosuke. As she approached, she saw he was a handsome, young stranger.

His beauty overwhelmed her. "My heart beats for this man," she said to herself. "Why shouldn't I give up Kurosuke? He's not good looking like this man. I already love him without sharing a single word with him!"

The man smiled and beckoned her. Smiling, she followed him into the forest.

She didn't return.

A few days later, Tamae, the sixteen-year-old daughter of Kinsaku, awaited her secret lover in the temple grounds near the statue of Jizo. A painfully handsome young man approached her from the forest. His beauty struck her, and she offered no resistance when he took her by the hand and led her into the forest.

A total of nine girls disappeared along with an equal number of immoral boys.

"It must be our children's immorality during the festival that angers Yenoki," the village elder said. "He might even be the one who carries them off."

The villagers started to lock themselves in their homes, neglecting their farms and their other work. When the Lord of Kishiwada heard of this, he summoned Sonobe Hayama, a skilled samurai.

"Sonobe, I want you to go and inspect this tree that houses the spirit of Yenoki. I don't know what is the best course of action. I leave it to you to decide how to solve the mystery of the disappearing girls."

Sonobe returned home where he bathed and fasted for a week to prepare. He arrived at the village in October. First, he visited the temple where he prayed to Fudo for a half hour. Then, he traveled to the tree of the one-eyed priest.

No paths led up the steep mountain. The village woodcutters avoided the area, but Sonobe was used to hard travel and solitude. But even Sonobe couldn't shake the feeling that someone watched him.

When he finally reached the tree, he bowed to it. "Honorable and aged tree. You have become the house of Yenoki's spirit. Yenoki, why do you rob the poor villagers below of their children? If you don't stop, I will make sure this honorable tree is cut down."

A warm wind blew across Sonobe's face. Overhead, dark clouds rolled in. Rain fell, and the earth shivered under his feet. Despite all of this, Sonobe stood calm and patient.

The figure of an old priest stepped out of the trunk of the tree. Transparent and thin, the ghost pointed at Sonobe, but the tough samurai didn't feel any fear.

"I admire your courage. Most men are cowardly and sinful. They fear to come near this tree. I don't speak evil to the good. The morals of the village have become so bad that I decided to teach them a lesson. Their customs have defied the gods. I want to make them godly, so I posed as a youth and carried away the worst of their children."

"And they are unharmed?" Sonobe asked.

The ghost nodded. "I've given them lectures each day, and they regret their sins. I know they will reform their village. You will find them further up the mountain, tied to trees." It pointed up the mountain. "Release them and tell the Lord of Kishiwada what the spirit of Yenoki, the one-eyed priest has done. I will always be ready to help him improve his people."

The spirit vanished.

Sonobe went where the ghost directed and found the girls and boys tied to trees. He cut them free and took them back to the village. He returned home to give an account to the Lord of Kishiwada.

The village reformed and became an example for other villages.

Trees and Plants

Green Willow

Tomodata served the Lord of Noto. He was a soldier, a courtier, and a poet. Despite his experience in war, he was handsome and had a good singing voice. His martial ability allowed him to dance gracefully. He was wealthy and generous with that wealth. The rich and the poor knew him as a kind man.

One day, the Lord of Noto summoned Tomodata. "Are you loyal?" the lord asked.

"You know I am, my lord."

"Do you love me?"

Tomodata knelt. "I do."

"Then you will carry my message," the lord said. "Ride fast, and don't spare your horse. Don't worry about the mountains or the province of the enemy. Don't stop for a storm or for anything. Give up your life if you must, but don't betray my trust. Above all, don't look any woman in her eyes. My message is that important. Go and send me word when you deliver my message."

Tomodata left and saddled his horse. He rode the straightest, fastest route. He pushed his horse with little rest. Three days into his journey, an autumn storm burst. Tomodata continued through the torrent. The wind howled through the pine trees. The horse struggled and could barely keep upright in the mud, but Tomodata urged it onward. He held onto his sodden cloak and clung close to his horse.

The storm's ferocity soon made navigation impossible. The strain and lack of sleep made Tomodata feel faint. The road disappeared, and he had no idea where he was. A marsh appeared out of the mist just as his horse collapsed, throwing him into the weeds. He stumbled to his feet and waited for his horse to recover enough to walk behind him. He decided to keep going in the same direction. It was as good a direction as any.

"Will I die in this wilderness and fail my lord?" he wondered.

The storm faded, and moonlight illuminated the harsh land. Ahead of him, a cottage sat on a hill. Smoke curled out of a hole in the roof, and three willow trees swayed in the wind. Tomodata secured the reins of his tired horse on one of the willow's branches and asked to be let inside the cottage.

An old woman peered through the open door. Her clothes were poor but neat. "Who's out on such a night?"

"I am a tired, lost traveler. My name is Tomodata. I'm a samurai who serves the Lord of Noto. I need food and rest for me and my horse." Tomodata tried to straighten, but his exhaustion threatened to overwhelm him.

"Come in." The old woman opened the door. "Warm yourself at our fire. We don't have much to offer, but you are welcome to eat your fill. I will have my daughter take care of your horse. He's in good hands."

Tomodata caught movement in the corner of his eye and turned. A young girl held his horse's reins. Her loose hair streamed in the wind. Tomodata wondered where she came from, but he didn't think about it long. The old woman led him into the warm cottage and closed the door. An old man sat next to the fire.

The old couple did what they could to feed and comfort Tomodata. They gave him dry clothes and warmed him with hot rice wine. Supper was as simple as the old woman said, but it was filling.

Tomodata began to feel more like himself when the daughter of the house appeared with more rice wine. She wore a blue robe of home-spun cotton, and her feet were bare. Her hair hung to her knees. She looked to be about fifteen years old, yet Tomodata had never seen a beauty like her.

She knelt beside him and poured the wine. Tomodata watched her. When she sat down the bottle, their gazes met, and what he saw captured him.

"What is your name?" he asked.

"I'm called the Green Willow."

"That's a good name." He gazed at her so long that she blushed. She smiled and looked away.

Tomodata cleared his throat and sang:

Long-haired lady, do you know that with the red dawn I must go?
My sleeve will hide the blush away,
The dawn will come whether or not I want it.
Never leave me. Never go.
I lift my long sleeve.
Oh, Green Willow. Green Willow.

Green Willow blushed deeper at the song, and her parents seemed to enjoy it.

That night, he lay in front of the fire. Sleep avoided him despite how exhausted he felt. He could only think of Green Willow. He knew he shouldn't, but he would have better luck not breathing. His mission for his lord weighed heavily on him.

As soon as the sun's first ray touched the horizon, he rose to leave. The rest of the family still slept. He left a purse of gold next to the old man. He readied his rested horse and rode through the mist of the early morning. Everything shined with the damp of last night's storm. Luckily, the sky was clear, and the turning leaves shimmered in the light. Yet the uplifting sight didn't touch Tomodata's sadness.

"Green Willow." He sighed.

Throughout the day's travel he could think of little besides the girl. He managed to find an abandoned shrine at which to spend the night. The shrine's quiet, sacred feeling lulled him to sleep.

The next morning, he washed in the nearby cold stream. When he returned to the shrine, he froze. Lying where he had the previous night was Green Willow. She lay face down with her black hair fanned around her. She looked up and grabbed Tomodata's sleeve. Tears slid down her cheeks. "Why did you leave?"

He swept her into his arms without saying anything. He held her for a time and then carried her to his horse. They rode together all day. Tomodata savored the feel of her as she moved against him.

They came to a city Tomodata didn't know. He used some of the jewels he carried to buy a house. In the quiet room, the two heard a garden waterfall behind the house. There they stayed together, reveling in their love and their newfound life.

In the autumn of their third year together, they went into the garden at dusk to watch the moon rise. As they watched, Green Willow began to tremble.

"My love," Tomodata said, "you tremble. The night is getting cold. Let's go back inside." He wrapped his arm around her.

She cried out as if someone had stabbed her and fell against Tomodata. Her face contorted with pain. "Tomodata," she whispered. "Pray for me. I'm dying."

He shook his head. "You are just faint." He carried her to the garden's stream. Irises grew everywhere. He lapped water onto her forehead. "What is the matter?"

"The tree." She cringed. "They are cutting down my tree." She opened her eyes and gazed at her love. "Remember me. Remember the Green Willow."

Then she was gone. Her silk clothes fluttered across his arms, and her straw sandals rustled the grass. Tomodata's stricken mind worked to figure out what had happened. He had felt her weight against him, and then she was simply gone.

The lack of answer haunted him, and he became a monk and traveled from shrine to shrine barefoot as penance for both the loss of his love and for giving up his lord's trust all those years ago.

One night, he found himself in a marsh. On top of a hill sat the ruins of a cottage. The door swung on broken hinges, and the roof had fallen in. In front of the ruin stood three willow tree stumps that had long ago been cut down. Tomodata stood in silence for a long time, remembering and realizing what had happened to his love those years ago.

He sang quietly to himself:

> Long-haired lady, do you know that with the red dawn I must go?
> My sleeve will hide the blush away,

The dawn will come whether or not I want it.
Never leave me. Never go.
I lift my long sleeve.
Oh, Green Willow. Green Willow.

"I'm a fool," he said. "I should have recited the Holy Sutra for the Dead."

How the Spirit of a Willow Tree Saved a Family's Honor

Gobei Yuasa lived in Yamada village. For many generations, his family had lived in the area. Despite the family having no title, people respected them and their wealth. However, Gobei cared little for managing his wealth. He spent his money freely. He enjoyed conversation, good food, and painting wall hangings. Whenever his steward would bring him monetary problems Gobei would say:

"The destiny of man is arranged by Heaven."

One day as Gobei painted, his friend visited. "Have you heard about the spirit? People have seen it at least three times. Even the village elder has seen it."

"Where do they see it?"

"It appears under your old willow tree between eleven and twelve at night."

Gobei put down his brush. "I don't remember anyone being murdered under that tree. My ancestors don't have any stories about the tree either. Come to think of it, I've always wanted to paint a ghost. I will watch for it tonight."

He went to bed early but took his time waking up that evening. He finally went into the garden at midnight and hid behind the bushes that faced the willow. It was a moonbright night. Gobei fought boredom as he waited. About an hour later, clouds passed over the moon. A thin tendril of white smoke snaked from the roots of the tree. The smoke coalesced into a charming girl.

Gobei gaped. He hadn't considered the possibility that a ghost could be beautiful. He had expected an old woman with protruding bones or something else that would freeze his bone marrow with fright.

The girl floated toward Gobei's hiding place.

He stood. "Who are you? You are too beautiful to be the spirit of someone dead. Whose spirit are you, and why do you appear under this willow tree?"

"I am not a ghost of a person," she said. "I am the spirit of the willow tree."

"Then why do you appear now after all these years?"

"I was planted here in the twenty-first generation of your family, about six centuries ago. One of your wise ancestors buried a treasure near me—twenty feet below the ground and fifteen feet east of my trunk. The money was buried to save your house when it was about to fall."

The spirit gave him a hard look. "That time has come." She lifted a finger at him. "You have brought ruin and disgrace upon your family by bringing it to bankruptcy. Dig up the treasure and save your family's name." She vanished.

Gobei returned to his house and summoned his most faithful servants. At daybreak, they dug where the spirit had indicated. When they struck the top of an iron chest, Gobei exclaimed with delight. His servants were also pleased to see they wouldn't be ruined with him. It took some time to wrestle the heavy chest out of the hole. When they broke it open, they found a collection of old sacks. Over one hundred gold coins stuffed each bag. They pulled out each sack until they reached the bottom of the chest. On the bottom waited a yellowed letter. Gobei carefully unfolded and read:

"My descendant who must use this treasure to save our family's reputation will read this letter aloud. I, Fuji Yuasa buried this treasure in the twenty-first generation of our family so a future generation may fall back on it in a time of need. You who read this letter must say these words aloud and in your heart."

Gobei took a deep breath. "I repent of my folly that has brought our family so low. I can only repay my ancestor by being diligent to my household affairs. I will show the willow tree which has so long guarded my ancestor's treasure all my kindness. I vow to change from this moment."

Gobei became a different man that day. He made sure his lands and farms were properly tended. His family prospered, and Gobei managed to replace the treasure that saved him from bankruptcy. He painted a wall hanging of the willow tree's spirit and kept it in his room for the rest of his life. Gobei fenced in the willow tree and tended it himself.

Jirohei and the Cherry Tree

Jirohei owned a large and prosperous teahouse. He claimed his success was due to an old cherry tree that stood right next to the building. He paid the tree the greatest respect and tended to its wants. He stopped boys from climbing it and breaking its branches. As the tree prospered, so did he.

One morning, a samurai traveling to Hirano Temple stopped at Jirohei's teahouse to enjoy the cherry blossoms. Jirohei came out to see if he needed anything.

"Are you the owner of this teahouse?" the samurai asked.

"I am. Can I bring you anything?"

The samurai shook his head. "What a fine tree you have."

Jirohei smiled at the tree. "I owe my prosperity to the tree. Thank you for the compliment."

"I want a branch off of the tree to give to a geisha."

Jirohei bowed. "I'm sorry, but I have to refuse. The temple priests told me that I have to protect the tree. They said not even the flowers can be plucked from the tree. Everyone has to wait for them to fall on their own."

The samurai's eyes narrowed. His voice held a dangerous edge. "When I say I want something, someone of your station is to give it to me. Go and cut it."

Jirohei straightened. "I must refuse."

"If you can't give it to me, I will take it by force." The samurai stood and drew his sword. He was about to slash off a low hanging branch when Jirohei grabbed his sword arm.

"I asked you to leave the tree alone! Take my life instead, but don't harm it."

The samurai flexed and cut off a branch. "Insolent fool. I will gladly do just that and still take the branch."

The samurai stabbed Jirohei to make him let go. Jirohei released the samurai's arm, picked up the branch, and ran to the tree's trunk. The samurai snarled and cut Jirohei down. Then he fled, leaving Jirohei dead with the blooming branch still clutched in his hand.

The teahouse's prosperity ended with Jirohei's life despite the efforts of his widow and family. Few people came, and most had little money to spend. The tree began to fade. In less than a year, it died. Jirohei's family had to close the teahouse on the same day the last brown leaf fell. Consumed by despair, Jirohei's widow hanged herself from the dead cherry tree that night.

Soon, people reported seeing ghosts around the tree and feared to travel near it. Neighboring teahouses and even the temple suffered.

Throughout this, the samurai kept his secret close. He told only his father what had happened.

"Father, I will go to the temple to see if what people say about the ghost is true."

"Don't go. You need to make amends for your past sins and the dishonor you caused," his father said.

"I did nothing wrong of my station. I need to see for myself what people are jabbering about."

The samurai traveled to the dead tree and hid behind a stone lantern to see what came out at night. Around midnight, the tree suddenly burst into full bloom. It looked just as it had the day he had killed Jirohei.

The sight of it enraged him. He wasn't about to let the spirit of such an insolent man live on inside the tree. He rushed toward it with his sword drawn and attacked. He slashed at the trunk. As his blade connected, he heard a scream that seemed to come from inside the tree. Thinking he was hitting Jirohei's spirit, he redoubled his attacks. After a half hour of cutting and slashing, he stopped. His arms felt heavy, and he breathed hard.

"Now I will wait until morning to see what damage I've done."

When the day dawned, the samurai found his father on the roots of the tree, hacked to pieces. He fell to his knees.

"Father must have come to try to stop me. What have I done?" He doubled over, crying. After some time, he sat upright and slipped his arms out of his clothing so his chest was bare. He said a silent prayer for forgiveness, pulled his short sword out, and stabbed himself in the stomach. Gritting his teeth, he pulled the blade across.

The cherry tree blossomed in his dying vision.

From that day, people debated if the ghost was the spirit of Jirohei, the spirit of his wife, or the spirit of the cherry tree.

The Camphor Tree Tomb

On the 17th of January, a great fire broke out in Homyoji Temple in Edo. The fire soon engulfed the entire city, burning down commoner and samurai homes alike. Lord Date Tsunamune decided make his new home the finest ever designed. He directed Harada Kai Naonori to oversee it. Harada summoned the best architect of the time, Kinokuniya Bunzaemon.

"Lord Date wants his palace to be the finest, second only to that of the Shogun. What are your ideas?"

"It will be expensive to build such a palace," Bunzaemon said. "Especially right now with the lumber scarcity."

"Don't worry about that," Harada said.

Bunzaemon thought a moment. "How about a palace like Kinkakuji in Kyoto? It was built by the Shogun Ashikaga. The problem will be finding the large camphor trees needed. There are only a few, and they are sacred. I know of one in the forest of Nekoma-myojin. If I can get that tree, I should be able to make a ceiling that would put all other palaces in second rank."

"I will leave it to you then," Harada said. "No expense needs to be spared so long as you work well and quickly."

Bunzaemon bowed. "I will do my best." He made his arrangements for everything except the camphor tree. He saved that part for last, knowing it would be a delicate problem.

With all the other arrangements complete, he traveled to Iwaki province to meet with the district's manager Fujieda Geki.

"My name is Kinokuniya Bunzaemon. I've come to get your help and permission to cut trees in the small forest called Nekoma-myojin near Yabukimura village." He saw the manager for the Shogun hesitate. "If you help me, I will build you a new house for nothing as my way of showing appreciation for your help." He pushed a gold coin toward him. "This is just a small deposit for your trouble."

Geki pocketed the money. "I will send for four local managers, and you can settle the matter with them."

Ten days later, four village leaders arrived in Edo and met with Geki. Mosuke, Magozaemon, Yohei, and Jinyemon had served Geki well for years. Geki filled them in. "I will leave the negotiation to you." He took them to where Bunzaemon waited.

"Let's discuss this over dinner," Bunzaemon said. He took them to a restaurant called Kampanaro and spared no expense on treating them.

After they finished eating, Bunzaemon said, "I hope you will allow me to cut timber from the forest in your village. I can't build on a large scale without it."

"Very well. You may," Mosuke said. "But there is one tree that cannot be cut no matter the circumstances. It is an enormous, sacred camphor tree near our shrine."

"That's fine. Just write me a permit, giving me permission to cut any tree except your sacred tree." Bunzaemon doubted any of them could write.

"Why don't you write it, Jinyemon?" Mosuke said.

"I'd rather Mago write it."

"Yohei would be able to word it better," Magozaemon said.

"I can't write," Yohei said.

"Would you sign a document if I wrote it?" Bunzaemon asked.

The villagers agreed and stamped the document. After celebrating further, they left the restaurant pleased with themselves. Bunzaemon also went home pleased.

The next day, Bunzaemon sent his foreman Chogoro and his team to the forest. They went straight to the great camphor and started to prepare for felling it. As they chopped off the lower branches, the keeper of the shrine, Hamada Tsushima, ran out to them.

"Stop! What are you doing? That tree is sacred," Tsushima said.

"They are doing what they've been ordered to do," Chogoro said. "I am cutting down the tree at the order of my master Kinokuniya. And he has permission from the village leaders."

"They told me," Tsushima said. "But this tree wasn't a part of—"

Chogoro pulled out the document. "Read it for yourself."

Tsushima took it and read:

To Kinokuniya Bunzaemon,
Timber Contractor, Edo.

In order to build a new mansion for our lord, all the camphor trees must be spared except the large one said to be sacred in Nekoma-myojin forest. In witness whereof we set our names.

Jinyemon; Magozaemon; Mosuke; Yohei
Representing the local county officials.

Tsushima sent for the four men. They protested that they had exempted the tree, but Chogoro waved the document at them.

"I have to go by this," he said.

"I cannot allow this!" Tsushima shouted. He stripped himself to the waist and pulled out his knife. "My spirit will go into the tree and care for it. I will have my vengeance on the wicked Bunzaemon." He thrust the knife into his stomach and drew it across. He collapsed onto the grass and died. The four village leaders lifted the caretaker and carried him off, intending to rush a message to the lord of the district.

Chogoro's men felled the tree. But when they tried to move it, it wouldn't budge. The branches came to life and attacked them. They slapped at the men and drove them back. The branches nearly crushed several of the men. Fortunately, the workers managed to escape with only broken arms and legs.

A horseman raced up to them. "I am one of the Lord of Sendai's retainers. The council has decided to leave the tree untouched. Lord Date is furious and will punish Bunzaemon for what he has done. Return to Edo. We cannot blame you for following orders, but give me that forged permit before you leave."

A few days later, Bunzaemon was found dead. People saw a masseur enter his room, but no one saw him leave. People whispered the masseur was the spirit of Tsushima seeking revenge. Troubled by this event, Chogoro returned to the camphor tree and used his savings to build a new shrine dedicated to it. Amazingly, the tree's leaves remained green and vibrant as if it wasn't cut down at all.

The Cherry Tree of the Sixteenth Day

A samurai lived in Iyo and loved his garden. The old cherry tree that grew there was his favorite. He had played under the branches of the tree as a child. His father and his grandfather accounted of their games under that venerable tree. Each spring, the family would hang poems written on colorful paper from the branches as they blossomed. But as an old man, the samurai had only his memories. He had out-lived his sons and daughters and had no grandchildren to share the joy of the family custom.

Then, one summer, the tree too died.

His neighbors brought him a young, beautiful cherry tree and planted it in an effort to comfort the old samurai. He pretended to be glad, but his heart remained full of pain. The tree was his last link to his ancestors and his children.

On sixteenth day of the first month of the year, the old samurai remembered a story his grandfather had told him. In the story, a man had revived a dead tree. Excited by the prospect, the old samurai went to the withered tree in his garden. He bowed to it.

"I'm sorry it took me so long to finally remember a way to bring you back to life. Please bloom for the future generations."

He spread a white cloth under the tree and knelt on it. He placed his dagger in front of himself and bared his chest. Unsheathing the dagger, he gazed up at the tree, seeing it blossoming in his mind, and plunged the dagger into his stomach. Using the last of his strength, he pulled the dagger across, freeing his spirit from his flesh.

When he breathed his last breath, the tree exploded into bloom.

Every year, the tree blooms on the sixteenth day of the first month, in the season of snow.

The Cherry Tree of the Milk Nurse

Tokubei served as the headman of Asamimura village. Although he was rich and successful, he and his wife didn't have any children. They often visited Saihoji Temple to pray to Fudo Myo for children. After several years, their prayers were answered. They had a girl named Tsuyu, but her mother was unable to nurse her. So they hired a wet-nurse named Sode.

Tsuyu grew to be a beautiful girl. But at fifteen she became sick. The doctors did what they could, but they didn't expect her to live. Sode had come to love Tsuyu as her own daughter. She went to Saihoji Temple and prayed for twenty-one days.

Tsuyu suddenly and completely recovered.

To celebrate the miracle, Tokubei held a feast and invited his friends. But on the night of the feast, Sode collapsed just as Tsuyu had. Tokubei summoned the doctor, and the family gathered around her bed.

The doctor shook his head after examining her. "There's nothing I can do."

Soda smiled at Tsuyu. "I have a little secret. I asked Fudo to let me die in place of Tsuyu. He's granted my wish." She wiped a tear from Tsuyu's cheek. "Don't be sad for me. I die gladly for you."

She looked at Tokubei. "I have one request. I promised Fudo that I would have a cherry tree planted in the garden of Saihoji Temple. I won't be able to plant that tree now. Please fulfill my vow for me."

She died moments later with a peaceful smile on her lips.

After they buried Sode, Tokubei planted the finest cherry tree he could find. The tree flourished. On the second month of the following year—the same day Sode had died—the tree blossomed. For the next two hundred and fifty-four years, it blossomed on the sixteenth day of the second month. Its pink and white flowers resembled the nipples of a woman's breasts, dewed with milk. People called the tree The Cherry Tree of the Milk Nurse.

The Dragon-Shaped Plum Tree

Hambei loved tending his garden and his prized plum tree. The tree resembled a dragon lying in a field. He had many memories of spending time near it with his father, grandfather, and his own children. In autumn, he tidied the tree's dead leaves. During winter, he sympathized with the tree's cold bareness. In spring, he loved to watch the buds erupt and bloom. People from the town liked to visit the tree and listen to Hambei tell stories from history while sitting under those blossoms. During summer, he enjoyed the plums and shade the tree provided.

A counselor in the Imperial Court heard of Hambei's tree and sent Kotaro Naruse to purchase it. When Naruse arrived, Hambei received him with the best hospitality he could provide.

"I've come to take your dragon-shaped plum tree to the Imperial Court," Naruse said.

Hambei didn't know how he could refuse someone of such a high rank. "I-I can't sell the old tree. I've refused many offers already."

"I never said I was sent to buy the tree," Naruse said. "I came to bring the tree to the court where it will be welcomed with ceremony and treated with the greatest kindness. Think of it as a marriage. You should be proud that the first counselor would want to marry your tree."

Hambei sweated. He didn't want to give up his tree, but what could he do as someone of such low rank? "I can't refuse someone as high as the first counselor. Please tell him it is a gift. I cannot sell it."

Naruse smiled and pulled a bag from his clothes. "Please accept this small gift in return then." He tossed the bag to the table. Gold coins spilled from it.

Hambei drew back. "I can't accept such a gift."

"You don't want to insult my master, do you?"

Hambei hung his head. "All right."

The moment Naruse left, Hambei regretted what he had done. He felt as if he had sold his own daughter.

He couldn't sleep that night. Toward midnight, his wife rushed into his room, shouting.

"You wicked old man! At your age too! Where did you get that girl? Don't lie to me."

Hambei thought his wife had gone off her head for good this time. "What girl? I don't know what you are talking about."

"I saw her when I went to get a cup of water. She was crying outside the door. How did you get a beautiful seventeen-year-old like her, you dirty old man?"

Hambei brushed his wife aside and went to see for himself. When he reached the door, he heard crying. A beautiful girl sat crying on his doorstep.

"Who are you?" he asked.

"I'm the spirit of the plum tree. I've heard that you arranged to have me moved to the counselor's gardens. I shouldn't complain to be moved to such a noble family. But I will miss you. Can't you let me stay with you for as long as I live?"

Hambei felt the truth of what she said. "I'd love to keep you with me. I will see what I can do."

She looked up and smiled. Then she disappeared. When Hambei turned away, he saw his wife gaping at where the spirit had sat.

When Naruse came with a cart and his team of men, Hambei told him of the spirit's visit and plea. He pressed the money back to the man. "Take the money back. Please tell your master my story. He will surely understand and have mercy."

"Have you been drinking? You can't fool me. Even if the spirit of the tree came to you, did it say it would regret going to my master's garden? How can I explain the insult of you returning my master's gift? You've broken your word. I will take the tree, or I will kill you in place of it."

He kicked Hambei to the dirt and drew his sword. He raised it to take Hambei's head when a gust of plum-scented wind rushed between them. The spirit of the plum tree stood between them with her arms outstretched.

"Get out of my way," Naruse shouted.

"Kill me instead of killing a poor innocent old man. I am the spirit that has brought such trouble on my family."

"You are an old fox, not the spirit of the tree. I will kill you first." Naruse brought his sword down, expecting the illusion of the girl to disappear. Instead, he felt the blade sink into wood. The girl disappeared. In her place lay a severed, blooming plum branch.

Naruse stared in shock. He sheathed his sword and picked up the branch. "I'm sorry I didn't believe you." He swallowed. "I will take this branch to my master and tell your story."

When the counselor heard the story, he was so moved he sent a letter to Hambei telling him to keep the tree and the money. However, by the time the letter arrived, the tree had withered and died despite Hambei's care.

The Go-Board Cherry Tree

People knew Oda Sayemon for his bravery in battle and his temper when he lost a game of *go*. He struck anyone who won against him across the face with a heavy iron fan. Even the boldest samurai dreaded the call to play his lord at the game. All the samurai soon agreed it was better to let him win than to suffer a slap with his iron fan. As a result, Sayemon's ability grew worse even though he thought he was more skilled than anyone else.

On the 3rd of March, he threw a dinner party in honor of his little daughter Chio. When the feast finished, he called Saito Ukon, one of his oldest and most faithful samurai, to play *go* with him. Ukon took the case of white stones and placed them as if he was the superior player.

Sayemon's temper flared at the insult, but he kept his face smooth. He was confident he could win and force Ukon to apologize for taking the white stones.

Ukon won the game.

"I must have another game." Sayemon said. "I was careless in that one. I will show you how I can beat you when I decide to try."

When Ukon won that round, Sayemon's face flared red with his anger. "You will play a third game."

Ukon won again. Sayemon seized his iron fan and swung for Ukon's face. Ukon caught him by the wrist and gazed into his lord's eyes.

"My Lord, it is the better player who wins while the inferior player must fail. If you failed to beat me at *go*, it is because you are the inferior player. Is this how a defeated samurai behaves? Don't be so hasty in your anger. It doesn't befit your high position."

"How dare you speak to me like that," Sayemon said. "I will take off your head." He stood and reached for his sword.

"Your sword is to kill your enemies, not your retainers and friends," Ukon said. "Sheathe your sword, my Lord. You don't need to bother killing me." Ukon opened his clothes and showed an immense cut across his stomach. He grimaced at the motion. "I did this to offer you the advice you need and save the others from you."

Sayemon stared.

"If you learn nothing from this," Ukon said. "Learn this. You need to control your anger and treat your subjects better."

Sayemon seized his sword. "Not even by your death will I let the likes of you give me advice." He cut at Ukon's head. He missed and cleaved the go-board in two instead. Ukon paled and sagged. The sight of his dying retainer and the slashed go-board finally pushed Sayemon from his anger.

"I regret seeing you die, Ukon. I'm losing my oldest and most faithful retainer," Sayemon said. "I will take your advice."

"Even in death my spirit will be with you and watch over you as long as you live," Ukon said. He fell to his side and died.

Sayemon had Ukon buried in his own garden and buried the broken go-board with him. Sayemon changed his behavior and treated all his subjects with kindness. All of his people grew happy.

A few months after Ukon's death, a cherry tree sprang from his grave. Three years later, on the anniversary of Ukon's death, Sayemon went out to water the tree. He was surprised to find the tree in bloom. He saw a faint figure standing by the tree's trunk.

"Ukon?"

He rushed over, and the figure disappeared. At the base of the trunk, the roots had grown to the size and shape of a go-board. The bark even divided into squares. For years afterwards, until Sayemon's death, the spirit of Ukon appeared on the 3rd of March.

The Holy Cherry Tree of Musubi-no-Kami Temple

A man named Sodayu once lived in Kagami village. He was a widower but had a lovely seventeen-year-old daughter named Hanano. Sodayu decided it was time to find her a suitable husband.

"When I find you a husband," he told her, "I hope you will approve of him because it will be your duty to marry him."

She bowed to her father's statement, but she confided in her servant Yuka that she wouldn't marry a man she didn't love.

"What do you think I should do, Yuka?" she asked. "How can I find a man I can love? I want him to be handsome and not more than twenty-two years old. Father will likely find some old man for me to marry."

Yuka thought a moment. "Why not go to the shrine of Musubi-no-Kami and pray? He is the God of Love, after all. Pray that the husband your father will find will be handsome and after your own heart. I've heard if you pray at the shrine for twenty-one days in a row, your prayer will be granted."

Pleased by the idea, Hanano went with Yuka that afternoon to pray. They continued to visit each day. On the twenty-first day, they finished their prayers and were on their way home. They passed under the great cherry tree people called The Holy Cherry because of its great age. Standing near its trunk was a young man with a handsome, pale face and expressive eyes. He held a branch of cherry blossoms. As the women approached, he smiled at Hanano and bowed, walked toward her, and offered the branch without saying a word.

Blushing, Hanano took the flowers. The young man bowed again and walked away, still without saying anything. Hanano's heart fluttered as she watched him go.

Yuka gave her a knowing smile.

"Could he be the one of my prayers?" Hanano asked her servant. She clutched the cherry blossoms to her breast. "I haven't seen anyone so handsome. I wish he would've stayed and said something to me. I wanted to hear his voice."

She continued to muse to Yuka on their way home. The first thing Hanano did was put the cherry blossoms into a vase in her room. "Yuka, I need you to find out what you can of the young man. But don't tell father."

Over the next several days, Yuka tried to find out more about the mysterious young man. She found nothing, but she did learn about another young man who had fallen in love with Hanano. Tokunosuke intended to apply for Hanano's hand. Sadly, Tokunosuke's looks couldn't compare to those of the mysterious man under the cherry tree.

During Tokunosuke's visit with her father, Hanano was called to serve tea. He remained formal and polite toward her, and she to him. She didn't feel the spark the man under the cherry tree fanned, however. Soon after he left, her father called her to him.

"I've decided you are to wed Tokunosuke. He is desirable in every way, and his father is a friend of mine. The young man has loved you secretly for months now. He is certain to treasure and take care of you."

Hanano didn't say anything, but her tears betrayed her. She bowed and fled.

Sodayu called Yuka to him. "I found a desirable young man for Hanano, but she ran off crying. Do you know why?" His eyes narrowed. "Does she have a lover I don't know about?"

Yuka swallowed at the tone of his voice. Thinking it might benefit Hanano, she told Sodayu of the encounter under the cherry tree.

"Thank you for being honest with me," he said. "Please bring Hanano back."

Hanano's eyes were still red when she returned. "Yes, Father?"

"I want you to bring your lover to me—You look surprised. Of course I've known about him. If he will not meet with me, you will marry Tokunosuke."

The next day as Yuka and Hanano left to find the mysterious young man, Tokunosuke appeared.

Hanano bowed to him. "I'm sorry, but I cannot love you. I love another, and I don't even know his name. I leave to find him. Please excuse me." She weaved around him and hurried away with Yuka in tow.

Tokunosuke frowned after them. "How could she love a man whose name she doesn't even know?" He followed after the women, determined to discover who his nameless rival was.

He followed Hanano and Yuka to the temple. After they prayed, they passed under the Holy Cherry Tree where a young man waited for them. He smiled and gave Hanano another branch of blossoms. The man didn't say a word.

Tokunosuke could tell the two didn't know each other.

After a moment, they all bowed, and the women left. The young man watched them go.

Tokunosuke stormed out of his hiding place to confront the youth. "Just who are you? Why do you tempt Hanano to love you?" He reached out to snatch the man by the collar, but the nameless rival jumped back. A sudden gust of wind blew, causing a shower of blossoms to fall so thick that Tokunosuke lost sight of his rival.

When the shower ended, the handsome youth was gone, but Tokunosuke thought he heard a strange moaning sound from inside the cherry tree.

Just then, one of the temple priests dashed toward him, brandishing a club. "What are you doing? Don't you know this tree is sacred and contains a holy spirit? It sometimes appears in the form of a young man. That was what you tried to touch with your filthy hands. Get out of here and never come back!"

Tokunosuke ran from the temple. He ran straight to Sodayu's house. There, he accounted everything that had happened.

"She can't marry a spirit," he said. "Maybe now she will consent to marry me."

"I will speak with her. Go home for now, Tokunosuke." Sodayu told a servant to fetch Hanano.

"I've discovered the identity of your lover," he told her. He repeated what he had learned.

"What sin have I committed?" Her shoulders trembled. "I've fallen in love with a spirit?"

"You will have to let any illusions you had go," Sodayu said. "Tokunosuke will make a fine husband for you."

"I need to go to the temple and pray for forgiveness," Hanano said.

She and Yuka returned to the temple. She prayed for a long time for forgiveness for her foolishness. She also resolved to devote the rest of her life to the temple and refuse to marry. When she told her father of her decision, he consented. He knew nothing else would bring her peace. So she shaved her head and became one of the caretakers of the Holy Cherry Tree. There she remained, looking after her love for the rest of her life.

The Memorial Cherry Tree

Kihachi owned a little shop in Kyoto. He didn't have much to sell, but what he had was high quality. People came to his shop just to see what wonder he managed to find that week. One day, a court noble walked into Kihachi's shop.

He wandered the little place for a moment before turning to Kihachi. "You have many pretty and interesting things here. Would you mind if I wait here and look until it stops raining? My name is Sakata."

"By all means, stay. Some of my things are pretty, but a merchant wants to live two lives of one hundred years. The first of distress and trouble that lets him collect things for cheap. The other is of peace so he can sell and enjoy the proceeds. Sadly, I'm in the first life, but I love the things I buy and look at them long before I sell them. I see you are traveling. Where are you heading?"

"I'm going to Toba in Yamato province. My friend has suddenly gotten sick. He may not live long enough for me to get to him."

Kihachi pursed his lips. "Toba. My I ask your friend's name?"

"Matsui," Sakata said.

Kihachi made a noise in his throat. "Your friend is the same man people gossip about."

Sakata cocked his head. "Gossip?"

"They say he killed the spirit of a cherry tree near Toba. The spirit appeared to him in the form of a beautiful woman, and Matsui killed it. Since then, he's been sick. The tree also withered and died." Kihachi paused a moment. "So people say, anyway."

"Thank you for the information," Sakata said. "Looks like the rain has let up for the moment. I must be on my way." He left and made his way to Shonen Temple where Matsui stayed.

Soon after the court noble left, the drizzle turned into snow. It looked like it was going to snow for some time, so Kihachi closed his shop and went to his living quarters in the rear.

Late in the evening, he heard a knock. Kihachi called out from his warm bed. "Come back in the morning. The shop is closed."

The voice of a young girl filtered through the back door. "I was sent to sell you a good painted wall hanging."

Kihachi sighed, but curiosity made him brave the cold air. He opened the door. The thick snow glittered in the moonlight. A fifteen-year-old girl stood barefoot in it. She held the folded wall hanging.

"I'm the daughter of Matsui. I've been sent to sell you this." Her teeth chattered.

"Come in and warm yourself," Kihachi said. He stoked the remaining embers to life so he could see what the girl brought.

She handed him the painting and warmed herself over the fire. The painting was of a beautiful woman looking over her shoulder. Her long hair cascaded down her snowy back. The artist had obvious skill.

"I will give you a ryo for it," Kihachi said.

"I'll take it," she said.

Kihachi wondered if she had stolen it because of how quickly she accepted his offer. He pressed the coin into her hand, and she ran off into the snow. Kihachi closed the door.

"Most likely she stole it," he said. "But what am I to do about that? It's worth at least 50 ryo."

He hung the painting in his room and sat back to admire it by the light of his lamp. As he watched and mused about the actual value of the painting, the woman morphed. The delicate face contorted with pain. Red blood streaked it. The painting's eyes blinked, and the mouth opened.

Kihachi shook his head. "I'm just tired." He climbed into his bed and covered his head with his blanket.

He remained awake the rest of the night.

When morning finally arrived, the painting had returned to a beautiful woman. He supposed he had dreamed the transformation in his excitement. However, that night the painting transformed again. This time it shrieked at him all throughout the night. Kihachi decided to return the painting to Matsui and be done with it.

He reached Shonen Temple after two days of walking. After asking to see Matsui, the priests ushered him in. Matsui sat on his bed. His daughter stood beside him.

"Take this back." Kihachi handed the painting over.

Matsui paled when he unrolled the painting. With a cry, he and his daughter leaped and ran toward the temple's large fire. They both jumped into the fire with the painting in hand and burned to death.

The governor of Kyoto, Prince Nijo, heard of the event and had his servants look into the case. They interviewed a shaken Kihachi. After more searching, they concluded that Matsui had indeed killed a venerable cherry tree. Nijo concluded that the painting was the spirit of the tree taking a form to haunt Matsui.

Prince Nijo had a cherry tree planted on the spot of the old one Matsui had killed. People called it the Memorial Cherry Tree. As for Kihachi, he continued to buy and sell in his little shop, but he refused to buy any wall hanging brought to him.

The Peony Flower

Aya was the only child of the Lord of Omi Province. Because of his duties to the Shogun, she rarely saw him. Her mother died in childbirth, so she lived with her nurse and with the other women in her father's castle.

When Aya was sixteen, her father came home after winning a battle for the Shogun. She went to the gate to meet him, dressed in her best.

"My lord and father," she bowed as was proper for her station. "Welcome back."

"Is that you, Aya? How you've grown!" he said. "How old are you?"

"Sixteen, my lord."

"By the gods, you have become quite a young lady. I had lost track of the years and brought you a doll for a gift." He laughed.

Soon after he settled home, he began to look for a fitting husband for her. He knew the peace they had at the moment wouldn't last, so he wanted to take advantage of it for his daughter's sake.

The Lord of Ako had three sons. Each were fine men and warriors. Aya's father gave it some thought and settled on the middle son. So Aya became betrothed, and the provinces rejoiced. The Lord of Ako sent the customary gifts. Aya sat with her seamstress and helped make the bolts of silk into fine new clothes. With her marriage looming, she savored the moments with her friends. They told her stories about her future husband's adventures and about how beautiful he was.

One evening, they slipped into the garden to enjoy the cool air and the scent of the flowers.

"The moon is such a lonely lady," one of Aya's friends, Sada, said. "Look at how pale and wane she is. That cloud is like she is hiding her eyes with a sleeve."

"So true," Aya said. "But have you seen her sister? She looks even sadder."

"Who is the moon's sister?" Sada asked.

"Yes, who is it?" the other girls asked.

"I'll show you." Aya led them along the paths to a still pond. Fireflies danced above it, and frogs sang. The peonies Aya had planted the previous year blossomed.

"Look at the water," Aya said.

Her friends looked into the water and saw the moon's sister. They laughed and began to play in the water. Aya's foot slipped on a smooth stone. She screeched as she fell toward the water, but out of nowhere a young man appeared and caught her in his arms. He righted her and immediately disappeared with a shimmer, leaving Aya dry but trembling.

"Did you see that?" she asked.

"I did," Sada said. "He just appeared as you were falling and disappeared again. He was beautiful!"

Sudden sadness filled Aya. The brief glimpse of the strange young man lingered with her. Without saying a word, she turned and walked back through the garden. Her head hung. The other women left her, except for Sada, who followed her to her room.

Aya sat and traced the pattern on her clothes with a finger. Sada sat next to her and waited.

"He was a great lord," Aya said.

"That he was."

"He saved my life, you know. I can't swim." Aya sighed. "And I didn't even thank him."

"The moon shined on his jeweled sword, and his clothes were embroidered with peony flowers," Sada said. She paused. "What of the young Lord of Ako?"

"What of him? I haven't even seen him."

After that night, Aya fell into a deep depression. She sighed throughout the day and sometimes cried at night. Her wedding clothes and gifts made her sad, and she stopped going into the garden to spend time with her friends. She spent her time in her room. Her father sent for doctors, but no one could heal her sickness.

Finally, Sada told the Lord of Omi of the moonlight encounter with the young man.

"She dies for her love for this man," Sada said.

"It's impossible for a samurai to sneak in as you seem to think happened," the lord said. "The garden is protected by high walls and by my men. What do you think would happen if such a foolish story reaches the Lord of Ako?"

Sada began to cry. "My mistress will die."

The lord threw up his hands. "I can fight in war and navigate the Shogun's Court. But gods preserve me from the affairs of women! They are too hard for me to understand."

He ordered his men to search the castle and grounds for any signs or sightings of a stranger, but no one found anything.

That night, Aya needed to escape the heat of the castle. They took her out into the garden where she lay in Sada's lap. The family's musician played his biwa and sang:

> Music of my lute, is it born? Does it die?
> Is it truth or a lie?
> Whence and where, enchanted air?
> Music of my lute is mute.
> Sweet scents in the night
> Do they float, do they seem
> Are they essence of a dream?
> Or are they the thoughts of the dead?
> Sweet scents of the night, such a delight.

As the musician sang, a young man stood up from the peonies by the pond. Everyone saw him—his jeweled sword and his peony embroidered clothes. Aya cried out and ran toward him with her arms outstretched. When she reached him, he disappeared.

The minstrel watched this and sang:

> Love stranger than death
> Is it longer than life, is it hotter than strife?
> Strong and blind, transcending and kind.
> Love stranger than death or breath.

The peony samurai again stood up and gazed at Aya.

Just then one of Aya's bodyguards saw the man. He leaped down among the peonies. As he neared the peony samurai, a cloud darkened the moon. A hot wind blew from the south, extinguishing all the torches in the garden and blowing the women's sleeves about them. The wind scattered the petals of the peonies like snowflakes.

When the wind quieted, the bodyguard stood panting and pale. He still held his sword. In his left hand he held a perfect peony flower.

"I have him." He held up the flower.

"Give me the flower," Aya said.

The bodyguard did as he was ordered. Aya went to her room. She clutched the peony to her breast and fell asleep. For nine days, she kept the flower, sleeping with it each night. Color returned to her face, and she regained her cheerfulness.

She placed the peony in a bronze vase. The flower didn't wilt or fade. Instead, it grew larger and lovelier.

On the tenth day, the young Lord of Ako's company arrived for the wedding. Although people celebrated, Aya looked pale and wane.

The same day, the peony withered and was thrown away.

The Pine Tree of the Lovers

Matsue lived with her parents at Takasago. Their house sat under an ancient fir tree said to have been planted by a god just before he died. Matsue loved to sit among the soft, fallen needles of the tree while she weaved clothes for the villagers in the area. She loved the sea, the birds, and every living thing. She often joined the local fishermen and tried to catch a glimpse of the Palace of the Ocean Bed. The fishermen would tell her the story of the jellyfish who lost his shell or of the Island of Eternal Youth. In exchange for their kindness, she would sing them songs to cheer them while they worked.

One day, Matsue sat on her bed of fir needles working when a young traveler named Teoyo passed by. As Matsue weaved, she sang:

No man is so callous that he won't sigh
when over his head the withered cherry flowers
flutter down. The spring's soft showers
maybe are tears shed by the sorrowing sky.

Teoyo stopped and listened to her. As he did, he felt as if a spell clamped over his heart. When she stopped singing, he approached her. "I've traveled far and seen many fair women. But none of them are as fair as you. Take me to your parents so I can speak with them."

Teoyo's mannerisms and rich dress told Matsue that he was of quite a high rank. As she gazed at his kind face, she felt as if a string tied her heart to his. She could almost see its shimmering thread between them. She took him to her parents as he asked.

Teoyo offered his introduction to them and told them about himself. "I've traveled a long way, yet your daughter has snared me with her singing. I would like your permission to marry her."

Pleased that someone of such a station would be interested in their daughter, Matsue's parents consented. Teoyo decided to stay in Harima with her parents. The countryside and its people had impressed him more than any other placed he had visited. So they lived happily under the great fir tree. Years passed, and Matsue's parents eventually died of old age. Matsue and Teoyo remained in the house under the fir tree, enjoying the sea and forest and their children and their grandchildren.

A pair of cranes built a nest in the topmost branches of the tree. For many years, the couple watched the birds rear their young. A tortoise also started living next to them.

"We are blessed with a fir tree, a crane family, and a tortoise. The God of Long Life must have taken us in his care," Matsue said.

And so the couple lived long in years. When they finally died, they died together on the same hour. The villagers found them curled together on the bed of needles. Matsue's long white hair flared around her like the wings of a crane. Teoyo smiled as if he dreamed sweetly. On moonbright nights, villagers would sometimes see a young Matsue and a young Teoyo together under the tree, raking the needles and laughing together. People started calling the tree, "The Pine Tree of the Lovers."

The Spirits of the Lotus

Disease once broke out across Japan. The beloved Lord Koriyama contracted it, adding to the despair of the people. One day, Tada Samon, the highest official under Koriyama, was pondering various problems when a servant entered.

"A visitor waits by the gate," the servant said. "He says he has a cure for our master."

Samon had his doubts, but he kept an open mind. "Bring him in."

A mountain recluse entered and bowed low. "The illness of our master is evil business, caused by a spirit. You lack defense against them. The saints of old told us to plant a lotus in every moat to drive away and protect against evil of all sorts. Let me fill the dry northern moats and plant lotuses. Only then can Lord Koriyama and his family be saved."

Samon thought a moment. They had plenty of money, and such an action would help people see efforts to help their master. It would do well for their morale and keep them from being idle. If something so simple could help his master, all the better. He agreed and made the recluse the administrator of the project.

The recluse washed and prayed for the evil spirit to leave the castle. He had the people assigned to him fill the moats with water and plant lotuses. As soon he set the men to work, he disappeared. But the men worked with amazing energy, completing the immense project in less than twenty-four hours.

A few days later, Lord Koriyama and his family recovered. A week later, they were able to walk. Another week later, they had returned to health. Samon held a celebration, and people flocked to the castle to see the lotus strewn moats. The villagers renamed the castle the Lotus Castle.

Some years later, Lord Koriyama died, and his son succeeded. Lord Koriyama's son neglected the moats and their lotus flowers, so their beauty became a shadow of a memory. One evening, a young samurai walked along one of the moats and saw two beautiful boys, about six or seven years old, playing.

"It's not safe to play so near the moat," the samurai said. "Come cover here to me." He walked up to take them by their hands, but they sprang into the water. Water sprayed over him.

He rushed to the moat, but the boys didn't surface. Not sure what to think, he ran into the castle and told the high officials. He feared that the boys may have been kappas. The officials decided to have the moats dragged and cleaned, as they should've done when Lord Koriyama died. They didn't find any kappas or the bodies of the boys and supposed the young samurai was daydreaming.

A few weeks later, another samurai named Murata Ippai returned from visiting his sweetheart. As he walked along the moat, he admired the lotus blossoms, thinking about his love. Then he noticed a dozen beautiful little boys playing on the water's edge.

"These must be the kappas everyone talked about. No doubt they took the form of humans to try to fool me," he said. "They will find it hard to escape my sword." He cast off his clogs, drew his sword, and crept toward the boys. He stopped a few yards away to watch.

The boys seemed to be normal children except for their flawless skin and a strange scent that wafted from them. The sweet scent made Ippai think of lotuses. He considered sheathing his sword as he watched the boys play. Instead, he gripped his sword tighter. He rushed at them, slashing and cutting. He felt his sword hit and heard dull thuds of something falling. When he stopped and looked back, a cloud of colored light blinded him and then faded. Determined to see the results of his decision, he waited for dawn.

When morning came, he saw only the stalks of lotuses sticking out of the water.

He frowned. "My sword struck more than lotus stalks." He walked up and down the moat, thinking. Finally, his stomach twisted as he realized what he had done. "If I wasn't killing kappa, they must have been the spirits of the lotus. What have I done? The spirits of the lotus had saved Lord Koriyama and his family."

He collapsed to a flat stone surrounded by the shredded remains of the lotus flowers. He pulled his knife out, bared his torso, and disemboweled himself. The lotus continued to bloom, but no one saw the lotus spirits again.

The Willow of Mukochima

Ayame and her son, Umewaki, lived near Shinji Lake. Ayame worshiped the descendants of Izanagi and Izanami. Each day, she and her son would greet the rising sun together and pray. Then, Ayame would weave and leave her son to play and wander in the woods. She trusted the gods to keep him safe.

One evening, Umewaki didn't return home. She stepped out of their small house and called for him. Only the echo of her voice answered. Irritated and more than a little afraid, she went out to search for him. No person she asked had seen him. She searched until close to midnight.

"Maybe he is waiting for me at the house," she said to herself. She wanted to keep searching, but she knew it would be pointless in the darkness.

The house remained empty.

She began to cry and plead with the gods to bring her son back safe. The night seemed to take a month to pass. As soon as it was light enough to see, she set out to search. She soon learned that a band of thieves with a boy matching her son's description were seen heading toward Edo.

Meanwhile, Umewaki tried to figure out how to escape the thieves that had kidnapped him. In just a short day, the men had taken him through several towns of the like Umewaki had never seen. They used him to carry their provisions and to set their camps. Time passed, and soon the leaves began to fall. As they neared Edo, Umewaki collapsed. No matter how much the men kicked him, he was unable to move. Finally, they stripped him of their loads and left him on the side of the road. A kind man of Mukochima found him and carried him home.

Despite the kind man's efforts, Umewaki's health declined. On the fifteenth day of the third month, he called to the kind man. "Tell my mother that I love her. I want to stay with her, but Amaterasu calls me, and I must obey."

He died shortly after.

Ayame happened to pass through Mukochima in her search when she overheard people talking about a boy who had been abused to death by a band of thieves.

"Where is he?" she asked them. "Take me to him! I'm his mother."

They took her to the kind man's house.

"I'm sorry," he said. "I did all I could, but he told me that he loved you and that Amaterasu called him to her side. I can show you where he is buried."

The man had buried Umewaki under a sacred willow tree. As the wind blew, Ayame heard the tree rustle. It sounded similar to her son's soft voice. She settled into the district and began to visit the tree every evening. Soon other people began to visit the willow to listen to its unique rustling.

Whenever it rained on the fifteenth day of the third month, people would say "Umewaki weeps."

The Willow Wife

A great willow tree grew in a village. For generations, the villagers loved it. It provided shade during the summer, and many lovers spent a moonlit night under its branches. No one loved the tree as much as Heitaro. Each morning, it was the first thing he saw when he awoke. When he returned from the fields, he relished its familiar shape. He also would pray under its branches.

One day, the village chief came to Heitaro and explained that the village needed to build a bridge over the river. "We want the great willow for its strong timber."

"My dear willow turned into a bridge?" Heitaro said. "Never, old man. How can you even suggest it?" He took a deep breath. "I will give you some of my trees if you forget about the willow."

The old man accepted the offer.

One night sometime later, Heitaro sat under the willow when a beautiful woman appeared beside him. She looked down at him and then looked away.

Heitaro stood. "I will go home since you are waiting for someone." He smiled.

"He won't come right now," she said.

"Has his love for you grown cold?"

She shook her head.

"So why doesn't he come to you?"

She smiled at him. "He has come. His heart has always been here under this willow tree." She vanished.

Heitaro blinked, wondering if he had been dreaming.

The next night, she waited for him under the willow. After they spoke for some time, Heitaro asked her name.

"Please call me Willow. Just don't ask me about my past. I don't have a father or mother."

They met each night after that to talk. She loved to hear him compose poems about the willow.

Finally, one night, Heitaro took her hand. "Will you be my wife?"

"Yes, my heart, yes!"

They married a few days later. They had a son and called him Chiyodo. They lived happily together.

Several years later, the village buzzed with excitement.

"What happened?" Heitaro asked his neighbor.

"The ex-Emperor Toba wants to build a temple to Kannon in Kyoto. We've been ordered to present the great willow tree to him."

"We can't! There are other, much larger and stronger trees that would better serve the temple," Heitaro said.

"None of them are as grand as the willow."

Heitaro did what he could to change the villagers' minds, but he failed. He went home, feeling sadness he had never felt before.

"What's the matter, my love?" Willow asked.

"The villagers are going to cut down our dear willow tree. Before I married you, I couldn't have dealt with it, but because I have you, I supposed I will get over it someday."

That night, a cry woke Heitaro. Beside him, Willow writhed in pain. He grabbed her hand and shoulder. "Wha—"

"Are you there, Heitaro? I can't see."

"I'm right here. Tell me what's wrong."

She cried out in pain. "The villagers are killing me!" She snatched his hand and placed them on her stomach. "It hurts so much. If you put your hand there, the axes can't hit me, can they?" She shuddered under his hands. My love. I'm the spirit of the willow tree." Tears slide down her stricken face. "Our love can't be cut down by axes."

Confusion and helplessness quick-silvered in him.

"I will wait for you and Chiyodo. I love you." She stiffened and fell against him.

A crash outside shook the house. Heitaro felt the weight of his wife lift from him. Her clothes fluttered over his arms.

Yosoji's Camellia Tree

Yosoji felt helpless as smallpox ravaged his village. His mother also contracted the disease. Yosoji did what he could for her, but she grew weaker each day. Feeling desperate, he left to speak with the fortuneteller Kamo Yamakiko.

"Your mother has only one chance," Yamakiko said. "There is a small shrine near a brook on the southwestern side of Mount Fuji. Worship the god enshrined there and bring your mother the water from the brook. If she drinks it, she will be cured. But beware. It is a wild, dangerous country."

Yosoji left early the following morning, leaving his mother in the care of a neighbor. Toward midday, he arrived at a three-path intersection. While he debated which to take, a beautiful girl dressed in white approached him from the forest. Yosoji made to flee, but the girl called out.

"Don't run away. I know why you are here. You are a brave and faithful son. Let me guide you to the stream. Its waters will cure your mother. The road is dangerous, but don't be afraid." She turned and walked a short distance down the trail.

Yosoji didn't know where to go, so he decided to trust her. The two walked through the forest in silence. The ancient trees blocked out the sun. Strange howls and other sounds came out of the darkness. The trail angled upward. Abruptly, the forest ended. A small shrine stood near a cleft rock, and a silver stream gurgled from the rock. Yosoji had never seen such clear water.

"Fill your gourd and drink of the water yourself," the girl said. "The water will prevent you from catching the plague. But hurry. It's getting late. I will take you back to where I met you."

Yosoji drank the sweet, cold water. He had never tasted anything so fresh. He filled his water bottle to the brim. The girl guided him downhill. When they reached the intersection, Yosoji bowed low to her.

"Thank you for your kindness."

"It's a pleasure to help a dutiful son like you," she said. "In three days, you will need to fetch more water for your mother. I will be here when you come."

"May I ask your name?"

She smiled. "No. I can't tell you."

Yosoji felt perplexed, but he bowed and hurried home. When he arrived home, his mother had grown worse. He helped her drink a cup of water and told of his adventure. Throughout the night, he tended her. By morning, she had improved. By the third day, she had finished the water, and Yosoji left to keep his appointment with the lady in white.

She waited for him on a rock at the three paths. "Your mother is better." She smiled. "I can see it in your smile. You will have to come again in three more days. It will take five trips. You may also give the water to the sick villagers."

So Yosoji went with the mysterious girl five times. His mother recovered, and Yosoji shared the miraculous water with his surviving neighbors. As he spoke of the white-dressed girl, people wondered who she was. They had heard of the shrine, but no one knew where it was. The survivors sent gifts to Kamo Yamakiko to express their gratitude for his information.

Despite his success, Yosoji remained uneasy. He felt as if he had failed to express his gratitude to the mysterious girl. Besides, he wanted to know who she was. So he set out one last time to visit the shrine. He knew the road well now and didn't stop at the intersection. It was the first time he had traveled the trail alone, and he felt afraid despite its familiarity. He couldn't say why.

When he arrived at the shrine, the stream had dried up. But Yosoji wasn't interested in the water anyway. He knelt before the shrine and thanked the God of Long Breath for providing the means of curing his mother and his neighbors. He prayed for his guide to reveal herself one more time so he could thank her for her kindness. When he stood, she stood beside him.

"You must not come here," she said. "This is a place of great danger for you. Your mother and neighbors are cured. You had no reason to come here again."

Yosoji shook his head. "I had every reason. I haven't thanked you properly or expressed my gratitude for your help. I would've never found this spring without you. I want to know your name so we can erect a shrine in our village."

"You don't need to know who I am," the girl said. "We must part now."

She swung a camellia branch over her head. A cloud came from the top of Mount Fuji, enveloping her in mist. She rose into the air. Yosoji realized the girl was none other than the Goddess of Mount Fuji. He fell to his knees and prayed to her. The goddess smiled and tossed the branch of the camellia down to him.

Yosoji carried the branch home and cared for it. It grew into a large tree in two short years. The village built a shrine near the tree, attracting visitors from all over.

Bibliography

Ayrton, M. Chaplin. *Child-Life in Japan and Japanese Child Stories.* Boston: D..C Heath & Co. 1909.

Chamberlain, Basil Hall. *Aino Folk-Tales.* Private Printing. 1888.

Chamberlain, Basil Hall. *Things Japanese: being notes on various subjects connected with Japan for use of travelers and others.* London: John Murray. 1905.

Davis, Fredrick Hadland. *Myths & Legends of Japan.* London: George G. Harrap & Company. 1912.

Davis, Hadland F. *Myths & Legends of Japan.* London: George G. Harrap & Company. 1912.

Freeman-Mitford, Algernon Bertram. *Tales of Old Japan.* Macmillan and Company. 1890.

Griffis, William Elliot. *Japanese Fairy World Stories from the Wonder-Lore of Japan.* London: Trubner & Co. Ludgate Hill. 1887.

Hearn, Lafcadio. *Glimpses of an Unfamiliar Japan.* BostonL Houghton, Mifflin and Company. 1894.

Hearn, Lafcadio. *In Ghostly Japan.* Boston: Little, Brown, and Company. 1899.

Hearn, Lafcadio. *Japanese Fairy Tales.* New York: Boni and Liveright. 1918.

Hearn, Lafcadio. *Kwaidan: Stories and Studies of Strange Things.* Boston; Houghton, Mifflin and Co. 1904.

James, Grace. *Japanese Fairy Tales.* London: Macmillan and Co. 1910.

Ozaki, Yei Theodora. *Japanese Fairy Tales.* New York: A.L.Burt Company. 1908.

Ozaki, Yei Theodora. *Romances of Old Japan.* New York: Brentano. 1920.

Ozaki, Yei Theodora. *Warriors of Old Japan and Other Stories.* Boston: Houghton Mifflin Company. 1909.

Rinder, Frank. *Old-World* Japan Legends of the Land of the Gods. London: George Allen. 1895.

Ryunosuke, Akutagawa. *Rashomon.* Teikoku Bungaku. 1915.

Smith, Richard Gordon. *Ancient Tales and Folklore of Japan.* London: A&C Black. 1918.

Wilson, Epiphanius. *Japanese Literature Including Selections from Genji Monogatari and Classic Poetry and Drama of Japan.* The Colonial Press. 1900.

34216561R00239